THE OLD TESTAMENT
AND MODERN STUDY

A Generation of
Discovery and Research

ESSAYS BY
MEMBERS OF THE SOCIETY FOR
OLD TESTAMENT STUDY
EDITED BY

H. H. ROWLEY

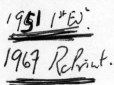

JMSinkler.
1915.

Including NH Snaith (Headingley)
CR North, J Anderson
(Hawshott)
Dr T Loines (St Caths).

OXFORD UNIVERSITY PRESS
LONDON   OXFORD   NEW YORK

1951 1st Ed.
1967 Reprint.

Oxford University Press, Ely House, London W.1

OXFORD LONDON NEW YORK
GLASGOW TORONTO MELBOURNE WELLINGTON
CAPE TOWN SALISBURY IBADAN NAIROBI LUSAKA ADDIS ABABA
BOMBAY CALCUTTA MADRAS KARACHI LAHORE DACCA
KUALA LUMPUR HONG KONG TOKYO

First issued as an Oxford University Press paperback 1961
First published by the Clarendon Press 1951
This reprint 1967

PRINTED IN GREAT BRITAIN

PREFACE

THE members of the Society for Old Testament Study have issued two earlier volumes of essays, the first edited by A. S. Peake and published under the title *The People and the Book* (1925), and the second edited by H. Wheeler Robinson and published under the title *Record and Revelation* (1938). Both volumes have been widely useful to those who have shared the deepening interest in the Old Testament and who have desired to be abreast of the work that was being done by scholars in this field. The present volume does not aim to be a replica of either of these, merely bringing their chapters up to date. It aims rather to survey the significant work that has been done during the last thirty years in order to bring out the changes that have come about and the new trends that have appeared. On some of the subjects dealt with in the earlier volumes there is little fresh to be said in this connexion, and students will continue to find those previous volumes valuable. On other subjects much that is in the older essays is gathered up and carried forward here.

The occasion which prompted the preparation of this volume was the fiftieth meeting of the Society. Yet it did not suppose that this occasion was of interest to people beyond its own membership or marked any epoch in Biblical studies. It happened that the life of the Society had extended through a generation of great activity and importance in Old Testament study, and it seemed to its members that it might render a service to many outside its own fellowship by a review of this period. It is much to be regretted that neither of the editors of the earlier volumes is still with us to edit the present work. The Society gave me the same freedom in planning the volume and choosing the writers which it gave to them. Some of the contributors have written essays for the previous books, while others appear here for the first time in this series of volumes. One only has contributed to all three volumes, and that is Professor T. H. Robinson, who was one of the founders of the Society and who for nearly thirty years served it as Secretary. To him the Society is mindful of its debt, and his influence on Old Testament studies in this country is probably far greater than any of us realize—not alone through his own writings, but through the influence of the Society which he did so much to organize.

It is a particular pleasure to me that I have been able to call on some of the Honorary Members of the Society for essays, as Dr. Wheeler Robinson also did. The essays of Professors Eissfeldt and Baumgartner were written in German, and for their translation Mr. D. R. Ap-Thomas, M.A., B.D., of Bangor, has been responsible. Professor Eissfeldt needs no introduction to students of the Old Testament in any country, while Professor Baumgartner is known for the masterly surveys of literature which he has from time to time published. The other Honorary Member who has contributed is Professor Albright, who is the foremost living authority in the field of Biblical Archaeology. For the rest, ordinary members of the Society have been called on. They have been given freedom to treat their subjects in their own way, their only briefing being a single sentence in which the aim of the volume was defined. In the matter of Bibliography each has gone his own way, some confining this to their footnotes, others supplementing these with a bibliographical appendix, and yet others combining in that appendix titles occurring in their chapters and supplementary titles. Complete uniformity in this and in some other respects is difficult to secure; though so far as possible uniformity of detail has been sought.

A measure of overlap between the essays is inevitable, though this will be found to be less than it might easily have been. Moreover, disagreement between the authors is much less than it might easily have been, and most readers will be impressed by the measure of agreement in the point of view that will be apparent in these primarily objective surveys. If they bewilder by the variety of view which they record, they will also help the reader to keep his bearings and to emerge with a balanced judgement on the problems that confront the student of the Old Testament today.

The Society is indebted to the Oxford University Press for the publication of this volume, as for its predecessors; and I would acknowledge the patience and the skill on which I have been able to rely for its production, as well as the speed with which it has been printed and published.

For the preparation of the Subject Index I have to thank the Rev. E. T. Ryder, M.A., B.D., of Cardiff University College, and for the preparation of the Author and Scripture Indexes my eldest daughter, Margaret.

H. H. R.

Manchester University
1951

CONTENTS

St.
@Marines·

ABBREVIATIONS

A.A.	Alttestamentliche Abhandlungen.
A.A.S.F.	Annales Academiae Scientiarum Fennicae.
A.A.S.O.R.	*Annual of the American Schools of Oriental Research.*
A.f.O.	*Archiv für Orientforschung.*
A.J.A.	*American Journal of Archaeology.*
A.J.S.L.	*American Journal of Semitic Languages and Literatures.*
A.K.	*Archiv für Kulturgeschichte.*
A.O.	*Archiv Orientální.*
A.O.T.	H. Gressmann, *Altorientalische Texte zum Alten Testament,* 1926.
A.P.A.W.	*Abhandlungen der preußischen Akademie der Wissenschaften,* Phil.- hist. Klasse.
A.R.I.	W. F. Albright, *Archaeology and the Religion of Israel,* 1942.
A.R.W.	*Archiv für Religionswissenschaft.*
A.S.A.E.	*Annales du Service des Antiquités de l'Égypte.*
A.T.D.	Das Alte Testament Deutsch.
A.T.R.	*Anglican Theological Review.*
B.A.	*The Biblical Archaeologist.*
B.A.S.O.R.	*Bulletin of the American Schools of Oriental Research.*
B.H.	R. Kittel, *Biblia Hebraica.*
Bi.Or.	*Bibliotheca Orientalis.*
B.J.P.E.S.	*Bulletin of the Jewish Palestine Exploration Society.*
B.J.R.L.	*Bulletin of the John Rylands Library.*
B.M.B.	*Bulletin du Musée de Beyrouth.*
B.N.Y.P.L.	*Bulletin of the New York Public Library.*
B.S.O.A.S.	*Bulletin of the School of Oriental and African Studies.*
B.W.A.N.T.	Beiträge zur Wissenschaft vom Alten und Neuen Testament.
B.W.A.T.	Beiträge zur Wissenschaft vom Alten Testament.
B.Z.A.W.	Beihefte zur *Zeitschrift für die alttestamentliche Wissenschaft.*
C.A.H.	*Cambridge Ancient History.*
Camb. B.	Cambridge Bible.
C.B.Q.	*Catholic Biblical Quarterly.*
Cent. B.	Century Bible.
C.I.S.	*Corpus Inscriptionum Semiticarum.*

C.R.A.I.	*Comptes rendus de l'Académie des Inscriptions et Belles Lettres.*
D.L.Z.	*Deutsche Literaturzeitung.*
E.B.	Études Bibliques.
E.B.	*Encyclopaedia Biblica.*
Echt. B.	Echter Bibel.
E.H.A.T.	Exegetisches Handbuch zum Alten Testament.
E.H.P.R.	Études d'Histoire et de Philosophie religieuses.
E.T.	*Expository Times.*
E.Tr.	English Translation.
F.R.L.A.N.T.	Forschungen zur Religion und Literatur des Alten und Neuen Testaments.
F.S.A.C.	W. F. Albright, *From the Stone Age to Christianity*, 1940, ²1946.
F.u.F.	*Forschungen und Fortschritte.*
G.T.	I. Engnell, *Gamla Testamentet: en traditionshistorisk inledning*, i, 1945.
H.A.T.	Handbuch zum Alten Testament.
H.J.	*Hibbert Journal.*
H.K.	Handkommentar zum Alten Testament.
H.S.A.T.	E. Kautzsch (ed. by), *Die Heilige Schrift des Alten Testaments*. (4th ed., edited by A. Bertholet.)
H.S.A.Tes.	Die Heilige Schrift des Alten Testamentes (Bonner Bibel).
H.T.R.	*Harvard Theological Review.*
H.U.C.A.	*Hebrew Union College Annual.*
I.C.C.	The International Critical Commentary.
J.A.O.S.	*Journal of the American Oriental Society.*
J.B.L.	*Journal of Biblical Literature.*
J.E.A.	*Journal of Egyptian Archaeology.*
J.E.O.L.	*Jaarbericht Ex Oriente Lux.*
J.H.C.R.	L. Finkelstein (ed. by), *The Jews, their History, Culture and Religion*, 1949.
J.J.S.	*Journal of Jewish Studies.*
J.N.E.S.	*Journal of Near Eastern Studies.*
J.P.O.S.	*Journal of the Palestine Oriental Society.*
J.Q.R.	*Jewish Quarterly Review.*
J.R.A.S.	*Journal of the Royal Asiatic Society.*
J.S.O.R.	*Journal of the Society for Oriental Research.*
J.T.S.	*Journal of Theological Studies.*

K.A.T.	Kommentar zum Alten Testament.
K.–B.	Koehler–Baumgartner, *Lexicon in Veteris Testamenti Libros.*
K.E.H.	Kurzgefaßtes exegetisches Handbuch zum Alten Testament.
K.H.C.	Kurzer Hand-Commentar zum Alten Testament.
L.U.Å.	Lunds Universitets Årsskrift.
M.A.O.G.	*Mitteilungen der altorientalischen Gesellschaft.*
M.D.O.G.	*Mitteilungen der deutschen Orient-Gesellschaft zu Berlin.*
M.G.W.J.	*Monatsschrift für Geschichte und Wissenschaft des Judenthums.*
M.V.A.G.	*Mitteilungen der vorderasiatischen Gesellschaft.*
Ned. T.T.	*Nederlands Theologisch Tijdschrift.*
N.J.D.W.	*Neue Jahrbücher für Deutsche Wissenschaft.*
Nor. T.T.	*Norsk Teologisk Tidsskrift.*
N.T.T.	*Nieuw Theologisch Tijdschrift.*
O.L.Z.	*Orientalistische Literaturzeitung.*
O.T.S.	*Oudtestamentische Studiën.*
P.A.A.J.	*Proceedings of the American Academy for Jewish Research.*
P.A.P.	W. F. Albright, Pelican *Archaeology of Palestine*, 1949.
P.A.P.S.	*Proceedings of the American Philosophical Society.*
P.E.F.Q.S.	*Quarterly Statement of the Palestine Exploration Fund.*
P.E.Q.	*Palestine Exploration Quarterly.*
P.J.B.	*Palästinajahrbuch des deutschen evangelischen Instituts für Altertumswissenschaft des Heiligen Landes zu Jerusalem.*
Pr. J.B.	*Preussische Jahrbücher.*
R.A.	*Revue d'Assyriologie et d'Archéologie orientale.*
R.B.	*Revue Biblique.*
R.E.S.	*Revue des Études Sémitiques.*
R.E.S.-B.	*Revue des Études Sémitiques et Babyloniaca.*
R.G.G.	*Die Religion in Geschichte und Gegenwart.*
R.H.P.R.	*Revue d'Histoire et de Philosophie religieuses.*
R.H.R.	*Revue de l'Histoire des Religions.*
R.Th.Ph.	*Revue de Théologie et de Philosophie.*
S.A.T.	Die Schriften des Alten Testaments in Auswahl.
S.B.O.N.T.	The Sacred Books of the Old and New Testaments.

S.B.U.	*Svenskt Bibliskt Uppslagsverk.*
S.E.A.	*Svensk Exegetisk Årsbok.*
S.H.A.W.	Sitzungsberichte der Heidelberger Akademie der Wissenschaften, Phil.-hist. Klasse.
S.K.G.	Schriften der Königsberger gelehrten Gesellschaft.
S.P.A.W.	Sitzungsberichte der Preussischen Akademie der Wissenschaften, Phil.-hist. Klasse.
T.L.B.	*Theologisches Literaturblatt.*
T.L.Z.	*Theologische Literaturzeitung.*
T.R.	*Theologische Rundschau.*
T.S.K.	*Theologische Studien und Kritiken.*
T.U.	Tekst en Uitleg.
T.Z.	*Theologische Zeitschrift.*
U.U.Å.	Uppsala Universitets Årsskrift.
W.C.	Westminster Commentaries.
W.J.L.	*Wiener Jahrbuch für Literatur.*
W.Z.K.M.	*Wiener Zeitschrift für die Kunde des Morgenlandes.*
Z.A.	*Zeitschrift für Assyriologie.*
Z.A.W.	*Zeitschrift für die alttestamentliche Wissenschaft.*
Z.D.M.G.	*Zeitschrift der deutschen morgenländischen Gesellschaft.*
Z.D.P.V.	*Zeitschrift des deutschen Palästina Vereins.*
Z.N.W.	*Zeitschrift für die neutestamentliche Wissenschaft.*
Z.S.	*Zeitschrift für Semitistik und verwandte Gebiete.*
Z.S.T.	*Zeitschrift für systematische Theologie.*

TRANSLITERATION

of Oriental words normally accords with the following system.

HEBREW

א	= '	ח	= ḥ	פ	= p
בּ	= b	ט	= ṭ	פ	= p̲
ב	= b̲	י	= y	צ	= ṣ
גּ	= g	כּ	= k	ק	= ḳ
ג	= ḡ	כ	= k̲	ר	= r
דּ	= d	ל	= l	שׂ	= ś
ד	= d̲	מ	= m	שׁ	= š
ה	= h	נ	= n	תּ	= t
ו	= w	ס	= s	ת	= t̲
ז	= z	ע	= '		

Short vowels unmarked; long vowels as ū or û according to whether written defectively or plene; *Šᵉwā* small raised letter.

Proper names follow familiar forms in English.

ARABIC

ء	= '	ز	= z	ق	= ḳ
ب	= b	س	= s	ك	= k
ت	= t	ش	= š	ل	= l
ث	= t̲	ص	= ṣ	م	= m
ج	= ǧ	ض	= ḍ	ن	= n
ح	= ḥ	ط	= ṭ	ه	= h
خ	= ḫ	ظ	= ẓ	و	= w
د	= d	ع	= '	ى	= y (or i)
ذ	= d̲	غ	= ġ	ة	= t (in Construct)
ر	= r	ف	= f		

Transliteration

RAS SHAMRA

as in Cyrus Herzl Gordon's *Ugaritic Handbook*, Rome, 1947,
here arranged in the order of the recently recovered alphabetic tablet.

1.	a		17.	n
2.	b		18.	ẓ
3.	g		19.	s
4.	ḫ		20.	ʿ
5.	d		21.	p
6.	h		22.	ṣ
7.	w		23.	q
8.	z		24.	r
9.	ḥ		25.	ṯ
10.	ṭ		26.	ǵ
11.	y		26a.	ġ
12.	k		27.	t
13.	š		28.	i
14.	l		29.	u
15.	m		30.	ś
16.	ś			

INTRODUCTION

IT is said that about a quarter of a century ago a British
Orientalist confided to a friend that he intended to turn his
attention in future to studies outside the Hebrew and Old
Testament field, since there was nothing more to be done within
that field. The problems of the Old Testament had all been
studied and stable conclusions reached, so that all that remained
for scholars to do was to go on repeating what had already been
sufficiently said. While this was never strictly true, there seemed
a substantial measure of justification for it. When the Society for
Old Testament Study was formed, during the First World War,
there was a broad agreement amongst the scholars of the world
on a large number of questions concerning this book. There were
conservative writers who stood outside the general body of
critical scholars and who rejected most of their conclusions, but
they did not seriously affect the position. For while many of them
had considerable learning, they made little secret of the fact that
they were employing their learning to defend positions which
were dogmatically reached. Their work had little influence, therefore, amongst scientific scholars who were concerned only with
the evidence, and the conclusions to which it might naturally lead.

Towards the text of the Old Testament, as represented by the
Massoretic Hebrew, there was a rooted suspicion, and commentators vied with one another in the ingenuity with which it
was emended. Where any version could be invoked in favour of
a change its support was welcomed, but where no version could
be laid under contribution it mattered little. Any guess was to be
preferred to a text which was assumed to be untrustworthy.
That this is an overstatement, and in some degree a caricature,
is doubtless true; yet there was a very substantial justification for
it, and the innumerable emendations that filled every commentary may be appealed to in evidence.[1]

[1] In Gunkel's *Die Psalmen* (H.K.), 1926, more than 250 new emendations were
proposed, in addition to very large numbers of others that were adopted.

On questions of the date and authorship of the books of the Old Testament there was also wide agreement. Individual scholars could be found who differed more or less as to the precise date of the sources of the Pentateuch, or as to the exact delimitation of the sources, and different writers had their own preferences as to the age to which the majority of the psalms were to be ascribed. Yet all of these differences affected details only and not the broad picture of the growth of the Old Testament.

There was scant interest in the theology of the Old Testament because the very term implied a unity that was felt to be wholly lacking. The course of the development of Israelite religion could be traced from its primitive beginnings to its heights in the pre-exilic prophets, and its decline in the post-exilic priestly religion which triumphed over the prophetic. The neat literary analysis of the various books was paralleled by the sharp anti-thesis between Yahwism and Baalism, between priest and prophet, between pre-exilic and post-exilic ages.

Like all generalizations, this broad summary of the position will be misleading unless it is recognized that on every question there were diversities of view, and some scholars pressed the general standpoint which has been indicated much farther than others. Nevertheless, given that recognition, this is not an unfair summary of the position at the beginning of the period surveyed in the present volume.

Today the whole scene is changed, and the student of the Old Testament is living in a very different climate. We have passed through a generation of activity, and even of excitement, in the study of the Bible that could not have been foreseen. Many of the conclusions that seemed most sure have been challenged, and there is now a greater variety of view on many questions than has been known for a long time. It is therefore much more dangerous and misleading today to speak of the consensus of scholarship on many questions than it was. Such a consensus would represent a far smaller proportion of the scholars of the world in any generalizations that might be made than was the case earlier in this century. This does not mean, however, that scholars have turned their backs on the work of their predecessors, and have repudiated them and all their ways. That would be but folly. Without their work ours would be impossible, and we are wise to remember with honour those who worked before us, though without being bound by all of their conclusions. New sources of knowledge have come to light, and new lines of approach to old problems have been tried, so that there has been progress, rather than revolution, in this field of study.

It must be emphasized that not all of the changes that have taken place have been due to new knowledge which has demonstrated the wrongness of old conclusions. While there has been much new knowledge to assimilate, and while this has led to much modification of positions, it has rarely yielded anything like proof of the wrongness of the conclusions of former scholars, and the interpretation of its evidence is usually a matter of opinion, on which scholars are not agreed. Moreover, many of the most significant changes that have come over the scene are due less to new sources of knowledge than to new approaches to already available sources of knowledge, and to the turning of the critical method against some of the conclusions that had been too easily accepted. These tendencies had already begun to appear before the beginning of our period, indeed, and some of the most significant developments which are recorded in the present volume had their first beginnings quite early in this century. It is therefore quite misleading to suppose that the changes in attitude and approach are the results of archaeological finds. There has been no sudden revolution, but a gradual and almost imperceptible change, and it is mainly in retrospect that we can see how considerable has been the movement. For even the excitement of the new discoveries and abundant new materials that have been laid before us have stirred scholars more by the new tasks they have brought than by their revolutionary evidence for the overturning of older conclusions.

In general, it may be said that there has been a tendency towards more conservative views on many questions than were common at the opening of our period. These more conservative views are not shared by all scholars, though they are widespread, and any assessment of the position today is bound to give prominence to them. They are hailed sometimes as evidence of the failure of critical scholarship, and as the justification of the older conservatism that has been mentioned. This is quite inaccurate and misleading. For they are reached by the critical method, and hence must be accounted among its fruits. On the other hand, their conservatism is both other and firmer than the older conservatism, just because it is critically, and not dogmatically, based, and because it is built squarely on the evidence, instead of merely using the evidence as a support where it is convenient, and explaining it away where it is not.

In the present volume an effort is made to survey the work of the last thirty years, in order to bring out the change that has come over the scene, and the newer trends that have been referred to. The Society for Old Testament Study held its fiftieth meeting in 1950, when it was felt that such an enterprise would be useful both to its own members and to others. The choice of a starting-point for the survey was not alone due to the Society's own history, but to the fact that it roughly coincided with the end of the First World War,[1] and that it gave a period of a full generation for the survey, and hence provided an adequate opportunity to estimate the trends that have become evident. For the scholar in this field this may be not without value, since it will help him to take stock of the position, while for scholars in other, and related, fields it may have greater value, since they are not always aware of the changes that have taken place. To the general reader who wishes to be reasonably well informed of the progress of Biblical studies, it will bring ample evidence that there is no stagnation so far as the Old Testament is concerned.

Perhaps never has it been more difficult to prepare such a volume. In contrast to the large measure of unity that prevailed a generation ago, there is today an almost bewildering diversity of view on many questions, and it is necessary to speak of trends,

---

[1] The first meeting of the Society was held in January 1917, nearly two years before the war ended. Its activity during the war was restricted, however, and in any case it was largely cut off from scholars abroad. The fact that its fiftieth meeting was held on the thirty-third anniversary of the first was due to the suspension of its meetings during war-time.

rather than of a single trend, in our studies. On a number of subjects contrary tendencies have appeared in various quarters leading to a greater fluidity in the field as a whole than has been known for a long time. Older views have been challenged from more than one side, without being overthrown, so that though they are more lightly held by many than they once were, they are still held, until their challengers can offer more solidly based views to take their place, which can command wider support than the views they seek to displace.

For some of the chapters it has been necessary to choose writers who are familiar with the work of Scandinavian scholars, and who have access to their work in the Scandinavian languages, as well as in the more usual international languages of scholarship. One of the most notable features of the past generation has been the activity of Scandinavian scholars, and today they occupy a more conspicuous place in our field of study than they have ever done. The penetrating study of Israel's life and culture by Pedersen is widely known to English readers, and scarcely less so the creative brilliance of much of the work of Mowinckel, though less is available in the English language. The wide range of Nyberg's learning, and his contribution to the development of the so-called Uppsala school, may be less widely known, while the sound judgement and balanced wisdom of Lindblom is even less widely known, since a larger proportion of his major works has been written in Swedish. Beside these, a large number of younger scholars of great energy and erudition, of whom perhaps the two most brilliant and inspiring are Widengren and Engnell, have focused attention on Scandinavia in a remarkable way, and one of the chief purposes which the present volume will serve will be the review of the important work which has been done there, and the indication of the special trends of study which have become manifest there.[1]

It is impossible here to anticipate all that will be said in the

[1] Perhaps the most indefatigable of all the Scandinavian scholars is the learned and judicious Bentzen, who has made accessible to English readers in his *Introduction to the Old Testament*, 2 vols., 1948–9, a good deal of information about recent developments in Scandinavian scholarship. Cf. also his article 'Skandinavische Literatur zum Alten Testament, 1939–48', in *Th.R.*, N.F. xvii, 1948–9, pp. 272–328.

following chapters, and all that can be done is to summarize in a few words the main trends that will be traced through the detailed surveys that will follow. Each chapter is written by an acknowledged expert in its particular field, save that the acknowledgement of the *expertise* of Professor Anderson will probably follow the publication of his essay, since to many readers he will be a new writer. The editor has reserved for himself only the task of indicating in a general way the tendencies that will appear in various ways in different parts of the field and in different aspects of our study.

The new sources of knowledge have come principally in the field of archaeology, and will be found referred to in the chapters dealing with archaeology, epigraphy, and textual criticism. Between the wars there was a great outburst of activity in this field throughout the entire Near East, and new materials were brought to light much faster than they could be dealt with. The excavation of Palestinian sites went on apace, and important texts in Egyptian and in Hebrew were found, while non-textual evidence of the greatest importance was provided by a number of sites. From Egypt, too, new and important materials came, while the excavations of the ancient sites of Nuzu, Ugarit, and Mari provided sensational finds which will occupy scholars for many years. In addition, many other sites of Mesopotamia and Syria brought fresh evidence to light of no little importance for the Biblical scholar. All of this material must be studied primarily for itself, and for the knowledge it can give us of the ancient peoples from whom it has come down to us; yet it is valuable to the student of the Old Testament because of the indirect light it sheds on many problems.

Exaggerated claims are sometimes made as to the significance of all the new archaeological material. It is suggested that it has proved the accuracy of Biblical records, or that it has conclusively settled such questions as the date of the Exodus. Such unfounded and misleading claims are dangerous. The evidence of archaeology is rarely as simple and clear as we should like to have it, and its bearing on Biblical questions is more often indirect than direct. Not seldom it complicates our problems rather than solves them.[1] Nevertheless, it is true that in a broad way archaeology has tended to bring about a more conservative attitude to some questions. It has not proved the historical accuracy of the patriarchal narratives; but it has shown the historical credibility of those narratives by its evidence that they reflect the situation and the outlook of the patriarchal age in a remarkable way.[2] It has brought about a greater disposition to credit many of the poems of the Bible, both in the historical books and in the Psalter, with a higher antiquity than was once thought likely, by its demonstration that similar poetry was known in Canaanite civilization even before the time of Moses.

It will be noted that there is no chapter in the present volume devoted to the history of Israel. On a number of the details of Biblical history there has been new knowledge, such as the definite fixing of the date of the fall of Nineveh and the clearer understanding of the policy of Josiah. But such knowledge as has come has been brought to us through the work of the archaeologists and the decipherers of the texts which excavation has brought to light. Reference is therefore made to its most significant elements in the chapters which deal with these subjects. For the knowledge of Israel's history our main source is, and must continue to be, the Bible, and our acquaintance with its record has not been seriously modified during the period of our survey.[3] Certainly no new trends can be discerned in the treatment of Israelite history. There are, of course, many outstanding problems in this field, such as the obscure post-exilic period[4] and the development of the Samaritan schism, and to the research on these problems which has taken place during the last generation

[1] The present writer has surveyed the archaeological and other evidence bearing on the vexed question of the date of the Exodus in his Schweich Lectures, *From Joseph to Joshua*, 1950.

[2] Cf. the writer's 'Recent Discovery and the Patriarchal Age', in *B.J.R.L.* xxxii, 1949-50, pp. 44-79.

[3] It may be noted, however, that the largest original English work devoted to the history of Israel was published within our period in Oesterley and Robinson's *History of Israel*, 2 vols., 1932.

[4] The important third volume of Kittel's *Geschichte des Volkes Israel*, devoted to the post-exilic period, has appeared within the period covered by this survey, in 1927-9.

reference is made in one or other of the chapters of this book. Nevertheless, it remains true that the chief developments in Old Testament study in recent years have been less in the historical than in other spheres.

The value of the archaeological material that has been brought to light lies less in its contribution to the solution of historical problems, such as the date of the Exodus, than in its enrichment of our knowledge of the historical, cultural, and religious background of Israel's life and thought, and here it has contributed notably to the tendencies that have made themselves apparent during our period. One of the main trends of our time has been the emphasis on the links between Canaanite culture and Israelite. No longer can we think of a simple battle between Israelite Yahwism and Canaanite Baalism, in which all of the ways of the latter were repudiated by the champions of the former. Israel's religion has behind it a background of the common culture of the ancient Near East, and while it had a character of its own, which it did not share with the Canaanites or with any others, it could express itself through many forms which it did share with them. There were forms which could not be integrated into Yahwism, and which were always repudiated by the champions of Yahwism though accepted by many in Israel; but there were other forms which were taken over and adapted to the worship of Yahweh and made the organ of Israelite religion.

Here, however, we find during the period covered by our survey a variety of tendencies among scholars. Some have so emphasized the links between Israel and her neighbours as to obscure the unique elements in her life and faith, while others have called afresh for attention to the theology of the Old Testament with the desire to concentrate on those unique elements, and to see in the Old Testament a Christian book. The revived interest in the theology of the Old Testament is indeed to be welcomed, provided it is governed by an historical sense, and recognizes that out of which Israel's religion came as well as that to which it was led. The history of Israel's religion and the theology of the Old Testament must be studied side by side. There were primitive ideas and practices which were outgrown and shed within the period of the Old Testament, which must be studied in any history of Israel's religion, but which have no place in a theology of the Old Testament. This rather concerns itself with those elements in Israel's own religion which were incipient from the beginning and which became clearer and richer in the course of her story, and which gathered to themselves elements of older or even alien origin which could be related to her faith and made the vehicle of its expression, but which also gradually eliminated other elements of her ancient inheritance as well as resisted other alien elements because they were inconsistent with its own genius. The unity of such a theology is a dynamic unity, rather than a static unity. Its study is quite consistent with research into the history of the forms of the religion, and the recognition that many of these had much in common with the forms of Canaanite religion. How far this recognition can be pressed, however, is a more disputed question. Some find evidence of divine kingship in the Old Testament, and see in Yahweh a dying and rising God, at whose festivals a *hieros gamos* with all its accompaniments took place, while others hold this to be going beyond the evidence, and maintain that Israel adopted into Yahwism and adapted to it other elements of Canaanite practice, such as the ritual combat and the mimed representation of the triumph of Yahweh, but without the elements above mentioned, which were fundamentally alien to Yahwism. Large fields of study are opened here, which are not without importance for any ultimate theology of the Old Testament.

Another notable tendency has appeared in the study of the prophets. This has been the recognition that priests and prophets are not to be set over against one another in quite the sharp antithesis that was formerly common, but that prophets were cultic persons alongside priests in the service of the shrine. Here again there are disagreements as to how far this should be pressed, and it is probable that we should not regard all the prophets as priestly persons, or draw sharp lines of distinction within the prophetic circles. We have to beware of isolating Israel too completely from the ways of her neighbours, and equally of reading into her life all that we find amongst her neighbours. Her prophets cannot all be reduced to diviners with particular techniques, nor can we sharply distinguish spiritual prophets from false prophets, as unofficial and official prophets. There were many varieties of prophets, and within each type there were good and bad, some who were more and some who were less attuned to the mind of God, and so exercising a ministry of varying spiritual quality.

Closely connected with all this has been the tendency to interpret many of the Biblical texts as rituals. Parts, or the whole, of some of the prophetic books have been read as ritual texts, composed for use in the Temple service on particular occasions. Some of the historical narratives have similarly been held to be ritual texts, used in the annual festivals to give them a specifically Israelite and Yahwistic character, so that not mythology but Israel's own history supplied the terms in which she celebrated the divine victory. Still more important, many of the psalms have been ritually interpreted, or have been attributed to cultic prophets who composed them for liturgical use. Of few books of the Old Testament has recent study been so profoundly modified as the Psalter. At the beginning of our period one of the principal aims of every commentator was to determine the date and historical background out of which the psalms came, and each had his own favourite period to which large numbers were ascribed. Today the tendency is rather to ask for what purpose the psalms were written, and to what ritual use they were applied. There are still disagreements, as there were when the approach was historical; but the change in approach is shared by many scholars.

Coupled with this again has been the tendency to find a greater measure of unity in the Old Testament than was formerly found. The bringing of prophets and priests together as cultic persons, sharing in their differing ways in the service of the shrine, has as its counterpart the lessening of the antithesis between prophets and priests in their attitude to the cultus. Before the mention of cultic prophets, indeed, there were many scholars who held that the great canonical prophets did not repudiate all the forms of worship as necessarily bad, or condemn sacrifice as wrong *per se*, and who found priests and prophets to be less at cross purposes than some had held. This point of view has been stressed within our period, though there are still scholars who adhere to the other view. That there was a difference of emphasis as between prophet and priest is undeniable, and that there were varieties of worth amongst priests as there were amongst prophets, may reasonably be allowed. But that good priests thought that the ritual act was effective whether it really expressed the worshipper's attitude or not need not be assumed, any more than we may reasonably assume that the good prophet supposed that a right attitude of mind could dispense with all the forms of worship. It is commonly agreed that the prophetic books were collected and cherished in the post-exilic period, in which the later sections of the Law were prepared and the whole edited, and in which, too, the collection of the Psalms was made. All of these, therefore, expressed in their varying ways the interests of post-exilic Judaism, which is to be understood in terms of them all, and not in terms of one element alone. It is this greater willingness to see a fundamental unity in the Old Testament amid all its still recognized diversity that has prepared the way for that return to an Old Testament theology, to which reference has been made.

In the field of Lower, or Textual, Criticism, the most significant tendency of our period has been seen in the greater respect paid to the Massoretic text. Sometimes this has been carried to the extent of holding that the text is completely inviolable, but this has been an overpressing of the tendency. It has often to be recognized that the Hebrew text that has come down to us is not in its original state, though nothing like so often as was formerly held. Here we are unwise to put too much reliance for the present on the Dead Sea Scroll of the book of Isaiah, in view of the uncertainty of its age. If it should be established that it comes from the second century B.C., the large measure of its agreement with the Massoretic text would be of great significance, though the measure of its disagreement would still require to be remembered. If it should be established that it comes from a much later age, its agreement with the Massoretic text would be less significant, though it is probable that in any case the manuscript will be recognized to be of great importance. Yet quite apart from this manuscript, and long before it had been heard of, the attitude of growing respect for the Massoretic text was apparent. The new literature from the neighbouring peoples and the epigraphic texts that have become available have shed much light on Old Testament texts, while the recognition that many Old Testament difficulties may be resolved by finding in the passages rare words whose meaning may be preserved in much later literature in the cognate languages has avoided the necessity for a great deal of needless emendation. Occasionally archaeology has turned up the actual word which has long bothered interpreters and established its meaning beyond a peradventure, and thus saved the necessity for emendation. Such a case is that of the word *pîm* in 1 Sam. xiii. 21. Nevertheless, it is idle to deny that there are many corruptions in the Hebrew text. In the verse just referred to, for instance, the mere identification of the word *pîm* by no means solves the difficulties of the text. Sometimes the versions will enable us to restore a text with reasonable certainty, though we should beware of supposing that any of the versions in its entirety will compare with the Massoretic text for reliability. Often conjectural emendation may be quite convincing, as in the familiar case in Amos vi. 12, where the simple division of the strange plural of a collective noun, *beqārîm*, into two words, *bāqār yām*, at once restores sense, grammar, and rhythm. But more often, when we recognize the text to be no longer original, we are content to confess that we have not the means to restore it, and that the eager readiness to rewrite the text as we should like to have found it is less profitable than the attempt to understand it as it has come to us. Hence conjectural emendation is the last resort, rather than the first resort, of the commentator and is less pursued than it was. It has, however, still a legitimate place in textual criticism, and we must beware of letting our reaction against an overuse carry us too far in the other direction. The same is true of the use of metrical considerations in textual criticism. There were commentators who were dominated by metrical theories, and who mauled and mutilated the texts they dealt with to make them conform to their theories. Some have reacted against this so strongly that they have repudiated metre entirely as an instrument of textual criticism. Cautiously applied, however, it can still be of real service, especially where, as in the case above mentioned, its evidence reinforces other considerations.

In the field of Higher Criticism various tendencies have appeared. On the one hand, there has been an intensification of the process of literary analysis, and on the other, there has been a rejection of that process altogether, with various intermediate attitudes in between these extremes. In the Pentateuch new sources have been detected, or old sources subdivided; while yet some scholars have sought to reduce the number of sources by eliminating the E source altogether. Where the main sources are still recognized we find efforts to shift their dates, and consequently to reshape the whole story of the compilation of the Pentateuch. Some have carried the date of Deuteronomy, on which the entire ordering and dating of the sources depends, to a much later period, while others have pushed it back much earlier. It is here that the greatest fluidity in the whole field of Old Testament study is to be found today, though it cannot be said that any agreed pattern is emerging from the welter of challenge to the older views.

From Scandinavia comes a more radical challenge with the attack on literary criticism as an instrument of scholarship and the claim that a traditio-historical approach can solve more problems. That oral traditions lie behind our oldest written traditions would be widely agreed by many who still adhere to literary criticism, and indeed in literary critical circles much attention has been paid during our period to the question of the sources behind the main sources of the Pentateuch. For embedded in the main sources which have been recognized are fragments drawn from much older sources, carrying back the literary history of the Pentateuch far behind the earliest of the main sources. When to this is added the recognition that ancient traditions lie behind all the sources, and traditions whose verisimilitude has been established to no small degree by the recently available texts from Mesopotamia, we are carried back in our study of the Pentateuch a long way farther than many have been content to go.

Less radical have been the challenges to older views and approaches to problems concerning the other books of the Old Testament, with the exception of the Song of Songs and the Psalter. In the case of the Song of Songs the view has been propounded that we have here a cultic liturgy of the type that has been already mentioned, but one that was composed originally for the Adonis-Tammuz cult and later adapted to Temple use. While this view has secured an influential following, it is no necessary concomitant of the view which finds close links between Israelite and Canaanite usage, and there are signs that its popularity is waning.

So far as the Psalter is concerned, we have here one of the major fields in the Old Testament to which Form-criticism has been applied with important results. This approach goes back much beyond our period, but it has come most into prominence within our period. To this reference has been made above, and to its effort to determine the character of the psalm and the purpose for which it was written. Fundamentally the work of Gunkel, it has been applied by Mowinckel in ways that have brought new life into the study of the Psalter.

It is not alone in the Psalter, however, that there has been the development of this line of approach. Much attention has been paid to the forms of literature found in the Old Testament as a whole, and the rich variety of literary material gathered here has been brought into much clearer focus. Moreover, particular study has been given to the legal forms in the various codes of the Pentateuch, and attempts have been made to identify the conditions out of which the various forms arose. Not all scholars accept the conclusions that have been drawn, which assign the casuistical laws to a Canaanite background and the apodictical to an Israelite. Nevertheless, there is great value in the recognition that behind the oldest of the legal codes of the Pentateuch there lies a history, and that none can be treated as a simple unity.

Again, there has been a notable interest in the psychology of the Hebrews during our period. Of outstanding importance here has been the work of Pedersen, whose two volumes[1] give an unrivalled insight into the working of the Hebrew mind. In England, Wheeler Robinson devoted unwearied attention to this subject, and while in some particulars A. R. Johnson is supplying a corrective to his views, his work will long continue to bear fruit. His name is especially associated with the idea of 'corporate personality', though he was not the only one, or even the first, to draw attention to the phenomenon of thought which the term denotes. It was he who brought it into special prominence, and who applied it fruitfully to some of the outstanding problems of the Old Testament, and in particular to the question of the 'I' of the Psalms and to that of the Suffering Servant. Here again Johnson has taken up the idea of Wheeler Robinson, but this time less to offer a corrective than to apply it in another sphere, where its theological importance has been as yet inadequately appreciated.

To the psychology of prophecy also much attention has been devoted. Somewhat before our period opened, Hölscher had brought into prominence the ecstatic theory of prophecy which has characterized much of the writing on this subject. While this theory has been pushed to great extremes by some writers, and too sharply repudiated by others, it is probably to be recognized that there was an ecstatic element in all the prophets. At the same time the prophetic psychology is not sufficiently fathomed when we have recognized this element, and it demands more penetrating study than has yet been given to it.

In every generation there has been much writing on the Suffering Servant, and these thirty years have been no exception. They have seen the advocacy of a new theory, which has had considerable popularity in various modified forms. Here, once more, it was from Scandinavia that the new impulse came in the suggestion of Mowinckel that the Suffering Servant was the prophet himself.[2] In the Ethiopian eunuch's question this solution

---

[1] *Israel: its Life and Culture, I–II*, 1926; *III–IV*, 1940.
[2] *Der Knecht Jahwäs*, 1921.

was raised as a conceivable possibility, but it had secured no following amongst scholars anywhere until Mowinckel advanced it. Alongside this tendency, however, has been another in the direction of the messianic interpretation that was once almost universal, but that has been widely rejected in modern times. Here the work of Wheeler Robinson has borne fruit in the application of the fluidity for which he argued in a somewhat different way from that which he himself adopted, and the consequent interpretation of the Servant in terms of a fluidity which oscillated between the community of Israel and a future individual who should embody its mission and lead it to the acceptance of that mission.

It will be seen that the movement towards more conservative views has been along more than one line, and that running through a great deal of the work of our period has been the treatment of the Old Testament as a fundamentally religious book. Its records have been treated not merely as records, but as texts written for a religious and even for a liturgical and ritual use; its prophets not so much as statesmen and social reformers as religious figures, concerned with both ritual and life and recognizing that their divorce is fatal to both; its psalmists less as private singers calling on their muse to interpret their own thoughts or contemporary history than as religious figures composing texts which accompanied ritual acts to express their meaning and by that expression to complete their efficacy. Beyond that it has been emphasized, as the concluding chapter of the present book will show, that the Old Testament is a book through which Divine revelation of enduring importance to men is given. It not only comes down from the past and demands study in relation to its contemporary world, but it comes down to our generation with a message which calls for translation into the terms of our contemporary situation. It cannot be read as a Christian book, yet it is part of the Christian Bible, and the Christian message is impoverished if it does not gather into itself the abiding lessons of this part of our heritage.

Equally clearly it will be seen that there is still much work to be done on the Old Testament, and that there is room for scholars of wide equipment and of profound penetration to work in this field for a very long time to come. If the publication of the present volume stimulates some younger students to share our tasks it will have achieved a further purpose, beyond those mentioned earlier in this Introduction.

H. H. ROWLEY

I

THE OLD TESTAMENT AND THE
ARCHAEOLOGY OF PALESTINE

No subject related to biblical research has changed more
rapidly and more completely during the thirty years from
1919 to 1949 than Palestinian archaeology.[1] When the
writer first arrived in Palestine at the end of 1919, this subject
was in such a complete state of chaos that it seemed hopeless to
a neophyte. Nor did a year of extensive reading in it appreciably
alter the writer's feeling of helpless desperation. Bliss and the
earlier Macalister contradicted the chronology of the later
Macalister so sharply that in most matters of direct interest to
the Old Testament student they were actually in head-on
collision. Mackenzie's Beth-shemesh chronology differed from
the dates of the later Macalister even more violently than from
those of the earlier Macalister.[2] Watzinger's chronology con-
flicted with Macalister's and Mackenzie's, often by as much as
500 years or more. Percy Handcock's valiant attempt to produce
a synthesis out of chaos in his *Archaeology of the Holy Land*
(1916) only yielded greater confusion, since each chapter included material really belonging to several different archaeological phases; he even covered a thousand years in one chapter
where he should have covered three centuries, and then covered
much of the same ground in the next chapter under the impression that he was dealing with a new period!

Under such circumstances it was virtually impossible to utilize
archaeological data from Palestine to illustrate the Old Testament except with regard to inscriptions and to generalities such as
the average size of towns. Moreover, the few inscriptions which
did turn up were generally misinterpreted, and the fortifications

---

[1] On this see the writer's chapter on 'The Present State of Syro-Palestinian
Archaeology' in *The Haverford Symposium on Archaeology and the Bible* (New Haven,
1938), and especially the survey in *P.A.P.*, pp. 23 ff., 110 ff., &c.

[2] Ibid., pp. 30 ff.

and house-plans which were excavated received as a rule quite erroneous dates. Canon Driver's admirable critical survey of the subject in his introductory volume of Schweich Lectures, *Modern Research as Illustrating the Bible* (1909), did far more good by warning students against the dangers of 'archaeology' than it did harm by discouraging those biblical scholars who were inclined to leap too hastily into the archaeological arena. Ten years after its publication S. R. Driver's book had lost none of its pertinence—quite the contrary. But many biblical scholars of today seem to think that the situation has not changed since 1909 or 1919. They are sadly mistaken, and their error is now handicapping the progress of Old Testament research by per-petuating innumerable hypotheses and assumptions which cannot stand for a minute in the light of contemporary archaeology.

The writer is not going to devote any of the limited space in this chapter to describing how the complete change in our picture has come about. Interested readers will find the matter explained in his recent Pelican *Archaeology of Palestine* (1949). The chronology of Palestinian pottery has now been so com-pletely fixed by a combination of stratigraphic and typological research that differences between competent scholars over most periods have become very minor indeed. Except for the very earliest times, the dates given in this book will be found identical in essential respects with those given by such younger scholars as G. L. Harding, R. de Vaux, Nelson Glueck, G. Ernest Wright, I. Ben Dor, B. Maisler, Ruth Amiran. It may safely be said that none of these scholars would differ by much over a century in dating characteristic groups of pottery consisting of a number of types belonging to a single burial or room from the middle of the Early Bronze Age to Roman times. There is still difference of opinion with respect to the absolute chronology of earlier times, but very little with regard to relative chronology. The further progress of radiocarbon research will probably soon reduce differences in late prehistoric and early historic dates to equally minor oscillations. Future archaeologists are likely to spend much less time on chronology and much more on the meaning and purpose of their finds.

Palestine does not enter into the biblical story until the migration of Abram from Harran, which can scarcely be dated before the end of the third millennium B.C. on any hypothesis and may fall centuries later.[1] The traditions of Genesis clearly reflect a Middle Bronze background between the twenty-first and the sixteenth centuries. We shall, therefore, abstain from describing the extraordinary transformation in the state of our knowledge of Palestine before this period, thanks to archaeological discovery since 1929. Suffice it to say that we can now follow changing styles in artifacts and modes of life from the quasi-sedentary communities of the Mesolithic (Natufian), in the seventh or sixth millennium, through the sedentary and semi-nomadic societies of the Neolithic (fifth millennium) and Chalcolithic (fourth millennium) to successive phases of Early Bronze (third millennium). Abram came at least two thousand years after the first sedentary occupation of sites like Megiddo and Tell el-Fârʿah in central Palestine. Moreover, we know that the dominant ethnic strain during this long period was Semitic and that Palestine was already at the cross-roads of ancient trade and empire building in the fourth millennium.

Since 1930 there has been revolutionary progress in our understanding of the Middle Bronze Age. Excavation of comparable series of superimposed layers of occupation from this period at Megiddo and Tell Beit Mirsim has yielded virtually identical stratification, proving that the ceramic culture of Palestine developed along closely parallel lines in southern and northern Palestine.[2] The period between *c.* 2100 and *c.* 1550 B.C. is marked by three principal phases of culture: (1) a transitional stage following Early Bronze IV and the ensuing main phase of Middle Bronze I, which is derived from the caliciform-pottery stage of Syria;[3] (2) Middle Bronze II A, which was contemporary with Tell Beit Mirsim G–F and the Royal Tombs of

[1] See the most recent surveys of the present situation with respect to the Patriarchal Age in the excellent monographs of R. de Vaux, *R.B.* liii, 1946, pp. 321 ff., lv, 1948, pp. 321 ff., lvi, 1949, pp. 5 ff., and H. H. Rowley, *B.J.R.L.* xxxii, 1949, pp. 3–38.

[2] *P.A.P.*, pp. 83 ff.

[3] *B.A.S.O.R.*, No. 95 (1944), pp. 3–11, on the pottery of Bâb ed-Drâʿ and its affiliations.

Middle-Bronze Byblus; (3) Middle Bronze II B, which represents the Hyksos Age and came to an end with the invasion of
Asia by the troops of Amosis I. Since it is possible to date these
successive periods by objects of known Egyptian origin, coming
from the chronologically fixed Middle Empire, our dates are
not affected by possible oscillations in Mesopotamian chronology.

Excavations and soundings in Western Palestine, combined
with the results of Nelson Glueck's surface explorations in
Transjordan (supplemented again by soundings on the part of
various scholars), give us an excellent picture of the history of
occupation. It is true that doubt has been cast by several archaeologists on the validity of Glueck's method of surface exploration.
Having carried out many similar surface explorations himself,
and being familiar with the details of Glueck's work, the writer
can state with absolute confidence that the latter's conclusions
are sound, though this or that detail will doubtless have to be
modified. Outside of the Jordan Valley and south of northern
Gilead there are scarcely any true tells, with superimposed strata
of occupation. Where there is stratification, as at Ader,[1] it seldom
reflects more than a few centuries of occupation, and it is virtually everywhere possible to determine the principal periods of
occupation in a given site or group of sites by careful surface
exploration. Where there are true tells, surface exploration is
inadequate and sometimes yields quite erroneous results, since
whole strata may just not be reflected by finds of sherds on the
top or slopes of the mound. Soundings are also sometimes misleading, and extensive digging is sometimes required to elucidate
a complex history of settlement. Tomb groups, such as the
valuable series recently discovered by Harding near 'Ammân in
Transjordan, do not necessarily prove the existence of a town
near by, since there is strong evidence that pottery was buried
with semi-nomadic chieftains and members of their families.
The writer first became aware of this fact when he failed to find
any evidence of a Middle-Bronze settlement in the Wâdi Sâmieh
in central Palestine, in spite of the fact that there had been a rich
necropolis of this period there, many of whose groups are now

[1] *B.A.S.O.R.*, No. 53 (1934), pp. 13–18.

in the Harvard Semitic Museum. Since then this phenomenon has become familiar, and it would appear to have been especially characteristic of the Hyksos Age, during which vast material wealth was brought back from Egypt by the native chieftains of Palestine who had served with the Hyksos. While most of the objects found in the tombs are of local Palestinian manufacture, many of the weapons and much of the jewellery came from Egypt, and part of the wealth brought from that country was naturally traded for familiar objects of native origin. This situation throws light on the cave of Machpelah near Hebron, in which the Hebrew chieftains of Genesis were buried. Of course, once semi-nomadic notables had adopted the sedentary mode of burial in rock-cut tombs or enlarged grottoes, they also followed the sedentary custom of burying food and drink in pottery vessels with the deceased.

The evidence of excavations and surface explorations, strikingly confirmed by the contents of the Execration Texts (on which see the next chapter), proves that sedentary occupation became thinner all over Palestine toward the end of the third millennium and especially in the course of the twentieth century B.C. Probably before 1900 B.C., and certainly not long afterwards, Transjordan was almost entirely abandoned to the nomads and semi-nomads, while most of Western Palestine was in the hands of semi-nomadic tribes. The situation changed rapidly thereafter, and by the eighteenth century towns were being reoccupied all over Western Palestine. Many new towns were founded and became the fortresses of feudal princes, who had taken the place of the earlier tribal chieftains of the Execration Texts. In the process of displacement the Semitic inhabitants were driven out or subjected by intruders from the north, often of non-Semitic origin. The fortresses and towns of these feudal princes were mostly in the lowlands and river valleys, and there were a number scattered here and there in the hill-country, as at Hebron (probably), Beth-zur, Jerusalem, Bethel, Shechem, &c.

It is now generally recognized that the topographical allusions in Genesis fit the archaeological indications of the Middle Bronze

Age extremely well.[1] Of course, this does not mean necessarily that we can equate the situation presupposed in the patriarchal narratives precisely with any given archaeological situation or group of situations. There are likely to be some anachronisms (such as in the allusions to domesticated camels),[2] some dislocations, and some folkloristic embellishment. But by and large there is astonishing similarity between the background provided by archaeology and that presupposed in Genesis. The semi-nomadic Patriarchs play exactly the role of the semi-nomadic chieftains who lived in the hill-country between thinly scattered fortresses, who moved northward and southward according to the season, and who buried their dead according to the recipes of that day. Even the social organization of the Patriarchs resembles the Amorite background of the Mari and Nuzu documents. Abram and his *hanakîm* correspond almost exactly to the chieftains of the twentieth century with their *hnkw* or *hanakū*.[3] The constant intercourse with Egypt depicted in the Genesis tradition is remarkably reminiscent of the evidence from Egypt and Palestine for continuous movement between the two countries in that period.

Of course, the archaeological evidence from Palestine does not force us to place Abram, for example, in the period of the Execration Texts and the Beni Ḥasan reliefs rather than in the Hyksos Age, and the writer has oscillated between these two alternatives. If we could date Gen. xiv, our task would be simpler, but though evidence continues to strengthen the case for underlying historicity of this chapter, the four kings cannot yet be identified with historical persons. Latest among the names to be identified is 'Arioch', obviously the *Ariyuk*[4] of the Mari

[1] This was first emphasized by the writer, *B.A.S.O.R.*, No. 35 (1929), pp. 10 ff., and often subsequently, as new material pointing in the same direction has been discovered.

[2] See now the discussion by R. de Vaux, *R.B.* lvi, 1949, pp. 7 ff., with full references to recent discussions by the writer. The evidence is steadily increasing in support of the late arrival of the domesticated camel in the Fertile Crescent, and the evidence from camel bones alleged to have been found in Bronze Age deposits is very flimsy.

[3] See *A.f.O.* vi, 1931, p. 221; *B.A.S.O.R.*, No. 94 (1944), p. 24, n. 87 (which is too cautious).

[4] Cf. R. de Vaux, *R.B.* lv, 1948, p. 333. The anomalous *Ariwuk* must be discarded,

documents, but this discovery merely proves that the name was employed by the ruling dynasty of Mari in the eighteenth century B.C. Thanks to the Mari finds we can confidently say that Gen. xiv does not refer to events between *c.* 1750 and 1680 (low chronology), but we are still left undecided between an earlier or a later date. After lowering his preferred date for Abram to the late seventeenth century in 1942,[1] the writer has oscillated back to the twentieth or nineteenth century, but the evidence is still quite inadequate for a real solution of the problem.

It has often been urged of late that the Patriarchs should be dated in the Late Bronze Age, immediately before the time of Moses. This view is opposed by an increasing mass of evidence, in agreement with the Israelite tradition of a long interval between the two periods. Patriarchal names and traditions fit far better into the Middle Bronze background than into that of the Late Bronze. The significance of Late Bronze archaeology for the student of the Old Testament consists particularly in the light it sheds on the immediate background of the Mosaic Age and on conditions immediately before and after the Conquest.

The Late Bronze Age escaped relatively intact from the confusion of periods which demoralized Palestinian archaeology thirty years ago; it had already been correctly dated by Bliss at Tell el-Ḥesi and later by Macalister at Gezer, though the German excavators subsequently confused it to some extent with the Middle Bronze. Most of the finds of cuneiform tablets from Palestine had already been made before 1919, though more tablets have since been discovered at Shechem and at Amarna in Egypt. But great progress has been made during the past decade in interpreting the Canaanite letters from Palestine and Egypt, and it now becomes clear how far we were thirty years ago from being able to utilize their contents fully for historical and philological purposes. Several publications on this subject by

since the sign *PI* was already pronounced *ya, yi, yu* as well as *wa, wi, wu* in the Mari tablets, as demonstrated by a great many clear cases. In the Canaanite Amarna Tablets the former alternatives are exceedingly common and were long ago accepted. The name appears to be of Hurrian (Horite) origin, cf. de Vaux's remarks.

[1] *B.A.S.O.R.*, No. 88 (1942), pp. 33–6. For his present point of view see the historical sketch in *J.H.C.R.*, i, p. 4.

the writer and his pupils are expected to appear soon, and the very great significance of Amarna Canaanite for our understanding of Hebrew grammar (especially syntax) and vocabulary will then become clear. Naturally we are greatly indebted to the light shed on these matters by the decipherment and publication of the Ugaritic tablets (for which see the next chapter).

Among the discoveries which are of special significance to the student of the Old Testament are early inscriptions in the Canaanite alphabet. Since they belong together, regardless of where they were found, we shall briefly sketch their significance here. First comes a group of at least three very short inscriptions from Gezer, Lachish, and Shechem, all datable by material or context to Middle Bronze II B, roughly between 1700 and 1550 B.C. The forms of several characters, notably of the head (presumably *r*) and open hand (presumably *k*), are distinctly more archaic than the forms of the next group of inscriptions belonging to this category. This group was discovered in and near Serābîṭ el-Khâdem in Sinai by Sir Flinders Petrie; it was then partly deciphered by Sir Alan Gardiner before the beginning of our thirty-year period. Since that time the number of inscriptions has been more than doubled by several subsequent expeditions, and in 1948 the writer succeeded in continuing and nearly completing Gardiner's decipherment (at least to his own satisfaction) by the use of the rich material now available for North-west Semitic dialects of the second millennium B.C.[1] Since the resulting linguistic picture fits neatly into the phonetic, morphological, syntactic, and lexicographical framework of the Late Bronze Age, and since it is self-consistent, it has an excellent chance of being proved substantially correct. Of course, we need more and longer inscriptions to confirm or correct it in detail. Discoveries made during the two years that have passed since the decipherment bring striking corroboration of certain points.[2] The writer's

---

[1] *B.A.S.O.R.*, No. 110 (1948), pp. 6–22.

[2] In November, 1949, M. Claude Schaeffer resumed work at Râs Shamrah and discovered a small tablet bearing a complete ABC of the cuneiform alphabet of Ugarit. There were thirty letters in it, the twenty-two Phoenician characters being found in correct order, but separated occasionally by one or another of the five consonants which disappeared from North-west Semitic speech in the thirteenth and twelfth

new dating about the early fifteenth century B.C. is some three centuries later than the commonly accepted one, but agrees with Petrie's view and fits the archaeological picture much better than the early date. Moreover, the language, as deciphered by the writer, follows Late Bronze grammatical forms, and would not fit into Middle Bronze or Early Iron context. Further, the script is distinctly later and more cursive than that of the three Middle Bronze II B inscriptions which we have mentioned, and yet is materially more archaic than that of the thirteenth-century inscriptions from Palestine. The fact that the sculpture and line-drawing of the miners to whom we owe the inscriptions are provincial Egyptian and emphatically not Palestinian combines with other evidence to make the origin of the miners in Egypt certain, though not all of them need have been natives of that country. There is, accordingly, a decided possibility that the Serābît inscriptions reflect the background of the Hebrews in Egypt 150–200 years before the Exodus. Both language and content of the inscriptions point in that direction, but until the writer's readings can be controlled by new material, the whole matter must be left in abeyance.

Probably more than two centuries later than the Serābît inscriptions are two alphabetic inscriptions dating from the last years of Canaanite Lachish, and hence to be dated roughly between 1250 and 1220.[1] Unfortunately both are fragmentary,

centuries B.C. At the end of the twenty-seven consonants in question, evidently copying the order of the contemporary linear alphabet, were three additional letters without special consonantal significance. For the past twenty-five years the writer has been insisting that the Canaanite alphabet had about twenty-seven distinct phonemes, and his reconstruction of the Proto-Sinaitic alphabet shows twenty-seven letters. Another interesting point is that the most archaic South-Arabic dialect, Qatabanian, shows uses of enclitic *m* more closely parallel to Proto-Sinaitic as deciphered by the writer than does any other Semitic tongue, though Ugaritic approaches it closely.

[1] They undoubtedly belong to the latest Canaanite occupation, and the 'ewer' on which one inscription appears had been smashed in the last destruction of the Fosse Temple. On the date see especially *B.A.S.O.R.*, No. 74 (1939), pp. 20 ff.; it should now be lowered from c. 1230 to c. 1220 in view of the convincing new accession year for Ramesses II (1290 B.C.) calculated by M. B. Rowton, *J.E.A.* xxxiv, 1948, pp. 57–74. After much correspondence with Rowton, the writer has been convinced that his results are very probable indeed.

but there is general agreement about the reading of several words in them. To about the same period belongs apparently the Beth-shemesh Ostracon, inscribed on both sides. Most of the inscription is effaced, but two personal names, *Ḥanan* and *Gumʿ ân*, or the like, are clear. A gold ring, found by the Chicago expedition at Megiddo, bears a short incised inscription which is dated by the context of the tomb in which it was found to the first half of the twelfth century (considerably later than the date given it by the excavators); the forms of letters, so far as they can be identified, agree very well with this date. The earliest inscription of this general category which can be read as far as it is preserved is the so-called enigmatic inscription from Byblus, which was partly deciphered by H. Grimme and partly by the writer; most of the characters are already identical in form with the letters on tenth-century inscriptions from Palestine and Phoenicia, but the position of several is so different that they must be reversed or turned upside down before their identity is realized.[1] A date about 1200 B.C. seems reasonable, though there is no external evidence for dating. Since the forms are intermediate between forms of the thirteenth and tenth centuries but closer to the former than to the latter, this date may safely be adopted provisionally.

Archaeology necessarily plays a decisive part in any current discussion of the date of the Israelite Conquest of Canaan, on which the dates of the Exodus and of Moses' career depend so closely. Owing to continuous disturbances in Palestine since 1936, there has been no further archaeological work bearing directly on it since 1938. However, publication since then of numerous definitive excavation reports furnishes rich material for comparative study, and we are thus in a far better position to control our data than was possible a decade ago, when I published my most recent treatment of the problem in detail.[2] Unfortunately, I have not yet published the detailed report on the excavation of Bethel, for which I must apologize very humbly; many

---

[1] See provisionally the writer's discussion of this inscription in *B.A.S.O.R.*, No. 116 (1949), pp. 12–14.
[2] Ibid., No. 74, pp. 11 ff.

points will become clearer after this publication. One minor change of ten years must now be made in my chronology, as a result of M. B. Rowton's demonstration that the reign of Ramesses II is to be set at 1290–1224 instead of at 1300–1234, with Borchardt, whom I have been following for many years.[1] We must then date the shallow bowl with a hieratic inscription from the fourth year of some Pharaoh who immediately succeeded Ramesses II in 1221/1220 or possibly a little later. Since Israel was already menacing the Canaanite towns in force before the following year, according to the famous Israel Stele of Marniptaḥ, we may safely date the fall of Canaanite Lachish in 1220 or shortly thereafter. This is a decade later than my previous date. At the same time my preferred date for the Exodus also comes down about a decade, to *c.* 1280 B.C. Tell Beit Mirsim certainly fell into the hands of the Israelites about the same time as Lachish; Bethel fell not long before, at some time in the course of the thirteenth century. The problems of Bethel and Jericho are substantially identical; in my earlier discussions I failed to give due attention to the fact that both Garstang and I found only empty rooms in the ruins of the latest Canaanite occupations at these two sites; the Late Bronze pottery on which Wright and I based our previous argument[2] came from the débris washed down after the destruction of certain loci of the latest Canaanite occupation of Jericho, and did not represent either débris of occupation or necessarily débris of the final destruction of the town. Our arguments were valid as far as they went, disproving Garstang's date for the destruction about 1400 B.C.; but they did not necessarily establish a date for the final destruction before 1300. We must await further careful excavation before passing judgement; Vincent's date about 1250 B.C. remains possible, though extremely difficult.

Iron I, from the twelfth to the tenth centuries B.C., was scarcely known at all before the excavations which followed the

---

[1] See p. 9, n. 1.

[2] G. Ernest Wright, *B.A.S.O.R.*, No. 86 (1942), pp. 32 ff., with which the writer concurs. But I continued for years to overlook the possible implications of the rooms with well-preserved floor-levels from the latest Canaanite occupation of Jericho and Bethel, which Garstang and I found absolutely empty.

First World War. It is true that Mackenzie had established the chronological relation between the importation of Mycenaean and Cypriote wares into Palestine and the emergence of Philistine pottery, and had shown that there was a period of substantial duration between the end of Mycenaean ware and the first appearance of Philistine pottery at Beth-shemesh. But this observation remained isolated, and the Philistine problem was not cleared up until the thirties. Moreover, virtually no evidence had been found bearing on the period of the United Monarchy, from *c.* 1020 to *c.* 922 B.C.,[1] and the character of the preceding Israelite occupation remained almost wholly obscure. Since that time excavations at Gibeah (Tell el-Fûl), Beth-shan, Tell Beit Mirsim, Tell en-Naṣbeh, Beth-shemesh, Shiloh, Bethel, Tell Abu Huwam, Tell el-Fârʿah in the Negeb, and, most recently, Tell el-Qasîleh near Tel-Aviv, to select only the most significant sites of this period, have enormously increased and refined our knowledge. We can now say with confidence that the Philistine conquest of the southern coastal plain about 1175 B.C.[2] was followed by a period of internal consolidation and slow spread of Philistine influence into neighbouring districts of Israel. Then, about 1050 B.C. or a little later[3] came the destruction of Shiloh by fire, certainly following the defeat of Israel by the Philistines at the battle of Ebenezer. About the same time clear pottery evidence from Tell Beit Mirsim and Beth-zur shows that there were local destructions by fire in these towns.[4] The ceramic evidence is complex but clear; the destructions of the two towns took place before painted Philistine ware had gone out of use, but after Cypriote perfume juglets of Black-on-Red I type had begun

---

[1] For the chronology see *B.A.S.O.R.*, No. 100 (1945), pp. 16–22, to which additional Tyrian and Egyptian evidence may be added; e.g. Hiram of Tyre was a long-time friend and ally of David, and his reign is fixed by the Tyrian annals, as reported by Menander of Ephesus, to 969–936 B.C. The writer's date for David, c. 1000–961 B.C., agrees very well with this synchronism, but higher dates do not.

[2] The lowering of this date follows Rowton's new chronology (cf. p. 9, n. 1). Note, however, that the writer long defended the same date for Ramesses III, c. 1180–1150, before he provisionally accepted Borchardt's chronology (1195–1164 B.C.).

[3] The evidence for this date is historical and genealogical; cf. *A.R.I.*, pp. 201 f., n. 18. Some lowering is possible and now seems probable to the writer.

[4] See *A.A.S.O.R.* xxi–xxii, 1943, pp. 8 ff., 36 ff.

to be imported. Moreover, Beth-zur was destroyed before the collar-rimmed store-jar (*pithos*) had gone out of use between the fall of Shiloh and the period of Saul's fortress at Gibeah.[1] It may be added that Maisler's date for the disappearance of painted Philistine pottery at Tell el-Qasîleh, *c.* 1050,[2] is too high; it may have lasted as late as 1000 B.C. On the other hand, Gjerstad's dates for his early geometric Cypriote wares are generally much too low, as will be shown by Young and Van Beek.

Space is lacking for a full discussion of the archaeological evidence for the date of the Song of Deborah. The arguments of Engberg and Simons[3] against the writer's date between Megiddo VII and VI are both squarely contradicted by the evidence now succinctly presented in *Megiddo II*, which shows that there was a complete break in the occupational history then, with a drastic interruption in the continuity of town-planning. The writer's brief surrender to Engberg on this point was motivated mainly by an erroneous assumption that the latter (who left Megiddo before work was undertaken at these levels) was better informed than he proved to be. Rowton's reduction of the date for the reign of Ramesses III by fifteen years (which marks a return to the date long previously held by the writer) compels us to date the fall of Megiddo VII after *c.* 1140 B.C., and a date for the Song of Deborah in the interval before Megiddo VI was occupied, *c.* 1125 B.C., remains probable from every angle.

The archaeology of the United Monarchy is far better known today than it was even a decade ago, thanks to recent excavations and to publication of previous finds. It is true that our knowledge of the archaeology of Saul's reign stands about where the writer left it in 1933 after his second season at Tell el-Fûl (which remains unpublished except for the preliminary report),[4] and that we have only scraps of evidence with regard to the buildings and culture of David's reign. But evidence for the culture of

[1] Cf. *P.A.P.*, pp. 118 f.

[2] See *B.J.P.E.S.* xv, 1949, p. 12; though Maisler's date for Stratum X seems 25–50 years too high, his stratification will be exceedingly valuable.

[3] See *B.A.S.O.R.*, No. 78 (1940), pp. 4–9, and *O.T.S.* i, 1941–2, pp. 38–54; cf. my remarks in *J.H.C.R.*, i, p. 58, n. 52.

[4] *B.A.S.O.R.*, No. 52 (1933), pp. 6–12.

Solomon's time has increased enormously. The excavation by P. L. O. Guy and others of the Solomonic stables at Megiddo was followed by Nelson Glueck's excavation of the copper refinery and Red Sea port at Ezion-geber (Tell el-Kheleifeh). Hazor and Tell el-Ḥesi have also yielded evidence of Solomonic constructions which could not previously be dated. On the other hand, Schumacher and Macalister had recognized the Solomonic date of certain masonry at Megiddo and Gezer; their attributions have since been confirmed. It is true that J. W. Crowfoot and Kathleen Kenyon have been inclined to reject as too high the Solomonic date of Megiddo IV B, the Davidic or Solomonic stratum of the excavators, but their evidence is simply that the earliest pottery of Samaria (founded about 870 B.C. according to my chronology) is virtually identical in some respects with the pottery of IV B at Megiddo. Since the latter was almost certainly burned by Shishak about 918 B.C. (the mention of the town in his Karnak list is confirmed by the finding of a fragment of a monument of his at Megiddo), there was a period of less than fifty years between the end of Solomonic Megiddo and the foundation of Samaria. Since there was no sharp change in pottery styles in the interim, the actual situation is exactly what one would expect *a priori*. As for the argument that the Stables are later than the Palace Enclosure, it is disproved by the fact that the plaster pavements of both show exactly comparable indications of extensive repair after destruction; both complexes were in more or less continuous use from their construction by Solomon after about 950 B.C. until their final destruction by the Syrians somewhere about 815 B.C. (see below). Careful analysis of the excavation reports by G. Ernest Wright and H. G. May, following the writer's suggestions, shows that Megiddo IV B was much more important than had been thought by the excavators, who had attributed extensive areas of Megiddo IV B to IV A or V A. Actually there is no adequate evidence for two successive phases of V, which was a short period, lasting from late in the eleventh century to somewhere between *c.* 990, when David began to expand Israel, and *c.* 950, when Solomon took Megiddo over to be rebuilt as a chariot city.

As already stated, there was little reliable knowledge of Iron II, the period of the Divided Monarchy, in 1919 when the writer first came to Palestine. Owing to the fact that Reisner's two massive volumes on Samaria did not actually appear until 1924, the results of his splendid excavation did not become available to scholars until long after the close of the dig. When J. W. Crowfoot attacked the site again in 1931, he was able to bring the results of a decade of scientific excavation after the end of the First World War to bear on the site. He was naturally able to correct and refine the conclusions of Reisner in many details. One assured result of Crowfoot's work, obtained by close collaboration with Kathleen Kenyon and I. Ben Dor, was that the famous ostraca of Samaria must be dated much later than Ahab, almost certainly in the reign of Jeroboam II. Since they were found in the second and last constructional phase of the Israelite palace complex and since the first phase, begun under Omri, can scarcely have been finished until well along in the reign of Ahab, the view of Reisner is categorically impossible. The script is, of course, good cursive of the eighth century, as we now know from fairly extensive comparative material. Aside from the valuable ostraca, somewhat augmented in number by recent finds, Samaria has yielded important data for Israelite architecture in the ninth-eighth centuries and reliable evidence for the development of pottery in northern Israel, though we must await Miss Kenyon's publication for details. The ivories of Samaria have also provided us with most significant insight into Phoenician influence on Israelite art in the same period.

Owing to the accidents of archaeological history, comparatively few sites of importance for the period of the Divided Monarchy have been adequately excavated during the past thirty years, though a great many sites of this period have been examined. Like Gezer, Beth-shan remained unoccupied. Megiddo, Tell Beit Mirsim, Beth-shemesh, Tell en-Naṣbeh, and Lachish have been our chief sources; from them it has been possible to build up a consistent ceramic chronology and to gain a good general idea of the development of civilization and the vicissitudes through which Israel passed. The discoveries at

Megiddo since 1925 have thrown light on both the ninth and the eighth centuries, less on the seventh. Tell Beit Mirsim has given us by far the clearest idea of life in the seventh and early sixth centuries in Judah. Beth-shemesh had yielded interesting details of life in the ninth and eighth centuries, but very little for the following period. Tell en-Naṣbeh has also furnished valuable information for the ninth and eighth centuries, less for the latter part of our period. Lachish has already proved invaluable for the last century and a half of the monarchy of Judah; its excavators have barely begun to disclose the information about the Monarchy which must be buried there.

One of the most striking features of the excavations during the past generation has been a steady rise in our respect for the material civilization of the Israelites during the Divided Monarchy. We have already referred to the extraordinary change in the attitude of historians to the period of Solomon brought about by work at Megiddo and Ezion-geber. At the commencement of the past generation Macalister's exceedingly low opinion of the material culture of Iron II held the field and still influences biblical scholars, who do not realize that it was based on erroneous dating of an inferior settlement of Iron I. The writer's work at Tell Beit Mirsim gives an entirely different picture of the life of common men in a typical provincial town of Judah in the seventh and early sixth centuries. Houses were well built and clean, being provided with cisterns and adequate drainage; cattle were kept outside the town, and the members of a household slept upstairs, not on the ground (at least as a rule). Moreover, writing was very common in the eighth and seventh centuries, as shown by many short graffiti on pottery and other objects, as well as by beautifully written ostraca and occasional formal inscriptions. A multitude of inscribed seals, only one of which may safely be attributed to the ninth century,[1] shows a steady increase in the use of writing and enables us to check the development of script by royal seals and private seals standing in known genealogical relationship. Among recent additions to the list of

---

[1] This is the seal which appears in Diringer's book, *Le iscrizioni anticoebraiche palestinesi* (1934), pl. xx: 10. *Mem* and probably *aleph* are very archaic.

seals bearing identifiable royal names or names of officials are those of Ahaz, Jotham, Shubna ('Shebna'),[1] and Gedaliah. The jar-stamps inscribed 'belonging to the king' can also be arranged in chronological order according to their types, and their general date is quite certain.[2]

Thanks to the Lachish Ostracon and the ostracon from Ophel, as well as to the two recently published ostraca from Tell el-Qasîleh,[3] it is now possible to study the development of the Hebrew cursive hand in the century and a half following the Ostraca of Samaria. Previously there was always a possibility that the material on which the Siloam inscription and numerous graffiti are inscribed might mislead us into regarding their scripts as lapidary rather than cursive. We know today that (with due caution in detail) they can be regarded as true reflections of the ordinary scribal hand of their time. In the near future we may confidently expect further discoveries to make it possible for us to date inscribed objects from the Divided Monarchy within narrow limits. It will also be possible by careful comparative method to throw much light on Hebrew phonology and linguistic usage during our period, with new opportunities for dating and interpreting Old Testament literature composed at that time.

One of the most important historical results of excavation in the past three decades has been to fix the periods of occupation and the time of destruction in many biblical sites of Palestine belonging to the Monarchy. The combination of documentary and archaeological data required for this type of research still requires a critical attitude, but the great advance of knowledge in recent years has stabilized the situation. First in significance for our period comes the invasion of Shishak about the year 918 B.C. It is true that 1 Kings mentions only his capture of

[1] For the vocalization and meaning of this name and the fuller *Shubnayahu* (Shebaniah) cf. already *B.A.S.O.R.*, No. 79 (1940), pp. 28 f., n. 1; No. 82 (1941), p. 17. The vocalization is proved by cuneiform (Neo-Babylonian) *Šubunuiama* (pronounced approximately *Šubnyau*), LXX *Sobnas*, and now also by the full writing *Šwbn'* of the new Isaiah Scroll from the second century B.C. (Burrows, *J.B.L.* lxviii, 1949, p. 205).

[2] See Diringer, *P.E.Q.*, 1941, pp. 91–101; the writer, *A.A.S.O.R.* xxi–xxii, pp. 73 ff.; Diringer, *B.A.* xii, 1949, pp. 70–86.

[3] See Maisler, *B.J.P.E.S.* xv, pl. v: 1–2. His date in the eighth century B.C. is certainly correct.

Jerusalem, but the report in 2 Chron. xii. 2 ff. says that the fortified towns of Judah were captured and lists his army as consisting of Libyans, *Sukkîyîm*, and Ethiopians—all barbarians who undoubtedly sacked and burned whatever towns they stormed. The historical accuracy of the Chronicler has been recognized increasingly by archaeologists, and there is not the slightest reason to suspect his account as a whole, though there may easily be exaggeration in detail. The hitherto mysterious *Sukkîyîm* have at last made their appearance as foreign troops in Egyptian service from the twelfth century onwards; their origin remains, however, obscure.[1] It is certain that Megiddo, which is among the towns named in the Shishak List, fell into Egyptian hands, since a fragment of a Shishak stele was discovered there by Fisher in 1925; evidence of destruction at the end of Megiddo IV A fits exceedingly well into this situation, *c.* 918 B.C. Tell Beit Mirsim and Beth-shemesh were destroyed about the same time, and contemporary destruction levels will doubtless turn up as more sites are adequately excavated.

The end of Megiddo IV A is graphically illustrated by the account of the humiliation of Israel and the almost total destruction of its chariotry by Hazael, *c.* 815 B.C. (2 Kings xiii. 3–7). Since Megiddo was one of the principal Israelite fortresses, standing in a key position and housing at least 400 chariot horses, it is incredible that it escaped destruction at this time. The archaeological indications are in perfect agreement with this date, and the stables were never rebuilt after Hazael's destruction.

The problem of the identification of Tell el-Fâr'ah, near Nâblus, with Tirzah, sketched originally by the writer twenty years ago, will be solved largely by similar methods, since Tirzah seems to have disappeared from the scene after the time of Omri. So far R. de Vaux has failed to find any signs of occupation after the ninth century B.C.[2] This is only one example; there are many others which must be passed over for lack of space. The writer's demonstration that the list of Levitic towns in Joshua reflects

---

[1] See Gardiner, *The Wilbour Papyrus* (1948), ii, p. 81, n. 1. Spiegelberg had long previously divined the equivalence of the Egyptian and Hebrew words, but without adequate proof.   [2] *R.B.* lv, 1948, pp. 570 f.

the latter part of David's reign is based very largely on similar arguments.[1] It is already probable that most of the fortified Israelite towns of Galilee were destroyed by the Assyrians in 733 and that many of them, like Hazor (Tell el-Qedaḥ) and Chinnereth (Tell el-'Oreimeh), were never reoccupied.

But the outstanding example of the importance of archaeological research *sensu stricto* in establishing historical fact on a large scale is in connexion with the Chaldaean conquest of Judah and the subsequent history of the country. While there is evidence for partial destruction of some towns in or about 701 B.C., when Sennacherib invaded Judah,[2] the devastation then caused cannot be compared in any way with the total destruction of the towns of Judah in 589–587 B.C. Nor can the partial destruction of towns like Tell Beit Mirsim and Lachish in 598 B.C. be compared with the devastation which we find in excavating the ruins of towns captured a decade later. This last destruction was total, and there is as yet no evidence for any immediate reoccupation. At Tell Beit Mirsim there was no reoccupation at all after about 588 B.C., and the same situation is found in surface exploration of all the mounds in that vicinity, such as Tell Khuweilifeh, Tell 'Aiṭûn, and Tell Muleihah. Tell ed-Duweir (Lachish) offers the same picture, except that a Persian villa was erected there in the fifth century and a small settlement grew up around it. Beth-shemesh tells a similar story; it was not reoccupied until Byzantine times. And this we find to have been the case wherever we can examine the site of an ancient fortified town of pre-exilic Judah within the territory held by its last kings. There is strong evidence that the Negeb proper was no longer part of Judah in the last years before the Chaldaean conquest. It is not, therefore, surprising to find Jewish settlements continuing there—presumably without serious interruption—into the the fifth century B.C., or to find the Edomites established at the same time in the southern hill-country around Hebron, Adoraim (Adora), and Maresha (Marisa), which had been completely depopulated by the Chaldaeans. Outside the territory

---

[1] See *Louis Ginzberg Jubilee Volume* (1945), English Section, pp. 49–73.
[2] See *A.A.S.O.R.* xxi–xxii, 1943, pp. 65 f.

held by the last kings of Judah northward of Jerusalem we have
a similar situation. Gibeah (Tell el-Fûl) was probably on the
northern boundary of Judah at that time. North of it we have
no evidence of general destruction in the early sixth century, and
there can scarcely have been such a destruction at Tell en-
Naṣbeh, to judge from the results of Badè's excavation, while
there most certainly was no destruction at Bethel until decades
after the Chaldaean invasion (as shown unmistakably by the
pottery found in the ruins of the great conflagration which
destroyed Bethel somewhere in or about the latter part of the
sixth century).

The historical importance of the Lachish Ostraca is by now
sufficiently well known to require no commentary here, and
their date in 589 or 588 B.C. is recognized by all scholars who
have dealt competently with the material. It is perhaps not so
generally known that the two stamps from the seal of 'Eliakim
steward of Yaukin', found by the writer in the ruins of the last
partial rebuilding of Tell Beit Mirsim after the capture and
partial destruction of the town in 598, are identical with a similar
stamp found in the remains of the latest pre-exilic town of Beth-
shemesh; all three were made by the same seal. Moreover, Père
Vincent's correct identification of Yaukin with king Joiachin,
accepted and developed by the writer,[1] who showed its historical
implications, has been fully confirmed by Weidner's publication of
several tablets listing the rations given to captive Yaukin, king
of Judah, and five royal princes in or about 592 B.C. The spellings
of the name reflect exactly the same pronunciation, leaving no
possible doubt about the identification. Such seals as those of
Gedaliah, found at Lachish, and Jaazaniah, discovered at Tell
en-Naṣbeh, help further to round out the picture of officialdom
in the last days of the First Temple.

In contrast to the overwhelming mass of evidence from
archaeology for the total devastation of Judah at the time of
the Chaldaean invasions, there is comparatively little evidence
directly affecting our historical picture of the Persian period.
Reoccupation was slow at places hitherto excavated, such as

Beth-zur and Bethel, especially the latter. Since there is no indication of a destruction at either site for several centuries following the reoccupation in the fifth century B.C., our evidence for occupation is scanty and rather haphazard, consisting mainly of sherds, coins, and fragmentary foundations. Whenever the archaeologist finds complete or even partial destructions he has before him stratigraphic evidence of clear-cut nature. But when he deals with sites where occupation was more or less continuous and where the absence of fortifications prevented the accumulation of débris, he is severely handicapped. So it is at Beth-zur and Bethel. When we find a seal-impression with latish pre-exilic characters, inscribed with the name of 'Gealiah, son of the king', at Beth-zur,[1] we may safely identify the owner with the Davidide Yig'al of I Chron. iii. 22, who was the son of Nehemiah's contemporary, Shemaiah son of Shecaniah. This identification, first made by B. Maisler, commends itself at once to all who are familiar with the shifts of personal names in Hebrew[2] and is confirmed by the archaizing script, so different from the flowing lines of real pre-exilic epigraphs.

E. L. Sukenik's identification of the name *Yehûd*, 'Judah', on jar-stamps and coins of the fifth–third centuries B.C.[3] has thrown much light on the organization of the post-exilic Jewish state under Persian rule. The coins bearing this inscription all belong to the fourth and perhaps the early third century B.C. The date of the jar-stamps is not so clear, since we lack adequate comparative material, but there can be no doubt that none precedes the fifth century or is later than the beginning of the second (at very latest). The same is true of the stamps containing the pentagram and the name 'Jerusalem'. All of this material combines to prove that there was some kind of autonomous priestly control of the Temple treasury, with the right to levy excise taxes or tithes in order to keep its extensive cult going. It is of peculiar interest to note that the coins used at that time in southern

---

[1] *B.A.S.O.R.*, No. 43 (1931), pp. 8 f. At first we dated the seal too early.

[2] Cf., e.g., the various forms attested for the name of Joiachin, especially *Yekōnyāhū* and *Kōnyāhū*, *•Yauyākîn (Yoyākîn)* and *Yaukîn*.

[3] See especially *B.A.S.O.R.*, No. 53 (1934), pp. 20–2.

Palestine, including the 'Judah' coins, follow the Attic standard and are mostly transparent imitations of Athenian coins, with the owl and head of Athene. This proves that the Chronicler was quite correct in writing of drachma collections (*darkemônîm* is plural of a **darkemáh*, or the like) in the Persian period (properly in the time of Nehemiah).[1]

Light from Palestinian archaeology on the Hellenistic period, while very respectable, seldom bears directly as yet on the interpretation of the Old Testament. However, one recent discovery promises to illuminate text and canon of the Hebrew Bible in a way previously unhoped for by the most optimistic scholar. I refer, of course, to the finding of the Dead Sea Scrolls in 1947. The following spring, after several scrolls had been purchased by the Syrian Monastery of St. Mark in Jerusalem and a roughly equivalent number had been bought by E. L. Sukenik for the Hebrew University, they were brought to the attention of the world and promptly created a sensation. Now, early in 1950, all the scrolls hitherto sold by the Bedouin finders (who are credibly reported to be hiding some in the hope of obtaining higher prices) have either been completely unrolled or have at least been identified by detached fragments. There prove to be seven extensive documents, besides a part of a scroll and many hundreds of fragments found in the cave afterwards. These seven documents include: a complete scroll of Isaiah from about the second half of the second century B.C.; another more fragmentary scroll which contains material from the last third of Isaiah in a later hand; a partly preserved commentary of midrashic character on the first two chapters of Habakkuk; a 'sectarian' document containing many interesting details bearing on the beliefs and organization of an unidentified Jewish sect of the second century B.C., together with a long poetic composition belonging to the same sect; a long collection of thanksgiving hymns (the so-called *Hôdāyôt*), put together from what were originally four distinct scrolls or remains of scrolls; a text of apparently eschatological character, describing the war of the Children of Light against

[1] Cf. the writer's discussion of this subject in his paper 'The Judicial Reform of Jehoshaphat' in the *Alexander Marx Jubilee Volume* (New York, 1950, pp. 61–82).

the Children of Darkness; finally, part of the long lost Book of Lamech, showing very close affinities to the first part of the Book of Enoch as well as to the so-called 'Book of Noah', imbedded in our extant Enoch. The first six of these texts are, of course, in Hebrew, while the seventh is in an Aramaic which is distinctly later than the Aramaic of Daniel (now ascribed by many scholars to the third century B.C.) but considerably older than any otherwise known Jewish Aramaic texts (as distinct from inscriptions).

When the new scrolls first became known they were dated palaeographically to the last two centuries B.C., since it was immediately clear to a number of scholars that they were considerably later than the Edfu papyri and ostraca belonging to a Jewish colony of the third century B.C. in Upper Egypt, and yet earlier than most of the graffiti, dipinti, and formal inscriptions of the Herodian and immediately preceding period found increasingly in recent years in the area of Jerusalem. This date, vigorously defended by the writer and S. A. Birnbaum, has been confirmed in the most conclusive way by the excavation of the cave itself by G. Lankester Harding and Père R. de Vaux, early in 1949.[1] The masses of sherds and larger remains of pottery found in the cave are characteristically late Hellenistic in type and cannot possibly be dated after the development of the Herodian phase of early Roman pottery. The homogeneous character of the pottery has impressed itself on all ceramic experts who have seen it, and it may safely be labelled as not later than the first century B.C. Since most of it must have been specially made for storing the scrolls, none of it can be appreciably earlier or later than the latest scrolls. The excavators prefer a date for the sealing of the cave somewhere about the end of the second century or the beginning of the first century B.C. I agree that this date is entirely possible, but see no good reason for placing the *terminus ad quem* before the third quarter of the first century B.C.; Birnbaum's date about 50 B.C., adopted before the excavation of the cave, seems reasonable. In any case palaeography and archaeology agree most strikingly in fixing the date at which

[1] See now *R.B.* lvi, 1949, pp. 586–609. The dates given by Harding and de Vaux for the late Hellenistic pottery found in the cave may be a little too high.

the scrolls were stored in this cave not later than the middle decades of the first century B.C., somewhere in the transition from Maccabaean to Herodian times. This also happens to be the writer's *terminus ad quem* for the famous Nash Papyrus, found in Egypt and dated by the writer in the Maccabaean period.[1] This fragment has a great deal in common with the scripts and hands employed in the scrolls, but it is not yet certain whether it belongs with the later or earlier group of the latter, since the palaeographic evidence is not altogether clear.

Since there were over forty jars, each capable of holding several scrolls, there must have been two hundred or more complete rolls at one time. Besides the seven documents already identified, there are scores of different texts represented by hundreds of fragments. Among them have been identified bits of Genesis, Exodus, Leviticus, Deuteronomy, Daniel, Jubilees, &c., besides hitherto unknown works. All are in contemporary Aramaic script except five fragments of the Holiness Code of Leviticus, written in an archaic Samaritan or possibly late pre-exilic script which the excavators would date in the third or fourth century B.C. The writer does not see his way clear to dissociating this script from the Samaritan alphabet *sensu stricto*; he is impressed by its radical departure from the normal cursive tradition of the last two centuries before the Exile. To him it appears to be modelled on the archaistic lapidary of the Persian period (e.g. the Gealiah seal mentioned above) and to have many striking points of contact with the archaizing script of the Maccabaean coins. He is not, therefore, ready to date it before the second or preferably early first century B.C. However, only the future can determine what is true in this instance.

The new biblical texts will provide textual critics with a wealth of new material. Since the Greek translators of the third and early second centuries B.C. probably employed old scrolls of the fourth and third centuries where possible, we must not be surprised to find our new evidence from a later date supporting the Masoretic Hebrew against the Greek most of the time where the two texts diverge. One thing is already certain: though the

[1] See *J.B.L.* lvi, 1937, pp. 145–76; *B.A.S.O.R.*, No. 115 (1949), pp. 10–19.

Hebrew text was far from being fully Masoretic in the period between *c.* 150 and *c.* 50 B.C., it was already fixed, and the differences between it and our printed Bibles are seldom significant. The new texts from the first century B.C. in familiar quasi-Masoretic consonantal orthography are very close to the Masorah, though they sometimes prefer LXX readings. The Isaiah Scroll is written in a drastically divergent orthography, which goes even farther than the Nash Papyrus in employing vowel-letters to indicate vocalization. Though the text itself is careless and may have been based on a specially dictated prototype, as thought by H. M. Orlinsky, the spelling yields a rich harvest of morphological and lexicographical details hitherto unknown, since they were lost long before the period of the Masorah.

One thing is certain: the days when Duhm and his imitators could recklessly emend the Hebrew text of the poetic books of the Bible are gone for ever; so also is the time when Wutz felt free to reinterpret the original Hebrew *Vorlage* of the LXX to suit himself. We may rest assured that the consonantal text of the Hebrew Bible, though not infallible, has been preserved with an accuracy perhaps unparalleled in any other Near-Eastern literature. Moreover, the discovery of the Hymns (*Hôḏāyôt*), which were composed not later than the second century B.C. in a strange mosaic pattern whose constituent elements come from all parts of the Bible, including the latest Psalms and Job, deals the *coup de grâce* to the hypothesis of Maccabaean Psalms, while the Habakkuk Commentary from the same period makes it impossible seriously to accept the idea that there are Hellenistic elements in the Prophets. Incidentally, the mere fact that the translators misunderstood the meaning of innumerable words and phrases in Hebrew poetry so completely when putting the latter into Greek in the second century B.C., should give us pause before suggesting that some of these poems had been composed in the very same century. No, the flood of light now being shed on biblical Hebrew poetry of all periods by Ugaritic literature guarantees the relative antiquity of its composition as well as the astonishing accuracy of its transmission.

Archaeology and its ancillary disciplines are only beginning to yield the information which our pupils will be able to derive from them, and the possibilities now seem almost without limit. The next chapter will illustrate how they are magnified when the entire ancient Orient shares in this inspiring task!

W. F. ALBRIGHT

II

THE OLD TESTAMENT AND THE ARCHAEOLOGY OF THE ANCIENT EAST

In the preceding chapter we sketched the results of thirty years of research in Palestinian archaeology and its bearing on the Old Testament. Here we shall describe some of the most important finds bearing on the Hebrew Bible which have been made in other lands of the ancient East since the end of the First World War. There have been many surprises of the most sensational character, such as the discoveries at Ugarit and Mari; there has also been steady progress almost all along the line. In Egypt, for instance, it was widely supposed thirty years ago that we were entering a period of diminishing returns in archaeology. This is not true at all; I shall never forget the vivid impression made on me at the end of 1947 by a tour around the Cairo Museum during which M. Étienne Drioton, director of antiquities, showed me the outstanding finds made during the twelve years of his incumbency up to that time.

Since it will obviously be impossible even to list all the discoveries of biblical significance made in the lands of the ancient East outside of Palestine during the past thirty years, we shall have to select a few items from the rich material. Above all, we must omit any characterization of the most important contribution of all: the extraordinary advance in the interpretation and correlation of finds, both written and unwritten, anepigraphic artifacts as well as literary compositions. Thanks to the astonishing development of stratigraphy and typology, we can now correlate most remains of human civilization over the entire ancient East with comparatively little disagreement among competent scholars. Thanks equally to the devoted grammatical and lexicographical investigations of scholars like Sir Alan Gardiner and Benno Landsberger, we can interpret ancient inscriptions with far greater confidence than was possible a generation ago.

Despite the fact that a century of archaeological investigation had already preceded the year 1919, the past thirty years have seen new peoples resurrected from the oblivion of millennia, new scripts brought to light and deciphered, new literatures disclosed, and whole worlds of unsuspected culture unveiled. At the outset of our period the Hittites were little known and the Horites (Hurrians) known only by name; the Ugaritic alphabet and the Byblian syllabary were equally unknown; the long-lost literature of Hittites, Horites, and Canaanites remained to be discovered, and little was known about Sumerian literature; the civilization of the third millennium B.C. in India was just as unknown as that of the Sumerians had been seventy years before.

The tremendous significance of the new finds for the Bible can be realized in part by listing a few of the outstanding achievements of the spade: the revival of the Patriarchal Age through the excavations at Nuzu and Mari; the flood of light on Hebrew poetry and language as a result of the excavation of Ugarit; the vivid illumination of the beginnings of Mosaic legislation through the publication of Hittite and Assyrian, Sumerian and Eshnunna codes; new light on the Persian period of Jewish history from Egypt and Iran. But again it must be emphasized that the really great contribution of ancient Eastern archaeology has been in the total picture, which enables us to see the life of the Chosen People against the background of the surrounding world. This is a contribution before which everything else must fade into insignificance.

We shall pass the principal lands of the ancient Near and Middle East—Syria, Mesopotamia, Asia Minor, Egypt—rapidly before our eyes, selecting only developments of major importance for biblical scholars, though not forgetting the fact that isolated finds mean little except in context. Syria must come first because it had remained archaeological *terra incognita* until after the formation of the French Mandate immediately following the end of the First World War, and so all the most sensational finds in that rich land come within our thirty-year period.

A few finds in Syria have already been described because of their intimate connexion with similar finds in Palestine.

Byblus has been disappointing, probably because much of the ancient citadel of the city has long since disappeared beneath the waters of the Mediterranean. Aside from the one great temple, no public buildings have been recovered, and the stratified deposits hitherto encountered in digging the old site throw little light on the development of the city and its civilization during the third, second, and first millennia B.C. And yet accidental finds, seldom in context, have revealed something of the prodigious antiquity of the holy city of Gebal, port of the cedar trade with Egypt from time immemorial. Dunand's discovery and publication of the syllabic Byblian inscriptions in hieroglyphiform characters from the early centuries of the second millennium—perhaps even earlier—have disclosed the possibilities still latent for our future knowledge of higher Canaanite culture.[1] The discovery of numerous Byblian inscriptions from about the tenth century has thrown very important direct light on the evolution of Hebrew script and orthography.[2]

The accidental discovery of the great ancient site of Ugarit, modern Râs esh-Shamrah or Râs Shamra, in 1929 and its subsequent excavation by C. F. A. Schaeffer, have completely altered our picture of Canaanite civilization.[3] Though repeated

---

[1] For the excavations at Byblus see especially Pierre Montet, *Byblos et l'Égypte* (text and plates, Paris, 1928); Maurice Dunand, *Fouilles de Byblos*, vol. i (plates, Paris, 1937; text, Paris, 1939); Dunand, *Byblia Grammata* (Beyrouth, 1945). E. Dhorme's decipherment of the Proto-Byblian inscriptions is a *tour de force* which must remain *sub judice* for the present; see especially Dhorme, *Syria*, xxv, 1946–8, pp. 1–35, and in criticism R. de Langhe, *Bi. Or.* v, 1948, pp. 81–3. Among principal weaknesses of Dhorme's decipherment are the want of grammatical and phonetic consistency, the limitation of the number of consonants to twenty-three, whereas we now know that there were about twenty-seven (thanks to the recent discovery of an Ugaritic ABC based on the twenty-seven letters of the linear Canaanite alphabet, to which three specifically Ugaritic letters have been added), and the failure to attribute accompanying vowels to their consonants in assigning values to the syllabic characters of Proto-Byblian.

[2] See my treatment of these inscriptions in *J.A.O.S.* lxvii, 1947, pp. 153 ff.

[3] In addition to the annual reports and supplementary articles in *Syria* (since vol. x, 1929), see Schaeffer, *Ugaritica I* (Paris, 1939), *Ugaritica II* (Paris, 1949), and R. de Langhe, *Les Textes de Ras Shamra-Ugarit et leurs rapports avec le milieu biblique de l'Ancien Testament* (2 vols., Gembloux & Paris, 1945). The Ras Shamrah

efforts have been made to separate Ugaritic and Ugaritic literature from Canaanite, it remains certain that Ugarit formed an
integral part of the domain of Canaanite culture stretching in
the Late Bronze Age from Gaza in the south to Ugarit in the
north. Pottery and material culture of this territory remained
virtually identical through the Middle and Late Bronze, from
before 1800 to after 1200 B.C. Language and religion were also
virtually identical; the languages of Ugarit and Byblus were only
dialectally different, and the religions of the two cities differed
mainly in the Horite tinge of Ugaritic pantheon and ritual. As
soon as we cross the massif of Casius into the valley of the lower
Orontes we find substantial changes in pottery and other forms
of material culture, and the Horite and 'Amorite' elements in
higher culture become dominant, as we know from the excavations of Sir Leonard Woolley at Alalakh (Tell 'Aṭshânah), as
well as from du Mesnil du Buisson's work at Qaṭna (el-
Mishrifeh). But along the coast there is no real change, and
Ugarit was regarded in Byblus as the wealthiest of all the Canaanite cities, as we are informed in an Amarna letter.

It is rather superfluous to recall the circumstances of the
discovery of the previously unknown Canaanite cuneiform
alphabet at Râs Shamrah in 1929, or its decipherment by Hans
Bauer and Dhorme in 1931 and its definitive interpretation and
the publication of the tablets inscribed in it by Virolleaud in
subsequent years. In 1932 Virolleaud published the first instalment of tablets belonging to the great Baal Epic, and by 1940
he had published most of the literary material, and the first
scientific grammar of Ugaritic had been published by C. H.
Gordon, following the principles of H. L. Ginsberg. In 1946
a new edition of the *Ugaritic Grammar* appeared, with complete
transcriptions and vocabulary, as an *Ugaritic Handbook* (Rome).
This makes it possible for all biblical scholars and Semitic
philologians to take part in the interpretation of these priceless monuments of Canaanite religious literature. To be sure,
Gordon's useful translation of all significant texts, both literary

bibliography has kept swelling until it is now formidable in bulk and often difficult of
access.

and documentary, in his *Ugaritic Literature* (Rome, 1949) shows clearly how much remains to be done before we can really understand the Canaanite epics, but he has provided an exceedingly valuable foundation on which others can build.

There has been much misunderstanding of certain basic matters in discussions of the Ugaritic epics and other religious texts. There can be no doubt, in the writer's opinion, that we have only an insignificant fragment of the total content of the epics of Baal, Keret, and Aqhat. It is probable that the Baal Epic contained at least 5,000 lines and perhaps even two or three times as much; the other two epics were probably shorter, but the breaks between the now extant tablets indicate that many more tablets must be lost. Thus the Keret Epic, three tablets of which have been preserved in more or less fragmentary form, may easily have had twelve or more tablets. Under these conditions it is idle to attempt to distinguish between different compositions belonging to the Baal cycle, or to analyze it into allegedly parallel strands in the manner of the documentary hypothesis of Old Testament scholars.

The date of our copies of these tablets is certain; they belong in the main to the reign of Niqmadda, who was a contemporary of Suppiluliuma of Khatti. Among his letters from Amarna there is one in which his name is spelled out as indicated by our transcription.[1] But the original composition of the epics may have been considerably earlier. Keret and Aqhat contain traces of a later stage of Canaanite literary development, and references to chariots and horses in the former and to typical Middle-Bronze names in the latter suggest a date of composition after *c.* 1800 B.C. The Baal Epic, however, is much more archaic, and may easily contain elements little changed for many centuries before the date of our copies. It would not be at all surprising if it goes back in substantially its extant form to the third millennium B.C. To judge from many indications of mistakes brought about by dictation from oral sources in these epics, especially in Keret and Aqhat, the date of original reduction to writing did not much

---

[1] This point (still overlooked by many writers) has been demonstrated in my paper, *B.A.S.O.R.*, No. 95 (1944), pp. 30–3.

precede the early fourteenth century B.C., to which our copies belong.

The provenience of these three epics can be confidently designated as Phoenicia Proper, that is, the coast of Lebanon between Galilee and the Eleutherus Valley. In support of this inference are many data. The geographical names which can be identified with confidence, such as Lebanon and Shariyânu (Sirion), Tyre and Sidon, belong there, and plausibly identified place-names such as *Smk* and *Hrnm* belong in the immediate hinterland, north of Lake Ḥûleh and in the Biqâʿ of Syria, respectively. The pantheon of the epics is more characteristically Canaanite than are the names of deities occurring in liturgic texts, &c. As we learn more about Phoenician language and literature, parallels with Ugaritic literature become more evident; a considerable number of such parallels have been discovered in the Byblian inscriptions of about the tenth century B.C. and also in such recently published Phoenician texts as the Arslan Tash incantations and the Karatepe bilinguals. Thus the extraordinary similarity in language and style between Ugaritic literature and the earliest (and some of the later) poems of the Bible is hard to explain unless we equate 'Ugaritic' with 'Canaanite' in describing the pre-Israelite literature which directly influenced Israelite poets.

The question of the language of Ugarit is extremely important for the biblical scholar because of the innumerable parallels in diction between Ugaritic and Hebrew. There are two schools of thought with regard to the linguistic affiliations of Ugaritic; one school, headed by Albrecht Goetze, maintains that it is really a distinct language, which stands between Canaanite and Accadian and may have closer affinities to 'Amorite'. The other school, represented by H. L. Ginsberg and the writer among others, holds that Ugaritic, South Canaanite, and Hebrew are different dialects of North-west Semitic, and that the term 'Canaanite' may safely be used for them all (with certain precautions, of course). The main difference, that of the *s*-causative in Ugaritic as contrasted with the *h*-causative in Hebrew, is strictly comparable to the difference between Sabaean and Minaean, the former of which has an *h*-causative whereas the latter has the *s*-causative. Actually, there are some *s*-causatives in Hebrew (notably *yištahawêh*, Ugaritic *yšthwy*)[1] and there are almost certainly many causatives without *s* in Ugaritic (e.g. *ymlk*, 'he causes to reign'). The remaining differences between Ugaritic and later Hebrew or Phoenician largely vanish as we go back into the Bronze Age, and the ancestral dialects of the Middle Bronze must have been very close together in most respects. As we apply Ugaritic and other Canaanite data recovered during the last twenty years to Hebrew poetry, especially to our earliest compositions, we find that many grammatical peculiarities known from Ugaritic or Amarna Canaanite, or from both, reappear in the astonishingly conservative Hebrew consonantal text.[2]

This is not the place to expatiate on the extraordinary illumination of Hebrew literature by Ugaritic parallels, or on the rewriting of the literary history of the Old Testament which is now possible through critical use of the new data.[3] Suffice it to say that the generally accepted date for the Song of Deborah is confirmed, and that the Song of Miriam (or Moses) in Exodus xv is added to it as an outstanding example of early triumphal poetry. The Oracles of Balaam[4] receive strong support for their antiquity from Ugarit, and a number of psalms turn out to date back to the tenth century or earlier.[5] Moreover, the great age of the Blessings of Jacob and of Moses is confirmed, and it becomes difficult to date the psalm transmitted in I Sam. xxii = Psalm xviii after the tenth century B.C. Interested scholars will find

[1] The discovery of the Ugaritic form has antiquated all previous attempts to find the etymology of the Hebrew word. The stem is *ḥwy*, 'to gather'; for the development of meaning cf. Arab. *taḥawwā*, 'be contracted, coil up'. A reflexive of a *šaf'el* naturally proves the prior existence of the latter.

[2] Cf. my remarks, *C.B.Q.* vii, 1945, pp. 22–5.

[3] See provisionally *Studies in Old Testament Prophecy* (Edinburgh, 1950), pp. 2–9.

[4] See *J.B.L.* lxiii, 1944, pp. 207–33, and cf. p. 35, n. 2, below.

[5] Several papers and theses by my students on this subject may be expected in the next few years. In my opinion Psalm lxviii is a collection of incipits (roughly about thirty in number) of hymns, a kind of catalogue composed not later than about 900 B.C. and preserved because of the otherwise unrecorded content. A paper on this subject is appearing in the *Hebrew Union College Jubilee Volumes*.

these matters treated in the writer's papers and in those of his students, David N. Freedman and Frank M. Cross, Jr.[1]

Before we leave Ugarit, we shall glance briefly at the valuable material of strictly monumental character unearthed there by M. Schaeffer. The temples of Baal and Dagon from the Late Bronze Age and the numerous inscribed and uninscribed stelae from the same general period have revolutionized our understanding of Canaanite cultic architecture and art. Thanks to them it has been possible to identify buildings and representations from Palestine, previously obscure, and they also furnish vivid illustrations of the mythological poems. Ugarit has greatly enriched our knowledge of mortuary cult among the Canaanites —in fact, our previous knowledge of this important subject was virtually zero. Palestinian archaeology and Israelite higher culture are both clarified by our new knowledge of mortuary beliefs and practices.

After Ugarit the great site of Tell el-Ḥarîrî, ancient Mari on the Middle Euphrates, has already yielded most, and its ultimate value will scarcely be less than that of the coastal city.[2] As is well known, M. André Parrot and his colleagues have recovered a large palace of the Middle Bronze Age, flourishing in the late eighteenth century according to our low chronology (which fixes the reign of Hammurabi c. 1728–1686 B.C.).[3] In this palace they have unearthed unique mural paintings and other art remains. Above all, however, they have recovered nearly 20,000 tablets and fragments from the eighteenth century B.C.,

[1] As a first instalment see Cross and Freedman, 'The Blessing of Moses', *J.B.L.* lxvii, 1948, pp. 191–210.

[2] The preliminary reports of the excavator will be found in *Syria*, vols. xvi–xxi (1935–40). A detailed bibliography of Mari publications is given in *Studia Mariana* (Leiden, 1950), pp. 127–38. Among the most valuable recent surveys of the tablets and their content, we may refer to Georges Dossin, *Correspondance de Šamši-Addu* (Paris, 1950); J. R. Kupper, *Correspondance de Kibri-Dagan* (Paris, 1950); W. von Soden, 'Das altbabylonische Briefarchiv von Mari', *Die Welt des Orients*, 1948, pp. 187–204.

[3] In spite of strong opposition from certain quarters, this low date for Hammurabi and his age is gaining ground steadily. Even if it should prove to be a few years off, there can be little doubt, in my opinion, that the truth lies in its immediate vicinity. Sidney Smith's argument from Middle Minoan synchronisms is extremely weak; cf. my discussion, *Bi. Or.* v, 1948, p. 126.

virtually all in Accadian, but often in an Accadian influenced by the 'Amorite' tongue native to most of the scribes. As MM. Dossin, Jean, Kupper, and others publish these texts, we are learning to know the Western Asia of that day with a vividness and precision even surpassing our knowledge of the Assyrian Empire of Asshurbanapal. The value of this new material, which now bursts the dikes of the Old Testament field of research, will be largely indirect, but it will be no smaller for that reason, since the international culture of the Patriarchal Age underlies all subsequent developments in Western Asia. Before long it should be possible to reconstruct much of 'Amorite' grammar and vocabulary from the transparent Accadianized 'Amorite' written by many of the native scribes of Mari. And this language, which also underlies the personal names of the Mari documents, appears to have been substantially identical with the language of the Hebrew patriarchs. Certainly it was practically identical with the speech reflected by the personal names of Palestinian nomadic and sedentary chieftains listed in the Egyptian Execration Texts of the twentieth and nineteenth centuries B.C.[1]

In addition to the sensational excavations at Byblus, Ugarit, and Mari there have been many other undertakings in Syria during recent years. The excavations at Antioch and Dura seldom throw direct light on the Old Testament, though Dura does possess great importance for our knowledge of the Hellenistic age in Syria and Mesopotamia. On the other hand, Sir Leonard Woolley's excavation of ancient Alalakh (Tell 'Aṭshânah) on the lower Orontes and Harald Ingholt's work at Hamath on the middle Orontes have both yielded very significant results for our purpose. Alalakh has disclosed a flourishing phase of Syrian culture during the Late Bronze, with inscriptions, constructions, and art objects. Of particular interest is the autobiography of king Idrimi of Alalakh, inscribed on his statue about 1450 B.C.[2]

---

[1] Cf. my study of personal names from the two sources, *B.A.S.O.R.*, No. 83 (1941), pp. 30–6.

[2] Published by Sidney Smith, *The Statue of Idrimi* (London, 1949); see also my detailed treatment of the narrative part of the inscription in *B.A.S.O.R.*, No. 118 (1950). Among new points brought out in the latter study is the identity of the homeland of Balaam, spelled '*MW* both in the Masoretic Bible and in the Hebrew

In its artless naïveté (from our point of view) it illuminates life in northern Syria at that time; particularly interesting to the student of the Bible are several motifs recurring in the story of Joseph, which may well have been at that very time in process of formation around a nucleus from the Hyksos period. Idrimi's story also tells of the hostile jealousy of his older brothers and subsequent reconciliation, of a seven-year period (repeated in two different forms), and of divining by different methods in order to scry the future.

At Hamath Ingholt has worked out a valuable stratigraphic series, which now forms the basis for our relative chronology of Syria in the Bronze and early Iron Ages.[1] Individual finds have helped greatly to reconstruct the culture of Hittite and Aramaean Hamath when it was a rival of Israel and Damascus. Less important than Hamath are the excavations of R. du Mesnil du Buisson at Qatna, modern Mishrifeh, south-east of Hamath.[2] Of indirect value to our subject are the lengthy inventories of the temple treasure of the goddess Beltekalli, an Accadian deity which became popular among the Horites under the slightly altered form Pentikalli, dating from the fifteenth century B.C. There is much new material for Hebrew lexicography in these lists.

The excavations of the University of Chicago at three mounds near Rîḥānîyeh in the southern part of the Plain of Antioch are of considerable value for the Iron Age.[3] In particular Tell Tainât has yielded the remains of a temple plan of about the ninth century B.C. which resembles the plan of the tenth-century Temple of Solomon more closely than any other hitherto known structure of that general age.[4] Inscriptions of great value for

text underlying the third-century LXX translation, with the North-Syrian land of 'Amau, mentioned both in Idrimi and in an Egyptian text from the same general period.

[1] See Harald Ingholt, *Rapport préliminaire sur sept campagnes de fouilles à Hama en Syrie* (1932–8), Copenhagen, 1940; P. J. Riis, *Hama: les cimetières à crémation* (Copenhagen, 1948).

[2] See the preliminary reports in *Syria*, vols. vii–xi, and his book, *Le Site archéologique de Mishrifé-Qatna* (Paris, 1935). The remarkable inventories of the goddess Beltekalli have now been admirably published by J. Bottéro, *R.A.* xliii, 1949, pp. 1–40, 137–215.

[3] R. J. Braidwood's long-awaited pottery volume is due to appear very soon.

[4] See provisionally G. Ernest Wright, *B.A.* iv, 1941, pp. 20 ff.

biblical history and philology have been discovered since 1919 in Syria and immediately contiguous lands. Among the most significant are the stele of Ben-hadad I (or II) of Aram,[1] the treaty of Matî''el of Arpad,[2] the Arslan Tash incantations published (and to be published) by R. du Mesnil du Buisson,[3] the Karatepe inscriptions from eastern Cilicia near the ancient Syrian frontier.[4] All these documents date from between *c.* 850 and 650 B.C., and their philological significance for the study of Hebrew is far from exhausted.

Babylonia and Assyria have contributed to biblical scholarship mainly through cuneiform texts, though the gain from excavations there for our over-all picture of ancient material civilization is very considerable. However, during the past thirty years few unknown reliefs have come to light; even the orthostates from Gozan (Tell Ḥalâf) were nearly all discovered before the First World War (though mostly published since then). Our knowledge of temple architecture from the beginning of the fourth millennium at Eridu to the Seleucid period at Erech (Warka) has increased enormously, but the significance of this rich new material for biblical archaeology is again indirect, though not negligible since it enables us to understand many cultic installations described in the Old Testament much better than had previously been possible.[5]

[1] Published by M. Dunand, *Bulletin du Musée de Beyrouth*, iii, 1939, pp. 65–76; on the date and meaning see also my remarks, *B.A.S.O.R.*, Nos. 87 (1942), pp. 23–9, and 90 (1943), pp. 32–4.

[2] Published by Ronzevalle, *Mélanges de l'Université St. Joseph*, xv, 1931, pp. 235–60. By far the best of subsequent treatments is by Hans Bauer, *A.f.O.* viii, 1932, pp. 1–16.

[3] See *Mélanges syriens offerts à M. R. Dussaud*, i (1939), pp. 421–34; Albright, *B.A.S.O.R.*, No. 76, 1939, pp. 5–11; T. H. Gaster, *Orientalia*, xi, 1942, pp. 41–79.

[4] Discovered by H. Th. Bossert since 1946, and already translated and discussed by many scholars from all countries; among the best treatments are those of A. M. Honeyman, *Muséon*, lxi, 1948, pp. 43–57, *P.E.Q.* lxxxi, 1949, pp. 21–39, and R. T. O'Callaghan, *Orientalia*, xviii, 1949, pp. 173–205, with eight plates. In spite of occasional denials, there appears to be no doubt that the Hittite hieroglyphic text is original, and that we must await complete publication of the Hittite text by Bossert (cf. already *Oriens*, ii, 1949, pp. 72–120, where the publication reaches word 128 of the Hittite) before feeling sure of our translations in ambiguous or obscure passages.

[5] Cf. especially H. J. Lenzen, *Die Entwicklung der Zikurrat* (Leipzig, 1942), and André Parrot, *Ziggurats et Tour de Babel* (Paris, 1949), for the material. For an

First among the results of the past generation of scholarly work must be placed the magnificent accomplishments of S. N. Kramer and others (Arno Poebel, Thorkild Jacobsen, Adam Falkenstein) in recovering unilingual Sumerian literature. Among the long neglected treasures from the Nippur excavations now at Philadelphia and Istanbul, Kramer has recovered many previously unknown or little known literary texts.[1] Thanks to duplicates it is sometimes possible to reconstruct an almost perfect literary masterpiece from scores of broken fragments. These religious and didactic texts belong for the most part to the late third millennium and they have come down to us in copies or adaptations from the first centuries of the second millennium (nearly all antedating the middle of the seventeenth century). The original compositions thus belong in general to pre-patriarchal times. For our understanding of the spirit and letter of Mesopotamian higher culture these early tablets form a priceless key. In them we see the prototypes of many familiar biblical formulae, such as the introduction to the cosmogonies of Gen. i and ii ('when . . . then . . . created') and the form of secular jurisprudence ('if . . . provided that . . . then'). In them we also find the model for subsequent cosmogonies and systems of divination. As research proceeds and missing links are uncovered (as has been brilliantly demonstrated by H. G. Güterbock's recent publication and comparative study of Horite theogony)[2] the historical value of this early Sumerian literature will become clearer and clearer. Biblical scholarship will gain greatly, both positively and negatively, as similarities and contrasts are analysed.

Thanks to the excavation and publication of Old Babylonian and Old Assyrian tablets (from a settlement of the nineteenth century B.C. at Kanish in Cappadocia) during the past generation, our knowledge of cuneiform jurisprudence has increased enor-

illustration of its bearing on biblical archaeology *sensu stricto* see *A.R.I.*, pp. 150–2 (note that the illustrative data have swelled notably during the past few years and that a much stronger case can be made now).

[1] See especially his book, *Sumerian Mythology* (Philadelphia, 1944), in addition to which he has published a long series of monographs and papers on new Sumerian literary works since 1938.

[2] See his *Kumarbi* (Zürich, 1946).

mously. When we add the rich material recovered at Nuzu near Kirkuk since 1925 (fifteenth century B.C.), it can easily be seen how insignificant by contrast was our information thirty years ago. To the Code of Hammurabi (still classic) have been added the Sumerian laws of Lipit-Ishtar king of Isin[1] and the even earlier laws of Eshnunna,[2] written in a dialectal Accadian. The famous Code thus appears as a late-comer in Babylonia, where codes of laws must have been published in rather rapid succession over a period of centuries. Moreover, the Eshnunna Code, which is nearly two centuries older than the Code of Hammurabi, contains the first exact parallel to an early biblical law (Ex. xxi. 35, dealing with the division of oxen after a fatal combat between the animals). Since the Code of Eshnunna is on any rational theory at least five centuries earlier than the Book of the Covenant, this parallel becomes particularly interesting. Of course, it is now becoming a truism that the cultural background of the Book of the Covenant lies in the Bronze Age, not in the Iron; i.e., it must go back substantially to the Mosaic Age.[3]

Turning to the subsequent Middle-Accadian period, we note the publication of the cuneiform treasures excavated by the Germans at Assur, including especially the laws from the time of Tiglath-pileser I (probably based on earlier codes), first published in 1920.[4] These laws, dating about 1100 B.C. in their present form, are a century or two later than the copies of Hittite laws which we possess (also published during our period), and they show interesting contrasts to earlier Babylonian jurisprudence. In fact, the differences between these early codes of the second millennium are even more instructive than their similarities. Compared with all of them the Book of the Covenant exhibits a

---

[1] See Francis R. Steele, *A.J.A.* lii, 1948, pp. 425–50.

[2] See Albrecht Goetze, *Sumer*, iv, 1948, pp. 63–102; P. A. Pohl, *Orientalia*, xviii, 1949, pp. 126–9 and plates x–xx; W. von Soden, *A.O.* xvii, 1949, pp. 359–73.

[3] Cf. especially Albrecht Alt, *Die Ursprünge des israelitischen Rechts* (Leipzig, 1934); Henri Cazelles, *Études sur le Code de l'Alliance* (Paris, 1946); Philip Korngrun, *Ḥuqqê ham-Mizraḥ haq-Qadmôn* (Tel-Aviv, 5704 = 1943–4).

[4] On the laws in general see most recently G. R. Driver and John C. Miles, *The Assyrian Laws* (Oxford, 1935), and especially the invaluable article by E. F. Weidner, *A.f.O.* xii, 1937, pp. 46 ff., in which he fixes provenience and date of the tablets, besides publishing much supplementary material.

combination of simplicity in economic life and ethical humani-
tarianism in human relations which could have arisen only in
early Israel. This does not preclude Alt's sound differentiation
between casuistic and apodictic laws; it merely illustrates the way
in which the former were transformed by the religion of Moses.

The yield of new documents from Neo-Assyrian and Neo-
Babylonian times has been very respectable but not nearly as
sensational in its implications for biblical research. The most
important discovery for the Old Testament scholar has doubtless
been C. J. Gadd's publication of the Nabopolassar Chronicle in
1923, with its precise new information about the last years of the
Assyrian Empire.[1] Second we may list the publication by E. F.
Weidner in 1939 of the ration tablets from the time of Nebuchadnezzar, which repeatedly mention King Joiachin (Yaukîn) of
Judah and the five royal princes (see Chapter I).[2] Another
tablet, published by Eckhard Unger, confirms and explains the
list of Babylonian notables given in Jeremiah (xxxix. 3, which
had previously been cut to pieces by many exegetes).[3] The Cyrus
Panegyric (otherwise called 'the Persian Verse Account of
Nabonidus'), published by Sidney Smith,[4] has also been of the
greatest significance for our understanding of the background
of Second Isaiah and Ezra i.

Among the many miscellaneous literary discoveries bearing
more or less directly on the Old Testament is, of course, the list
of antediluvian kings of Babylonia, first published by Langdon in
1923. Subsequently Langdon and others published additional
material reflecting several variants of the list preserved in Greek
dress by Berossus.[5] These variants show that the origin of the

---

[1] *The Fall of Nineveh* (London, 1923). There is a very extensive secondary
literature.

[2] *Mélanges Dussaud*, vol. ii (Paris, 1939), pp. 923–35; cf. Albright, *B.A.* v, 1942,
pp. 49–55.

[3] See Unger, *T.L.Z.* l, 1925, cols. 88–98, and *Babylon, die heilige Stadt* (Berlin,
1931), pp. 282–94. This document dates from about 570 B.C.

[4] *Babylonian Historical Texts* (London, 1924), pp. 27–97; Th. Bauer and B.
Landsberger, *Z.A.* xxxvii, 1927, pp. 88–98.

[5] See especially Stephen Langdon, *Oxford Editions of Cuneiform Texts*, vol. ii
(Oxford, 1923), pp. 1 ff.; Th. Jacobsen, *The Sumerian King List* (Chicago, 1939),
pp. 1 ff., 69 ff.

two lists of antediluvian patriarchs preserved in Genesis is much more complex than had previously been guessed, and that any common source must go back at least to the third millennium. Literary influence was certainly present, but it is increasingly likely that there was no direct borrowing of content but only diffusion of a pattern.

Accadian literary texts of exceptional significance are the Epic of the King of Battle, describing the campaigns and exploits of Sargon of Accad in the twenty-fourth century B.C.[1] This epic was exceedingly popular, to judge from the portions of it found at Amarna in Egypt, at Assur, and at Khattusas (modern Boğazköy in Asia Minor), etc. This epic enables us to gain at least a faint idea of the poetic sagas underlying the story of Nimrod and the narrative in Gen. xiv. Another very significant literary composition is the triumphal poem celebrating the victory of Tukulti-Ninurta I over the Cossaean king of Babylonia in the late thirteenth century B.C.[2] From it may be drawn interesting illustrations of the Song of Deborah and other early Hebrew triumphal poems.

Among the most romantic phases of the rediscovery of the ancient East has been the reconstruction of the culture of the Hittites and to some extent that of the Hurrians (Horites). Our knowledge of Hittite material civilization during the Bronze and Iron Ages is derived from surface remains and excavations in Anatolia and Syria. Though mostly excavated before the First World War and deciphered by Hrozný about 1915, the Hittite cuneiform tablets from Boğazköy have nearly all been published since the beginning of our thirty-year period. Albrecht Goetze and H. G. Güterbock have been particularly active in publishing texts and in synthesizing their contents. We have already mentioned the Hittite laws; there are also innumerable texts of religious and mythological interest, including native Hittite myths like that of the god Telipinus and Horite myths translated

[1] See E. F. Weidner, *Der Zug Sargons von Akkad nach Kleinasien* (Leipzig, 1922); Albright, *J.S.O.R.* vii, 1923, pp. 1–20; H. G. Güterbock, *Z.A.* xlii, 1934, pp. 86–91.

[2] See R. Campbell Thompson, *The Excavations in the Temple of Nabu at Nineveh* (Oxford, 1929), pp. 126 ff.; Erich Ebeling, *Bruchstücke eines politischen Propagandagedichtes aus einer assyrischen Kanzlei* (*Mitt. der Altorient. Ges.* xii. 3, Leipzig, 1938).

into Hittite like that of Kumarbis, which has been so well edited and interpreted by Güterbock. Hittite prayers and rituals are of unusual interest in providing a background for Israelite religious literature, since Syria has so far provided us with little or no illustrative material belonging to these categories and Hittite-Horite practice was unquestionably nearer Syrian on the whole than was Mesopotamian.

One of the most fascinating achievements of our generation has been the reconstruction of the Horite (Hurrian) language and religion from scattered tablets in different scripts and from different periods. Hurrian texts come from Amarna in Egypt and from Boğazköy in Cappadocia, from Ugarit in north-western Syria and from Mari on the Middle Euphrates. Our most important source for Hurrian personal names is formed by the economic tablets found at Nuzu in the East Tigris country since 1925.[1] In 1941 E. A. Speiser published an *Introduction to Hurrian* which has been recognized everywhere as a model of its kind. The studies of H. G. Güterbock have confirmed the impression of experts that the role of the Horites as intermediaries in the westward diffusion of Sumero-Accadian civilization was of the highest significance.[2] To them, it would appear, are due some of the most significant elements in the higher culture of the Hittites and even, perhaps, of the earliest Greeks (at least to judge from such phenomena as the close dependence of Hesiod's cosmogony on its Hurrian precursor). The significance for the development of Syro-Palestinian culture which we may credit to the remarkable Hurrian-Indoaryan symbiosis (if we may be permitted to use this biological term), which has most recently been demonstrated by R. T. O'Callaghan,[3] is still unclear, but there are indications that it exerted strong influence on the composite civilization of later Canaan.

We come now in our survey to Egypt, that treasury of archaeological riches which seems yet to be almost inexhaustible (cf. above). It is true that the most remarkable finds of the past

---

[1] See I. J. Gelb, P. M. Purves, Allan MacRae, *Nuzi Personal Names* (Chicago, 1943). [2] See his *Kumarbi* (Zürich, 1946).
[3] *Aram Naharaim* (*Analecta Orientalia*, vol. xxvi, Rome, 1948), pp. 56–70.

generation relate to prehistoric and proto-historic Egypt, where successive excavations at such sites as Badari, Ma'âdeh, and Saqqârah have immensely enriched our knowledge of the evolution of Egyptian material civilization and its flowering in the first three dynasties. The mortuary temple of Djoser, founder of the Third Dynasty, is alone a find of the utmost significance for the history of art and architecture. Since the minimal date for this temple is about 2600 B.C.,[1] it is obvious that it possesses only indirect interest for biblical scholars. More directly significant to students of biblical background is the rich new evidence for interrelations of trade and conquest between Egypt and Syria-Palestine during the fourth and early third millennia. The correlation of the Ma'âdeh culture with the early post-Ghassulian of Palestine is made certain by Palestinian pottery found at Ma'âdeh.[2] The end of the Chalcolithic in Palestine is illustrated by finds at Abûsîr el-Meleq in Middle Egypt. The irruption of Asiatic elements of Mesopotamian origin into late predynastic Egypt about the end of the fourth millennium and the beginning of the third (minimal chronology) suggests invasion and certainly proves active trade between the Tigris-Euphrates and Nile Valleys at that remote date.[3] Finds of pottery from Palestine or Syria at Abydos and Saqqârah synchronize Early Bronze II with the First Dynasty, and similar finds in both Egypt and Palestine prove that the Pyramid Age was roughly contemporary with Early Bronze III.[4]

If we turn to early biblical times, the Execration Texts of the Twelfth Dynasty, published by Sethe in 1926 and by Posener in 1940, have illuminated the political and demographic situation within the Egyptian empire in Asia (Palestine, Phoenicia, and southern Syria) to a previously unimagined degree, confirming and illustrating the results of archaeological exploration in Palestine and Transjordan.[5] New studies of the long-known

[1] For this date, which the writer has held consistently since about 1925, see now Hanns Stock, *Studia Aegyptiaca II: Die erste Zwischenzeit Ägyptens* (*Analecta Orientalia*, vol. xxxi, Rome, 1949), p. 103.   [2] Cf. *P.A.P.*, p. 70.

[3] See especially H. Frankfort, *A.J.S.L.* lviii, 1941, pp. 329–58.

[4] Cf. *P.A.P.*, pp. 74 ff.

[5] See K. Sethe, *Die Ächtung feindlicher Fürsten, Völker und Dinge,* &c. (*A.P.A.W.*,

story of Sinuhe, narrating events from the beginning of the twentieth century B.C., have demonstrated that this story is not a mere romance, but must be based on intimate personal knowledge of life in Syria and neighbouring regions at that time.[1]

The Hyksos problem still remains difficult, but studies by such scholars as Winlock and Stock, as well as by the writer, are at last beginning to throw light on the sequence of events and the nature of the Hyksos movement.[2] We now know that it must be dated within the period from *c.* 1720 to *c.* 1550 B.C., and that it was led by Semites, not by Hurrians or Indo-Aryans as supposed by many scholars until recently.

The history and life of the New Empire from the eighteenth to the twentieth Dynasty are becoming better known all the time. Within our period falls the sensational discovery and publication of the tomb of Tutankhamen, which has thrown so much light on details of art and craft in Late-Bronze Egypt.[3] Among particularly striking finds may be mentioned the new stele of Tuthmosis III from Gebel Barkal in Nubia, published by Reisner,[4] the discovery and publication of the Memphis stele of

Berlin, 1926, No. 5), with the writer's detailed commentary, *J.P.O.S.* viii, 1928, pp. 223–56; G. Posener, *Princes et pays d'Asie et de Nubie* (Brussels, 1940), with the writer's papers, *B.A.S.O.R.*, No. 81 (1941), pp. 16–21, No. 83 (1941), pp. 30–6. There is a considerable additional literature, most of which is spoiled by lack of adequate knowledge either of Semitic or of Egyptian—or of both.

[1] Cf. *A.R.I.*, p. 62 and n. 90; Albrecht Alt, *P.J.B.*, 1941, pp. 19 ff. The best translation of the Sinuhe text is now that of Elmar Edel, in Kurt Galling's *Textbuch zur Geschichte Israels* (Tübingen, 1950), pp. 1–12, with an admirable running commentary. In this connexion it may be remarked that I have long restored the 'Amorite' name underlying the Egyptian *'mmw-nnśy* as **'Ammu-la-nasi*, on the model of *Ṣidqu-la-nasi*, &c.; the shift of sibilants is dialectal.

[2] See especially H. E. Winlock, *The Rise and Fall of the Middle Kingdom in Thebes* (New York, 1947), and Hanns Stock, *Studien zur Geschichte und Archäologie der 13. bis 17. Dynastie Ägyptens* (Glückstadt, 1942). Cf. also for the Palestinian and Syrian evidence my brief discussion in the *Waldo Leland Anniversary Volume, Studies in the History of Culture* (Menasha, Wis., 1942), pp. 21 ff., with reference to earlier treatments of details.

[3] See Howard Carter and A. C. Mace, *The Tomb of Tut-ankh-amen*, 3 vols. (London, 1923–5). The rich contents of this tomb are very far from being adequately published or even analysed as they should be. Their importance for biblical archaeology is enormous, but it remains for the future to assess it in detail.

[4] *Zeitschrift für Ägyptische Sprache*, lxix, 1933, pp. 24–39; cf. S. Yeivin, *J.P.O.S.* xiv, 1934, pp. 194–229.

Amenophis II, with its revolutionary information with regard to the 'Apiru and other peoples and groups of Syria-Palestine,[1] and the Beth-shan stelae of Sethos I and Ramesses II (included here, though found in Palestine).[2] Far more important culturally are the Chester Beatty papyri from the Ramesside period, with their revelations of the scope of Egyptian literature in that golden age.[3] Among them we may mention as particularly useful to biblical scholars the dramatic poem which so neatly foreshadows the plan of Canticles (though differing widely in detail) and the quasi-monotheistic hymn demonstrating the continuous influence of the solar monotheism of Amarna after it had been suppressed by the priests of Amun. To the following century and the twentieth Dynasty belongs the great work of publication of the buildings and reliefs of Medînet Habu by the Oriental Institute of the University of Chicago. Sir Alan Gardiner's publication of the great Wilbour Papyrus from the middle of the twelfth century B.C. gives us a complete treatment of an Egyptian analogue to the Domesday Book, containing extremely interesting lists of land-holdings and local proprietors.[4]

Turning to the period of the Israelite Monarchy, we have much new light on the obscure twenty-first Dynasty. The Wen-amun Report proves again to be authentic in its atmosphere and its picture of conditions in Palestine-Syria, and we are only beginning to utilize its information adequately.[5] Montet's discovery of royal

---

[1] Ahmed M. Badawi, 'Die neue historische Stele Amenophis' II' (*A.S.A.E.* xlii, 1943, pp. 1–23); cf. also B. Maisler, *B.A.S.O.R.*, No. 102 (1946), pp. 7–12. There is already a considerable bibliography dealing with this stele, but little of it has any permanent value because of neglect of the rich material now available for topography and phonology.

[2] See provisionally Alan Rowe, *The Topography and History of Beth-shan* (Philadelphia, 1930); cf. Elmar Edel in Kurt Galling's *Textbuch zur Geschichte Israels* (Tübingen, 1950), pp. 31 f. for the latest translation of the major Sethos stele, and B. Grdseloff, *Une Stèle scythopolitaine du roi Séthos Ier* (Cairo, 1949) for the text of the other stele.

[3] Alan Gardiner, *The Chester Beatty Papyri*, No. 1 (London, 1931); *Hieratic Papyri in the British Museum, Third Series*, vol. i (London, 1935).

[4] *The Wilbour Papyrus*, 3 vols. (Oxford, 1941–8).

[5] The best translation of this document is given now by Elmar Edel in Kurt Galling's *Textbuch zur Geschichte Israels* (Tübingen, 1950), pp. 36–43. Important contributions to our understanding of the contemporary allusions have been made by

and noble tombs from the Tanite and Bubastite (22nd) Dynasties at Tanis just before and since the Second World War has given us many accurately dated art objects, illustrating the great wealth of Egypt in the eleventh, tenth, and ninth centuries B.C.[1] The Shishak List has yielded some of its secrets, especially through the independent recognition by Martin Noth and the writer that there are many Edomite place-names in it.[2]

While there have been a good many interesting discoveries and publications throwing light on the civilization of later Egypt, such as the tomb of Petosiris,[3] the most important finds have been Aramaic and Phoenician papyri. Most interesting are a Phoenician letter from the sixth century B.C., published during the recent war by the late Noël Aimé-Giron,[4] and an Aramaic letter from king Adon of Ascalon (?), writing to Necho of Egypt about 600 B.C. (published by A. Dupont-Sommer).[5] The former goes far to establish the substantial identity of the Baalzephon of Exodus with later Daphne-Tahpanhes; the latter proves that Aramaic had already become the *lingua franca* of Palestine before the Chaldaean conquest, as implied by 2 Kings xviii. 26. Then there are numerous new finds of Aramaic papyri of the late sixth and fifth centuries B.C., including particularly a group of leather scrolls containing correspondence between the Persian viceroy Arsames, residing in Babylonia, and Egyptian officials toward the end of the fifth century B.C. (to be published by G. R. Driver). From Elephantine itself came a valuable lot of papyri in the

John A. Wilson (*J.N.E.S.* iv, 1945, p. 245) and the writer (*Leland Volume* [cf. p. 44, n. 2], pp. 36 f.). In a study in *A.J.A.* liv, 1950, pp. 162–76, entitled 'Some Oriental Glosses on the Homeric Problem', the writer shows how important this document is for the history of Palestine and Phoenicia at that time.

[1] Cf. Pierre Montet, *La Nécropole des rois tanites* (Paris, 1942, also in *Kemi*, vol. ix), *Tanis: douze années de fouilles dans une capitale oubliée du Delta égyptien* (Paris, 1942), *Les Constructions et le tombeau d'Osorkon II à Tanis* (Paris, 1947), &c.

[2] Cf. Martin Noth, *Z.D.P.V.*, 1938, pp. 277–304; Albright, *A.f.O.* xii, 1939, pp. 384–6 (independent of Noth).

[3] See G. Lefebvre, *Le Tombeau de Petosiris*, i–iii (Cairo, 1923–4).

[4] *A.S.A.E.* xl, 1940, pp. 433–60; see also A. Dupont-Sommer, *P.E.Q.*, 1949, pp. 52–7. For the biblical significance of this letter cf. my remarks, *Festschrift Alfred Bertholet* (Tübingen, 1950), pp. 9, 13 f.

[5] *Semitica*, i, 1948, pp. 43–68; see also H. L. Ginsberg, *B.A.S.O.R.*, No. 111 (1948), pp. 24–7, and John Bright, *B.A.* xii, 1949, pp. 46–52.

Brooklyn Museum (to be published by E. G. Kraeling).[1] Another important lot of papyri (to be published by Murad Kamil) was found at Ṭûna el-Gebel in Upper Egypt; here is mentioned, for instance, the Queen of Heaven, already known from several allusions in Jeremiah but not yet recorded anywhere else.[2] A very important collection of several hundred ostraca from Elephantine, excavated long ago by Clermont-Ganneau, is at last approaching publication (by A. Dupont-Sommer). Thanks to these and other finds, our knowledge of the Aramaic of Ezra and of life in the Jewish diaspora during the Restoration of Judah is being enormously increased, and the radical views of C. C. Torrey and Stanley Cook have been almost categorically disproved.

The foregoing sketch of discoveries in the lands of the ancient East which bear on the Old Testament is painfully inadequate, and for lack of space we have refrained from attempting to document our catalogue of finds in detail. References to the books and papers where these discoveries were first announced would alone swell the length of this chapter unduly, and any attempt to document all important research on these discoveries would be utterly impractical.

We may rest assured that the volume of research and publication will not decrease, but rather increase in coming years—unless Armageddon comes. These studies are too engrossing and their ultimate significance for history and religion too great to permit them to be wholly neglected in free countries, no matter how depressed may be the state of the humanities in general. No one who believes in the eternal mission of the Bible to the human spirit can fail to recognize the fundamental importance of our research for the future of mankind.

W. F. ALBRIGHT

[1] The writer has just been reading the manuscript of Professor Kraeling's forthcoming volume, which lies on his desk as he types these lines. The state of preservation of these juridical documents is almost throughout extraordinarily good, and the importance of their content for Egypto-Aramaic studies cannot easily be exaggerated.

[2] Cf. *Revue de l'Histoire Juive en Égypte*, 1947, p. 2.

III

PENTATEUCHAL CRITICISM

THIRTY years ago it looked as if the problem of the Pentateuch was reaching a definitive solution. Apart from a few fundamentalists, and an occasional solitary critic like Eerdmans,[1] the consensus of opinion was that the documents—and no one had the least doubt that it was a question of 'documents'—were to be arranged in the order J, E, D, P, with Ezekiel xl–xlviii as the middle term between D and P. Ezek. xl–xlviii and H were thought to be nearly contemporary, the priority between them being still undecided. The seventh century date of D had been practically unchallenged ever since de Wette (1805) identified it with Josiah's law-book, and the other documents were dated in relation to it. The Graf-Wellhausen theory had triumphed and it seemed that little or nothing remained to be done.

Nevertheless, within a decade, J. E. McFadyen was writing in *The People and the Book*:[2] 'To a superficial observer the situation to-day must seem like confusion confounded. . . . Everywhere uncertainties abound, and, like the dove after the Deluge, we seem to find no solid ground anywhere for the sole of our foot.' Not that McFadyen himself was seriously perturbed. Indeed, he characterized as a 'gross exaggeration' Hölscher's statement that 'of the work of Wellhausen and his school hardly one stone remains upon another'. After all, the only serious challenge so far was concerned with the absolute date of Deuteronomy, and it was a challenge which had come from Hölscher himself. A. S. Peake was quite unruffled, even positively reassuring. In a paper embodying extracts from his Presidential Address to the Society for Old Testament Study in January 1924[3] he summed up the situation in these words: 'The net result of the

---

[1] *Alttestamentliche Studien* i–iv, Giessen, 1908–12.
[2] 1925, pp. 183, 218.
[3] 'Recent Developments in O.T. Criticism', *B.J.R.L.* xii, 1928, pp. 72 f.

recent critical movement, it seems to me, is that we are left, in the main, where we were a quarter of a century ago. Reactionary and radical conclusions have still their representatives, new theories make their appearances from time to time. They probably contain their elements of truth and necessitate minor readjustments. I believe that critics will tend steadily to retreat from the extravagances of criticism represented by such names as Duhm, Marti, and Hölscher. But I am disinclined to anticipate that we shall see any great movement in the direction of reclaiming Deuteronomy for the pre-prophetic period, to say nothing of the Priestly Document. The relative dating of the codes advocated by the Grafians will, I am convinced, remain, and the absolute dating will also, I think, not be seriously altered.' He noted with satisfaction that even Hölscher retained 'the Grafian sequence' and admitted 'that the development goes from Deuteronomy to P with Ezekiel as its middle term'.[1] It was obvious that Hölscher's post-exilic dating of D necessitated 'drastic handling of Ezekiel', and this was one reason why Peake was 'out of sympathy' with his scheme. Nevertheless, notwithstanding that the book of Ezekiel has been as severely handled by subsequent critics as it was by Hölscher, Peake's anticipations have so far, on the whole, and outside Scandinavia, been justified, though it must be admitted that 'the regnant hypothesis' is now encountering very heavy weather.

Since it was Hölscher's challenge to the identification of Josiah's law-book with Deuteronomy—that 'point of Archimedes' in the subject, as Peake called it[2]—that heralded the subsequent discussion, it is natural to begin this present survey with a brief indication of Hölscher's position.[3] He does not deny that D embodies old laws, but the demand for a single sanctuary would have been a piece of 'impracticable idealism' if it had been made in pre-exilic times. Can we imagine that anyone would seriously propose that the entire population of the country, men and women, sons and daughters, slaves of both sexes,

---

[1] Ibid., p. 62.   [2] Ibid., p. 61.

[3] 'Komposition und Ursprung des Deuteronomiums', *Z.A.W.* xl., 1922, pp. 161–255; see also his *Geschichte der israelitischen und jüdischen Religion*, 1922, pp. 130–4.

Levites and *gērîm* (some 120,000 in all before the exile), should journey for a week at a time to Jerusalem, while their infants and farm-animals were left to look after themselves? (This seems hyper-critical; how did they do in New Testament times, when the one-sanctuary law was accepted without question?) What Josiah attempted, then, was to purify the worship at Jerusalem, not to abolish the 'high places', and 2 Kings xxiii. 8*a*, 9, is an expansion by a Deuteronomic redactor. The impression we get from Deuteronomy is of a closed community newly entered into Palestine, of a kind of second eisodus after the exile. Deuteronomy, accordingly, is not the programme, but a product or deposit of Josiah's reform. It is to be dated about 500 B.C., about half a century later than E, which, in Hölscher's opinion, extends to the end of 2 Kings and must itself, therefore, be exilic.

Quite independently of Hölscher, R. H. Kennett also proposed a post-Josianic date (sixth century) for Deuteronomy.[1] The earliest document was E, which was drawn up about 650 B.C. for the instruction of the mixed population of the Assyrian province of Samaria. J was compiled in Hebronite circles as a counterblast to the reforms of Josiah, and was the writing repudiated by Jeremiah (Jer. viii. 8). Deuteronomy presupposes the combined JE and must, therefore, be later than both of its components, the more so since in H, which has its closest affinities with Ezekiel, the law of sacrifice is 'undoubtedly earlier than the corresponding law in Deut. xii'.[2] It may be noted that Kennett assumed that documents which are approximately contemporary can be exactly related in time sequence to one another, as though every author was familiar with what his predecessors had written, and always proposed something which should be an 'advance' upon it. This assumption was usual thirty years ago, but few would insist upon it today.

No sooner had Hölscher assailed the seventh-century date of Deuteronomy from the one side than A. C. Welch attacked it from the other, maintaining that it was earlier than generally

---

[1] *Deuteronomy and the Decalogue*, Cambridge, 1920; *Old Testament Essays*, Cambridge, 1928.　　[2] *O.T. Essays*, p. 49.

supposed.[1] He sympathized with Hölscher's plea that the one-sanctuary law was impracticable in the seventh century. Emphasizing the primitive character of many of the laws, he proposed to carry the main part of them back to a time not far removed from that of Solomon, and to regard them as North Israelitish. With regard to the law of the one sanctuary, he asserted that the only place in the book which unambiguously demands centralization is xii. 1–7, in the phrase *mikkol-šib͟e͟tēkem*, 'out of all your tribes'. Elsewhere, the phrase *bᵉ'aḥad šᵉḇāṭêḵā* (xii. 14 +) is to be understood as 'in (any) one of thy tribes', and a plurality of sanctuaries is assumed. The law of the sanctuary in the original Deuteronomy was thus the same as in Exod. xx. 24. 'The constant note of the Deuteronomic code is not monotheism, but Yahwism.'[2] The section xii. 1–7, which introduces the law-code proper, was an *ad hoc* addition made in order to carry through Josiah's centralization policy, and it was against this piece of chicanery, as he regarded it, that Jeremiah protested (Jer. viii. 8).[3]

A still earlier date for Deuteronomy is proposed by Edward Robertson.[4] As he sees it, the Hebrews entered Palestine as an organized community possessing a nucleus of law comprising the Decalogue and perhaps the Book of the Covenant. Between the settlement and the rise of the monarchy this organized community became decentralized and split up into a number of religious communes, each with its own independent sanctuary.

---

[1] *The Code of Deuteronomy*, London, 1924; *Deuteronomy: The Framework to the Code*, Oxford, 1932. Welch's conclusions had been anticipated a year earlier by Theodor Oestreicher (*Das deuteronomische Grundgesetz*, Gütersloh, 1923), who characterized the Deuteronomic formula as 'nicht Kulteinheit sondern Kultreinheit'.

[2] *The Code of Deuteronomy*, p. 202.

[3] *Jeremiah: His Time and His Work*, Oxford, 1928, pp. 89–92.

[4] In a series of papers in *B.J.R.L.*: 'The Disruption of Israel's Monarchy: Before and After', xx, 1936, pp. 134–56; 'Temple and Torah: Suggesting an Alternative to the Graf-Wellhausen Hypothesis', xxvi, 1941, pp. 182–205; 'The Priestly Code: The Legislation of the Old Testament and Graf-Wellhausen', xxvi, 1942, pp. 369–92; 'The Riddle of the Torah: Suggesting a Solution', xxvii. 1943, pp. 359–83; 'Samuel and Saul', xxviii, 1944, pp. 175–206; 'The Pentateuch Problem: Some New Aspects', xxix, 1945, pp. 121–42; 'The Period of the Judges: A Mystery Period in the History of Israel', xxx, 1946, pp. 91–114: Investigations into the Old Testament Problem: The Results', xxxii, 1949, pp. 19–43. These have now been published together in *The Old Testament Problem with two other Essays*, Manchester, 1950.

At these sanctuaries there developed divergent though related traditions and laws. When the people were reunited under a king, it was necessary to bring about religious unity. For this purpose 'a summary of legislation, comprising a codification, after due investigation and review, of the law codes of the sanctuaries, was prepared under Samuel's guidance and immediate supervision. . . . This new code was the book of Deuteronomy and was designed to be the standard law book of the centralized administration.'[1] The remainder of the materials in the Pentateuch—the J, E, P, of the critics—'a seemingly confused mass of literary matter, the choicest literary fruits of the sanctuaries with all the disabilities of many and diverse origins, with consequent duplications, inconsistencies, and even contradictions, yet most carefully arranged on a definite plan, was added to serve as a preliminary to the book of Deuteronomy either at the same time as this great law code was composed or shortly after'.[2] When the monarchy was disrupted, Deuteronomy was rendered inoperative. 'Its re-discovery in the reign of Josiah was opportune for by then the Northern Kingdom had fallen, and "all-Israel" could be re-united under the same code.'[3] This reading of the situation is distinctly conservative, but it is not fundamentalist. Robertson no more asserts the Mosaic authorship of the Pentateuch than the normal critic does. Whether his construction is right or wrong is entirely a question of historical evidence. That Samuel is said to have 'told the people the legislation (*mišpāṭ*) of the kingdom, and wrote it in a book and laid it up before Yahweh' (1 Sam. x. 25) seems an inadequate foundation for the theory that it was he who composed Deuteronomy, and what we read of the early *nebî'îm* does not accord very well with the assumption that they were the authoritative interpreters of the newly codified law at the various sanctuaries. Nevertheless, Robertson has drawn attention to a factor which has been insufficiently appreciated by critics, namely, that many of the duplications, inconsistencies, and contradictions in the Pentateuch may be due to contemporary differences of ideas and usage, rather than to

[1] *B.J.R.L.* xxix, 1945, p. 122. [2] Ibid., p. 142.
[3] Ibid., p. 126.

different stages of development which must be arranged in time-sequence.[1]

It has long been remarked that the J sections in the primeval history (Gen. i–xi) are not homogeneous. In particular, there are stories which seem to know nothing of the Flood; e.g. the Cainite genealogy (Gen. iv. 16–24), the marriages of 'the sons of God' with the daughters of men (vi. 1–4), and the Tower of Babel (xi. 1–9). It had accordingly become usual to distinguish between J[1] and J[2].[2] In 1922 Otto Eissfeldt[3] proposed to separate the pre-Deuteronomic materials in the Hexateuch into three continuous strands, which he designated by the sigla L (*Laienschrift* or Lay-source), J, and E, his 'L' in Genesis being roughly equivalent to what had previously been assigned to J[1]. L is so called because it is at the other extreme from the sacerdotal P; it reflects the nomadic and Rechabite ideal, with its hostility to the Canaanite way of life, and is to be dated about the time of Elijah. Eissfeldt has since traced L through Judges[4] and even Samuel.[5]

Another solution of the problem of the disparate elements in the primeval history has been put forward by Sigmund Mowinckel,[6] without, however, any suggestion of a new document. It has generally been supposed that E began with Abraham, and that the earliest traces of it are in Gen. xv. Mowinckel argues that E must have related that Abraham came to Canaan and how he came there, and that Josh. xxiv. 2–4 ('E's recapitulation') knew that the patriarch had lived in Mesopotamia. He accordingly revived Dillmann's opinion that E was represented in the primeval history. His J corresponds roughly with J[1] (Eissfeldt's L) and his E with Eissfeldt's J. This involves the

[1] Cf. R. Brinker, *The Influence of Sanctuaries in Early Israel*, Manchester, 1946.

[2] So R. Smend, *Die Erzählung des Hexateuchs*, Leipzig, 1912, who even traced J[1] throughout the Pentateuch.   [3] *Hexateuch-Synopse*, Leipzig.

[4] *Die Quellen des Richterbuches*, Leipzig, 1925.

[5] *Die Komposition der Samuelisbücher*, Leipzig, 1931. In this the three strands are designated I, II, and III, but in his *Einleitung in das Alte Testament*, Tübingen, 1934, p. 306, Eissfeldt says that they are 'probably continuations of the three narrative threads of the Heptateuch—L, J, and E'.

[6] *The Two Sources of the Predeuteronomic Primeval History (JE) in Gen. i–xi*, Oslo, 1937.

assumption that E not infrequently employs the divine name
Yahweh in Genesis. Mowinckel sees no objection to this:
Exod. iii. 13 f. 'gives us no data for anticipating the author's
(E's) own usage before and after the revelation on Ḥoreb. In
reality, it is *not* E's view that Yahwe is here revealing a hitherto
unknown name to Moses. Yahwe is not *telling* his name to one
who does not know it. Moses asks for some "control" evidence
that his countrymen may know, when he returns to them, that
it is really the god of their fathers that has sent him. . . . The
whole conversation presupposes that the Israelites know this
name already.'[1]

Eissfeldt's is not the only attempt to discover additional
documents in the pre-Deuteronomic sections of the Pentateuch.
Julian Morgenstern[2] has proposed a document which he calls K
(= Kenite). It was a kind of biography of Moses, beginning
with his birth and culminating in the covenant between Yahweh
and Israel on the basis of what is usually called 'the Yahwistic
decalogue' of Exod. xxxiv. 14–26. Thereafter a covenant
relationship was established between the Kenites and Israel—
Morgenstern accepts the 'Kenite theory' of the origin of Yahwism—and the two peoples journeyed on together and at last
forced their way into Canaan from the south. Morgenstern's
thesis is that the original K 'was a document of considerable
magnitude, and that, composed in 899 B.C., in support of the
religious reformation of King Asa, it is truly the oldest document
of the Hexateuch'.[3] Only a few fragments of it, however,
survive in the present Hexateuch. Many of those that do survive
are found in Eissfeldt's L.

Another suggested document is R. H. Pfeiffer's S (= South or
Seir).[4] This is confined to Genesis, and, again, much of it
corresponds with passages in Eissfeldt's L. It appeared in Edom
about the time of Solomon, and additions (S[2]) were subsequently

---

[1] *The Two Sources of the Predeuteronomic Primeval History (JE) in Gen. i–xi*,
Oslo, 1937, p. 55.

[2] 'The Oldest Document of the Hexateuch', *H.U.C.A.* iv, 1927, pp. 1–138.

[3] Ibid., p. 135.

[4] 'A Non-Israelite Source of the Book of Genesis', *Z.A.W.* xlviii, 1930, pp. 66–73;
Introduction to the Old Testament, New York, 1941.

made to it at various times between 600 and 400 B.C. Of these the Flood Story (the usual 'J' portions) may be earlier than the exile, but others, notably the Melchizedek episode (Gen. xiv. 18–20), are 'clearly post-exilic'.

Not only has J been divided, but Gerhard von Rad[1] has divided P into two strands (P^A and P^B) of approximately equal length. Both A and B were intended as history-works, especially the former, whose author still speaks like a real story-teller of the old school. The whole grew, by a natural enrichment with narrative materials, out of a Book of Generations (*sēper tôl^edôt*) which still survives in Genesis (v. 1 *et passim*). Of the two strands of the main work, B is the more complex, and more priestly in outlook than A. They are, however, so similar that their combination is to be thought of rather as a genetic process of growth within the same school than as the work of an external redactor, the last phase, as it were, whereby the priestly literature reached its present form.

It must strike even the casual reader of Eissfeldt's *Synopsis* that, outside Genesis, many of the passages which he assigns to L are very fragmentary. According to Pfeiffer,[2] 'unless we assume that large portions are lost, no "sources" or "documents" can be reconstructed out of this literary debris'. Paul Volz, in a review of it,[3] said quite bluntly: 'I see in this Synopsis the culmination of the hitherto prevailing method, and I find that it proves exactly the opposite of what it is meant to prove, for the miserable fragments of narrative which for the most part the columns contain prove precisely that there were not four original narratives, and that this entire Pentateuchal Synopsis is nothing but the artificial creation of modern erudition.' Much the same might be said of Morgenstern's K and even of Pfeiffer's own S. It seems likely that with sufficient analytical ingenuity it would be possible to sort out more such documents—this is not to say that there may not have been such documents—especially if we suppose that they were subsequently cut down by redactors.

---

[1] *Die Priesterschrift im Hexateuch*, B.W.A.N.T., Vierte Folge, xiii, 1934.

[2] *Introduction to the Old Testament*, p. 159.

[3] In *T.L.Z.*, 1923, pp. 389 ff., quoted by Staerk in *Z.A.W.* xlii, 1924, p. 35; translation by McFadyen in *The People and the Book*, pp. 196 f.

Documentary analysis can be carried to such lengths as to result in a return to the old fragmentary hypothesis. Even von Rad leaves outside his synopsis of P, probably rightly, not only the *tôlᵉḏôṯ*-book, but other considerable sections like the regulations governing sacrifices (Lev. i–vii), and, of course, H (Lev. xvii–xxvi). Indeed, all that he includes of Leviticus is viii. 1–x. 7 and parts of xvi. The rest, presumably, if we are formally to label it P—and von Rad says of i–vii that 'it has nothing to do with Pᵍ'—must be considered to have been editorially incorporated into the complex we call P. Baentsch, it may be remembered, in his Leviticus Commentary (1900), worked with no less than seven P-sigla: P, Ps, Pss, Ph (xvii–xxvi), Po (i–vii), Pr (xi–xv), and Rp. Any one of the secondary sources might have a second (Phˢ, Prˢ) or third (Prˢˢ) hand, together with redactors (Rpo, Rph) and even secondary redactors (Rpˢ). We even meet with refinements like Po¹, Po², Po¹ˢ, Po²ˢ. This is surely the *reductio ad absurdum* of the analytical method and it is improbable that we shall ever see anything quite like it again.

The impression that a process of 'atomizing' has set in is further heightened by the many discussions, during the ten or fifteen years preceding the war, on separate units such as topographical lists, poems, and, of course, legal corpora like the Decalogue and the Book of the Covenant.[1] These discussions are carried on for the most part without reference to any bearing they may have on Pentateuchal Criticism, their object being to examine the passages as separate entities, to determine their origin and purpose, and even their actual or approximate dates. It has, of course, long been recognized that such lists, poems, and legal materials, could not very well have been the free compositions of 'authors' like J and E. Further, writers like Gunkel[2] and Gressmann[3] have examined single stories and

---

[1] A representative selection will be found *passim* in Eissfeldt's article 'Modern Criticism' in *Record and Revelation*, ed. H. Wheeler Robinson, 1938, pp. 75–90. Much interest attaches to the work of Albrecht Alt on the Origins of Israelite Law (*Die Ursprünge des israelitischen Rechts*, Leipzig, 1934). This bears, of course, upon the Pentateuch, but, since it is not specifically on Pentateuchal Criticism, it does not call for detailed treatment here.

[2] *Genesis*³, 1910.   [3] *Mose und seine Zeit*, Göttingen, 1915.

legends, and their gatherings into complex cycles, and it seems to be agreed that these had reached a certain fixity in oral tradition before ever they were incorporated into the putative documents. Even, therefore, if we think of J and E as individual authors rather than as 'schools', it must be conceded that they were dealing to a large extent with what were once fragments and which even now are only held together by the stamp of their individual genius. If the 'authors' go—and at the best they are anonymous—what is to become of the documentary hypothesis? And if they were 'schools'—which implies successions of unknown authors and redactors—have we any good reason for speaking of 'documents' at all?

As to authors, Volz proposed to do away with two of them, E and P.[1] We have already seen that he reacted strongly against what he regarded as the excessive analysis of Eissfeldt. What he now pleaded for was a return to something like the old supplementary hypothesis. He expressed himself as convinced 'that in Genesis we have before us only a single story-writer (whom we may call the Yahwist), that above all the so-called Elohist was not an independent story-writer, that the so-called Elohist, if he ever existed at all, was at the most a new editor of the great (Yahwistic) story-work, that into the great original (Yahwistic) story-work (whether by a so-called Elohist, or it may be by a Deuteronomic redactor) detached sections were for particular reasons inserted.'[2] Thus, the story of the sacrifice of Isaac (Gen. xxii), which has always been assigned to E, is not from E at all, but from J. Further, 'P' (note the inverted commas) was not a story-writer. Stories that have been assigned to P either do not come from P (e.g. Gen. xxiii, Abraham's purchase of Machpelah, is really from J), or else P has at the most here and there revised the (Yahwistic) story-work which he had before him (as in the Flood story). 'P is not a story-writer, but a legislator or an author of religious (*geistlicher*) documents like Gen. i and xvii.'

Volz only carried out his examination as far as Gen. xxxv. The Joseph-saga (Gen. xxxvii–l) was dealt with by Wilhelm

[1] P. Volz and W. Rudolph, *Der Elohist als Erzähler: Ein Irrweg der Pentateuchkritik?* B.Z.A.W. lxiii, 1933.　　　　　　　　　　　　　　　[2] Ibid., p. 13.

Rudolph, who collaborated with him and subsequently published over his own name a volume in which he examined the 'Elohist' from Exodus to Joshua.[1] The two scholars worked independently and their views, although similar, are not identical. Rudolph does not, like Volz, deny the existence of P, nor does he reject the documentary hypothesis as such: 'The doubts about the Wellhausen source-criticism which for a long time have more and more forced themselves upon me, are not directed against source-analysis in general: that J is the oldest and P the youngest source of the Pentateuch seems to me to be unshaken and unshakable.'[2] Further, Rudolph was rather more positive than Volz in his estimate of the supplementary materials. Some of them, to be sure, have no tendentious purpose, but are simply enrichments of the older stories; but a large part of them were intended to deepen and enrich the religious content of the earlier narratives, so that while we are to think in some sort in terms of a supplementary hypothesis, it is proper to regard the 'E' expansions as representing a conscious and higher stage of reflexion.[3] Presumably, therefore, 'E' may still be reckoned with in any history of Old Testament ethics and religion.

Mowinckel had already, in 1930, expressed himself about E in terms which anticipated Volz.[4] E is to be assigned to Judah, not to North Israel. Its stories about the old days always go back in the last instance to the parallel J-stories; it knows no traditions independently of J. E is not in the strict sense an author. What we have in E's remodelling is not a literary work or the work of a single man, but an oral process spread over several centuries. The Yahwist had not given final form to the first account of the sagas, nor had he robbed them of their original oral life. ' "The Elohist" is he who, after the fall of the State, set down the whole of the already collected material in his own peculiar idiom, and according to his own ideas altered, smoothed out, or omitted this or that. . . . It is this whole process which we designate and

---

[1] *Der 'Elohist' von Exodus bis Josua*, B.Z.A.W. lxviii, 1938.
[2] *Der Elohist als Erzähler*, p. 145.
[3] *Der 'Elohist' von Exodus bis Josua*, pp. 258–63.
[4] 'Der Ursprung der Bil'āmsage', *Z.A.W.* xlviii, 1930, pp. 233–71.

gather up in abbreviated form in the ideogram "E".'[1] (It may be remarked that this is hardly consistent with what Mowinckel was to say seven years later about J and E in the primeval history, of which he assigned the non-Flood sections to J and the Flood sections to E).[2]

We have seen that, according to Volz, there is in Genesis only one main story-work, namely J. It may be assumed that if he had carried out his examination to the end of Numbers, his conclusion would have been much the same. At this point it is pertinent to ask again what becomes of the documentary hypothesis if J is atomized? And from what Volz wrote about it, it is clear that even J can easily be atomized. He says[3] that 'the great story-writer (whom we call the Yahwist) was above all the great *collector* and that his stories were originally frequently detached legends, cult-legends, place-legends, &c. '. This, indeed, is recognized on all hands. It is generally recognized, too, that J is in some degree composite, no matter what sigla we employ (J[1], J[2], L, S) to indicate that compositeness. Whether we can speak of a single author, J, depends very much upon whether we can discern the presence of a master-hand controlling its disparate materials and arranging them to serve the purposes of a definite interpretation of history. It is generally believed that we can discern such a purpose,[4] but this belief is obviously difficult of convincing demonstration, and it is always open to an objector to say that the apparent purpose that runs through the saga was already stamped upon it while it was still current in oral tradition. Let the emphasis be laid upon oral tradition, and J, and with it the documentary hypothesis as a whole, is volatilized. We are obviously within sight of the position maintained from Uppsala.

The roots of what has come to be called 'the Uppsala School' are mainly three. Their enthusiasm for oral tradition goes back ultimately to Gunkel, but its immediate source is H. S. Nyberg,[5] himself a professor in Uppsala. The emphases upon divine-

---

[1] Ibid., p. 271.   [2] See *supra*, pp. 53 f.

[3] *Der Elohist als Erzähler*, p. 22.

[4] Cf. Pfeiffer, *Introduction to the Old Testament*, pp. 142 ff.; C. R. North, *The Old Testament Interpretation of History*, London, 1946, pp. 24 ff.

[5] *Studien zum Hoseabuche*, Uppsala, 1935.

kingship ideology and cultic prophecy which figure so prominently in their work go back ultimately to Mowinckel's
Studies in the Psalms,[1] but the proximate source of the kingship
ideology is the British 'Myth and Ritual School', somewhat to the
embarrassment of the representatives of that school. The antiliterary-critical polemic of Uppsala derives very largely from two
scholars, Volz, and Johannes Pedersen of Copenhagen. To
Pedersen also they are indebted for what may be called their
cultic and psychological approach to the Old Testament.

In 1931 Pedersen gave formal notice that he had abandoned
the documentary hypothesis in its usual form.[2] Wellhausen, says
Pedersen, had frankly acknowledged his great indebtedness to
Vatke, and Vatke was a thoroughgoing Hegelian. The result
was that in the Wellhausen scheme the rationalism of the eighteenth century was carried over, via Vatke, into the evolutionary
conceptions of the nineteenth. 'Thus Vatke's scheme, which
revived the conceptions of the eighteenth century in Hegelian
form, was taken over in its entirety by Wellhausen, though
without its obsolete terminology and other special peculiarities.
. . . This fact shows itself not only in the way in which the whole
presentation was closely bound up with literary criticism, but
also in something else. Vatke had laid it down that the history
of Israel followed a fixed line of development, and so it came about
that his Hegelian view passed over imperceptibly into the next
theory which came to be applied to the history of culture,
namely the evolutionary theory.'[3] But, continues Pedersen,
'While this source-critical method undoubtedly has its validity,
even for antiquity, when it is a matter of determining events and
external facts, it has severe limitations when it is a matter of
describing the culture of a people. Once we are clear about that,
we shall see that the neat (*schön*) separation of the different strata
of the Pentateuch and their distribution to definitely assigned
points of historical time, is highly problematical.'[4]

Pedersen then turns to the materials in the Pentateuch. The

[1] *Psalmenstudien*, *II*, Kristiania, 1922; *III*, ibid., 1923.
[2] 'Die Auffassung vom Alten Testament', *Z.A.W.* xlix, 1931, pp. 161–81.
[3] Ibid., pp. 173 f.   [4] Ibid., p. 175.

Priestly-writing can be separated out with comparative ease, and should obviously and quite rightly be referred as a whole to a late period. Its schematic narrative bears the stamp of late Judaism and its laws contain quite secondary constructions, which cannot derive from a living national life. The same applies to the so-called Law of Holiness. But underneath the schematism, and sometimes hidden in it, we find laws which cannot have been framed suddenly after the downfall of the State, because they point to a real life. This is true of both cultic and social laws, but is naturally more clearly discernible in the latter. A good example is to be seen in the laws relating to redemption (*ge'ullâh*) in Lev. xxv. 'How is it possible to date such laws? If a Bedouin sheikh had to write down the laws of his tribe in (say) the year 1700, should we be justified in saying that the laws dated from that year? By no means, because we know that the accepted customs were approximately the same in 600 and 1700.'[1] It is therefore impossible to carry through a clear distinction between old and new.

In Deuteronomy we have a series of laws which give us a clear picture of Israelitish life as it developed in the towns under the influence of the Canaanites and also in reaction against them. How can such laws have been framed at a particular time by a particular author, and how can they ever be dated? These laws are in a less schematic form than those of the Priestly-writing, but even D contains elements of a more arbitrary kind, like the demand for the centralization of the cultus and for the rooting out of non-Israelites. The demand for the one sanctuary *can* come from the time shortly before the exile, though this is not very probable; but the tension between Israelites and other peoples is more naturally referred to the post-exilic period. 'Behind the utterances of D we see a very self-contained society, fighting convulsively to preserve its individuality from the foreign innovations threatening it. . . . Through the struggles of the seventh century the ground was prepared for such a self-contained Israelite community as D takes for granted, but it did not come into existence before the exile.'[2] What is true of the

---

[1] Ibid., p. 175.
[2] *Israel: its Life and Culture, III–IV*, Engl. ed., 1940, pp. 583, 585.

Deuteronomic laws is equally true of the Book of the Covenant and of Exod. xxxiv. 'The laws are embodied in narratives with which they have no inner relation; literary criticism is therefore in this case entirely devoid of real interest.'[1]

With regard to J and E, it is clear that they contain much living material, like the stories of Tamar (Gen. xxxviii), and of Jacob's dealings with Esau and Laban, reflecting relations with neighbouring peoples which are only conceivable in pre-exilic times. But even here there is much that points to a later age, such as speculations about the divine name, and calculations about the claims of righteousness (Gen. xviii), and, above all, the leading theme of the reward of obedience to Yahweh, which carries us down towards later Judaism. The narratives themselves are old enough, but they received their present form after the downfall of the State. As to the plurality of sanctuaries, how are we to know that everybody in exilic and post-exilic times thought as Deuteronomy did? It is more likely that the stories derive from circles which sought the true Israelite life outside the great cities, in the life of shepherds and half-nomads, and they had no particular reason to esteem the demand of the Jerusalem priest-hood. Did not the revered ancestors build altars? And as for anthropomorphisms, if these are a proof of great age, then the Talmud is older than any biblical writing![2] The conception of J and E as two parallel narratives cannot be maintained. Far too often source-analysis rests upon a misunderstanding of ancient Israelite psychology.

According to Pedersen, then, JE, D, and P are designations of collections which do not admit of being arranged in exact order according to an evolutionary scheme; rather are they parallel and serve to give a picture of the many-coloured variety of Israelitish culture. 'All the sources of the Pentateuch are both pre-exilic and post-exilic. When we work with them and the other sources, we have no other means than that of intrinsic appraise-ment (*innere Schätzung*); in every single case the character of the material must be examined and the supposed background be in-ferred from that. That is precisely the task of the historian.'[3]

---

[1] *Z.A.W.*, op. cit., p. 177.   [2] Ibid., pp. 177 f.   [3] Ibid., p. 179.

The central corpus of the Pentateuch is, according to Pedersen, the description of Israel's distress in Egypt, the growing up of Moses, Yahweh's struggle with the Egyptians, and the deliverance of Israel.[1] 'This description (Exod. i–xv) is a cult legend of the Passover reflecting the annual re-living of historical events, as it took shape down through the ages.'[2] The obvious incongruities and irregularities in the text are not due to its having been made up from parallel stories put together like a mosaic, but to additions and alterations made in the course of time. 'This story, as well as the whole emigration legend, though inserted as part of an historical account is quite obviously of a cultic character, for the whole narrative aims at glorifying the god of the people at the paschal feast through an exposition of the historical event that created the people. The object cannot have been to give a correct exposition of ordinary events but, on the contrary, to describe history on a higher plane, mythical exploits which make of the people a great people, nature subordinating itself to this purpose. . . . The narrative is no report but a cultic glorification.'[3] If this means anything it would seem to imply that it is a hopeless endeavour to try to get behind the cult-legend to the precise historical events which gave birth to it. The section has no close inner relation to the tribal legends of Genesis, though, like them, it bears 'the mark of conditions both in the monarchical period and in post-exilic times'.[4]

This brings us at length to Uppsala, where the leading protagonist for a radically new theory of Pentateuchal origins is Ivan Engnell. Engnell has set forth his views in an Introduction to the Old Testament[5] and in a number of articles in the Swedish Bible Dictionary, now in process of publication.[6]

---

[1] 'Passahfest und Passahlegende', *Z.A.W.* lii, 1934, pp. 161–75; cf. *Israel III–IV*, Engl. ed., pp. 726–37.

[2] *Israel III–IV*, p. 726.   [3] Ibid., p. 728.

[4] Ibid., p. 736.

[5] *Gamla Testamentet. En traditionshistorisk inledning*, i, Stockholm, 1945. Only the first part of this has so far appeared, but the second part appears to be in proof, and Engnell and some of his colleagues occasionally quote from it.

[6] *Svenskt Bibliskt Uppslagsverk*, utgivet av Ivan Engnell och Anton Fridrichsen, Första Bandet, A–K, Gävle, 1948. Vol. ii is in the press, and Prof. Engnell has kindly placed at my disposal proofs of some of the articles which will appear in it.

Engnell calls his book 'A Traditio-historical Introduction', and in the early pages of it[1] he enumerates three stages through which Old Testament criticism has passed or is now passing. The first is the Literary- or Source-critical, associated especially with the name of Wellhausen. The second is the Form-literary, associated with the name of Gunkel. The third, which alone offers a satisfactory solution of the problems, is the Traditio-historical. It is characterized by a decidedly conservative attitude towards the Massoretic text, and by great emphasis upon the role played by oral tradition. 'Fundamental in a high degree for this view is the recognition of the role which oral tradition played and still plays in the Orient, and therefore also in Israel. To a large extent—although the conditions are very different within different "types of literature" in the Old Testament—the Old Testament existed as oral "literature" before its fixation in writing, and even after that it continued to a large extent to exist as oral tradition. Oral tradition and written fixation must not, therefore, be played off against one another as exclusive alternatives, but regarded as complementary to each other. Instead of sources and "redactors" we have to reckon with units of oral tradition, complexes of tradition, and collections of tradition, together with circles of traditionists and schools within which these traditions were handed on, often through several generations.'[2] Further, the traditio-historical view 'unites in itself analysis and synthesis, and adopts a much more positive attitude towards tradition in respect of its reliability'.[3]

As a preliminary to his onslaught upon literary criticism Engnell mobilizes[4] all the malcontents[5] who have raised their

---

[1] *G.T.* i, pp. 7–11.

[2] Art. 'Gamla Testamentet', § 6, *S.B.U.* i, col. 659.

[3] *G.T.* i, pp. 10 f.

[4] Ibid., pp. 178–209; art. 'Litterärkritik, *S.B.U.* ii.

[5] They include all those whose names have appeared in the foregoing, together with others, of whom two may be mentioned briefly, since their views have a certain similarity to Engnell's own. According to M. Löhr (*Untersuchungen zum Hexateuch-problem, I. Der Priesterkodex in der Genesis*, B.Z.A.W. xxxviii, 1924) there never was an independent document P. The Pentateuch is a compilation by Ezra and his associates, who put together groups of laws and narratives, and gave to these heterogeneous materials a certain semblance of unity. Umberto Cassuto (*La Questione della Genesi*,

protests against the documentary theory during the past thirty years. They appear to him to have brought about 'chaos within the well-ordered but entirely fictitious and anachronistic construction which constitutes the Wellhausenian fabric of learning'.[1]

One does not need, Engnell continues, to have any very profound insight into the history of the ancient East, its culture and literary history, 'to see that the whole literary-critical system rests upon a complete misunderstanding of its real conditions, that it represents a modern, anachronistic *book-view* (*boksyn*), and is therefore an interpretation in modern categories, an *interpretatio europeica moderna*. For a right judgement of the problem a "modified" or "moderate" view of literary-critical type is, therefore, not enough; what is demanded is a radical break with this whole method.—There never were any parallel continuous documents in the Mosaic books of the kind that are assumed. That large parts of the material in the Mosaic books were from the beginning or at a very early stage fixed in writing is quite another matter. Still more important, however, is a right appreciation of the function, extent, and significance of oral tradition. Because only from the starting-point of an originally oral transmission is there any explanation of, for example, the problem of the variants within the Mosaic books, whose occurrence in this kind of literature is a typical feature of precisely an oral transmission, which works among other things according to something which can be called "the epic law of iteration"—even though this is also true in some measure of "written" literature, of a cult-dramatic kind. That "obscurities" and "contradictions" are a natural occurrence at the culture- and language-stage at which we find ourselves in the Old Testament, ought also to be self-evident. Yet, in reality they are found again and again only by a western desk-logical mind, and in innumerable cases rest upon a deficient understanding of Hebrew psychology, and, what is

Florence, 1934) thought Genesis to be the work of a writer of genius, probably in the later years of David's reign, who made use of such stories of the patriarchs as served his purposes, and brought them together into a harmonious and organic whole.

[1] Art. 'Moseböckerna', *S.B.U.* ii. Quotations, in what follows, are from this article unless otherwise indicated. If much is in inverted commas, this is because I feel that it is the only way to convey what Engnell says without risk of misrepresenting him.

worse, upon a deficient knowledge of the Hebrew language, especially its syntax, against whose elementary rules it all too often breaks down. It almost seems as if, since the discovery of the universal expedients of source-analysis and emendation, we no longer believed ourselves to be in need of linguistic knowledge, which nevertheless is alpha and omega for exegetical study.'[1]

Coming now from general to more particular considerations, Engnell says that the only really relevant indication of the existence of continuous documents would be a consistency of stylistic differences such as are asserted to be present, partly of a theological and partly of a purely linguistic kind. With regard to purely linguistic 'constants' or *isoglossor*, he maintains that these can have no validity if they occur in more than one 'document'. A close examination shows that they do not fulfil this condition, and to set aside or emend the text is only to argue in a circle. The most important linguistic constants—which at the same time border on the theological—are the different names for God. But even this argument loses its evidential value from the fact that within the supposedly different documents the Hebrew manuscripts vary considerably (*kraftigt*) among themselves, and not least does the LXX differ *vis-à-vis* the Hebrew text. 'In reality the LXX shows inescapably that the variation in the divine names in the Hebrew text must to a large extent be the result of a later process of unification; the variation is not original.' Even more grave is the fact that the different 'sources' are not consistent in their use of the divine names which are alleged to be their distinctive marks. 'In so far as a certain "constant" change of divine names is really to be found, a closer examination shows that this does not rest upon change of documents but upon a conscious stylistic practice of the traditionist, something which is bound up with the fact that the different divine names have different ideological associations and therewith different import. Thus, Yahweh is readily used when it is a question of Israel's national God, indicated as such over against foreign gods, and where the history of the fathers is concerned, &c., while on the other hand Elohim, "God", gives more expression to a "theo-

[1] Cf. *G.T.* i, pp. 189 ff.

logical" and abstract-cosmic picture of God, and is therefore used in larger and more moving contexts. . . . So, then, it is the traditionist, the *same* traditionist, who varies in the choice of divine names, not the "documents".' As to the 'theological' constants, it can be stated without further ado that they fall under the same verdict as has already fallen upon 'obscurities', 'differences', and 'contradictions'. 'In reality such "criteria" rest upon nothing other than an *a priori*, evolutionistic way of looking at things, which goes hand in hand with and dictates the sources-analysis.'[1]

Engnell denies that Deuteronomy's demand for centralization of the cultus has any bearing upon the question of its date in relation to 'P'. 'The presence or absence of the demand for centralization is no criterion for the age of the respective documents, but simply an evidence of different interests and viewpoints which can quite well lie alongside one another in time.'[2] As to absolute chronology, neither in whole nor in part is Deuteronomy identical with Josiah's law-book. Indeed, the strongly North Israelitish provenance of Deuteronomy makes it not very probable that it should have been found in the Jerusalem Temple and made the programme for a reformation.

This brings Engnell to his positive presentation of the literary problem of the Mosaic books. Their huge and widely diverse kinds of tradition-materials belong to two different collections which had no primary connexion with one another. 'The first of these comprises Genesis–Numbers and can, with a certain accommodation to the usual terminology, be called the "*P-work*", not because it contains a "document" "P", but because it received its final shape and therewith its ideological tendency in *a traditionist-circle* which, with certain modifications, shows many of the features which are ascribed by literary-critical research to the "document P" or the "redactor P". Another conceivable name for it is the "Tetrateuch". The "P-circle" or "P-work" had from the beginning no connexion—or in any case no actual direct connexion—with the second great collection, "*the Deuteronomic history-work*", comprising Deuteronomy–2 Kings, which in its definitive shape was formed in another

[1] Cf. ibid., pp. 194 ff.　　　　　　　　[2] Cf. ibid., pp. 203 f.

circle of tradition, which may be called the "D-circle". .... For those who prefer to believe in documents the matter might be expressed in this way, that "J", "E", and "P" do not go beyond Numbers, while on the other hand "D" or "R^D" are not found in Genesis–Numbers.'[1]

This view of the matter, Engnell points out, has been pressed in some of the most recent literary criticism, notably by Martin Noth.[2] ' "P" in the new meaning of the traditionist-circle— possibly, but not very probably, the "tradent", and so an individual person—which gave to later ages the "P-work" or "Tetrateuch", is responsible at the same time for a quantity of tradition-material with a peculiar stamp which, so to say, is its own, handed down from ancient times within the circle itself, and by them collected together with a mass of other traditions, transmitted both orally and in writing. If anything like "documentary-research" is to be carried on or could be carried on with any hope of success within the Tetrateuch, it would in that case consist in the separation of this special "P-material", and there is no doubt that the "P(riestly-code)" of literary criticism does in a very large measure correspond to this material, even though the exact determination of it is often much less clear and reliable than was formerly optimistically supposed, and so cannot be pursued from verse to verse. On the other hand, it is quite out of the question to keep "J" and "E" in the meaning of strata of tradition. Although such strata of tradition were originally found in the Tetrateuch, they were already at the stage of oral tradition so woven together that it is now an impossible task to resolve them.'

The central complex in the P-work—this in dependence upon Pedersen[3]—is the 'Passover-legend' of Exod. i–xv. Originally this was a ritual text, but in its present form it has become 'disintegrated', deculticized, and historicized. Although it is impracticable, even by traditio-historical methods, to get behind the present text to any kind of 'Urform', or to reconstruct in

---

[1] Cf. *G.T.* i, pp. 209 ff.
[2] *Überlieferungsgeschichtliche Studien*, i, Halle-Saale, 1943.
[3] Cf. *supra*, p. 63.

detail the historical events that lie behind it, this does not exclude the possibility that actual happenings do lie behind it.[1]

There is no doubt that 'P' in its present shape emanates from Jerusalem, but its roots go back to Hebron and Kadesh-Barnea, and it thus represents a southern tradition. It has a marked anti-quarian interest. Its genealogical schematism may very well preserve much old oral 'history-writing', and its many archaisms, notwithstanding that many of them seem artificial, point in the same direction. The tabernacle-tradition undoubtedly goes back to pre-Jerusalem times, even though it is coloured by conditions in Jerusalem. Its legal matter is also to a large extent ancient, and is firmly anchored in actual life-situations. Its attitude to the tradition-materials it has taken over is positive, and they have been faithfully preserved, with but little overworking. The apportionment of the materials as between oral and written sources is a very complicated problem. Written fixation by no means implies something new, but a setting down in writing of what has already received a fixed form in units, complexes, and collections of tradition. Some traditionist-circles made predomin-ant use of oral tradition, others of written, but most of them em-ployed both methods side by side. It is to be emphasized that oral tradition, in a sacral literature so unique as the Old Testament, by no means involves greater risks of falsification than written; on the contrary in many cases. On the whole, it may be assumed that the narrative portions in the 'P-work' rest predominantly on oral tradition. The legal materials, on the other hand, were for the most part early fixed in writing, though oral repetition continued side by side with it. Such legal matter as is manifestly secondary or did not originate in living situations, but was first framed in more or less complete form in the final editing of the whole work, was naturally written *ad hoc*, and never circulated orally at all. Despite the relatively high antiquity of the 'P-work', its final redaction must be relatively late, in exilic and post-exilic times, indeed as late as the time of Ezra and Nehemiah.[2]

Engnell's views about the 'D-work' (Deuteronomy–2 Kings) may be summarized more briefly, if only because in this essay

[1] Cf. *G.T.* i, pp. 218 ff.   [2] Cf. ibid., pp. 229 ff.

we are only concerned with the Deuteronomy section of it. Here also, as in the 'P-work', it may be assumed that the legal portions were early fixed in writing, while the story-materials—with the exception of i. 1–iv. 43, which is from the Deuteronomic circle itself—depend mainly upon oral tradition. Many of the laws rest upon very ancient practice, while others are abstract-ideological and have a distinctly anti-Canaanite tendency. They certainly come from widely different localities and are in part of clear North-Israelitish origin. But in its final form the work is dominated by an intensely Jerusalemite tendency. Indeed, on the whole, it is more priestly in outlook than the 'P-work'. More, too, than 'P', ' "the Deuteronomist" or "D-circle" represents a real "author" or "school of authors", but this is not to deny that "he", faithful to the ancient transmission-principle, dealt, on the whole, very piously with the materials handed down by tradition, especially in those sections which have to do with the older time'. The theological standpoint is very similar to that of the reform-prophets. The date of the 'D-work' must be later than the liberation of Jehoiachin (562–61 B.C., cf. 2 Kings xxv. 27 ff.). All things considered it may be brought down to about the same time as that of the 'P-work', i.e. to the time of Ezra and Nehemiah.[1]

Very soon after their final composition the two 'serial-works' were united into one, in such a way that the beginning of the 'D-work' was built into the 'P-work'. This was the more easy because Deuteronomy was cast into the form of a long address by Moses shortly before his death. 'It is a likely hypothesis that the "P-work" itself originally related the death of Moses, but that this tradition was not included in its original place at the end of Numbers, the story about it being deferred to its present place in Deut. xxxiv.' Exactly when and by whom this was done it is impossible to say, but it is unlikely that it was by the Deuteronomist himself, since there is no trace of his hand anywhere in the 'P-work'. Once the two great works were united, the original unity of the 'D-work' was forgotten, and it was split up into its present 'books'.[2]

[1] Cf. *G.T.* i, p. 245. [2] Cf. ibid., pp. 246 f.

Before we attempt some assessment of the present position and future prospects of Pentateuchal Criticism, something must be said of the most recent German work on the subject. Most, if not all, of what has been published in Germany since the war has been written without access to the work of Uppsala, and two scholars, Martin Noth and Artur Weiser, expressly mention this in their Forewords. Yet notwithstanding that all recent German work presupposes 'documents', a certain measure of approximation to the Uppsala position is noticeable; or, if that is the wrong way of putting it, it is clear that German scholarship has moved a good way from the original documentary hypothesis, which could picture J, E, D, and P as the free compositions of individual authors, capable of being fixed—at whatever points—upon a single date-line. Much of Uppsala's polemic against 'Wellhausenism' is directed against the Wellhausenism of fifty years ago, and there is a good deal of banging upon doors that are no longer obstinately closed.

The most recent work of Hölscher[1] is on lines we should expect from him, and makes little concession to the newer tendencies. It is a study of the J document, which according to Hölscher extends to the account of the division of the monarchy (1 Kings xii). Like Mowinckel, Hölscher assigns the non-P sections of the Flood-story to E, so that in the primeval history his J corresponds very much to Eissfeldt's L.

In von Rad[2] the newer viewpoints find clearer expression. He still works with J (*circa* 950), E (perhaps 200 years later), D (after 701), and P (between 538 and 450). But these dates are conjectural and only relate to the completion of the sources. The question of the age of the traditions taken up into the actual writings is something quite different; e.g. in P we have the essence of the theological work of many generations of priests. 'The "composition" of such a work cannot, in view of the very slow development of such sacral traditions, be determined to a

---

[1] *Die Anfänge der hebräischen Geschichtsschreibung*, Heidelberg, 1942.

[2] *Das formgeschichtliche Problem des Hexateuchs*, B.W.A.N.T., Vierte Folge, xxvi, 1938; *Deuteronomium-Studien*[2], Göttingen, 1948; *Das erste Buch Mose, Genesis Kapitel 1–12, 9*, Das Alte Testament Deutsch, Teilband I, Göttingen, 1949.

year or even to a century. Even though in its final shape it must date from post-exilic times, it conceals, alongside late and theologically edited material, much that is very old in an almost unaltered and highly archaic form. . . . Many times, many men, many traditions and theologies have built up this colossal work. Only he who sees the Hexateuch not on a flat surface (*flächenhaft*), but reads it with an awareness of its dimensional depth (*Tiefendimension*), will come to a right understanding.'[1] Nevertheless J, though of course a collector, is to be thought of as in a real sense an author, who set his stamp upon the whole body of Hebrew tradition, even to giving to the Hexateuch its definitive form. After him E and P bring nothing essentially new.[2]

Noth's most recent work[3] is principally concerned with the history of the oral tradition of which the documents are the final precipitate. In an earlier work[4] he had detached Deuteronomy altogether from the Pentateuch—a course which Engnell hailed with enthusiasm[5]—asserting that there never was a 'Hexateuch', and that the original Books of Moses consisted only of Genesis–Numbers together with some portions of Deut. xxxi–xxxiv. J, E, and P do not extend beyond this truncated Pentateuch. For the rest, Noth's Pentateuchal criticism is along orthodox lines. P was a story-work, not a mere 'tradent' (Volz, Engnell). Into it as a framework the other documents were fitted, and Noth is sceptical of von Rad's attempt to separate out two parallel strands in it. E was originally a complete document, not, as Volz and Rudolph have attempted to demonstrate, so much expansion or revision of J. Nor does Noth find any place for Eissfeldt's L. He thinks there must have been a common basis (*Grundlage* = G) for J and E, but leaves open the question whether this existed in written or only in oral form. What he will make of the Uppsala attempt to account for the Tetrateuch entirely in categories of tradition-history, is hardly in doubt. It seems certain that he will insist on documentary analysis as the

[1] *Das erste Buch Mose*, p. 19.
[2] *Das formgeschichtliche Problem*, p. 69.
[3] *Überlieferungsgeschichte des Pentateuch*, Stuttgart, 1948.
[4] *Überlieferungsgeschichtliche Studien*, i, 1943.
[5] *Supra*, p. 68.

starting-point for any hopeful attempt to deal with the history of oral tradition.

The second edition of Weiser's 'Introduction'[1] is especially suggestive. He even uses the term *Traditionsgeschichte*. In his view, each of the three hypotheses, the fragmentary (Gunkel), the documentary (Smend, Eissfeldt, von Rad), and the supplementary (Volz and Rudolph), has its measure of truth, but each has also its limitations. No one method by itself can account for all the features in the tradition. The history of the formation of the Pentateuch is richer and more manifold; the sources-strata themselves are by no means literary documents which can be defined to the last detail. They were transmitted and woven together in the course of the religious and national history, and we cannot entirely account for the Pentateuch on the literary-critical assumption of a more or less mechanical addition of purely literary works into a fixed and unalterable form. The history of Old Testament literature, indeed even the bringing together of the sources by the hand of redactors, is more than a matter of arithmetic.[2] Nor are we in a position to understand the problems aright unless we recognize that the origin of the literature lies in the cult. Even after a tradition had become fixed in writing it might still be not inconsiderably altered and developed to conform to actual cultic pronouncements. It is probable that oral tradition continued for a long time side by side with written, and even influenced what had been written. For this reason it is conceivable that the neat separation of the sources from one another can never be entirely successful. Yet it would be going too far, on the ground of such considerations, to lose sight of the authors of the sources as individual persons, and to think instead, with Gunkel, in terms of Schools (JE). Even in their later historical development the sources did not lose the stamp of their individual authors. Finally, it is to be observed that the cultic repetition of *Heilsgeschichte* implies something other than simple adherence to the memory of the events of past history, and that the Pentateuch, originating as it did in the cult-festivals, is

---

[1] *Einleitung in das Alte Testament*[2], Göttingen, 1949, esp. § 13, Das Problem der Entstehung der Pentateuchquellen.   [2] Ibid., p. 67.

something rather different from historical literature in the modern sense. *Heilsgeschichte* is sacramental, realized and immediately experienced in the cult-act. For this reason the question of the origin of the Pentateuch is more than simply a problem of history and literary-history.[1]

And so to some attempt at synthesis. It is clear that the questions in dispute have to do with much more than the nomenclature and appropriateness of certain time-honoured labels. We are face to face with a fundamental problem, that of the interpretation of Old Testament religion. There are two aspects of this problem: (1) the first concerns the historical value of the Bible account of the world from the Creation to the death of Moses, more particularly of the events in which Moses is said to have been the leading figure; (2) the second concerns the value of the Pentateuch as a source for the history of Hebrew religion from the Exodus to the post-exilic period, on the principle that 'the Pentateuch is an epitome of the history of Israel's religion'.[2]

1. So far as the period of history covered by the Pentateuch is concerned—to the death of Moses—it has long been recognized that the Pentateuch is not history in the modern sense of the word. Whether we regard J as the first Hebrew attempt at historical writing (Hölscher), or the Court History of David (von Rad), or Deuteronomy (Noth)[3], it is conceded that all of these were written some centuries after the Exodus. Nevertheless, it has commonly been assumed that the story was intended as history and that historical events lie behind it, and further that, partly by a process of rationalizing its miraculous elements, it is possible to discover in some detail what those events were. But *Heilsgeschichte*, as we must now regard the Pentateuch, is not quite the same thing as legend with a nucleus of history, even though, like legend, it does contain a nucleus of history. There is much to be said for the view of Pedersen and Engnell that the story of the Exodus is a cultic glorification, and that the

---

[1] *Einleitung in das Alte Testament*[2], pp. 78 f.

[2] J. Estlin Carpenter, art. Introduction to the Pentateuch', in *Peake's Commentary*, p. 130*a*.

[3] Cf. Eissfeldt, *Geschichtsschreibung im Alten Testament*, Berlin, 1948.

only 'history' we can extract from it is history in very broad outline, not history in any precise detail. If we think of the crossing of the Red Sea as made possible by an east (or north-east) wind, it is difficult to see how the Israelites could have crossed the sea in the teeth of it. Or if we are attracted by the seismic-volcanic interpretation of the story, with a crossing at the northern end of the Gulf of Akaba, we must suppose, since the Egyptian cavalry only caught up with the Israelites after they had travelled some 150 miles (they were much cumbered with their children and flocks—Exod. xii. 37 f.), that it took them ten days or a fortnight to make up their minds to pursue them; a most improbable assumption. Pedersen is right when he says that the story is in a different dimension from ordinary history. We do not know when, or how, the Exodus took place, nor where the sacred mountain Sinai-Horeb was, nor what were the original terms of the covenant between Yahweh and Israel.[1] Tradition-history, the interpretation of history, is in many ways more important than 'history' itself. This does not mean that the 'history', if we could recover it, would not bear looking into, or that it would not support the interpretation which faith builds upon it. It only means that although, for Judaism and Christianity, history is the medium of revelation, the revelation does not consist in 'bare facts'. 'There are', as Wheeler Robinson never tired of insisting, 'no bare facts for the historian'. This is true even in the realm of secular history. Much more, in sacred history, salvation-history, the alleged 'bare facts' are trans-figured by faith until they can be almost unrecognizable. In the community experience of generations they become blended of time and eternity, of earth and heaven. That is the paradox of Judaism and Christianity: they are mediated through history, and yet at no point can we have a cinematographic reproduction of the history. Since it pleased God to reveal Himself in history, the *terminus a quo* of the revelation had to be the beginning of

[1] Attempts to reconstruct the history within the framework of an elaborate documentary theory can be highly subjective and unconvincing; cf. C. A. Simpson, *The Early Traditions of Israel: a Critical Analysis of the Pre-Deuteronomic Narrative of the Hexateuch*, Oxford, 1948.

the historical era. Equally, the *terminus ante quem* had to be before the elaboration of modern techniques. That Jesus should have delayed His coming until the age of press photography is a well-nigh intolerable thought. We have no photographs of Him, nor any descriptions of what He looked like. It is better so. He must be accessible to imagination and faith, and at the same time shielded from vulgar familiarity. Only as He is different to successive generations can He be 'the same yesterday, and today, and for ever'. And about the Exodus, which took place in the morning twilight of the historical era, much is, and probably must forever, remain obscure. 'Put off thy shoes from off thy feet, for the place whereon thou standest is holy ground.... Take heed to yourselves, that ye go not up into the mount.... They saw the God of Israel; and there was under his feet as it were a paved work of sapphire stone, and as it were the very heaven for clearness. And upon the nobles of the children he laid not his hand: and they beheld God, and did eat and drink.' This is *Heilsgeschichte*; and we need not break our hearts if we often have to be content with *Heilsgeschichte*, or with tradition-history, rather than with 'pure' history. This much we may concede to Copenhagen and Uppsala.

2. The second aspect of the problem concerns the value of the Pentateuch as a source for the history of Old Testament religion down to the post-exilic period. It has generally been assumed that the religious history of a millennium has been telescoped, so to speak, within the compass of the Pentateuch, and that by arranging the materials chronologically, mainly on the basis of the documents (in the order J, E, D, P), together with what external evidence can be gleaned from the rest of the Old Testament, and some arbitrament from the concept of evolutionary development, we could point most Old Testament ideas and institutions upon a single date-line. This whole procedure is now challenged. If, with Engnell, we do away with the documents, and are left with a mass of unco-ordinated traditions— however reliable the traditions may be in themselves; or if, with Pedersen, we regard the 'documents' as parallel, contemporary, and more or less co-terminous 'strata', and have no other means

than *innere Schätzung* for determining the age of the materials they contain, it is obviously going to be more difficult than we had supposed—indeed, perhaps, even impossible—to write the history of Old Testament religion. No one reading Pedersen can escape the feeling that he presents things on a flat surface, without dimensional depth. He can hardly complain at this criticism, since he says very definitely that it is quite impossible to carry through a clear distinction between early and late when we are dealing with culture and cult. His interest is in the psychology rather than in the history of Old Testament religion. The Uppsala scholars, for their part, seem again and again to select materials from anywhere they like, and to use them as they please. What we had supposed to be late, they confidently assume to be early. This is not surprising, in view of their polemic against 'evolutionism' and 'logicism'. It is always possible that they are right and the rest of us wrong, that with our Well-hausenian training and background we have been more optimistic about the possibilities of dating this and that than the evidence really warrants. We should much prefer a stereoscopic picture, if that is possible, something in relief, instead of in only two dimensions; history, rather than a mainly undifferentiated tradition-history. By all means let us abandon an *a priori* 'evolutionism'; even so, history is not static; it has movement, and there is not the slightest doubt that some ideas and institutions were early and others late. The question is whether we can discover what is early and what is late. If we abolish the documents that question must be answered mainly in the negative.

This brings us to the question of the documents. It seems quite clear that if we bury the 'documents', we shall have to resurrect them—or something very like them. Pedersen recognizes the presence of three kinds of materials, P, D, and (an undifferentiated) JE, though he thinks in terms of parallel 'strata' rather than of documents. Engnell's position is not dissimilar. He puts D in a category by itself. He grants that the 'tradent(s)' of the 'P-work' were responsible for a quantity of 'special "P-material"' which corresponds 'in a very large measure' to the P of literary criticism. What remains must be the JE of literary-criticism, since there is little that the critics leave outside their JEP scheme. Engnell even goes so far as to concede that something corresponding to separate 'J' and 'E' strata may once have existed, but says that they were already so fused together at the stage of oral tradition that it is now hopeless to try to disentangle them.

But if, as Engnell insists, 'oral "literature" ' can have all the fixity of 'written', does it matter whether the 'literature' is 'oral' or 'written', or—as he asserts of the Pentateuch—a mixture of both? Is there anything in principle wrong in the application of literary-critical methods to it? Quite obviously not. It may, of course, turn out to be a waste of time, and Engnell asserts that it is a waste of time, at any rate as applied to 'JE'. But, when all is said, the Pentateuch as we have it is literature, and it must have come to be what it is by literary processes. How could such a heterogeneous mass of materials have assumed the form in which we have them in the Pentateuch without 'redactors'? What were Engnell's circles of traditionists doing all the centuries they were at work? Have they left no traces of their activities? And if they were as faithful custodians of tradition as Engnell says they were, and as, indeed, to judge from the abrupt transitions from one style or story to another, we may readily believe they were, we should expect to be able to sort things out with comparative ease. If the literary critics had decided that the Pentateuch was the product of a single author, who went to his work like a modern historian, reading up his 'sources' and then writing a history in his own words, that would indeed have been an *interpretatio europeica moderna*. But to say that the traditionists preserved their materials more or less intact is not to propound an *interpretatio europeica moderna*, but to lay bare a *methodus hebraica antiqua*. That this was the Hebrew method is clear from a comparison of Kings with Chronicles, and Engnell admits that the author(s) of the 'D-work' incorporated written sources (e.g. the Court History), and that the tradent(s) of the 'P-work' did the same, at least in the legal sections. But it is no matter—since oral tradition had, *ex hypothesi*, such fixity—whether the sources were oral or written; they were sources. What Engnell denies is obviously not *sources*, but *parallel sources of considerable length*. But if there were different circles of traditionists, and if the circles of traditionists handled not only units but *collections of tradition*, it is not inconceivable that the Pentateuch will be found to contain something like parallel 'documents', whether 'oral' or 'written'; indeed, there is antecedent probability that it will. Let us suppose, for argument, that written 'books' only became common in Israel in exilic and post-exilic times;[1] nevertheless, if *collections* of oral tradition already existed in pre-exilic times, we are perfectly at liberty to apply source-critical methods to them. There can be no possible objection in principle to parallel sources even at the pre-literary stage. It is entirely a question of evidence. If we can speak of 'oral literature', it is all one whether the literature was oral or written.

This brings us to the question of 'constants'. And here, especially, Engnell overplays what in some ways was quite a good hand. To say of the divine names that within the supposedly different documents the Hebrew MSS. vary 'considerably' among themselves, is surely a gross exaggeration. That anyone in Uppsala, of all places, should say that 'the LXX shows inescapably that the variation in the divine names must to a large extent be the result of a later process of unification', is almost incredible.[2] Skinner's crushing reply to Dahse, to whom Engnell refers with approval in this connexion, is final: the agreement of divine names in the Hebrew and Samaritan texts extends to over 300 cases,[3] with difference in only eight or nine.[4] This agreement goes back to a time before the LXX was thought of, and is proof positive of the reliability of the Massoretic text. Again, granted that the different divine names have 'different ideological associations', is there any reason why, when Abraham lied to Pharaoh (Gen. xii. 10–20) the emphasis should be on 'Israel's national

---

[1] Though Geo Widengren, *Literary and Psychological Aspects of the Hebrew Prophets*, Uppsala Universitets Årsskrift, x, 1948, has cast serious doubt on this supposition.

[2] It is the habit of Uppsala to depreciate the LXX in favour of the MT.

[3] J. Skinner, *The Divine Names in Genesis*, London, 1914, p. 116. Engnell does not mention Skinner.

[4] Ibid., p. 38.

god', while when he similarly lied to Abimelech of Gerar (Gen. xx) it should be more 'theological' and 'abstract-cosmic'? Nor is it by any means a question of only a single 'constant' in a particular pericope. In Gen. xx. 1–17 and xxxi. 22–55 we have 'Elohim' *and* the dream motif (note also Abraham as a 'prophet'). This would seem to indicate that xx. 1–17 and xxxi. 22–55 are from a different stratum of tradition from xii. 10–20 and xxvi. 1–11. Further, in the account of the sale of Joseph into Egypt (Gen. xxxvii) there are variations which cannot be explained by 'the epic law of iteration' as that law is exemplified in, say, xxii. 6, 8 ('they went both of them together') and the recapitulatory speech of Abraham's servant in xxiv. 34–49. What we have in xxxvii. 28 seems sheer contradiction, and can only be accounted for on the hypothesis of the dovetailing of two divergent traditions.[1] There appear, therefore, to be cogent reasons for making some kind of distinction between J and E. And since, in Gen. xxxvii, J's association of motifs (the father's favouritism—Judah —the sale—the Ishmaelites) is parallel with E's (Joseph's dreams—Reuben—the pit—the Midianites), it would seem that E represents a different version of the tradition, not simply so much expansion of J. (It is, of course, impossible within the compass of this essay to argue the case for the parallel sources hypothesis *ab initio*; it can only be pointed out that if the attack on it fails, we are left in some sort where we were.)

If, then, we are to keep the sigla J, E, D, P, what do they signify? Are they 'strata', as Pedersen conceives of them?[2] Or are they 'documents' in the meaning of the older literary criticism? The truth lies, probably, somewhere between the two extremes. Let it be granted that all the 'documents' contain pre-exilic and post-exilic materials; let us even suppose that the *termini a quo* and *ad quem* of the materials they contain are approximately the same (though this seems less likely for E and D than for J and P). This must not be taken to mean that the 'gauge', if we may use the figure, of each is the same throughout its entire course.

---

[1] Cf. Aage Bentzen, *Introduction to the Old Testament*, ii, Copenhagen, 1949, p. 46.

[2] And as Bentzen, op. cit., pp. 62 ff., to a large extent agrees: 'All the strata contain both pre-Exilic and post-Exilic material. *They are as much parallel as successive.*'

The gauge of J is broader in the pre-exilic period than in the post-exilic,[1] while that of P is broader in the post-exilic period than in the pre-exilic. Nor should we do away entirely with the 'authors' of the 'documents' and speak only in terms of 'schools'. There is, about J at least, an architectonic quality which argues for an 'author' who flourished at some time in the ninth or tenth century B.C. He was, if we will, a 'collector', and additions were made to his work. But it was he who gave to Hebrew tradition its abiding form, a form which was determinative for subsequent ages.

In conclusion: as matters now stand, the history of any one of the 'documents' may well be as complicated as the history of the whole Pentateuch was conceived to be only thirty years ago. We can no longer use the figure of a single date-line, but must think rather of a dimensional area, and plot the ages of ideas and institutions upon it with as much precision as we can. The matter may be represented graphically, very approximately, so:

A. *The older Sources Hypothesis.*

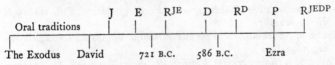

B. *The present (tentative) position.*

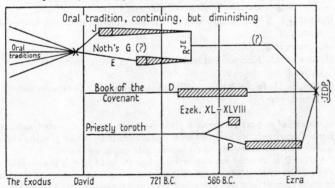

[1] Pedersen instances Abraham's intercession for Sodom (Gen. xviii. 22*b*–33*a*) as

This obviously does not mean that we are forced to adopt a prevailingly agnostic attitude to the history.[1] Nevertheless, on the whole, we must be less confident of our datings than was once customary. Yet the present position is not without its compensations. During the period we have had under review the contrast between the Theology of the Old Testament and the History of Israel's Religion has been so sharp and stubborn that the task of writing a Theology has seemed well-nigh impossible. But if we must now, perforce, be less dogmatic about the History than we used to be, we may perhaps essay to write the Theology with fewer misgivings.

C. R. NORTH

BIBLIOGRAPHY

(*The following list includes items which have not been mentioned in the preceding notes. Not all the items referred to in the notes are repeated here.*)

BAUMGARTNER, W. 'Wellhausen und der heutige Stand der alttestamentlichen Wissenschaft', *T.R.* ii, 1930, pp. 287–307.

— 'Alttestamentliche Einleitung und Literaturgeschichte', *T.R.* viii, 1936, pp. 179–222.

BENTZEN, A. *Introduction to the Old Testament*, Engl. Ed., 2 vols., Copenhagen, 1948–9.

COPPENS, J. *Histoire critique des livres de l'Ancien Testament*[3], Bruges, 1942.

EISSFELDT, O. *Hexateuch-Synopse*, Leipzig, 1922.

— *Einleitung in das Alte Testament*, Tübingen, 1934.

ENGNELL, I. *Gamla Testamentet. En traditionshistorisk inledning*, i, Stockholm, 1945.

— Articles in *S.B.U.*

HÖLSCHER, G. 'Komposition und Ursprung des Deuteronomiums', *Z.A.W.* xl, 1922, pp. 161–255.

HOOKE, S. H. *In the Beginning* (Clarendon Bible, Old Testament, vol. vi), Oxford, 1947.

an example of post-exilic material in J. He does so on grounds of *innere Schätzung*. But the same conclusion has long been recognized on literary-critical grounds. There is therefore no reason to play off the two methods against one another.

[1] Thus P, in its final form, does appear to legislate for an Aaronic priesthood at a single sanctuary. D acknowledges all Levites as priests. Ezek. xl–xlviii, with its tentative proposal for a Zadokite priesthood, is still the middle term between them. Such a development is natural enough and cannot be ruled out of court as 'evolutionism'.

HYLMÖ, Gunnar. *Gamla Testamentets Litteraturhistoria*, Lund, 1938.

LODS, Adolphe. *Histoire de la littérature hébraïque et juive*, Paris, 1950. (Posthumous.)

MICHELET, S., MOWINCKEL, S., and MESSEL, N.: *Det Gamle Testamente*, i: *Loven eller de fem Mosebøker*, Oslo, 1929–30.

MOWINCKEL, S. *The Two Sources of the Predeuteronomic Primeval History (JE) in Gen. i–xi*, Oslo, 1937.

NOTH, M. *Überlieferungsgeschichtliche Studien*, i, Halle-Saale, 1943.

— *Überlieferungsgeschichte des Pentateuch*, Stuttgart, 1948.

OESTERLEY, W. O. E., and ROBINSON, T. H.: *An Introduction to the Books of the Old Testament*[2], London, 1946.

PEDERSEN, J. 'Die Auffassung vom Alten Testament', *Z.A.W.* xlix, 1931, pp. 161–81.

— *Israel: its Life and Culture, III–IV*, Engl. Ed., London and Copenhagen, 1940.

PFEIFFER, R. H. *Introduction to the Old Testament*, New York, 1941.

ROBERTSON, E. *The Old Testament Problem with two other Essays*, Manchester, 1950.

RUDOLPH, W. *Der 'Elohist' von Exodus bis Josua*, B.Z.A.W. lxviii, 1938.

SIEBENS, A. R. *L'Origine du code deutéronomique*, Paris, 1929.

VOLZ, P., and RUDOLPH, W.: *Der Elohist als Erzähler: Ein Irrweg der Pentateuchkritik?* B.Z.A.W. lxiii, 1933.

VON RAD, G. *Die Priesterschrift im Hexateuch*, B.W.A.N.T., Vierte Folge, xiii, 1934.

— *Das formgeschichtliche Problem des Hexateuchs*, B.W.A.N.T., Vierte Folge, xxvi, 1938.

— *Deuteronomium-Studien*[2], Göttingen, 1948.

— *Das erste Buch Mose, Genesis Kapitel 1–12, 9*, Göttingen, 1949.

WEISER, A. *Einleitung in das Alte Testament*[2], Göttingen, 1949.

WELCH, A. C. *The Code of Deuteronomy*, London, 1924.

— *Deuteronomy: The Framework to the Code*, Oxford, 1932

IV
THE HISTORICAL BOOKS

JOSHUA

FORTY years ago it was generally agreed that Joshua has substantially the same literary history as the Pentateuch. It was permissible to speak of the Hexateuch, thus including Joshua in the full-orbed Graf-Wellhausen scheme. This involved a composite JE for the first twelve chapters, a D-revision, then a P-revision with possibly later additions. P is almost non-existent in the first twelve chapters, but predominant in the rest, especially where topographical matter is concerned, though xxiv is mostly E.

This trend of study has been continued by some scholars down to the present time. J. A. Bewer[1] is typical of the earlier group of these. There was an original JE-account of the conquest, completely rewritten by D with a marked predilection for E. Very little of J was thus left (xiii. 13; xv. 13–19, 63; xvi. 10; xvii. 11–18; xix. 47; cf. Judges i). A P-editor took this D-Joshua, introduced some P-elements (iv. 10, 16, 18 f.; part of v. 10–12; ix. 15b, 17–21; xii. 9–24), provided most of the details in xiii–xxiv, but kept the D-framework. Some J and E material was added later. The more modern developments of this position mostly deal with the relations between J, E, and D. R. H. Pfeiffer[2] thinks that the E-material has been edited out of all recognition by a JE-editor *ca.* 650 B.C., by D-editors *ca.* 550 B.C., and by a whole chain of annotators down to *ca.* 200 B.C. He can find no real trace of E apart from xiv. 6–14 and xix. 49 f., D having rewritten E to such an extent that it is not possible to recover E by removing the D-material. The D-editors had suppressed the J-material of the original JE-Joshua, eliminating the story of a piecemeal, and not always successful, invasion. The D-Joshua, which ended at xxiv. 31, was taken by

---

[1] *The Literature of the Old Testament in its Historical Development*, 1922, pp. 67, 80, 228, 278. [2] *Introduction to the Old Testament*, 1941, pp. 296–313.

a P-editor, who inserted some details in i–xii, provided most of xiii–xxii, but left xxiii alone, this being chiefly D. The last chapter (xxiv. 1–24, 32 f.) is E without any editorial traces, and was added later. G. Hölscher[1] allows much more for J than some of his predecessors, finding traces of J through to 1 Kings xii. 19. In Joshua he finds the J-elements mostly confined to odd verses and even parts of verses: viz. the spies in Jericho: ii, part of 1 a, 1 b, 8, 12 bβ, 13, 17 a, 18–21; the crossing of Jordan: parts of iii. 1; iv. 3; iv. 8; the capture of Jericho: v. 13–14 a; vi. 25; the capture of Ai: viii. 11 b–12, part of 14 a, 17 b, part of 19, 20 a, 21, 22 a, 24 aα, 24 b, 25; the covenant with the Gibeonites: ix. 4–5, 6 b–7, 12–14, 15 aβ, 16 aβ, 16 bβ, 22 bβ, part of 23. This marks a renewed attempt to disentangle the two strands in JE. Another attempt to carry this type of literary analysis to its utmost limits is that by C. A. Simpson.[2] His results have been carefully tabulated in O. Eissfeldt's[3] detailed and extended criticism. Simpson finds his late J2 source interwoven with E throughout, apart from D and P elements. The disconcerting feature of these studies by Hölscher and Simpson is that, careful and analytical as their treatment is, their results do not agree. They disagree also with the results of Oesterley and Robinson,[4] whilst Eissfeldt[5] has his own scheme, tracing J, E and his own suggested L source in Joshua and Judges i. 1–ii. 5, together with elements, sometimes extensive, from D and P. In iv, where S. R. Driver[6] found *a* and *b* narratives, Eissfeldt finds three, L, J, and E, but there is no common agreement throughout as regards sources between Driver and Eissfeldt, any more than between the others. Most recently A. Weiser[7] has

[1] *Die Anfänge der hebräischen Geschichtsschreibung*, S.H.A.W., 1942.
[2] *The Early Traditions of Israel*, 1948, pp. 280–322, adversely criticized by H. H. Rowley, *Bi. Or.*, Sept. 1948, pp. 139–40.
[3] *Die ältesten Traditionen Israels, ein kritischer Bericht über C. A. Simpson's The Early Traditions of Israel*, B.Z.A.W. lxxi, 1950, pp. 14–30.
[4] *An Introduction to the Books of the Old Testament*, 1934, pp. 69 ff.
[5] *Einleitung in das Alte Testament*, 1934, pp. 282 ff.; also *Geschichtsschreibung im Alten Testament*, 1948, p. 43, a monograph in which he discusses Hölscher's work, as well as studies by Noth and von Rad.
[6] *Introduction to the Literature of the Old Testament*[9], 1913, pp. 104–16.
[7] *Einleitung in das Alte Testament*[2], 1949, pp. 111 ff.

reaffirmed the orthodox point of view, but avoiding the pitfalls of minute allocation between J and E. Similarly C. R. North[1] in the main follows Driver, but contenting himself, like Weiser, with a composite JE, not seeking to disentangle them. He sees relics of the J-story of the conquest in scattered verses in xiii–xix (cf. Bewer's list above: the suggestion was originally Schrader's in 1869). Hölscher did not recognize these as J-material; Beatrice L. Goff[2] ascribes them to some other early source independent of both J and E; Eissfeldt[3] allocates them to L; and Simpson[4] to J2. Pfeiffer[5] grudgingly allows them to be J-material but summarized till the beauty of the J-style is gone. He envisages a J-history gaining popularity through the centuries until elements of it were at last inserted into the almost completed (D plus P) narrative.

It is plain that attempts to trace the Pentateuchal sources in Joshua have led to a far from unified result. W. Rudolph[6] roundly declares that there is no E-material at all in Joshua i–xii, and allocates it all to J, whilst R. E. Wolfe[7] finds no J, but D or P or both. It is not, therefore, in the least surprising that A. Bentzen[8] says that we have spent far too much time and energy on the 'supposition that the documentary tetragram JEDP must be maintained in Josh.'. All agree on the D-element being strong, and most scholars also agree that there are P-elements, but the real differences of opinion concern the material on which the D-editors worked. The wide differences of opinion make it unlikely that the stories were in any of the recognized Pentateuch sources.

Accordingly there has been a recent tendency to ignore the (by now) traditional literary analysis method so far as the pre-D material is concerned. M. Noth[9] finds much pre-D material

---

[1] *The Old Testament Interpretation of History*, 1946, p. 32.
[2] 'The lost Jahwistic account of the conquest of Canaan', *J.B.L.* liii, 1934, pp. 241–9.
[3] *Einleitung in das Alte Testament*, 1934, pp. 282 ff.
[4] Op. cit., pp. 280–322.   [5] Op. cit., p. 299.
[6] *Der Elohist von Exodus bis Josua*, B.Z.A.W. lxviii, 1938, pp. 164 ff.
[7] *J.B.L.* lx, 1941, p. 420.
[8] *Introduction to the Old Testament*, ii, 1949, p. 83.
[9] *Das Buch Josua*, H.A.T., 1938, pp. ix–xii.

throughout. In ii–xii he finds three main sources, a group of aetiological legends (ii–ix) preserved at Gilgal, and two locally preserved hero legends (x and xi. 1–9), one from the south and the other from the far north. The Gilgal legends are Bethlehemite in origin, but gained national importance because of Saul. All three date from the time between the disruption of the kingdom and the reign of Ahab. A. Alt[1] had already advocated an aetiological origin for i–xi generally, but saw in x a Joshua hero legend with an historical basis. Noth finds this also to be aetiological, arising as an explanation of the strange heaps of stone near the cave at Makkedah. I. Engnell[2] follows Noth in general. According to A. Lods,[3] viii–ix are based upon aetiological legends of the topography of Ai, a town actually destroyed *ca.* 2200 B.C., and never again occupied except for a small Benjamite occupation. Excavations show that the city which was destroyed in the Joshua invasion was Bethel and not Ai.[4] The two sites are close together, a mile and a half distant, and could therefore never flourish at the same time. A legend referring to the age-old destruction of Ai was transferred to the already long-distant destruction of Bethel, four times destroyed between 1200 and 1000 B.C.

And yet even in the aetiological legends there are interwoven strands. K. Möhlenbrink[5] has made this clear so far as iv and vi are concerned. In iv there are two stories concerning monoliths, one of twelve stones in the middle of Jordan (*v.* 9) and the other of monoliths still to be seen in Gilgal (*vv.* 21–4). Similarly in vi, there are two interwoven accounts of the fall of Jericho; in vii, variants concerning the fate of Achan, and again in viii of the sacking of Ai. And so Möhlenbrink[6] finds two cycles of

---

[1] 'Josua' in *Werden und Wesen des Alten Testaments*, B.Z.A.W. lxvi, 1936, pp. 13–29.

[2] *Gamla testamentet: en traditionshistorisk inledning*, i, 1945, pp. 235 ff.

[3] 'Les Fouilles d'Aï et l'époque de l'entrée des Israélites en Palestine', *Mélanges Franz Cumont*, 1936, pp. 847–57.

[4] W. F. Albright, *F.S.A.C.*, 1940, pp. 117, 219; more recently *The Archaeology of Palestine* (Pelican Books, 1949), pp. 30, 117; also G. E. Wright, *The Westminster Historical Atlas to the Bible*, 1945, p. 105.

[5] 'Die Landnahmesagen des Buch Josua', *Z.A.W.*, N.F. xv, 1938, pp. 238–68. Also H. H. Rowley, *The Growth of the Old Testament*, 1950, p. 54.

[6] Op. cit., pp. 266 f.

traditions, an E Ephraimite twelve-tribe cycle from Shiloh and a three-tribe cycle (Benjamin, Reuben, and Gad) from Gilgal, combined at a very early date and with Shechem substituted for Shiloh. To all this there was added a large secondary section, consisting of xi f. and xiii. In spite of Pfeiffer's[1] criticism, the fact remains that there are two strands, and it remains true that the complications cannot be removed by any simple solution, whether literary or aetiological. Whatever the history of these chapters, it is certainly complicated.

Dealing with the latter part of the book, Alt[2] holds that the list of towns in xv is based on a list of the twelve provinces of Josiah's kingdom (*ca.* 620 B.C.), and that[3] the tribal boundaries in xiii–xix are based on a document dealing with land laws in the pre-monarchy period. S. Mowinckel[4] believes that these chapters are post-exilic, composed by the P-editor from traditions. The lists are unlike other administrative lists. The twelve-tribe system belongs to the post-Davidic period, and earlier there were ten tribes. The details of Ephraim and Manasseh (xvi and xvii) assume the existence of schismatic Samaritans, and must therefore be quite late. To W. F. Albright[5] xxi is a list of Levitical cities of the times of David and Solomon, on the ground that not one town in the list was founded after 950 B.C. The views of Alt and Noth involve a combination of traditions into a story purporting to tell how Israel originally became possessed of the land. Later, the hero Joshua was worked into the story, and later still there was a re-editing of the D-Joshua. Albright[6] rightly criticizes a rash use of this new aetiological method when it is unsupported by any external evidence. He says that Alt and his followers are not justified in making Joshua only an insignificant local chief just because certain minor changes have to be made in the Jericho and Ai stories and elsewhere in the traditions. The

[1] Op. cit., p. 311 n.

[2] 'Judas Gaue unter Josia', *P.J.B.*, 1925, pp. 100–116.

[3] 'Das System der Stammesgrenzen im Buch Josua', *Sellin Festschrift*, 1927, pp. 13–24.

[4] *Zur Frage nach dokumentarischen Quellen in Josua 13–19*, 1946.

[5] *The Archaeology of Palestine*, 1949, p. 229; and earlier, in the *Louis Ginzberg Jubilee Volume*, 1945, pp. 49 ff.   [6] *F.S.A.C.*, 1940, pp. 38 ff.

course of events is much closer to the biblical tradition than these scholars allow (p. 329), and he himself has written in strong criticism[1] of the work of Noth and Möhlenbrink.

M. Noth[2] will not allow anything of J, E and P after Numbers, except only for Deut. xxxiv. 1 aα ... 7–9. A Deuteronomist, living in Bethel or in Mizpah, wrote the story of the waywardness of Israel, beginning with Moses (Deut. i) and ending with King Jehoiachin on parole in exile (2 Kings xxv). The D-Joshua is part of this long history. It included i. 1–6, 10–18, most of ii–xi; xiv. 6 aβ, 6 b–15 a; xii; with Joshua's parting discourse in xxiii, which is in good D-style. J. Pedersen[3] agrees to the extent that the Graf-Wellhausen theory cannot provide the final solution. We must start with Deuteronomy, closely allied with which are the stories in Joshua about the conquest and the allocation of territory, the subject-matter of which cannot be segregated by formal literary criteria. Pfeiffer[4] finds xv–xix to be sound as a description of fifth-century Palestine, and the date is confirmed by the topographical work of Albright, Alt, Elliger, and Noth.

E. Jacob[5] finds everywhere evidence of the large part played by the local priests in the preservation of the early historical material, but in the search for origins other than J and E, all rivals have been outdistanced by G. von Rad.[6] He starts from the little Credo in Deut. xxvi. 5 b–9. The D-style is plain, but the alliteration betrays an early origin. It is the feast-legend of the Feast of Weeks at Gilgal, brought into prominence by the importance of Samuel and Saul, and is associated with the land-allocation saga. There is a similar passage in Joshua xxiv. 2 b–13, which von Rad claims to be a free adaptation of a cult-lyric. Behind Deuteronomy, behind Exodus, behind Joshua xxiv there

[1] *B.S.A.O.R.*, No. 74, April 1939, pp. 11–23.

[2] *Überlieferungsgeschichtliche Studien*, i, S.K.G., 1943; also *Überlieferungsgeschichte des Pentateuch*, 1948, p. 19.

[3] *Israel, its life and culture, III–IV*, 1940, p. 725.

[4] Op. cit., p. 309; cf. Mowinckel (*supra*).

[5] *La tradition historique en Israël*, 1946, pp. 41–2.

[6] *Das Formgeschichtliche Problem des Hexateuchs*, B.W.A.N.T. xxvi, 1938; *Der Anfang der Geschichtsschreibung im Alten Testament*, A.K. xxxii, 1944, pp. 1–42.

is the same cult-motif. This consists of a recital of the events of Paran-Sinai and the people's apostasy (14 f.), promise of future faithfulness (16 f., 24), proclamation of the Law (25), the binding of the covenant (27), and the blessing and the curse (27 b; cf. viii. 34). All this (so von Rad, p. 35) is the original motif of the old vintage feast of Shechem. The real conclusion of the J-material is Joshua xxi. 43–5, rewritten by the D-editor, but concluding the long J-story of the way in which Jehovah fulfilled his promise to the patriarchs, gave them the promised land, but especially gave them rest. Here, say von Rad and Engnell[1] is the real continuity of the Pentateuch.

Bentzen[2] is much attracted by this cult approach coupled with aetiological and hero legends, but he is careful to point out that this does not do away with the older literary hypotheses.[3] It points to new ways in which these hypotheses are to be worked out. The ultimate solution is that the sources of the historical books, Genesis to the earlier part of 1 Kings, are these cult and other legends, many of them containing a considerable and sound historical nucleus, sometimes found in J and E and sometimes not found there, but welded, stage by stage, into a continuous narrative.

JUDGES

We are faced in Judges with the same general problem and the same diversity of solution as in Joshua. The 'remarkably varied and contradictory' picture of which Eissfeldt[4] wrote in 1938 has grown more varied and contradictory. On the one side, we find Pfeiffer (1941) and Hölscher (1942) continuing along orthodox lines and attributing the pre-D material to J and E, with Eissfeldt finding here, as before, three sources, J and E and his own L. On the other side, we have Bentzen (1949) tending towards the newer school of Alt, Noth, von Rad, and Engnell, who write in terms of aetiology and hero-sagas, and for the most part ignore

---

[1] Op. cit., p. 217.
[2] Op. cit. ii, p. 61.
[3] Cf. Albright's remarks, *F.S.A.C.*, pp. 209–11.
[4] 'Modern Criticism', *Record and Revelation* (ed. H. W. Robinson), 1938, p. 75.

the older type of literary criticism. Bentzen[1] writes of strata of traditions rather than of documents, referring to collections of legends woven together before they were gathered into the Deuteronomic net.

All are agreed[2] that there was at one time a D-Judges. The general opinion is that it contained the central core (ii. 6–xv. 20), but without the so-called 'minor' judges (Shamgar, Tola, Ibzan, Elon, Abdon), the Abimelech story (ix), and probably the last and least creditable of the Samson stories (xvi). But was there a pre-Deuteronomic Judges? The general opinion is in favour, and those who still adhere to the literary analysis school believe, for the most part, that it was a JE-Judges. Its date is *ca.* 630–600 B.C.[3] It had an introduction (ii. 6, 8–10, 13, 20 f.), and contained stories of Ehud, Deborah and Barak, Gideon (but not viii. 4–21), Abimelech, Jephthah, and Samson, and the summarized references to the five minor judges mentioned in x. 1–5 and xii. 8–15. The JE-editor omitted the J-material in i and the whole of xvii–xxi. The D-editor omitted the Song of Deborah (v), the references to the minor judges, the last story about Samson (xvi), going on from xv. 20 to 2 Sam. i–xii, and replaced the Abimelech story with viii. 30–5. All this JE-material was restored under P-influence, and in the third century the original J-material, which the JE-editor had omitted, was restored. There are obviously late elements in xvii–xxi. Pfeiffer follows W. R. Arnold[4] in ascribing them to a late marginal commentary, whilst Bewer[5] allots them to a P-editor who retouched i. 1–ii. 5 (adding i. 1 a, 4, 8 f., 18; ii. 1 b–5 a) and xx, adding a homily in xxi. 1–14, 24 f. Mowinckel[6] thinks that the P-author of Joshua xiii–xix knew Judges i (the only documentary source he did know).

Some such scheme of what Bentzen[7] depreciatingly calls this 'subtraction- and addition-theory' is adopted by all who seek to account for the evident absence of D-touches in some parts of

---

[1] Op. cit. ii, p. 90.
[2] Not C. F. Burney, *The Book of Judges*, 1918, p. xlvi, who thinks that what is usually ascribed to D is actually E².   [3] So Pfeiffer, op. cit., p. 332.
[4] *Ephod and Ark*, 1917, p. 101.   [5] Op. cit., p. 272.
[6] *Zur Frage nach dokumentarischen Quellen in Josua 13–19*, 1946.
[7] Op. cit. ii, pp. 88 f.

the book, in some of the earliest as well as in some of the latest parts. Bentzen finds it difficult to see how such scandalous stories could have been inserted at a time when the tendency was to idealize the past. He thinks that these stories were indeed in the D-Judges,[1] intended by the D-editor to account for the Philistine oppression recounted in 1 Samuel, being caused, according to the good old D-pattern, by Israel's apostasy and generally scandalous behaviour. But it was not everything in the past that was idealized: only those particular events which were dear to later writers. Dan was excluded from the life of the World to Come (cf. Rev. vii. 5–8) as being the apostate tribe, and apparently the name is avoided in the genealogy of 1 Chron. vii. 12. There is no reason why a late writer, strong for David, should not insert scandalous stories about Saul's tribe or Samson the Danite, or let the full story of Dan's idolatries be known. The D-editor, in any case, is responsible for ii. 7, 11–13; ii. 4–6; nearly all of iii. 7–11 (Othniel); iii. 12–15 a, 30 b; iv. 1–3; v. 31 b; vi. 1, 7–10; viii. 27 b, probably 28 b, 33–4, 35; x. 6–16, 17 f.; xiii. 1; xv. 20.[2]

But is it right to say that the pre-D Judges is a JE-Judges? The Ehud story is probably a unit,[3] but there are interwoven stories in iv: one, an account of Barak's defeat of Sisera; the other, the story of the fight of Zebulon and Naphtali against Jabin of Hazor (cf. Josh. xi. 1–9). The second of these stories is commonly ascribed to J (not by Hölscher, who finds no J in this chapter iv), and the first to E (but Eissfeldt says L). The Gideon-Jerubbaal stories are not easy to disentangle. Gideon is the J-hero (so Pfeiffer, Hölscher, &c., but Eissfeldt finds J and L interwoven) who rescues West Manasseh from raiding Midianites under their two kings, Zebah and Zalmunna. The torches and the ephod-image belong here. The E-narrative, according to Pfeiffer,[4] starts with a prophet warning a wayward people (vi. 7–10). Gideon destroys the Baal altar, is rescued by his father from

---

[1] So also Rowley, *The Growth of the Old Testament*, 1950, p. 62.

[2] North (op. cit., 1946, pp. 97 f.) includes also xvi. 31 b, since he apparently admits xvi into the D-Judges.

[3] E. G. Kraeling, 'Difficulties in the story of Ehud', *J.B.L.* liv, 1935, pp. 205–10; E. Jacob, op. cit., 1946, p. 63.   [4] Op. cit., pp. 328 ff.

the angry villagers, reduces his forces to three hundred men, and surrounds the enemy camp by night. The trumpets belong to this story, and so also the panic-stricken flight of the enemy, who are cut off by the Ephraimites and lose their chiefs Raven (Oreb) and Wolf (Zeeb). But Hölscher finds nothing of J in vii, which means that for him the torches and the trumpets both belong to the Oreb-Zeeb story, and so also for Oesterley and Robinson,[1] who say that there are two recensions of this story. For Pedersen,[2] the Jerubbaal story, as it is now told, is remote from the events. The name belonged originally to a time when there was no sharp distinction between Jehovah and Baal, and the story, as we now have it, tells of the change-over of a sanctuary from Baal to Jehovah, with the result that the original meaning of the name ('Baal is fighting') has become twisted to have a new significance.

There has been more agreement amongst the literary critics in respect of the other stories. For Pfeiffer, Oesterley and Robinson, Hölscher, the J-element in the Abimelech story is the Gaal intrusion (ix. 26–41), though Eissfeldt makes this L, together with ix. 1–5 a and 46–55. All are agreed that the main story is E and is one of the finest and best-told stories in the Old Testament. In xi–xii, the J-strand concerns an illegitimate Jephthah driven out by his brothers to become a bandit chief. The Gileadites promise to make him their ruler if he saves them from the Ammonites. He does this, and when the Ephraimites quarrel with him, he seizes the Fords of Jordan, cuts off every Ephraimite who has crossed east to attack him, and slays every one of them who cannot pronounce 'Shibboleth' (ford) with a 'sh'. The E-strand tells of a respectable householder of Mizpah, who saves his people from the Moabites, and sacrifices his daughter on his victorious return in fulfilment of his vow. This, says E aetiologically, is why Gileadite women annually observe a four-day mourning custom. Pfeiffer holds that the Samson stories are J, Hölscher J and E mixed, and Eissfeldt L and J mixed.

Scholars, however, are not agreed that these early strands are actually J and E. Pfeiffer, though he uses the symbols J and E,

---

[1] Op. cit., p. 80.   [2] Op. cit., p. 205.

causes confusion by saying[1] that he does not thereby mean that the J and E of Judges are identical with the J and E in Genesis. They are to be identified[2] with sources in Samuel rather than in the Pentateuch. L. Rost[3] and H. M. Wiener[4] do not think that JEDP are continued in Judges–Samuel–Kings. Wiener agrees that there are two sources throughout, and calls them N (for Nathan the prophet) and G (for Gad the prophet), these being substantially Pfeiffer's J and E. E. Jacob[5] does not think J and E go beyond Joshua. He writes of stories circulating in oral tradition, and at the time of their being written down they were of equal authority so that all were included. On the other hand, Mowinckel[6] finds JEDP right through into Kings; and so also do Hölscher and Eissfeldt,[7] the latter of whom finds LJEDP right through the historical books as far as 1 Kings xii.

The Samson stories are different from the rest and are true folklore, for Samson is the Trickster of Israelite folk-tales, corresponding to Mawi of the Maori tales, Robin Goodfellow (Puck) of England, the Coyote of the American Indians, and Qat of the Melanesians. Attempts have been made to find mytho-logical origins,[8] identifying Samson with the sun who loses his strength when his rays (Samson's hair) are cut off, and so forth, but the Trickster-motif of folklore is sufficiently well-estab-lished the whole world over for there to be no need for further search.

The Song of Deborah is one of the oldest Hebrew poems, and is at least as old as the twelfth century. Its genius is truly Canaanite and the style is closely similar to that of some of the Ras Shamra texts. There are passages with the same steady

---

[1] Op. cit., p. 315.

[2] So also Rowley, op. cit., p. 60.

[3] *Die Überlieferung von der Thronnachfolge Davids*, 1926.

[4] *The Composition of Judges ii. 11 to 1 Kings ii. 46*, 1929.

[5] *La tradition historique en Israël*, 1946, p. 62.

[6] 'Der Ursprung der Bil'āmsage', *Z.A.W.*, N.F. vii, 1930, pp. 233–71.

[7] *Die Quellen des Richterbuches*, 1925; *Einleitung in das Alte Testament*, 1934, pp. 288–301. In the *Eissfeldt Festschrift*, 1947, W. Rudolph pays a happy tribute to Eissfeldt's Judges-studies by contributing an article entitled 'Textkritische Anmer-kungen zum Richterbuch', pp. 199–212.

[8] G. F. Moore, *Judges*, I.C.C., 1898, pp. 364 ff.

repetitions in the Ras Shamra material,[1] and the same style is to be found in Jotham's parable of the trees (ix. 8–15), another very ancient piece.

The attitude of the more modern school of interpretation is well expressed by Pedersen.[2] He states that in his opinion literary criticism has limited itself to purely formal characteristics and has drawn greater conclusions from them than they can uphold. The Judges-material is too different from that in the Pentateuch ever to have belonged to the same original sources, and in any case he does not think any of either existed as a literary unit before the exile. What we actually have is[3] a small remnant of legends which told of the tribal wars and the feats of heroes from the time of the settlement onwards, together with legends concerning the founding of sanctuaries and also stories which are wholly aetiological in origin. With much of this we would agree, but we would not deny pre-exilic literary activity, and with Albright[4] would say that the course of events was much closer to biblical traditions than the modern aetiological school allows.

RUTH

It was the custom during the last century for the book to be ascribed to an early date, as early as the time of David, but latterly scholars generally have assigned it to the post-exilic period. The exceptions are Steinmueller[5] (early monarchy), Jepsen[6] (exilic period), and Bentzen[7] (any time from the later monarchy to post-exilic days).

There has been considerable discussion concerning the purpose of the book. With the ascription of the book to post-exilic days, there was developed also the theory that it was a fifth-century B.C. political tract directed against the exclusive policy of Nehemiah and Ezra, especially in relation to their mixed

[1] Cf. the texts translated by Cyrus H. Gordon, *Ugaritic Literature*, 1949; T. H. Gaster, *Thespis*, 1950; H. E. del Medico, *La Bible Cananéenne*, 1950.

[2] Op. cit., p. 727. [3] Op. cit., p. 654. [4] Re Joshua, *F.S.A.C.*, p. 329.

[5] *Companion to Scripture Studies*, ii, 1942, p. 82. So also C. Lattey, *The Book of Ruth*, 1936, pp. xxxiii–xl.

[6] 'Das Buch Ruth', *T.S.K.*, N.F. iii, 1937–8, pp. 416–22.

[7] Op. cit. ii, 1949, p. 185.

marriages policy (so Bertholdt in 1812–19 and latterly Bertholet, Cornill, Sellin, and Meinhold). Opinion is now veering away from this, though most would say that the book is universalist in its attitude without being polemical. Rowley[1] holds that it is just as easy to read the book as a defence of Nehemiah-Ezra's policy. Gunkel[2] and Gressmann[3] held it to be a straight novel without any real historical basis. For König (1893), Joüon (1924), Burrows[4] and others, it is the addition of the genealogy which has turned it into a polemic against the anti-mixed marriage policy. H. A. Brongers[5] regards the book as a social novel, designed to connect the g^e'ullâh and the levirate marriage. W. E. Staples[6] thinks the book was written during dark days for encouragement, with the birth of the child as the signal of a happier age. He maintains that all the proper names up to iv. 17 a have fertility-cult connexions, based on the cult of a god Leḥem (Laḥmu) whom he assumes to have been worshipped at one time in Bethlehem, to be supplanted later by Adonis. The latest discussion of the story itself is by E. Robertson.[7] He emphasizes the purely literary character of the book, with a plot carefully worked out, beginning with a famine and three widows in distress, a picture of the blackest destitution. The author uses the plot of the Judah–Tamar story and Hosea ix. 1, and from these two elements weaves a plot whereby Naomi cleverly traps Boaz into marrying Ruth, thus securing maintenance for both women.

The whole problem of the marriage of Ruth and Boaz in its relation to levirate marriage and the g^e'ullâh has been discussed recently by Rowley[8] and by Th. C. Vriezen.[9] Both reach the conclusion that there is no breach of the levirate laws. It is probable that in early times levirate marriage was not limited to a brother-in-law, that it neither required nor excluded full

[1] *Israel's Mission to the World*, 1939, pp. 46 ff.; also 'The Marriage of Ruth', *H.T.R.* xl, 1947, p. 78.

[2] *R.G.G.*[1], v, 1913, col. 107.

[3] *Die Anfänge Israels*, S.A.T., 1914, p. 284.

[4] *J.B.L.* lix, 1940, p. 450.   [5] *Ned. T.T.* ii, 1947, p. 1.

[6] 'The Book of Ruth', *A.J.S.L.* liv, 1937, pp. 145–57.

[7] 'The Plot of Ruth', *B.J.R.L.* xxxii, 2, 1950, pp. 207–28.

[8] 'The Marriage of Ruth', *H.T.R.* xl, 1947, pp. 77–99.

[9] 'Two old cruces : a, Ruth iv. 5', *O.T.S.* v, 1948, pp. 80–8.

marriage, and that it neither required nor excluded the un-
married condition of the levirate partner.[1]

SAMUEL

The two books of Samuel tell the story of the part which
three men played in the establishment of the Hebrew monarchy.
In 1 Sam. i–vii we have the story of Samuel; viii–xv deals with
Samuel and Saul; xvi–xxxi with Saul and David, whilst 2 Samuel
tells the story of David. This last story is concluded in 1 Kings
i–ii, a section which has been detached in order to form a prelude
to the history of Solomon's reign.

It is plain that there are at least two independent strata in
Samuel. These independent strata are to be seen in the different
accounts of how Samuel came to be king, of the way in which
David originally came to Saul's notice, and in various other
discrepancies and duplications throughout the two books.[2]
Advocates of a two-source theory have disentangled the two
sources in general as follows: belonging to the earlier source, in
1 Samuel, elements of i, ii, iv–vi, xviii, and xx; the whole of
ix. 1–x. 16; xi. 1–11, 15; xiii. 2–6, 15–23; xix. 1–46, 52; xvi.
14–23; xxii; xxiv; xxv; xxvii–xxxi (but not xxviii. 3–25); in
2 Samuel, i. 17–vi. 23; most of ix–xx; also xxi. 1–14, 15–22;
xxiii. 8–39; belonging to the later source, in 1 Samuel, most of
i–iii, elements in iv–vi, xx, xxi, xxiii. 1–13, 14–18; the whole of
vii. 2–7; viii; x. 17–25 a; xii, xv; xvii. 1–xviii. 5; xviii. 6–30;
xix; xxvi; xxviii. 3–25; in 2 Samuel, i. 6–10, 14–16.

Since the time of Karl Budde,[3] many scholars have identified
these two sources with J and E of the Pentateuch, but there
have been considerable variations of opinions here. T. Klähn[4]
amassed linguistic evidence to prove that the earlier Samuel
source is J. C. R. North[5] follows Budde, for he refers to 1 Sam.

---

[1] Cf. Rowley, op. cit., p. 97.

[2] For complete lists see the commentaries and Introductions, especially Oesterley
and Robinson, 1934, p. 88; Pfeiffer, 1941, p. 340; Bentzen, ii, 1949, p. 93; Rowley,
The Growth of the Old Testament, 1950, pp. 64–6.

[3] *Die Bücher Richter und Samuel, ihre Quellen und ihr Aufbau*, 1890, pp. 167–276.

[4] *Die sprachliche Verwandtschaft der Quelle J des Heptateuchs*, 1914.

[5] *The Old Testament Interpretation of History*, 1946, p. 36. He thinks (p. 98),

vii. 2–viii. 22; x. 17–24; xii as E (or E[2]), possibly retouched by D, not finding it easy to distinguish between D and the later strands of E.[1] Burney found JE as far as 1 Sam. xii, Hölscher (1942) through into Kings, and similarly Eissfeldt[2] for LJE. Bentzen[3] is doubtful, and so is E. Jacob.[4] For him J ends with the Settlement in Canaan, but there are undeniable resemblances between J and certain passages in Judges–Samuel–Kings. They belong to the same period, though not the same author. He sees in Samuel early examples of that literary art which is seen more fully developed in Ruth, Esther and Tobit. Pedersen[5] does not accept J and E in Genesis as two separated sources, so naturally finds neither here.

Eissfeldt,[6] following his three-source theory, allocates the Ark-stories to L (1 Sam. iv–vi; 2 Sam. iv), as also such biographical details as 1 Sam. xiv. 49–51; 2 Sam. viii. 16–18; iii. 2–5; v. 13–15; and David's lament over Abner (2 Sam. iii. 33–4). He allocates also to L certain details of the stories of establishment of the monarchy (1 Sam. x. 21 b–27; xi. 1–5, 6 b–15), whilst ix. 1–x. 16; xi, 6 a; xiii. 3–15 is J and viii; x. 17–21 b; xii is E. Amongst other allocations, 2 Sam. ix–xx is J, but ii–vi and viii are L. Oesterley and Robinson[7] are convinced that Eissfeldt is right so far as the story of the establishment of the kingdom is concerned, as, say they, a careful comparison of the above LJE passages shows. It is certainly true that two sources are scarcely enough to account for all the statements in 1 Sam. ix–xii. Eissfeldt's L-details do not readily fit into the other stories. Saul's having hidden himself (x. 21 b–27) comes in strangely, and it is curious that although the people wanted a king to save them from the Philistines (ix. 16: J), yet Saul actually established himself by saving the men of Jabesh-Gilead

contrary to most (cf. Pfeiffer, op. cit., p. 362), that it is going beyond the evidence to say that this author was inveterately hostile to the monarchy as such.

[1] He is not alone in this; cf. C. F. Burney, *Judges*, 1918, p. xxxviii.

[2] *Einleitung in das Alte Testament*, 1934, pp. 308 f., 336 f.

[3] Op. cit. ii, 1949, p. 95.   [4] Op.cit., 1946, pp. 82, 96.

[5] Op. cit., 1940, p. 727.

[6] *Die Komposition der Samuelisbücher*, 1931; *Einleitung in das Alte Testament*, 1934, pp. 302–17.

[7] Op. cit., 1934, p. 90.

from the Ammonites (xi). Again, Saul is made king three times, once by Samuel in private (ix. 26–x. 1), and twice publicly, at Mizpah (x. 17–24) and at Gilgal (xi. 15); David is thrice offered a daughter of Saul in marriage (xviii. 17–19; xviii. 21 b; xviii. 22–9 a); and David thrice makes a covenant with Jonathan (xviii. 3; xx. 16 and 42; xxiii. 18). Oesterley and Robinson[1] do not see the same necessity of a three-source theory for these later repetitions, and Pfeiffer[2] rejects it altogether. It is true that they can be fitted into a two-source framework, but they bear evidence of a certain amount of editing to make them fit in. At least this can be maintained, that if a documentary theory is insisted on for Samuel, then a plain two-source theory is not everywhere adequate.

A. Lods[3] holds that in the so-called early source there are two mutually exclusive narratives, a 'seer'-source and a Jabesh-source. The seer-source began with the folk-story of Saul seeking his father's asses (this is in Eissfeldt's L), whilst the Jabesh-source originally began with a legendary story of Saul's birth. This story (1 Sam. i) now tells the story of Samuel's birth, but *vv.* 20 and 28 contain puns on Saul's name, not Samuel's. He is followed in this opinion by J. Hempel (1930), I. Hylander (1932), and R. Press (1938), but Rowley (1950) thinks that there are plays on proper names elsewhere more far-fetched than this, and would let the story stand as a necessary prelude to the Shiloh-ark story. Rowley's argument, in our view, does not exclude Lods's suggestion, but merely explains the change. In any case, it is clear that the origin of these stories demands more than a simple, straightforward two-source theory.

As long ago as 1887, A. Klostermann[4] suggested that Ahimaaz son of Zadok was the author of the early source, which he considered to include 2 Sam. ix–xx, continuing through into 1 Kings i–ii, and to contain also 2 Sam. xvii. 17–21. Certainly the source of the details must have been ultimately either Jonathan son of Abiathar or Ahimaaz son of Zadok, unless Abiathar

[1] Op. cit., p. 90.   [2] Op. cit., p. 341.
[3] *Israël*, 1930, pp. 408–13.
[4] *Die Bücher Samuelis und der Könige*, 1887, pp. xxxii–xxxiii.

was responsible. This last (Abiathar) was B. Duhm's[1] suggestion, but Pfeiffer[2] prefers Ahimaaz, and, if so, then 'Ahimaaz . . . is "the father of history" in a much truer sense than Herodotus half a millennium later'. W. R. Arnold[3] thinks that Zadok's name stood originally in 2 Sam. vi. 4 in place of the strange 'Ahio'. This Zadok suggestion is found in Sellin (1924), and Budde (1934), and it is not necessarily disturbed by Rowley's[4] identification of Zadok as the pre-Davidic Jebusite priest of Jerusalem.

Much attention has latterly been paid to odd sections of the books. R. Press[5] has analysed the first three chapters of 1 Samuel, and finds the story of Samuel's childhood to involve an interwoven tradition in i; ii. 11, 18 b–21; iii and a double interweaving in ii. 13–16, 27–36. K. Elliger[6] thinks that 2 Sam. xxiii. 24–39 is a list of heroes admitted by David to the Thirty, dating in its present form from the Hebron days, but going back to Ziklag days. These concluding chapters (2 Sam. xxi–xxiv) form an appendix to the history proper, interrupting the main narrative, and having been reinserted into the D-Samuel. Here xxi. 1–14, 15–22; xxiii. 8–39 are commonly ascribed to the earlier of the two generally agreed main strands. There are six items in all, connected in pairs both in style and in substance, (*a*) xxi. 1–14, a famine and its ending, and (*f*) xxiv, a pestilence and its ending; into the middle of this (*b*) xxi. 15–22, exploits against the Philistines and (*e*) xxiii. 8–39, more exploits and heroes, were inserted; and into the middle of (*b*) and (*e*), (*c*) xxii (cf. Ps. xviii), David's song of deliverance and (*d*) xxiii. 1–7, David's last words, were inserted.[7] Probably the whole section belonged to the pre-D-Samuel, but was omitted by the D-editors.

[1] *Das Buch Jeremia*, K.H.C., 1901, p. 3.

[2] Op. cit., 1941, pp. 356–7.

[3] *Ephod and Ark*, 1917, pp. 61–2. Wellhausen, as long ago as 1871, proposed '*āḥîw* (his brother) for 'Ahio', *Der Text der Bücher Samuelis*, p. 167.

[4] 'Zadok and Nehushtan', *J.B.L.* lviii, 1939, pp. 113–41.

[5] 'Der Prophet Samuel: eine traditionsgeschichtliche Untersuchung', *Z.A.W.*, N.F. xv, 1938, pp. 177–225.

[6] 'Die dreissig Helden Davids', *P.J.B.*, 1935, pp. 29–75.

[7] Cf. amongst others, Pfeiffer, op. cit., 1941, p. 373; Rowley, *The Growth of the Old Testament*, 1950, p. 69.

2 Sam. vii has received special attention. H. van den Bussche[1] finds that both 2 Sam. vii and its parallel 1 Chr. xvii depend on an older text, with 1 Chr. xvii the nearer to it, both linguistically and theologically. It is evident that 2 Sam. vii has been written over again and again, as Mowinckel[2] has shown. The whole matter of these 'eternal' prophecies of the House of David (2 Sam. vii) and of the House of Zadok (1 Sam. ii. 27–36) is discussed at length by Pfeiffer.[3] Also, I. Hylander[4] posits two revisions of 1 Sam. ii. 27–36, one in favour of Zadokite supremacy and the other under P-influence. Pfeiffer[5] disagrees with Duhm's[6] idea that Ps. lxxxiv is partly a poetic paraphrase of 2 Sam. vii, and rightly holds that the evidence is the other way round. In this he is followed by North.[7]

The most likely *strictly* literary solution is that of A. R. S. Kennedy.[8] He finds five sources: history of Samuel's infancy: history of the Ark: favourable history of the monarchy: unfavourable history (D rather than E) of the monarchy: court history of David (cf. 2 Sam. ix–xx). A development from this position is that of A. Weiser,[9] who allows many separate traditions interwoven into two gathered groups, subjected to subsequent redactions. The separate original traditions included the story of Saul's battles (1 Sam. xi, xiii–xiv) and of David's Ammonite war (2 Sam. x–xi), popular account of the setting up of the kingdom (1 Sam. ix–x), the story of the Ark (1 Sam. iv–vi; 2 Sam. vi), the original Nathan prophecy in 2 Sam. vii, various lists and annals and David's laments (2 Sam. i. 17–27; iii. 33–4). The second stage was a gathering of traditions, the first beginnings of historical writing, into the story of the rise of Saul (1 Sam. ix–x, xi, xiii–xiv) and the story of the rise of David

[1] *Le Texte de la prophétie de Nathan sur la dynastie davidique*, 1948.
[2] Cf. his analysis of the chapter in *S.E.Å.* xii (Lindblom Anniversary Volume), 1947, pp. 228 f.
[3] Op. cit., 1941, pp. 368–71.
[4] *Der literarische Samuel-Saul-Komplex (1 Sam. 1–15) traditionsgeschichtlich untersucht*, 1932, pp. 41–2, 51–62.
[5] Op. cit., 1941, p. 371.   [6] *Die Psalmen*[2], K.H.C., 1922, p. 222.
[7] *The Old Testament Interpretation of History*, 1946, p. 99.
[8] *I and II Samuel*, Cent. B., no date, pp. 13–23.
[9] *Einleitung in das Alte Testament*[2], 1949, p. 130.

(1 Sam. xvi. 14–2 Sam. v or viii). This was, thirdly, worked together into some sort of chronological order, fourthly, edited by the prophetic school into a comprehensive historico-theological work, fifthly, a Deuteronomic redaction, and lastly, various late insertions (1 Sam. ii. 1–10; 2 Sam. xxii; xxiii. 1–7) and amplifications in 1 Sam. xvii and xviii.

A. Bentzen[1] finds himself driven to a modified strata hypothesis. He agrees generally with the literary analysis school, except that he makes reservations in identifying the earlier strands with J and E. There are two strings of stories in 1 Sam. i–2 Sam. viii, one in part from Gilgal and the other in part from Mizpah. These lead up to the Court History of David (2 Sam. ix–xx; 1 Kings i–ii), written soon after the events and perhaps Israel's best-told story. Into all this various items of older material have been inserted: David's laments (2 Sam. i and iii), the different lists (1 Sam. xiv, 49–51: Eissfeldt allocated these to L), probably the 'humorous' stories of the Ark (again in Eissfeldt's L), stories of David's relations with Ishbaal in 2 Sam. ii–vi, viii, and perhaps details of the relations between Samuel and Saul.[2] The stories of the Ark and the History of the Succession, together with Ps. cxxxii, he supposes to have had a cultic background, connected with the measures David took to secure the kingdom.

KINGS

These two books were originally one book, divided first in LXX and later (A.D. 1517) in Hebrew printed Bibles. The work falls naturally into three sections: 1 Kings ii. 12–1 Kings xi, the story of the undivided monarchy (1 Kings i–ii belongs properly to 2 Sam. ix–xx); 1 Kings xii–2 Kings xvii, the story of the divided monarchy; 2 Kings xviii–xxv, the story of the Kingdom of Judah down to the exaltation of Jehoiachin in exile in 561 B.C. Almost all scholars assume a double D-redaction, the second certainly being *ca.* 550 B.C. after the change of fortune of King Jehoiachin. This redaction belongs to the general D-edition of the great history of the Israelites which runs from Genesis

---

[1] Op. cit. ii, 1949, p. 93.　　　　[2] Cf. Hylander, op. cit.

through to 2 Kings (i.e. before the P-editing). Assuming that there was an earlier D-Kings, the question arises, Did this author write before or after the death of King Josiah at Megiddo in 609–608 B.C.? Pfeiffer[1] is very sure that this author knew of Josiah's death, but ignored it. He bases his argument on the authenticity of 2 Kings xxii. 1 and xxiii. 28, maintaining also that xxii. 2 proves that the author knew the details of Josiah's death. This last contention is hard to follow. Further, Pfeiffer agrees that the D-author must have written his work before the glamour of Josiah's days had passed away, but it is difficult to see what glamour was left after Josiah's tragic death, which denied the very core of his admirer's thesis. It is much better to regard this author as completing his book at 2 Kings xxiii. 25 a ('Moses'), and to assume that passages like 2 Kings xxii. 1 b and xxiii. 28 are from the 550 B.C. editor, who is maintaining here, as elsewhere, his predecessor's framework. This is Bentzen's[2] opinion. Also, he has argued[3] that there is a double narrative, one which knows nothing of Megiddo, and the other which is prophesying after the event.[4]

Rowley[5] thinks it probable that there was an original Kings, but goes no farther than a somewhat doubtful 'before the fall of Jerusalem in 586 B.C.'. Eissfeldt[6] thinks that there was a pre-D Kings, of which the constituent elements were L and J and E, whilst I. Benzinger[7] and G. Hölscher[8] maintain that J and E are to be found, and R. Smend[9] sees his own J[1] and J[2]. Such analysis is doubtful. A more fruitful line of approach is to recognize the sources which the D-author himself mentions; namely, the Acts of Solomon (1 Kings xi. 41), the Book of the

---

[1] Op. cit., 1941, p. 378.

[2] *Introduction to the Old Testament*, ii, 1949, p. 100.

[3] *Die josianische Reform*, 1926, p. 23.

[4] Cf. Eissfeldt, *Einleitung in das Alte Testament*, 1934, p. 321.

[5] *The Growth of the Old Testament*, 1950, p. 73.

[6] Op. cit., p. 335.

[7] *Jahwist und Elohist in den Königsbüchern*, B.W.A.T. xxvii, 1921.

[8] 'Das Buch der Könige, seine Quellen und seine Redaktion', *Eucharisterion für H. Gunkel*, 1923 (F.R.L.A.N.T., xix. 1), i, pp. 158–213.

[9] 'JE in den geschichtlichen Büchern des Alten Testaments', *Z.A.W* xxxix, 1921, pp. 181–217.

Chronicles of the Kings of Israel (1 Kings xiv. 19 plus sixteen other references), the Book of the Chronicles of the Kings of Judah (1 Kings xiv. 29 plus other fourteen). The first of these was biographical and designed not so much as a genuine history as to set forth the wisdom, riches, and magnificence of Solomon.[1] It was compiled from temple records and the royal annals, but contained also such folk-tales as that of Solomon's judgement (1 Kings iii. 16–28). The other two main sources are the royal annals of the two kingdoms. The author's method of dealing with the history of the two kingdoms was to deal with the whole reign of one king, and then to go back and deal with the reigns of all the kings who had begun to reign in the other kingdom during that king's reign. His chief difficulty was in the dating. He gives the year of the regnant king in the other kingdom, and he gives the length of the new king's reign, but the two systems do not agree, the discrepancies being three years one way from Jeroboam to Jehu, and twenty-one years the other way from Jehu to the fall of Samaria. Much attention has been given to this problem, rendered the more difficult because the first precise date we have from cuneiform records is 854 B.C., the year of the battle of Qarqar when Ahab fought in the Syrian confederacy against Shalmaneser II. J. Begrich[2] has supposed that the author used as many as five different chronological systems, but there are evidently errors in the sources themselves.

Into this original Kings (*ca.* 610 B.C.) a group of Northern tales was interpolated, probably by the 550 B.C. editor. The group consists of three cycles of stories which are concerned with the three outstanding Northern figures, Elijah, Elisha, and Ahab. There are considerable differences of opinion as to the limits of these cycles and as to the relations between them, but probably the Elijah cycle consists of 1 Kings xvii–xix; 2 Kings i. 1–18 and 1 Kings xxi; 2 Kings ix. 1–x. 31; the Elisha cycle, 2

---

[1] Cf. Mowinckel, *Stadholderen Nehemia*, 1916, *Ezra den Skriftlærde*, 1916. The so-called Memoirs are actually memorials after the oriental pattern, written to preserve the memory of great ones.

[2] *Die Chronologie der Könige von Israel und Juda und die Quellen des Rahmens der Königsbücher*, 1929. See also Pfeiffer, op. cit., pp. 393–5; Bentzen, *Introduction to the Old Testament*, ii, 1949, pp. 98–9.

Kings ii; iv; v; vi. 1–7; viii. 1–15; xiii. 14–21; the Ahab cycle, 1 Kings xx; xii. 1–38; 2 Kings iii. 4–27; vi. 8–vii. 20. There is also a group of southern stories in 2 Kings xviii. 13–xx, 19. These consist of the story of Sennacherib's attack on Jerusalem (xviii. 13–xix. 37), the account of Hezekiah's illness (xx. 1–11), and the story of Merodach-Baladan's embassy (xx. 12–19). In these Hezekiah traditions there are different strands, and these can be definitely isolated: 1) xviii. 13 (but not the date); xviii. 17–xix. 8; xix. 36–7; 2) xviii. 14–16; 3) xix. 9 b–35. The second is the most historical; the third the least historical. Apart from the addition of these stories, either by the 550 B.C. editor or by another, there have been numerous annotations and glosses, some under the influence of P and some as late as the second century B.C.[1]

The modern non-literary school finds less scope in Kings than in the earlier books, since it is plain that the three main sources were actually official chronicles. M. Noth[2] advocates one Deuteronomic author (*ca.* 550 B.C.), who wrote the history which reaches from Deut. i to 2 Kings xxv. His sources were partly the official annals, and partly various stories and legends collected in North and South. The way in which legends can be incorporated is shown not only in the story of Solomon's judgement (1 Kings iii. 16–28), but particularly in 1 Kings x, where in the Queen of Sheba we have an adaptation of the legend of the daughter of the jinni, whose legendary splendour is outshone by the magnificence of Solomon.[3] To Stewart Perowne[4] the story is the account of the first impact of Sabaean commerce on the Mediterranean world.

ESTHER

The roll of Esther is an historical novel used to account for the Jewish Festival of Purim. It has had, through the centuries, an extraordinary popularity amongst the Jews, especially during

[1] Pfeiffer, op. cit., p. 412.
[2] *Überlieferungsgeschichtliche Studien*, i, 1943.
[3] A. Chastel, 'La Légende de la Reine de Saba', *R.H.R.* cxix, 1939, pp. 204–25; cxx, 1939, pp. 27–44, 160–74.
[4] *P.E.F.Q.S.*, 1939, pp. 199–202.

times of bitter persecution. The story itself is without historical foundation, but the local colour is correct enough.[1] The historicity of the book has been defended by M. Wolff[2] and by J. Hoschander[3] who identifies the king with Artaxerxes II. To Pfeiffer[4] the whole book is fiction, and the author invented not only all the characters, but even the festival of Purim itself. Pfeiffer dates the book in the time of John Hyrcanus, making it reflect the fierce and jubilant patriotism of those times. A. E. Morris[5] sees in the book a reflection of the earlier years of Antiochus Epiphanes, and regards the author as advocating a policy of co-operation with the conqueror, in the hope of securing benefits for the Jews such as open resistance would destroy for ever. The book would thus date from the years before Antiochus IV deliberately set about seeking to destroy the Jewish religion. Rowley[6] agrees roughly with this dating, suggesting a few decades after 180 B.C., and that it was written to express the intense nationalistic feeling of Maccabaean days.

Attempts have been made to find a mythological background. Jensen[7] sees an original in the victory of the Babylonian deities Marduk and Ishtar over the Elamite deities Humman and Mashti.[8] It may be, as Bentzen[9] notes, that the names are purely personal, but the similarity of all four names to the names of deities is curious, and it is difficult to believe that the choice is wholly accidental. It is, of course, possible that the names have been adopted without a cultic or mythological association or background. J. von Hammer[10] and, following him, J. Lewy[11] identified Purim with the Persian festival *Farvardigan*, but not enough is known about Jews in the Eastern provinces of the

---

[1] H. Gunkel, *T.L.Z.* xliv, 1919, p. 214.

[2] *N.T.T.* l, 1916, pp. 75–120.

[3] *The Book of Esther in the Light of History*, 1923.

[4] Op. cit., pp. 732–47.

[5] 'The Purpose of the Book of Esther', *E.T.* xlii, 1930, pp. 124–8.

[6] Op. cit., 1950, p. 155.

[7] 'Elamitische Eigennamen', *W.Z.K.M.* vi, 1892, pp. 47 ff.

[8] Cf. L. B. Paton, *Esther*, I.C.C., 1908, pp. 87–94. More recently, J. Lewy, *H.U.C.A.* xiv, 1939, pp. 127–51.

[9] Op. cit. ii, p. 192; cf. A. S. Kapelrud in *S.B.U.*

[10] *W.J.L.* xxxviii, 1872, p. 49.   [11] Ibid., pp. 127–51.

Persian Empire, and it is there probably that this story originally arose.[1]

CHRONICLES—EZRA—NEHEMIAH

There is general agreement that all three (four) books were originally one work. A. C. Welch[2] denied this, holding that the author of 1 Chron. x. 1–2 Chron. xxxvi. 21 had nothing to do with either 1 Chron. i–ix or with Ezra–Nehemiah. His date was as early as *ca.* 520 B.C., with a later P-recension. Welch further held that Neh. x is as early as 586 B.C. But the majority of scholars fix the date of the whole series of writings between 350 B.C. and 250 B.C. Pfeiffer[3] advocates a date *ca.* 250 B.C. on general grounds of matter, style, and polemics. Oesterley and Robinson[4] prefer 350–300 B.C. and possibly later; Rowley[5] *ca.* 300 B.C.; and H. Wheeler Robinson[6] 300–250 B.C.

On the other hand, Rothstein and Hänel[7] hold the groundwork of the book to be soon after 432 B.C. (date of Nehemiah's return and renewed activity), with a redactor *ca.* 400 B.C., plus isolated interpolations. W. F. Albright[8] claimed Ezra as the author of the whole work and gave its date as 398 B.C. He has now[9] reverted to an earlier date for Ezra (427 B.C.), so presumably this will bring his proposed date correspondingly earlier and so to a date not far removed from that of Rothstein–Hänel. A. Weiser[10] agrees that the date cannot be earlier than 433 B.C., but favours *ca.* 300 B.C., mostly because he accepts a late date for the Aramaic portions. Bentzen[11] does not care to be more precise than to say 'fourth century as the earliest date', and that

---

[1] Bentzen, op. cit. ii, p. 193.

[2] *Post-exilic Judaism*, 1935, pp. 185–6; *The Work of the Chronicler*, 1939. Cf. C. R. North, op. cit., 1946, p. 116, where he agrees that 1 Chron. i–ix are readily detachable and may be later than the main work.

[3] Op. cit., 1941, pp. 811–12.　　　　　　　[4] Op. cit., 1934, pp. 111–12.

[5] Op. cit., 1950, p. 165.

[6] *The Old Testament: Its Making and Meaning*, 1937, p. 71.

[7] *Das erste Buch der Chronik*, K.A.T., 1927; also, J. Hänel, 'Das Recht des Opferschlachtens in der chronistischen Literatur', *Z.A.W.*, N.F. xiv, 1937, pp. 46–67.

[8] 'The Date and Personality of the Chronicler', *J.B.L.* xl, 1921, pp. 104–24.

[9] *F.S.A.C.*[2], 1946, p. 366.

[10] *Einleitung in das Alte Testament*[2], 1949, p. 237.

[11] Op. cit. ii, pp. 215, 211.

'something speaks for the assumption that the Ezra-legend has been told by a contemporary of Ezra'.

Actually the critical point of the debate is the date of the Aramaic portions, Ezra iv. 7–vi. 18; vii. 12–16. Otherwise there is a great deal to be said for a date close following the success of the separation policy, which is 432 B.C. if Nehemiah's second attempt was decisive, or 397 B.C. if we accept this late date for Ezra's arrival. Apart from the matter of the Aramaic, there are two items usually mentioned as favouring a late date for the Chronicler. One is the genealogy of 1 Chron. iii. 19–24, which is alleged to give eleven generations from Zerubbabel. This makes the date *ca.* 300 B.C., even if we allow, with Kittel,[1] no more than twenty years to a generation. It is plain that the Versions interpreted the section in this way, but *v.* 21 (on which this mostly depends) is difficult and suspect, and it is more than likely that a later hand has been at work (Rothstein, Bentzen, &c.), originally only four generations being involved. In any case, the first nine chapters may well be later than the main body (cf. Welch, North). They are of miscellaneous origin; ix is a duplication of Neh. xi. 3–22 and 1 Chron. viii. 29–38, whilst the details of the Levitical duties in ix. 35–44 are comparable to those detailed in 1 Chron. xxvi. 20 ff. M. Noth[2] saw in ix. 29–38 a list prepared soon after the death of Solomon for the organization of the military levy in the territory of Judah. The second item, which is alleged to show a late date, is the lists of high-priests in Neh. xii. 10, 22. Both lists include Jaddua, who, according to Josephus,[3] was high-priest in the time of Alexander the Great, though then a very aged man. The lists are probably not as late as the mention of Jaddua suggests. The phrase 'and Jaddua' looks very much like an addition in Neh. xii. 22, whilst the whole clause 'and Jonathan begat Jaddua' could easily have been added in Neh. xii. 10.

There are wide differences of opinion in respect of the

---

[1] *Die Bücher der Chronik*, H.A.T., 1902, p. 26.

[2] 'Eine Siedlungsgeographische Liste in 1 Chron. 2 und 4,' *Z.D.P.V.*, 1932, pp. 97–124.

[3] *Ant. Iud.* XI, vii, 8.

Aramaic portions. W. Baumgartner[1] dates the Aramaic *ca.* 300 B.C., and so also Torrey, Hölscher, Bauer and Leander, Pfeiffer and Rowley. On the other hand, Albright suggests 400–350 B.C., whilst Cowley, Sachau and Batten all think the style approximates to that of the fifth-century Elephantine papyri. Bentzen thinks the Aramaic belongs to the time of Artaxerxes I (i.e. middle of the fifth century). The verdict to be gained from the evidence of the Aramaic is therefore uncertain,[2] and there is a great deal to be said for fixing the date of the Chronicler as soon after the success of the separation policy as possible. This involves the idea that, just as the original compiler of Kings wrote in the full flush of his enthusiasm at the success and prosperity of the good (Deuteronomic) King Josiah, so the Chronicler wrote in the full fervour of the success of the Nehemiah–Ezra separation policy. The abruptness of the conclusion is therefore due to the fact that there was nothing more to be said.

A certain amount of recent study has concerned the relation of the Chronicler's work to D and P. This is an important factor, not only in the dating of his work, but also in the estimation of his whole purpose and intention. J. A. Bewer[3] found two fundamental principles throughout: the prophetic-Deuteronomic principle of retribution, and the belief that P had been in force since the time of Moses. So strong is the D-element that M. Noth[4] holds that the Chronicler used only the Deuteronomic history, all the rest being due to mannerisms on his part. G. von Rad[5] emphasized the firmness with which the Chronicler held to this prophetic-Deuteronomic principle. It is shown by the way in which the kings are warned by prophets who predict good fortune or bad according to the measure of the king's piety or wickedness. The Chronicler shows his firm determination most of all in the cases of Josiah and Manasseh. The Kings redactor of *ca.* 550 B.C. had found Josiah's early death a great

---

[1] 'Das Aramäische im Buche Daniel', *Z.A.W.*, N.F. v, 1927, p. 123.

[2] Cf. Bentzen's discussion on the Aramaic of Daniel, op. cit. ii, p. 200.

[3] *The Literature of the Old Testament in its Historical Development*, 1922, pp. 293–301.

[4] *Überlieferungsgeschichtliche Studien*, i, 1943, p. 178.

[5] *Das Geschichtsbild des chronistischen Werkes*, B.W.A.N.T. iv, 3, 1930.

stumbling-block, since he above all other kings was the pattern of all that a Deuteronomic king should be, and ought therefore to have prospered and lived long. The redactor's explanation was that not even Josiah's piety could lift the dead weight of sin created by Manasseh's apostasy and general wickedness. The Chronicler has another explanation (2 Chron. xxxv. 22), namely that Josiah did not obey the Word of the Lord which was spoken through the heathen Necho of Egypt. Further, the Chronicler has his own difficulty in Manasseh's long reign. He ought to have died early and in misery, since he was the worst of all kings according to Deuteronomic ideas. The Chronicler says that Manasseh repented, and that this was why he lived long. Such a repentance is in the highest degree improbable, but, as Pfeiffer[1] says, the Chronicler was 'a writer of great originality, vivid imagination and granite conviction'. This determined adherence to Deuteronomic ideas explains why it is that the Chronicler makes Hezekiah the great reformer rather than Josiah. Hezekiah ultimately prospered, but Josiah came to an unfortunate end. Therefore, Hezekiah must have been a better Deuteronomist than Josiah, and so forth.

The relation of the Chronicler's writings to the JEDP scheme is confused. J. Pedersen[2] holds that it is not possible to say what the literary relation is. Bentzen[3] finds the work to be based on the Deuteronomic ideology, but says that the Chronicler knew the whole Pentateuch including the cultic theory of P. Against this, the reference to the whole Pentateuch concerns largely the first nine chapters which may well be a later addition, and further, the relation to the P-cultus is confused. Bentzen says, for instance, that the Levites play a part corresponding not to D but to P, but in the same paragraph (p. 215) he allows that the Levites and singers surpass P and have a more important place than they are allowed in P. He suggests further that the reforms are P rather than D (cf. Exod. xii and Num. xviii). Our judgement is that nowhere do we find straight P, but sometimes more and sometimes less. For instance, 2 Chron. xxix. 34 says that the priest

[1] Op. cit., 1941, p. 806.   [2] *Israel III–IV*, 1940, p. 722.
[3] Op. cit. ii, 1949, p. 215.

ought to have flayed all the burnt offerings, but that the Levites had to help because of the very great number. But in Lev. i. 5 (P), it is the worshipper who flays the offering. The same general mixture, partly D, partly P and partly neither, is shown in Neh. viii by L. E. Browne,[1] who places the details of Neh. viii, and D and P in parallel columns. The net result of the comparison is that Neh. viii is closer to D than to P, but that there are items where neither is followed.

There is another section of the Old Testament where a situation is described which never existed, namely Ezek. xl–xlviii, the sons of Zadok being there given an exclusive priority which they never did in fact possess in the post-exilic temple. These nine chapters are Zadokite propaganda, presumably against the Aaronite priesthood. This parallel gives additional point to Pfeiffer's[2] remark that the Chronicler is taking an active part in the struggle between the sons of Aaron and the Levites. The Chronicler gave the Levites a higher place than they ever actually had. Pfeiffer thinks of the guilds of singers and gate-keepers being organized between 400 and 250 B.C., and still struggling for recognition.[3] His reason for fixing the lower date (*ca.* 250 B.C.) is that he estimates that to be the date of the Chronicler's work (mostly on linguistic grounds), but if there was such a struggle, it is much more likely that it took place as early as 400 B.C., at the beginning of the period which he suggests. Levitical interests are certainly strong in the book. G. von Rad (in the *Procksch Festschrift*) finds in 1 Chron. xxviii. 2–10 and 2 Chron. xv. 27 examples of contemporary Levitical preaching. These same Levitical interests are recognized by Noth, Engnell, and Bentzen. E. Jacob emphasizes the virtual substitution of David for Moses and sees in it a polemic against the P-tradition.

It is evident that the relations between the Chronicler and D and P are still obscure. Rothstein-Hänel think in terms of a later editor who followed P, but Oesterley and Robinson consider the first writer to be guided as a rule, though not wholly, by P, and a later writer to have been under D-influence. Kittel (1902) finds

---

[1] *From Babylon to Bethlehem*, 1926, pp. 51–5.
[2] Op. cit., p. 795.   [3] Ibid., p. 801.

four writers, two of them Levite, one Midrashic and the last the Chronicler. Welch holds that the annotator (a generation after the exile) was thoroughly out of sympathy with Ezek. xl–xlviii, so that P is a compromise between Chronicles–Ezra–Nehemiah and Ezek. xl–xlviii.

The last few years have been notable for a revival of discussion concerning the date of Ezra's arrival in Jerusalem. Both in Europe[1] and in Britain[2] there has been a renewed advocacy for the traditional date (457 B.C.) which makes Ezra's arrival take place in the seventh year of Artaxerxes I, and thus many years before Nehemiah arrived. This new departure has been thoroughly discussed by H. H. Rowley,[3] who holds to the 397 B.C. date. The attitude of J. Pedersen[4] is that the arguments usually brought forward are indecisive either way, but that the date 397 B.C. provides the more likely and reasonable solution. This is the date publicized by A. van Hoonacker[5] in 1890. It fixes Ezra's arrival in the seventh year of Artaxerxes II. Thus Nehemiah and Ezra never met, and it was Ezra who was the founder of Judaism. The traditional view, whereby Ezra's activity commenced before Nehemiah's arrival, makes Nehemiah and not Ezra the actual founder of Judaism.

There has always been agreement concerning the authenticity of Nehemiah's Memoirs (Neh. i. 1–4; i. 11 b–ii. 6; basis of ii. 7 b–9 a; ii. 9 b–20; iii. 33–vii. 5 a; basis of x. 30–40; xi. 1–2; xii. 27–43; xiii. 6–31), though not always as to their precise extent. Mowinckel[6] has maintained, with a very great

[1] B. Balscheit, *Der Gottesbund, Einführung in das Alte Testament*, 1943; H. Höpfl, *Introductio specialis in Vetus Testamentum⁵*, 1946; E. Johannesen, *Studier over Esras og Nehemjas Historie*, 1946; B. D. Eerdmans, *The Religion of Israel*, 1947, pp. 210–16; A. Weiser, *Einleitung in das Alte Testament*, 1949, p. 237; M. Rehm, *Esra und Nehemias*, Echter Bibel, 1950.

[2] W. M. F. Scott, Nehemiah–Ezra?, *E.T.* lviii, 1947, pp. 263–7; C. T. Wood, Nehemiah–Ezra, *E.T.* lix, 1947, p. 53; J. S. Wright, *The Date of Ezra's Coming to Jerusalem*, 1947.

[3] 'The Chronological Order of Ezra and Nehemiah', *Ignace Goldziher Memorial Volume*, 1948, pp. 117–49.   [4] *Israel III–IV*, 1940, p. 607.

[5] *Néhémie et Esdras, une nouvelle hypothèse sur la chronologie de l'époque de la restauration*, reprint from *Le Muséon*, ix, 1890, pp. 151–84, 317–51, 389–401; modified by L. W. Batten, *The Books of Ezra and Nehemiah*, I.C.C., 1913.

[6] *Stadtholderen Nehemia*, 1916; *Ezra den Skriftlærde*, 1916.

deal of probability, that the so-called Memoirs, both of Nehemiah and of Ezra, are actually memorials after the oriental pattern, written to preserve the memory of the great ones, whilst emphasizing the wickedness of their foes. It has been generally agreed that Nehemiah's Memoirs, at any rate, formed an integral part of the original work, but this has been lately challenged by S. Granild,[1] with whom A. Bentzen[2] agrees, who holds that the Chronicler did not use any Nehemiah material, but that this was inserted later by a post-Chronist editor, who inserted all the Aramaic, and wished to give Nehemiah, rather than Ezra, the credit for the foundation of post-exilic Jewry.

There has been wide variation of opinion concerning the historical and factual value of Ezra's Memoirs. Many have rejected them altogether as being to any degree reliable, maintaining that Ezra himself is the invention of the Chronicler.[3] Pfeiffer barely allows Ezra as an historical person. F. Ahlemann[4] maintains that the Ezra Memoirs were written by a surviving contemporary of Ezra (458 B.C.), still alive in the years 430–420 B.C. Except for Ezra vii. 1–26 and viii. 1–14 they are a unified whole, unshortened, and a valuable source of information. They were written with great skill, partly to exalt Ezra over Nehemiah and partly to inform the people generally. The probability is that Ezra was indeed a real person, who came to Jerusalem and did substantially what the Chronicler says he did. He abolished the mixed marriages and enforced the Law. It is unlikely that he had the extraordinary powers of Ezra vii. 22–7, but that he depended upon the effectual action of such vigorous men as Shecaniah.

The discussion concerning the date of Ezra's arrival depends in the first instance upon the possibility of him and Nehemiah having been in Jerusalem at the same time. Those who find it difficult to suppose that they were active at the same time (they

---

[1] *Ezrabogens literære Genesis, undersogt med Henblik paa et efterkronistik Indgreb,* 1949.

[2] Op. cit. ii, p. 210.

[3] M. Vernes (1889), C. C. Torrey (*Ezra Studies,* 1910), H. P. Smith (1903), G. Hölscher (1923, but not in 1900), A. Loisy (1933), and apparently W. A. L. Elmslie (*How Came Our Faith,* 1949).

[4] Zur Esra-Quelle, *Z.A.W.,* N.F. xviii, 1942–3, pp. 77–98.

persistently ignore each other; the three contexts where they are both mentioned, Neh. viii. 9; xii. 26; xii. 36, are all suspect) must find a suitable alternative date. W. H. Kosters (1895) proposed 'thirty-second' for 'seventh' in Ezra vii. 7, but an easier emendation is 'thirty-seventh' (Bewer, Albright in 1946), i.e. 427 B.C. Many scholars have held that Ezra came to Jerusalem between 432 and (say) 426 B.C., i.e. between Nehemiah's two visits, for there is no need to assume that Nehemiah returned as early as 432 B.C.: so A. Bertholet (1902), R. H. Kennett (1909), W. F. Albright (1932) and most recently W. Rudolph.[1] This involves the suggestion (cf. Rudolph) that Ezra raised such a hornet's nest that Nehemiah had to come back to straighten things out again; at any rate something must be assumed to account for a failure on the part of Ezra. There is a great deal to be said for some such solution as this, but, as Rowley[2] points out, Nehemiah's contemporary as high-priest was Eliashib, and probably Jehoiada his son during the second visit, whereas Ezra's contemporary was Eliashib's grandson, Jehohanan. It is true that Jehohanan is nowhere actually called high-priest, and attempts have been made to rebut the assumption that he (Jehohanan, Johanan, Jonathan) was active in Ezra's time, or that he was the grandson of Eliashib. The most likely solution, in our judgement, is that Ezra arrived in 397 B.C., and that he was successful where Nehemiah had twice failed. This involves a dislocation of material, such as is in part evident in LXX.

There remains only to mention the recent study of the Septuagint text of Chronicles by G. Gerleman,[3] who rejects quite definitely the theory that the translation included in LXX is that of Theodotion.   NORMAN H. SNAITH

---

[1] *Esra und Nehemia*, H.A.T., 1949.
[2] Loc. cit., pp. 133 f.
[3] *Studies in the Septuagint II, Chronicles*, L.U.Å., N.F. Avd. 1, Bd. xliii. Nr. 3, 1946.

V

THE PROPHETIC LITERATURE

THE investigation of Israelite prophetism belongs to those sections of the wide field of Old Testament study that, during the last two or three decades, have taken on a greatly altered aspect, though it is certainly true that many observations by earlier generations of scholars still retain their value. Books like W. Robertson Smith, *The Prophets of Israel* (1882), ²1895; C. H. Cornill, *Der Israelitische Prophetismus* (1894), ¹³1920; G. Hölscher, *Die Profeten*, 1914; B. Duhm, *Israels Propheten* (1916), ²1922; H. Gunkel, *Die Propheten*, 1917; J. Skinner, *Prophecy and Religion* (1922), ²1926, have still much to contribute to anyone concerned with a real understanding of Israelite prophetism. The same may be said about the commentaries on the prophetic books that appeared towards the end of the nineteenth and the beginning of the twentieth centuries, such as the Isaiah commentaries of B. Duhm (1892), ⁴1922, and G. B. Gray, 1912. To neglect the insight into the nature of Israelite prophetism gained by the preceding generation would inevitably wreck our whole understanding of that phenomenon. In this field, no less than in that of Pentateuchal criticism, we must be careful to safeguard continuity of research with the work of earlier scholars. This continuity is especially necessary in the study of the prophets, just because such a diversity of new forms of treatment has appeared. For experience teaches us that the significance of each new form of treatment tends to be over-rated, and is liable to be regarded not as a means to a better understanding of the subject, but as superior to it and even an end in itself; with the result that such truth as it has becomes lost.

Moreover, as we shall see, the new approach to the study of the prophets is limited to certain specified traits in them and in the books which bear their names. Other traits are not at all, or only lightly, touched upon, and so the attitude to them is still essentially that of the last generation. One of our objects therefore must still be to illumine the historical background of the prophets and their individual sayings. Similarly, we still recognize the necessity to determine by the methods of style- and form-critical investigation the limits of the original, independent, literary units, which are only unsatisfactorily and often even wrongly indicated by the traditional *Parashah-* and chapter-division of the prophetic books. In this connexion, the distinction between 'prose' and 'poetical' passages still plays a part, leading on to a closer metrical examination of the latter.

Literary criticism differentiated between 'authentic' passages, attributable to the prophet whose name the book bore, and 'unauthentic', whose origin lay elsewhere. Textual criticism, on the other hand, occupied itself with discovering and correcting the errors of text which had crept into the prophetical books during their transmission. Neither of these has entirely lost its significance for us. But, as we shall show below, even when from the new way of looking at the prophetic books we get quite a different view of their composition and transmission from that of an earlier generation, the new approach will not entirely displace the attempt to find out what really belongs to the individual prophets, and so what is the content of their message; nor will it give up those textual emendations of earlier scholars which bear the imprint of obvious correctness.

Finally, we must mention also the numerous contributions that have appeared during the last two or three decades, aimed at throwing light on the inner life of the prophets, their consciousness of their own call, and of their vocation, and also on the marvellous acts attributed to them. These studies, too, link up with older investigations of the same kind, and are similarly concerned to demonstrate what belongs to the sphere of psychology, what is to be assigned to the realm of religion and morals, and what is to be taken as revelation in the theological sense.

If the books and articles on Israelite prophetism published during the last two decades in many cases give the impression that they are ploughing an entirely new furrow, and that little or nothing of earlier conceptions remains, the impression is largely due to the fact that the new ideas are unusually illuminating with regard to many aspects of our subject with which they do not directly deal. Actually there are only two or three forms of treatment which can really rank as new or even relatively new, at least in the sense that they display a methodical exposition of independent observations occasionally already made earlier. First and foremost we must set the close linking up of the prophets, including the so-called writing, reform, or opposition prophets (like Amos and Hosea, Isaiah and Jeremiah), with the cultus, and their membership in organized cultic associations charged with particular functions. This connexion puts the pronouncements of these prophets in a new light, in that it makes it antecedently probable that cultic customs and conceptions were normative for them also.

Then, secondly, but not without connexion with the above-mentioned enrolment of the prophets in associations of cultic functionaries, the conception of the way in which the prophetic books came into being, and their transmission from generation to generation, has altered considerably. No countenance at all will now be given to the theory that the prophets after whom the books are named themselves put down in writing their individual oracles or smaller collections of them. It is regarded as much more likely that the words of the great prophets were treasured in the memories of their disciples, i.e. the members of the associations of cultic prophets to which the Master had belonged, and transmitted to later times within the cult-prophetic organization by word of mouth alone. In this process, the words of the master prophet became adapted to the contemporary scene—'actualized' —and, at the same time, they were expanded and enlarged by sayings of a different origin which, however, appear suitable to the context. In general, writing down took place only when the prophetic books had attained their final form in the oral tradition —the form in which we have them—so that even the books called after the older prophets were first put into writing in post-exilic and even late post-exilic times. In fact, this writing down gives us simply the mechanical preservation of an already completed structure.

Thirdly, there is the question whether the prophets were 'ecstatics' or not, and if so, in what sense. We use the word 'ecstatic' here as it is almost unavoidable in spite of its ambiguity. Here the newer approach, as we have observed, has borrowed much from the statement of the case by the previous generation; but in its investigations into the details of the inner life of the prophets and the remarkable character of many of their actions, it has introduced a welcome clarification by determining and making known the limits of psychological investigation, so that the religious and theological evaluation of the prophets is seen to be wholly independent of individual judgements on the psychology of their behaviour. We shall discuss below what the present generation of scholars has to say on the matter.

Although these three questions concern all the prophets, and the new answers given make all the prophets and all their books appear in a more or less new light, yet each prophetic figure and each prophetic book still has its own problems; and it was only to be expected that these would be investigated anew and solved in a fresh manner. This has in fact happened. During the period under consideration, there have appeared books and treatises, and especially commentaries, on each prophetic book, which have enhanced our understanding in one respect or another, and have given new and better answers to old questions. A bare catalogue of the relevant publications would alone far exceed the space at our disposal. Since the opinions expressed on the problems occurring in some of the prophetic books have been particularly stimulating, the solutions proposed for those problems have a title to receive careful consideration. First, we may mention 'Deutero-Isaiah', i.e. Isa. xl–lv, and, more especially, the 'Ebed Yahweh songs; of these again, more particularly the fourth and last, Isa. lii. 13–liii. 12. Next come Jeremiah and Ezekiel. Joel, Nahum, and Habakkuk have also been re-examined recently, and in the works devoted to them, the conception of the prophets as cultic functionaries has resulted in new interpretations of great interest and importance.

Accordingly, out of the almost boundless scholarly literature about the prophetic books that has appeared during the last two or three decades, the works on Isa. xl–lv, on Jeremiah and Ezekiel, and on Joel, Nahum and Habakkuk deserve to be regarded as the most significant. If we single these works out, it is not because they are regarded as distinguished above all others in worth, but only because they exhibit a conception of Israelite prophetism in general, or of one of its exponents, in particular, which is especially characteristic for our period. Whether that particular conception is right, or at least contains an element of truth, the future alone can really decide. This principle should be understood to apply generally to the selection from the literature of the last thirty years which is to be found in our necessarily compressed review. The fact that a book is not mentioned does not mean that it is disregarded, or valued less highly than those that are mentioned. As with T. H. Robinson, *Prophecy and the Prophets in Ancient Israel* (1923), [2]1944, and J. Lindblom, *Profetismen i Israel*, 1934, it is often the case that works not specifically referred to here have a very real importance, since they may well guide the present-day study of the prophets from many a by-road or wrong track back on to the right path.

I. CULTIC PROPHETS

It is obvious, and is universally admitted, that in Israel, as among the Canaanites (1 Kings xviii. 19–40; 2 Kings x. 19), organized associations of prophets ($n^e\underline{b}\hat{i}\hat{i}m$) existed in close relationship with the cultus, and were to be found most particularly at the sanctuaries. G. Hölscher, *Die Profeten*, 1914, p. 143, discusses 1 Sam. x. 5 ff., where a group of prophets, roused to a high pitch of excitement by means of music, is recorded as coming down directly from a high-place, he adds this remark, 'The enthusiasts spent their time at these old sanctuaries, indeed they belonged in a certain sense to the cultic staff of the sanctuary ... alongside the priests... as in Baal worship.' But this connexion with the cultus was normally assumed only in the case of the popular prophets. Any official organizational connexion between the reform or writing prophets and the cultus was for the most part denied. How could they else, so the argument ran, have asserted God's distaste for sacrifice and cult practice with such incisiveness as was actually done by an Amos (iv. 2–5; v. 25–7) or an Isaiah (i. 10–17)? The revolution in the conception of the facts which led to the opinion that the reform prophets also, at least by and large, belonged to the cultic staff, and are to be regarded as members of cultic prophet associations, is due to S. Mowinckel, *Psalmenstudien III: Die Kultprophetie und prophetische Psalmen*, 1923. As the main title of the book (*Studies in the Psalms*) showed, the investigation undertaken in it actually concerned not the prophets, but the psalms. It was therefore only a by-product if new consequences for the prophets emerged in the process. But in spite of this, new consequences for the prophets did emerge, and have had reactions at least as strong as those provoked by the conclusions on the real subject of the book, namely, the psalms.

Two observations resulting from Mowinckel's investigation, although directed primarily on to the psalms, are relevant to the prophets also. Firstly, many psalms, such as lx, lxxv, lxxxii, cx, exhibit sections in which Yahweh speaks in the first person, and look exactly like prophetic utterances. This phenomenon, according to Mowinckel, is to be understood only if we regard such passages as 'words which give a divine reply to a request made in a particular cultic situation by a cult ministrant who is regarded by himself and by his contemporaries as prophetically gifted, even though perhaps permanently employed in such work' (p. 3). Mowinckel then comes to the conclusion 'that the Nebiim were originally representatives of the congregation, seized by the ecstasy of the orgiastic tumult of the cult festival; they were filled by divine power to raving point as, ideally and theoretically, should happen to the whole congregation . . . they stand forth out of the congregation by the side of the priest-seers as the actual *religiosi* of the congregation' (pp. 16 f.). Clear traces of connexion may then be observed between the older cultic prophets and the later temple singers counted amongst the Levites (1 Chron. xv. 22, 27; 2 Chron. xx). The organizations of cultic prophets, so it may be explained, have gradually become guilds of temple choristers. The connexion of the prophets with the cultus makes it understandable that, as in many psalms, so too in their pronouncements, the complexes of ideas associated with the two most important cultic rites, those of the New Year festival and those of the royal ceremonial, mutually penetrative as they are, play a great role. Admittedly Mowinckel, in pursuing the indications of connexion between prophetism and the cultus, pays less attention to 'the persons and ideas in Old Testament religion—met with, amongst other places, in the so-called 'writing prophets'—that prefer to emphasize the ethical and anti-cultic, and indeed, in part, personal side of religion'; he concentrates much more on those that, 'in the commissions of the company, as well as of the congregation's deity', impart 'on demand, the necessary information about religious matters direct from their divine source, in virtue of a supranormal endowment of power'. On this point, Mowinckel remarks that such prophets are to be found in the Babylonian-Assyrian religion, as in the Greek and Syro-Anatolian cults, and indeed universally in primitive religions (p. 5). But we do find him drawing a line of demarcation between the popular $n^e b\hat{\imath}\,\hat{\imath}m$ and the great prophets. This boundary line is emphasized by the affirmation that it was the prophetic institution, which elsewhere 'in many places contributed nothing to the further development of religion on to a higher plane', that in Israel 'became the vehicle of one of the most significant elements in religious and moral development' (p. 6). Yet this distinction is almost immediately blurred by the fact that not only Joel, but also Habakkuk—who is characterized as a 'nationalistic prophet of weal, taking his place on the side of the Deuteronomic school'—is claimed as a cultic prophet (pp. 27–9). It is therefore understandable if in subsequent years the inclination to regard others of the writing prophets, or even the whole of them, as members of cultic prophet organizations has grown ever stronger.

At all events, the first chapter of Mowinckel's *Psalmenstudien III*, entitled *Einleitendes und Grundsätzliches*, whose most important trends, so far as relevant to our purpose, have been described above, shows us the seed from which, in the two or three decades since, a large number of similarly oriented investigations has grown. To enumerate them all, even omitting any comment, is quite impossible. We must be content with mentioning in the first place the collective works edited by S. H. Hooke entitled, *Myth and Ritual: Essays on the Myth and Ritual of the Hebrews in relation to the Cultic Pattern of the Ancient East,* 1933, and, *The Labyrinth: Further Studies in the Relation between Myth and Ritual in the Ancient World,* 1935. These books derive all mythical conceptions from cultic rites and emphasize the close connexion of Israelite myths and rituals in general—but particularly the ideas and customs concerning the enthronement festival and sacral kingship—with those of Israel's neighbours. They exhibit the tendency to relegate both the prophet and his word entirely to the cultic sphere, and in a form as extreme as their endeavour to explain Israel's prophets and their sayings as far as possible by analogy with similar phenomena in neighbouring cultures. The effect of this has been, that in these books the external analogies have been given precedence over the illustrative material to be found within the Old Testament itself, so that the latter has not been fully worked out. For the rest, the present position may be sufficiently indicated by reference to the works of three scholars—Aubrey R. Johnson, Alfred Haldar, and Ivan Engnell. Relevant in this connexion are: Johnson, *The Cultic Prophet in Ancient Israel,* 1944, Haldar, *Associations of Cult Prophets among the Ancient Semites,* 1945, and Engnell's article in the Lindblom Festschrift, 'Profetia och Tradition' (*S.E.Å.* xii, 1947, pp. 110 ff.) and his study, *The Call of Isaiah: An Exegetical and Comparative Study,* 1949. Engnell has also written articles in the *Svenskt Bibliskt Uppslagsverk,* i, 1948, and numerous other essays, including 'The 'Ebed Yahweh Songs and the Suffering Messiah in "Deutero-Isaiah"' (*B.J.R.L.* xxxi, 1948), which will be mentioned later in connexion with Deutero-Isaiah.

Johnson has set himself the task of proving that at all Yahweh sanctuaries, but in particular at the temple in Jerusalem, the prophets stood side by side with the priests, and played at least as important a role, having indeed a double function, first, to be the mouthpiece of Yahweh, and as such to deliver oracles, and second, to represent the people before God, and in that capacity to bring their concerns, and those of their own associates, in prayer before God (pp. 6, 63). This same conclusion may be drawn from a study of the writing prophets. The latter's sharp protest against the popular prophets of their time does not condemn their cultic functions as such, but the misuse of them— as is quite clear from such passages as Mic. iii. 11, or Jer. xxiii. 17. Consequently, prophetic guilds are to be thought of as a permanent element of the Jerusalem temple staff. Jer. xxxv. 4 refers explicitly to a temple chamber belonging to one of the 'sons', i.e. disciples or associates, of the 'man of God', namely, the prophet Hanani ben Igdaliah. Following up the line indicated by Mowinckel, Johnson then sets out how the associations of cultic prophets at the Jerusalem temple finally turn into the guilds of singers attested by the Priestly Code and Chronicles. As a reason for this development, Johnson adduces the fact that the cultic prophets lost more and more of their authority after the catastrophic fall of Jerusalem because, according to statements in Jer. v. 30 f., xxvii. 16, xxviii. 1 ff., Ezek. xiii. 10, 16, Lam. ii. 14, they had lulled the people into a false sense of security. Probably the study on *The Cultic Prophet and the Psalter*, announced by Johnson at the beginning of his 1944 work, will develop these ideas still further.

Johnson does not discuss the question how far, if at all, the writing prophets are to be thought of as members of the cultic prophets' associations. Nor does he do more than touch on the possibility that there existed amongst Israel's neighbours, and indeed throughout the ancient Near East, phenomena similar to those of the Israelite cultic prophets, and demanding comparison with them. Nor, finally, does he pursue the question of some sort of influence on the Jerusalem cultic prophets arising from the field of rites and myths associated with the enthronement festival and divine king ideology.

In Haldar's book, on the other hand, not only do these questions take up a good deal of space, but they are given very definite and decided answers. The question whether the writing prophets belonged to the cultic associations is answered with an emphatic affirmative, and it is plainly laid down that no more difference is to be made between the writing prophets and their predecessors in this respect than in any other. Indeed, in the case of Amos, the fact that he is called *nōḳēd* and *bōḳēr*—'shepherd' and 'neatherd'—(Amos i. 1; vii. 14), is taken as proof that he belonged to the cultic ranks, since these epithets are really designations of cultic functionaries. With similar confidence Haldar champions the thesis that the prophets of the Old Testament, including the writing prophets, portray in part a phenomenon current throughout the contemporary Near East; and so, wherever the data of the Old Testament concerning any particular point are ambiguous or insufficient, they must be interpreted by analogy with more fully preserved details from perhaps Sumerian or Babylonian and Assyrian sources.

In Sumerian and Accadian texts the king is described as the head of the *bārū-* and *maḫḫū-*guilds, which are taken to be organizations of cultic prophets. From this, Haldar deduces that such was the case, not only in Ugarit, but in Israel too. The evidence for Ugarit is as follows: in the colophon of I.AB occurs the phrase *rb khnm rb nḳdm* 'chief of the priests, chief of the shepherds', which is applied to the king (p. 79). For Israel, consideration of David's power of command over Nathan, in the first place, and, secondly, the injunction of Ahab, king of Israel, and Jehoshaphat, king of Judah, to 400 prophets to impart an oracle concerning the issue of the campaign planned against the Aramaeans, leads Haldar to the conclusion that here both kings are envisaged as leaders of associations of cultic prophets (pp. 138–40). Again Isa. xxi. 1–10 is taken as proving that the king as chief has given the leader of the group of cultic prophets in question his commission to arrange for a 'spy' from their midst, who shall divine and expound an oracle from the movements of human and animal pairs seen in a vision (pp. 104–7, 143). Haldar's efforts to fit the utterances of the prophets into definite cultic situations, and to find in them references particularly to the ritual of the New Year festival or the sacral king ideology, take up much of the book, and are even allowed space where their inconclusiveness is quite patent, as in the explanation of the menace of the Foe from the North (Jer. vi. 22 ff.; l. 41 ff.) as a historicization of one element in the ritual of the Babylonian

New Year festival, namely, the sham fight in which the Foe from the North plays a role (pp. 157 ff.).

For this last point, as for much else, Haldar appeals to Engnell's book *Studies in Divine Kingship in the Ancient Near East*, 1943. Here, as may be gathered from the title, the ideas and customs of the ancient Near East, that clustered around the Divine King conception, are investigated. Furthermore, the passages in the Old Testament which have, or appear to have, a bearing on it, are discussed; and signs which suggest that associations of cultic prophets existed in Israel are picked out. In his later contributions mentioned above (p. 122), Engnell pursues the matter further; he emphasizes the correspondence between the prophets of Israel, including the writing prophets, and the associations of cultic prophets to be found in the Israelite *milieu*. He goes to great pains to trace out in detail this correspondence, with individual examples, as in Isaiah's call vision, where the cultic circle in which the prophet moved is seen throughout against a background formed by the intermingled rites and myths of enthronement festival and sacral kingship. In his *Call of Isaiah*, 1949, the way in which Isaiah's call vision, described in Isa. vi, was conditioned by the coincidence of the New Year festival with the Enthronement Day, is vigorously emphasized, as well as its peculiar 'royal' character, in relation to which many points receive their explanation—though, in fact, simpler explanations may lie a good deal nearer to hand. A connexion is suggested between the seraphim mentioned in Isa. vi. 2–4 and the Beings corresponding to them in the Babylonian language, and found in connexion with the Akitu festival (pp. 33 f.). The cleansing of Isaiah's guilt is then taken as an echo of a ceremony from the ritual of the sacral king, which took place at the New Year festival, namely, the portrayal of the king as bearer and expiator of the people's sins (p. 40). Similarly, to quote just one further example, the mention of *maṣṣēbet*, oak, and terebinth in Isa. vi. 13 is taken to allude to cultic events or ideological conceptions from the realm of sacral kingship, which were immediately recognizable as such to Isaiah's contemporaries (pp. 49 f.). In what way Engnell would have us understand these demonstrations of this or that religio-historical parallel is shown on pp. 43 f. of his *Call of Isaiah* in these words, 'The similarities only confirm what is the inescapable result of recent research of the 'myth and ritual' or 'pattern' type: the occurrence of a basic cultic mode of thought—though *of course* with special characteristic features in the different formations—common to the ancient Near Eastern unity culture, a cultically rooted world of thoughts with a fund of tradition-bound words, expressions, and phrases, from which the Israelite prophets also draw. I am quite convinced, however, that when Isaiah speaks in "the categories of his own time", his words mirror at the same time living cultic conditions, the core of which is, in its turn, the sacral kingship. But I do not mean that Isaiah is merely reflecting in an unoriginal way these "common conceptual forms" ... On the contrary, his personally experienced and original religious practice finds contemporaneously clear expressions'.

II. THE ORIGIN AND TRANSMISSION
OF THE PROPHETIC BOOKS

For the first half of our period, from about 1920 to 1935, the particularly characteristic, if not standard, treatment of the origin and transmission of our prophetic books is that in the volume on the prophets by T. H. Robinson mentioned above (p. 119), also his commentary on the first six of the Minor Prophets (H.A.T. i, 14, 1938), and, in addition, many of the articles indexed in the bibliography of his works on pp. 201–6 of the T. H. Robinson Festschrift *Studies in Old Testament Prophecy*, 1950. Of these latter we may single out 'Die prophetischen Bücher im Lichte neuer Entdeckungen' (*Z.A.W.* xlv, 1927, pp. 3–9), and 'Neuere Prophetenforschung' (*T.R.*, N.F. iii, 1931, pp. 75–103). According to Robinson, the prophetic books, or at least the majority of them, have undergone a continuous development in three easily recognizable stages. First came the oral pronouncement by the prophet himself, mostly in short sayings dealing with particular contemporary events. These sayings were then orally handed on by the hearers and later, often after the death of the prophet, united into small collections and written down. Individual sections of our books, particularly amongst those containing accounts in the first person, may indeed have been written down or dictated by the prophet himself. Other pieces again, namely, those in which the prophet's life and fortunes are related in the third person, were at first passed from mouth to mouth among his followers, and later, having been gathered into small collections, written out. At this point many sayings crept in that did not in reality come from the prophet himself, but were beloved of the collector, and appeared to be worthy of the master. Hence, at the second stage in the history of our prophetic books, one or more collections existed for each prophet, containing both 'authentic' and 'unauthentic' material side by side. Here and there the principles on which these smaller collections were arranged may still be recognized. There is a clear case of arrangement according to subject matter in the collections of woes against foreign nations, which can be quite assuredly separated out from the books of Isaiah, Jeremiah, and Ezekiel: there is a manifest desire to have like with like. In other cases, the guiding principle of arrangement has been that of some purely formal similarity, such as associating sayings that begin with the same word—the catchword principle. In dealing with collections concerned with the fate of Israel, editors were very prone to end the main body of prophetic utterances, which consisted mostly of woes, with a word of cheer. In the case of prophecies against foreign nations, on the other hand, the colours were made still more sombre wherever possible. The editors felt no qualms on the question of whether the words of cheer which were put in to soften the harsh threats against Israel, or the extra punch added to the woes against foreign nations, really came from the prophet to whom they were now ascribed. Rather, such editors quite *bona fide* held the view that the master they so highly revered must obviously have understood his own message in the way in which the desires and requirements of their own later day demanded. The third stage is that in which the smaller or medium-sized collections ascribed to the individual prophets were worked up into the books as we have them, by redactors. At this stage also all manner of 'un-authentic' matter has crept in.

Here, for the most part, we are dealing with written transmission in the case of the smallest units, the intermediate collections, and the complete books, i.e. a type of transmission which we normally associate with works of literature. This does not mean that oral tradition is shut out. On the contrary it is indubitably to be reckoned with in the early stages, and it played its part in the later formation of the prophetic books as we have them. Particularly, we may say, the 'unauthentic' passages were found and taken up by the collectors and redactors from the contemporary oral tradition. But, by and large, it is true that this study of the origins of our prophetic books envisaged mainly literary ante-cedents, which were consequently to be explained by literary-critical means. Further, since these books contain material which for the most part goes back to the prophet whose name the book bears, its disentanglement becomes the supremely important task, attended up to a certain point with assured results.

The impulse towards a far-reaching change started with H. S. Nyberg's book *Studien zum Hoseabuche: zugleich ein Beitrag zur Klärung des Problems der alttestamentlichen Textkritik*, 1935. For although, as the sub-title shows, it belongs primarily to the text-critical class, it contains some sentences which touch on questions of the origin and transmission of the books of the Old Testament in general, and with those of the prophets in particular. These remarks, strongly buttressed by the erudition of their author, have had a marked influence; they are as follows: 'The written O.T. is a creation of the Jewish community after the Exile; what preceded it was certainly only in small measure in fixed written form. . . . Only with the greatest reserve can we reckon . . . with writers among the prophets. . . . We must reckon with circles, sometimes centres, of tradition, that preserved and handed on the material. It is self-evident that such a process of transmission could not continue without some change in the material handed on, but we have to do, not with textual corruptions, but with an active transformation. . . . For the rest, O.T. scholarship would do well to consider earnestly what possibility it can ever have of regaining the *ipsissima verba* of Old Testament personalities. We have nothing but the tradition of their sayings, and it is . . . in the highest degree unlikely that any but oral forms of transmission ever existed for them' (pp. 8 f.). Later, H. Birkeland followed up these suggestions in his book *Zum hebräischen Traditionswesen: die Komposition der prophetischen Bücher des Alten Testaments*, 1938. He sought to clear up the question of the composition of the individual prophetic books in accordance with the guiding principles he there lays down: the fixed written form in which we now have the prophetic books came about at a quite late period, and is nothing other than the literally accurate representation of an already petrified oral tradition (p. 20). The individual prophet was surrounded by a circle, at first small, but then growing ever wider, that after his death continued his work; and it was among these that the earlier, living transmission of the prophetic utterances found its home. Here, through generations, the prophetic sayings and complexes were handed down and underwent a constant remoulding (p. 20). Just because this happened, any hard and fast distinction between what comes from the prophet himself, and what had its origin in the *traditio*, is no longer possible; so that, in most cases, we must give up the attempt 'to get back to the product of the great Genius himself' (p. 23). In consequence, we must banish from our study of the prophetic books such ideas as 'notes', 'larger literary pieces', 'the writer at his desk'—expressions which have been shaped according to literary patterns. We must rather substitute for these such expressions as are suitable to the oral process of transmission, which alone needs to be considered, i.e. such terms as 'tradition', 'complex', 'circle'. Further, we must duly recognize the fact that 'questions about the *ipsissima verba* of the prophets . . . can only be solved, if at all, not on literary-critical, but on traditio-historical grounds' (p. 22).

The point of view put forward by Nyberg and Birkeland bears more on matters to do with the books of the prophets than on the prophets themselves and the question of their membership in associations of cultic prophets. But in the works of Haldar and Engnell it becomes united with the view started by Mowinckel, that the prophets were members of cultic associations, and obtains strong support in the process; for now these circles of tradition, which Nyberg and Birkeland made responsible for the transmission of the prophetic sayings and complexes, but which, nevertheless, remained very shadowy figments, are given flesh and blood. It is these very organizations of cultic prophets that preserved the inheritance from the great prophetic figure that arose from their ranks, and, with adaptations to the exigencies of the times, handed it down within their own ranks from generation to generation. Because this is so, and because, with our prophetic books, it is a matter of collections of traditions which have arisen in various circles of cultic prophets, and have been handed down by the same agency, it is inadmissible—here Haldar emphasizes similar statements by Nyberg and Birkeland—to seek any clearcut prophetic personality in and behind our books of the prophets (p. 122). On the contrary, the books of Amos and Hosea contain several Canaanite cult-lyrical elements, adapted to the Yahweh religion, with the result that any clear indications concerning the person or the ministry of either prophet is scarcely possible (p. 122). Engnell has delivered himself of similar sentiments in his article 'Profetia och tradition' (*S.E.Å.* xii, 1947, pp. 94–123), and its continuation in his 'Additional Note' in *The Call of Isaiah*, 1949, pp. 54–60. Here he has been able to take into account two works, by Mowinckel and Widengren, which will be considered again later, namely, S. Mowinckel, *Prophecy and Tradition*, 1946, and G. Widengren, *Literary and Psychological Aspects of the Hebrew Prophets*, 1948. Engnell still maintains his previous thesis, that the greater part of the Old Testament literature was first written down during or after the Exile; he also defines this happening more closely by stating that it was merely the establishment in written form of a corpus already definitively fixed during its oral transmission. He re-emphasizes that the transmission, primarily oral, of the prophetic sayings, which were regarded as sacred cult-material, was carried out with extraordinary care, and consequently the text that has come down to us may be regarded as tolerably dependable. At the same time, he does so far minimize the role that oral transmission played in the handing down of prophetic sayings and in their collection, that he divides prophetic literature into two groups: the first group he designates the 'Diwan type', the other, the 'Liturgy type'. In the first class he puts the books of Amos and Isaiah i–xxxix, regarding them as predominantly shaped by oral transmission. In the second class he puts Nahum, Habakkuk, Joel, and also Deutero-Isaiah, which were set down in written form from the beginning. We see from this that Engnell now somewhat limits the scope of oral tradition in connexion with the prophetic books, though he still, as before, brands 'the literary-critical approach and method with reference to the prophetic literature—especially its differentiation between "primary" and "secondary" sayings, and its emendations and reconstructions of the "original text" '—as an 'anachronistic method' which must under all circumstances be regarded as overthrown (p. 60).

Scandinavia has been the forcing-frame for the idea that in dealing with the origin and transmission of the prophetic books, both as we have them and in the smaller underlying collections, we must reckon for the most part, if not entirely, with oral tradition; and that, further, the heretofore beloved literary-critical mode of approach must be banished in favour of the 'traditio-historical'. But this point of view has been challenged. In Holland, for example, J. van der Ploeg has published 'Le Rôle de la tradition orale dans la transmission du texte de l'Ancien Testament' (*R.B.* liv, 1947, pp. 5 ff.). Even in Scandinavia itself opposition has been raised; and here the books of Mowinckel and Widengren mentioned above (p. 130) claim attention. Mowinckel readily recognizes many results from the new method of study that calls itself 'traditio-historical' in a special sense, and he takes sufficient account of it to modify some of his earlier conclusions accordingly. In his investigation, *Die Komposition des Buches Jeremia*, 1914, he designated the passages marked out as Deuteronomistic as a separate source, C, but now he would prefer it to be regarded as the product of a 'circle of tradition of their own, within which certain of the sayings of Jeremiah have been transmitted and transformed, according to the ideas and style that prevailed in the circle—in fact, the Deuteronomistic ideas, style and interests' (p. 62). Mowinckel thinks of the tradition as being both oral and written, and not simply the former; but, bearing this in mind, he agrees with Birkeland and Engnell that the transmission of the individual prophetic sayings, and of both the smaller and larger collections of them, was taken in hand by certain circles of traditionists, who always adapted the material of the tradition to the needs of the times. The consequence of this is to be seen, not only in the adaptation to the circumstances of the day, but also in the addition and insertion of 'unauthentic' material (pp. 73, 76). Mowinckel further recognizes connexions between individual prophetic sayings and certain cult-mythical concepts. He holds, especially, that there are traits in them that are due to the cult-mythical 'scheme' or 'pattern' underlying the enthronement festival, where the people are first shown in distress, then the temple prophet is bidden to announce 'the coming of Yahweh to the destruction of the enemy and the salvation of Israel'. This is the ritual pattern that is responsible for the expansion of prophecies of woe through the insertion of words of promise to form 'the scheme: disaster—salvation' so often followed by the collectors of prophetic sayings (pp. 79–81).

But elsewhere Mowinckel refuses explanations of other phenomena in the behaviour and speech of the Israelite prophets as based on 'ritual patterns' as too hasty and unfounded (p. 81). He also utters a *caveat* against over-estimating the influence deriving from the enthronement festival in the origin of the scheme: disaster—salvation, and thereby overlooking the fact that the real historical experience of Israel, and the spirit which lived on among the followers of the individual prophet, are, in this respect, of far greater moment than all cultic schemes and patterns (p. 83). Elsewhere, too, Mowinckel warns the modern traditio-historical school against making all-inclusive claims, and thereby bringing into discredit what is really true at the same time. The sole principle should be to gain a picture of the formation of the prophetic books in an historical perspective. To this end all media which promise any success must be employed, literary criticism as well as the form- and style-criticism introduced by Gunkel and

Gressmann, and also the traditio-historical method that is now the battle-cry of Engnell and others. Particular attention must be directed towards laying bare the manifold strata that lie concealed in the prophetical books, so that eventually we may get back to the very words of the individual prophet, and thereby have in our hand the key to a reconstruction of the manner in which they prophesied (pp. 84, 86).

Widengren's book falls into two parts, the shorter of which will be considered later, since it deals with the psychology of the prophet. The longer section starts off, as with Nyberg and Birkeland, in the lands surrounding Israel—to be more explicit, the pre-Islamic and early Islamic Arabs. But he comes to conclusions diametrically opposed to theirs. The latter refer to oral and not written transmission as being the authoritative form amongst the ancient Arabs and in the ancient East generally, and consequently in Israel also. From this datum they deduced a similar state of affairs with respect to the origin and transmission of the prophetical books. Widengren, on the other hand, believes that he can show that just the opposite was in fact the case, and that this situation in the surrounding countries needs to be taken into account for Israel in connexion with the origin of the books of the Bible, and especially, once more, with regard to the setting down of the prophetical books in writing. If they can be upheld, the proofs adduced by Widengren of the importance of written transmission among the Arabs will have consequences for our study; here reference can be made to only two extremely important facts, providing a parallel with the composition of the prophetical books. On pp. 81 ff. there is shown an agglomeration of poetic pieces and homiletic addresses, such as is characteristic of the book of Jeremiah, found among the utterances which issued from the lips of Muhammad. Again, on p. 86, the four types of literary material that are found in the prophetical books, viz. 'oracles, poetry, autobiographical narratives in prose, and biographical prose narratives', are put side by side with relevant passages from the writings of Abū Saʻīd ibn Abī-l-Khayr. a mystic of Chorasan, who was born A.D. 967. The latter are put under the headings 'a) sayings of Abū Saʻīd, b) autobiographical

narratives in prose, and c) biographical parts in prose. The first
literary type comprises both sayings in prose and verses recited
by the shaykh'. For the rest, Widengren draws attention to the
relevant passages in the individual prophetical books that point to
the conclusion that not only Isaiah, Jeremiah, and Ezekiel but
even Amos and Hosea themselves wrote down or dictated at least
a part of their message, and that in no case can we speak of a
purely oral transmission of their sayings (p. 77). We must reckon
rather, so Widengren considers, with both possibilities. The
writing down of prophetic utterances and of collections of these
probably began early, and alongside it there went the oral transmission. This latter will most readily be recognized in connexion
with the biographical sections of the prophetical books (pp. 92 f.).
It is significant that Widengren supports his warning about a
one-sided favouritism of a single method with references to the
prudent judgements of scholars of the last two generations of Old
Testament study, namely, passages in the Isaiah commentaries
of A. Dillmann (1898) and G. B. Gray (1912).

III. THE SUPRANORMAL EXPERIENCES
OF THE PROPHETS

The nature and significance of the supranormal experiences
of the prophets is a psychological question. Closely connected
with it is the historical question about the form of Israelite
prophetism. On the one side we have the $n^e\underline{b}\hat{\imath}\hat{\imath}m$, as described in
1 Sam. x. 5–12 and similar passages; on the other, figures such as
Amos and Hosea, Isaiah and Jeremiah—who are also described
as $n^e\underline{b}\hat{\imath}\hat{\imath}m$—and others like them. Was this institution borrowed
by Israel from the Canaanites, to appear in their midst for the
first time after the settlement in Canaan, or are we dealing with a
phenomenon common to the whole ancient Near East, and so
one with which Israel was already familiar in pre-Canaanite
times? Following in the path of earlier scholars, G. Hölscher,
in his above-mentioned book on the prophets, expressly proclaims his allegiance to the first theory, which he buttresses with
what may or may not be a true observation, that the peculiar

ecstasy characteristic of every appearance of Israelite prophetism is restricted to the territory of Syria and Asia Minor, where it is found from early times, whereas, on the other hand, it is not found among the early Arabs, or among the Babylonians and Assyrians; consequently it could only have become known to Israel on entry into the Syria–Asia Minor region, i.e. at the settlement. This argument has been adopted and repeated frequently, e.g. by A. Jepsen, *Nabi: soziologische Studien zur alttestamentlichen Literatur und Religionsgeschichte*, 1934. Jepsen brings in as further support the following three arguments: (1) that before the entry of Israel, nebiism was already known in Palestine; (2) the Old Testament tradition concerning Israel's pre-Canaanite period knows nothing of nebiism; (3) after the time of Samuel, Israel possesses an unbroken line of $n^e \underline{b} \hat{i}$ *îm*. Others have expressed themselves similarly, e.g. T. J. Meek, *Hebrew Origins*, 1936, pp. 145 ff., who follows earlier scholars in associating the rise of nebiism in Israel with the national feeling aroused by the Philistine oppression of Israel; and Harold Knight, *The Hebrew Prophetic Consciousness*, 1947, who appears to be in general agreement with Hölscher, to whom he explicitly refers when he asserts 'that ecstatic prophecy was not a native product of the religion of Israel, that it is an element of that Canaanite culture which so profoundly modified Israel's religious outlook' (p. 25). On the opposite side, Haldar, as we have seen (pp. 123 ff.), strongly champions the thesis that Israelite prophetism represents an offshoot of a phenomenon common to the whole ancient East (pp. 118 f.), particularly the Sumerians, Babylonians, and Assyrians (p. 25). Parallel to this set of alternatives—whether Israel's prophetism was in all things similar to that of the remainder of the ancient East, or whether it was an element which they absorbed for the first time on Canaanite soil—we have a second set: whether there existed a sharp distinction between the reform or writing prophets, and those popular prophets whom they oftentimes branded as false, or even Baal, prophets. This disputed point brings us back once again to the investigation of the nature of the supranormal prophetic experience described by a term which has become a catchword—'ecstasy'. This investigation has been carried out along many lines, but, putting aside the many slight shades of difference that exist, we may divide the results roughly into two groups: those who strongly emphasize the ecstatic element in the reform prophets classify them with the popular prophets on the psychological issue; whereas those who deny the presence of any supranormal psychological elements in the reform prophets, or at least restrict it to a minimum, find a deep gulf between them and the popular prophets.

The discussion of the nature of the strange experiences and mysterious actions of the Israelite prophets, to which the term 'ecstatic' is applied, important as it is, has also attracted much further attention during the last two or three decades. The main reason for this is that this question touches, or appears to touch, the religious and theological value of the prophets, since, according to the thinking of many scholars, the admission of an abnormal or even a supranormal state of experience and action would endanger the worth of the divine revelation in the pronouncements of the great .prophets, and much more so if one admits that there was great similarity between them and the 'false' prophets whom they denounced. As a consequence of this, the division of forces is not so much along the opposing fronts of the historico-critical school versus those who lay more stress on extracting the abiding content of Old Testament religion—as is otherwise very common in Old Testament questions; rather, a most unusual interpenetration of forces has become evident. No one who has really and truly sought to comprehend the personality and message of the great prophets of the Old Testament can avoid the impression that here we have men not only speaking a word to their own generation, but having something of value for us today also. Consequently, scholars who otherwise strive to view the prophets as historical beings, and so feel themselves bound, by the information accessible, to emphasize the supranormal-ecstatic element, at the same time strongly assert the timelessness of their message. Sometimes they go so far that some supposedly supranormal or ecstatic feature threatens to become overlooked or to be interpreted symbolically or allegorically.

Since this is the case, it should be made clear that the religious and theological value of the prophets and their message stands quite independently of the historical and psychological explanations of their experiences and actions, which can neither confirm nor dispute them. This is so because the former deal with the spiritual content of the message, and not with the human and temporal elements in the medium. Fortunately we may say that, on the whole, this point of view has steadily gained ground during the period with which we have to deal.

An important cause of difficulty in the discussion of the actual nature of prophetic experiences and acts is the lack of clear and distinctive definitions for the phenomena in question. Above all, the apparently inescapable word 'ecstasy' is susceptible of numerous interpretations. J. Lindblom has rendered a considerable service, apart from his large volume mentioned above (p. 119), by many articles (listed in the Lindblom Festschrift, *S.E.Å.* xii, 1947, pp. 343–73) which aim at clarifying the relevant terminology. We may mention in particular his article 'Die Geschichte der Propheten' (*Studia Theologica*, i, 1935, pp. 7–28). His latest essay is his contribution to the Bertholet Festschrift (pp. 325–37), on 'Einige Grundfragen der alttestamentlichen Wissenschaft'. Here he pursues farther the question whether, and in what sense, the term 'ecstasy' may be used in relation to the prophets of the Old Testament. His findings will receive general assent, at least in as far as he distinguishes two different kinds of ecstasy, and declares that only one of these may legitimately be applied to the prophets. Lindblom draws a sharp distinction between the 'absorption ecstasy', in which the personality loses itself in a fusion with the Universal, and the 'concentration ecstasy', which entails a deep concentration of the soul on a single feeling or notion, and has the result of extinguishing normal consciousness and putting the outward senses out of function. The latter alone, Lindblom argues, can be considered in connexion with the prophets. This holds good at least in so far that Old Testament religion represents God as a clear-cut personality, and not a neutral Unity and Universality in which one can lose oneself and be absorbed.

Nevertheless, the use of the ecstasy idea in connexion with the prophets, even in this more narrowly defined way, leaves room for quite different interpretations. Some would confine the relevant phenomena to the time of the prophets, regarding them as unavailable to modern man, out of the ordinary, even bordering on the abnormal; whereas on the other side are those who conceive of them as merely heightened forms of psychic experience which could quite well be experienced, at least to a certain degree, even today by men of similar gifts. All studies published on this subject during the last three decades and earlier belong somewhere between these two extremes; some tend to stress more the mysterious, well-nigh unbelievably strange, prophetic behaviour, while the others veer towards supposing that modern man, or certain particular representatives such as the poet, come very near the inner experiences of the prophet. It must, however, again be emphasized that it is not only those scholars who accept or incline to the latter alternative that would uphold the eternal value of the prophetic message; this is the case with the others also, and one gets the impression with some of them that they expose this mysterious and astonishing character of the Old Testament prophets as it intruded into history so clearly only because they can then with a clearer conscience and firmer voice testify to the eternal truth of their message.

T. H. Robinson, with acknowledgements to the previous work of Hölscher in the same field, holds very firmly to the opinion that the prophets (i.e. the reform prophets of the Old Testament) had special capacities denied to ordinary mortals. He considers that they, like their prophetic predecessors and opponents, were ecstatics, and that their hallmark lay, not only in the ethical and religious content of their message, but also in their supranormal psychic capacity. The first section of his survey, entitled 'Neuere Propheten-Forschung' (*T.R.*, N.F. iii, 1931, pp. 75–105), which deals with the psychology of the prophets, ends with these words: 'Scarcely a doubt exists that, in one form or another, Hölscher's theory will for the future hold the field. ... Modern study of prophetic psychology is only in its infancy, and we may expect far-reaching results from the next generation.' Much has, in fact, taken place in this respect during the last two decades. Mowinckel has again and again set himself to find a solution to the problem which here faces Old Testament scholarship. It will be noticed from his writings how the upholding of the peculiar value of the prophetic message, which is present in embryo from the first, gradually becomes the main interest. He himself, in his 'Postscript', 1937, to be mentioned again in a moment, brings this fact into connexion with his complete adherence meanwhile to the Oxford Group movement. Yet, at the same time, even after 1937, he argues clearly in favour of the view that we must reckon with a particular psychical endowment of the prophets, i.e. they were ecstatics. The *Norsk Teologisk Tidsskrift* (xlv, 3, 1944), which was presented to Mowinckel on his sixtieth birthday under the sub-title *Acta Mowinckeliana*, contains a classified bibliography of his writings, compiled by H. Harboe and O. Kolsrud, that provides evidence on this point. A. Bentzen's article in the same volume also provides an appreciation of Mowinckel's contribution to Old Testament scholarship in general, whilst that by N. Messel is more particularly concerned with his services to the translation and exposition of the prophetic books. Here we must be content with references to four or five of Mowinckel's articles on the ecstatic character of the prophets, viz. 'The "Spirit" and the "Word" in the Pre-exilic Reforming Prophets' (*J.B.L.* liii, 1934, pp. 199–227), with a 'Postscript' (*J.B.L.* lvi, 1937, pp. 261–5); 'Ecstatic Experience and Rational Elaboration in Old Testament Prophecy' (*Acta Orientalia*, xiii, 1935, pp. 264–91; xiv, 1936, p. 319); 'Die Erkenntnis Gottes bei den alttestamentlichen Propheten' (*Nor. T.T.* xlii, 1941, 2, supplementary vol.); 'Ekstatiske Innslag i Profetenes Oplevelser' (*Nor. T.T.* xlix, 1948, pp. 129–221). The last-named is a thorough-going rejoinder to I. P. Seierstad's *Die Berufungserlebnisse der Propheten Amos, Jesaja und Jeremia*, 1946. Mowinckel very decidedly rejects Seierstad's attempt, in the interests of the moral and religious content of the message, to deny any extraordinary psychical characteristics to the prophets, or at least to reduce them to a minimum. Mowinckel again makes use of the term ecstasy in reference to their experiences and acts; at the same time, of course, he reiterates the distinction between the reform prophets and their predecessors and opponents, which he has maintained in earlier essays, and which has, too, been maintained by others, particularly in A. Jepsen's work entitled *Nabi*, 1934. He argues in this connexion that for the reform prophets, the 'Spirit' (*rūaḥ*) of Yahweh—i.e. an irrational force—was not, as for the others, the stimulus of their peculiar experiences and acts, but that their stimulus came rather from the 'Word' (*dāḇār*) of Yahweh, perceived in the clear light of reason. This, he would say, applied at least to the majority of the writing prophets. As the title, given above, shows, Mowinckel's article published in 1934 is devoted to making clear the distinction between the 'spirit' and the 'word' prophecy. The reform prophets avoided connecting their experiences and actions with the 'spirit' of Yahweh just because the popular prophets derived their grossly ecstatic behaviour from this very spirit; and the reform prophets wished to draw a distinction between that and their own pronouncements, which were shaped in the light of reason. Ezekiel stands on the same high moral and religious level as the other writing prophets with regard to his message, and yet, in manner, was an ecstatic in the same sense as the older *nᵉḇîʾîm*, and had no misgivings on that account against bringing his own particular experiences and actions into connexion with the spirit of Yahweh. In his 1935 article, again, Mowinckel lays down a boundary line between the reform prophets—even those described as *nāḇîʾ*, like Isaiah, Jeremiah, and Ezekiel—and the popular prophets; at the same time, the reform prophets do have such mysterious and unusual experiences, that we must conclude 'that there is an ecstatic element in all this' (p. 271). And yet, their certainty that they are commissioned by Yahweh rests, in the last resort, not on such experiences, but on the certainty that they have received 'Yahweh's word'; and the decisive criterion that it has really come from Yahweh, is 'the clear, intelligible, moral and religious contents' (p. 287). 'The great prophets apply a rational, religious and moral standard to the secret experiences which come to them' (p. 289). His 1941 article moves along similar lines: viewed from the standpoint of psychology, he maintains, prophetism implies a transition from ecstatic orgasm to inspiration and revelation, in a sphere of quiet reflection and spiritual clarity. Ecstasy, in the sense of a concentration of body and soul on a single idea, is certainly to be found among the reform prophets, but not ecstasy in the sense of visible and violent excitement. In his 'Postscript', 1937, Mowinckel puts his attitude to the whole question in these very characteristic words: 'I am no longer primarily interested in unravelling the processes of the prophet's psychical experiences, in discussing how far the factors hold good in general, that caused the particular experience to take on an ecstatic character and to assume the form of visions, auditions, &c., &c., &c. That is a task for the psychologist, and it is not the duty of a theologian to become a professional psychologist' (p. 264). It can hardly be said that such expressions quite follow the lines laid down by T. H. Robinson in his 1931 programme (see above, p. 138) for the future study of the prophets.

The contributions of H. Wheeler Robinson, H. H. Rowley, and Harold Knight more nearly approach the requirements of that programme, though they all differ considerably from T. H. Robinson's theory of ecstaticism in their views of the mental make-up of the prophets. Prophetic psychology is not examined in their publications for its own sake, and so they cannot very well be put side by side with Hölscher's 1914 book; but yet, they all make it quite clear that the prophets, including the writing prophets, underwent unusual psychic experiences and performed extraordinary actions that were attributable, not to the reason, but to some compelling force which could not be opposed—in short, the great prophets, like the popular ones, were ecstatic. H. Wheeler Robinson has devoted many valuable essays to this problem. We can mention only two of them here, his 'Prophetic Symbolism' (in *Old Testament Essays*, 1927, pp. 1–17), and *Inspiration and Revelation in the Old Testament*, 1946. In the latter work, after establishing a distinction between the classical prophets and common $n^e\underline{b}\hat{i}$'$\hat{i}m$, Robinson makes further reference to the former in these words: 'But their visions, their symbolic acts, and their other abnormal experiences, most visible, of course, in Ezekiel, but not absent even from Jeremiah, make

apparent an affinity of form, however different the substance.
It is therefore much the sounder view to regard the classical
prophets as the culmination of a long development, though the
contrast between origin and result is here, as often in the history
of religion, so marked' (p. 177). Two at least of H. H. Rowley's
works that are relevant at this point may here be mentioned,
first, his contribution to the Eissfeldt Festschrift, 1947, entitled
'Was Amos a Nabi?' (pp. 191–8), and secondly, his article 'The
Nature of Prophecy in the Light of Recent Study' (*H.T.R.*
xxxviii, 1945, pp. 1–38). In the first, Rowley answers the
question referred to in the title—i.e. should *lōʼ nābīʼ ʼānōkī weʼlōʼ
ben nābīʼ ānōkī* be rendered 'I am no prophet or son of a prophet',
or, 'I was no prophet or son of a prophet'?—very illuminatingly in
favour of the latter, so that Amos is really establishing the moment
of his call as the beginning of his nabi-ship. Further, Rowley also
demonstrates that the word *nābīʼ*, though of uncertain etymology,
cannot be used as an argument for the ecstatic nature of the
prophets, as is so commonly done. His 1945 work gives an almost
exhaustive enumeration of all publications which appeared
between the end of the First World War and the last year but
one of the Second. He also provides a most fruitful review of
what scholarship of the last quarter of a century had done towards
clarifying the problems connected with Israelite prophetism. By
this means, he has given us an important addition to our knowledge, which anyone really interested in this matter will neglect
at his peril. Although it is a review of the work of others, the
article affords clear glimpses of the author's own standpoint.
Rowley, for instance, rejects as unsatisfactory the attempt to
make an essential distinction in mental experience and outward
manifestation between the popular and the reform prophets.
Furthermore, he produces considerations against the view held, as
we saw by Mowinckel, that the reform prophets, or the majority
of them, opposed the derivation of their call from the spirit of
Yahweh because the popular prophets invoked it. It would also
be a denial of the truth to confine the title ecstatic to the popular
prophets, and hold it to be inapplicable to the classical ones; one
should, and indeed must, admit these ecstatic experiences. But

these neither express the essence of their nature, nor do they constitute the difference between them and the popular prophets. The essential element that differentiates the classical prophet from his popular counterpart is the religious and moral content of his message, which constrains him with an unopposable 'must' from Yahweh, and which is conditioned by his relationship to Him. 'While, therefore, true and false prophets both provided evidence of abnormal psychology, and both forecast the future, the nature of prophecy is not to be defined in terms of these things. What is really vital is the relation of the prophet and of his word to God. The prophet who is properly so called was a man who knew God in the immediacy of experience, who felt an inescapable constraint to utter what he was profoundly convinced was the word of God, and whose word was at bottom a revelation of the nature of God no less than of His will, who saw the life of men in the light of his vision of God, and who saw the inevitable issue of that life, who therefore declared that issue and pleaded with men to avoid it by cleansing and renewing their lives. He was a true prophet in the measure of his experience of God, and the measure of his experience was the measure of his receptiveness and of his response to it' (pp. 37 f.). Harold Knight, *The Hebrew Prophetic Consciousness*, 1947, follows much the same lines as Wheeler Robinson and Rowley.

It will be noticed that whereas the three above-mentioned scholars recognize the presence of supranormal elements in the classical prophets, they make no actual attempt to explain their psychology more explicitly. Whether consciously or unconsciously they resign themselves on account of its uncertainty to giving up the investigation of the question whether by the methods and with the conceptions of modern psychology we can ever hope to penetrate the psychic make-up of these figures of nearly 3,000 years ago.

Widengren, however, in his already mentioned book (see above, pp. 130, 133 f.), tackles this mysterious realm of the prophets' inner life with renewed heart in the fourth chapter, entitled 'The Prophetic Leader, his Parapsychic Experiences, and their Importance to the Literary Fixation of the Revelations'. After

adducing parallels from outside the Old Testament, he gives a
review of all the powers possessed by, and acts performed by, the
Old Testament prophets that derived their source from parapsychic powers, remarking that these prophets make use of all
the telepathic and telekinetic possibilities. Next, he turns his
attention more particularly—though still bearing in view related
phenomena from outside the Old Testament—to the peculiar
experiences and acts of Ezekiel. He attributes the narrative in
Ezek. iii. 1–3, which tells how Ezekiel at Yahweh's command
devoured a book-roll and had the sensation as of eating honey,
to a vision connected with hallucinatory taste sensation. The
vision of Yahweh's judgement on the abomination in Jerusalem
and His departure from the city (Ezek. viii–xi), he explains as
follows: 'The prophet . . . must have experienced some phenomena of levitation. These are . . . connected with visions and
auditions, giving the accompanying levitation phenomena an
interpretation that relegates the parapsychic phenomenon in
itself more to the background, thus stressing what is seen and
heard and said by the prophet . . . When now the phenomena of
levitation are felt extremely strong, the prophet or seer must
have had the feeling that he was not experiencing a vision where
he imagined himself to be carried away, but that he was subjected
to a real transportation. In such cases . . . the expressions are in
the direction of a real transportation' (p. 110). We shall see later
(p. 157) that this solution of the psychological problem encountered in Ezek. viii–xi is of importance in finding an answer to
questions about the composition of the book of Ezekiel.

Out of the host of those who reject the standpoint of ecstatic
possession for the writing prophets, or a majority of them, we
have already (pp. 135, 139 f.) mentioned the books of Jepsen
and Seierstad. In the case of the latter, reference may be made
to a characteristic foretaste of his book published under the title
'Erlebnis und Gehorsam beim Propheten Amos' (*Z.A.W.* lii,
1934, pp. 22–41). Seierstad explicitly rejects the ecstatic theory
propounded by Hölscher, Gunkel, and others, and maintains
firmly that the constraint of which Amos speaks no more had its
origin in an ecstatic compulsion than had the 'I can no other'

attributed to Luther. Rather is it to be identified with the conscience bound to God. We must be satisfied with drawing attention to two more works only of those which belong here: they are H. Junker, *Prophet und Seher in Israel*, 1927, and A. Heschel, *Die Prophetie*, 1936. Junker calls Hölscher's approach a 'Psychologism, that sees the origin of all that appears in the field of religion, including prophetism, in the subconscious realm of the mind's workings' (p. 13). Though willing to admit that in certain circles of Israelite prophetism ecstatic traits may have crept in, he replaces that theory, in the case of the writing prophets, by one that brings them nearer to present day ethical and religious ideas and practices, and so represents them as conscious proclaimers of the divine will. Heschel, however, lays stress on a correct evaluation of the God of the Old Testament—whom he would represent as a personality swayed by dynamic feeling, and not some static passive Being—rather than on a complete understanding of prophecy itself. With such a God, no ecstatically motivated prophet can be correlated, but only a prophet whose consciousness is in such sympathetic union with the *pathos* of God, that he can bring that union to bear in any given set of circumstances. 'The *sympatheticos* is a religious type of its own, and to be regarded as the antitype of the ecstatic. *Sympatheia* also, in opposition to the tumultuous, momentary ecstasy, is a constant state' (p. 168). This religious sympathy, which represents an anthropological category, is 'of essential importance for what is a completely independent religious type, particularly in the make-up of the prophetic personality' (pp. 172 f.).

IV. THE INDIVIDUAL PROPHETS

The changes in the conception of the nature of the prophets and the composition of the books that bear their names which have come about during the last two or three decades have affected the figure of each prophet and every prophetic book in consequence. But some books have been particularly affected. The drawing of the writing prophets into connexion with the cult, and their enrolment in the associations of cultic prophets, was bound to bring the books into a new light, so that they will now much more readily be regarded as 'liturgies', i.e. collections —be it directly for actual cultic use, or merely literary imitations representing such cultic use—of many and varied, originally separate, units, such as laments, petitions, hymns, promises, &c., worked up into a larger structure. This applies, above all, to the books of Joel, Nahum, and Habakkuk. The book of Habakkuk, which during the last thirty years has been subjected to as many different interpretations as it was previously—whether it be on grounds of its historical setting and composition, or the identification of whoever is stigmatized therein as the 'godless' with some foreign power (and if so, which), or with some individual or group inside Judaism—has now been subjected to a new and rigorous examination by Humbert in *Problèmes du livre d'Habacuc*, 1944, with the following conclusions: the book originated with a cultic prophet working in the Jerusalem temple in the last quarter of the seventh century B.C. Humbert bases his case on the two oracles, i. 5–10 and i. 11–17, which were both actually delivered by the prophet in the temple at Jerusalem. Habakkuk has skilfully worked these oracles up into the book we now have, ready for a cult festival planned for 602 or 601 B.C. in the Jerusalem temple, in face of the threatening invasion of Nebuchadnezzar, and directed against the despotic rule of Jehoiakim. It is an open declaration of war therefore against the latter hated tyrant. In Habakkuk, 'prophecy and cult unite and shake hands' (p. 297).

The book of Nahum is ascribed by A. Haldar, *Studies in the Book of Nahum*, 1947, to a cultic prophet who foretold about 614 B.C. the nearly approaching destruction of Nineveh by Yahweh, and who utilized the images and expressions normally used in depicting the cult-mythical struggle of Yahweh against his foes. These motifs are paralleled in Sumero-Accadian and Ugaritic texts and so, where they are not clear, they may be illustrated from the latter. Still more strongly than Haldar in his exegesis of Nahum, A. S. Kapelrud in his *Joel Studies*, 1948, has been influenced in his explanation of the book of Joel by the cultic prophet theory and by research methods which lay stress on ancient oriental cult-myth patterns. As a consequence, his book has had to face strong criticism; but it still retains its importance as the most consequential application of these two hypotheses in any one single case.

Quite apart from the fresh aspects introduced by the new turn in the study of the prophets, each prophetic book offers its own problems. These have been dealt with extensively, during the period with which we are concerned, in commentaries, collective works, and monographs of every description. This labour can be brought under review only with reference to a few of the prophetic books, and there again with only a restricted selection from the publications dealing with them that have appeared during the last quarter of a century. We may mention as particularly stimulating and informative the scholarly studies published during this period on Deutero-Isaiah (Isa. xl–lv),—especially on the 'Ebed Yahweh songs found there—on Jeremiah, and on Ezekiel. Consequently we shall deal somewhat more fully here with the results of the discussions concerning these three prophetic books, and so follow up what was said on the subject in *Record and Revelation*, 1938 (pp. 90–102).

In connexion with Deutero-Isaiah, I. Engnell with his 'The 'Ebed Yahweh Songs and the Suffering Messiah in "Deutero-Isaiah" ' (*B.J.R.L.* xxxi, 1948, p. 13 and often) has extended the liturgy theory to include Isa. xxxv, xl–lv; i.e. this complex, including the 'Ebed Yahweh songs, is explained as the 'prophetic imitation of a cult liturgy', or, more exactly, 'an actual New Year Festival liturgy'. It is connected with Proto-Isaiah to the extent that 'behind it stands a traditionist circle—possibly also an individual poet—with direct personal and topical connecting lines to the latter' (p. 13). This is certainly a new and original treatment of Isa. xl–lv. Sidney Smith, *Isaiah Chapters XL–LV: Literary Criticism and History*, 1944, on the other hand, though certainly using a great deal of previously unculled material from outside the Old Testament, takes his way over previously travelled paths. He concerns himself with the task of very carefully tracking the references to historical events of the years 547–538 B.C., which are to be found in Isa. xl–lv, and then, having determined the separate sections of Isa. xl–lv by their composition at different

times within these ten years, he proceeds to set them out on
literary lines as speeches that were delivered by the prophet, and
then distributed as pamphlets. At the end of his book he lists
twenty-two speeches (including the otherwise separately named
first three 'Ebed Yahweh songs, Isa. xlii. 1–4; xlix. 1–6; l. 4–9)
delivered during eight different periods between 547 and 538
B.C.; these speeches are briefly defined according to form and
content, and then the section lii. 13–liii. 12, which is assigned
to a ninth period, is connected with the death of the prophet
and analysed after this fashion: lii. 13–15, Oracle of YHWH
addressed to Israel; liii. 1–10, Lament for the 'servant of
YHWH' by members of a community to which he belonged;
liii. 11–12, Utterance of YHWH concerning the 'servant'.
This utterance states, 'that the prophet by bearing the sins of
others has justified the greater part of Israel. The prophet's
part in the booty of Cyrus is to be the exiles whom he redeemed'
(p. 193). Critical reviews of the book have shown that the author's
rejection of the Gunkel-Gressmann type-analysis method
(*Gattungsforschung*), whereby Isa. xl–lv was divided up into about
fifty units, composed of promises, hymns, message-oracles, judge-
ment-sayings, &c., and, instead, his suggested division of this
complex into twenty-two speeches or pamphlets, in addition to
the above described special section lii. 13–liii. 12, has met with
strong opposition. This is also true of his suggestion that the
anonymous prophet of the time of the Babylonian exile, whom
we call Deutero-Isaiah, was the head of an underground movement directed against the Babylonians, and proclaimed Cyrus to
be the king appointed by Yahweh to rule over Judah, and was
therefore put to death by his own compatriots for high treason,
and that by his martyr's death he then made possible the edict
of Cyrus which commanded the rebuilding of the Temple at
Jerusalem, and the restitution of its cult furniture. Finally,
many of the references in Isa. xl–lv to definite situations in the
years between 547 and 538 B.C., as supposed by Smith, appear
in the eyes of the critics to be either wholly or largely questionable. The book, however, has a high value as a contribution to the
history of the years 547–538 B.C., and moreover, its attempt to

link the great unknown prophet behind Isa. xl–lv with the happenings of his age as closely as normally happens with the Isaiah of the last four decades of the eighth century B.C., who composed the core of Isa. i–xxxix, without at the same time losing sight of the eternal significance of utterances which sprang out of the temporary circumstances of the day, provides a salutary example of interpretation for the theologians who are generally only too wont to find in these chapters evidences for truths of eternal and universal validity, and to neglect the limitations of time and space.

The 'Ebed Yahweh problem is dealt with by S. Smith, as we saw, to the extent that he questions our right to extract Isa. xlii. 1–4; xlix. 1–6; l. 4–9 out of the run of other prophetic speeches, as separate entities of a different sort. He himself applies xlii. 1–4 to Cyrus, xlix. 1–6 and l. 4–9 to the prophet himself, and lii. 13–liii. 12 is reckoned as a retrospective view of the latter's death. But, as may easily be surmised, the 'Ebed Yahweh problem has received a great deal of further notice on its own account during the last two or three decades, particular attention being paid, as previously, to the pericope lii. 13–liii. 12. The answers given to the questions posed by this pericope group themselves around the same alternatives as before: collective or individual reference? is the Servant past, present, or future? 'Of whom speaketh the prophet this? of himself, or of some other?' (Acts viii. 34). Yet in spite of all continuing differences, a synthesis of opinion seems to be slowly coming into shape with reference to the understanding of Isa. lii. 13–liii. 12 that, using whatever truth is contained in the many earnest attempts made at its interpretation, presents the meaning of the pericope in this way: suffering and privation, contempt and an ignominious death are to be taken, despite all natural human inclination, not as proof of dereliction and guilt, but as vicarious self-sacrifice, voluntarily undertaken for others; further, this has made available a hitherto unheard of depth in the conception of life and the universe, which has become one of the richest possessions of mankind. A greater or lesser degree of emphasis is laid on the point that the lot and sentence of the figure pictured in Isa. lii. 13–liii. 12

links up most closely with the nature and value of Jesus' suffering and death and resurrection, and to that extent the latter can fittingly be described as 'fulfilment' of the 'prophecy' contained in Isa. lii. 13–liii. 12.

That such an interpretation of the 'Ebed Yahweh figure, so far at least as he is described in Isa. lii. 13–liii. 12, is winning more and more ground may be illustrated from two important works, H. S. Nyberg, 'Smärtornas man: en studie till Jes. 52, 13–53, 12' (*S.E.Å.* vii, 1942, pp. 5–82), and Christopher R. North, *The Suffering Servant in Deutero-Isaiah: an Historical and Critical Study*, 1948. Nyberg presents a highly accomplished comparative review of the collective and individual theories, and the historical and cult-mythical interpretations of this pericope, and at the same time justifies its application to the vicarious suffering and death of Jesus. In respect of mythological influence, Nyberg reckons with three circles of ideas: the belief in youthful dying and rising vegetation gods, the notion of a king who vicariously does penance for his people, and the certainty of the ancestor's continued existence in the community which had its origin in him. He sees the figure of an historical person in the picture of the 'Ebed, in so far that he believes that some great figure from among the prophetic circles, perhaps Jeremiah, must have been taken as a pattern. This pericope, however, takes its place suitably and legitimately among the lessons for Good Friday, since the supra-temporal conception appearing in the 'Ebed of Isa. lii. 13–liii. 12 is made manifest universally in historical persons, though, of course, most clearly and completely in the person of Jesus Christ. 'For in the Lord of the Church this Word has for all time taken human nature and become flesh' (p. 82). North gives an exhaustive survey of the explanations offered during the last 2,000 years of the 'Ebed Yahweh songs in general, and the fourth, Isa. lii. 13–liii. 12, in particular, and gives a considered critical examination of these attempts. Amongst them he singles out as important the use of the term 'myth'—understood in a special sense—by W. F. Lofthouse and others for the 'Ebed figure. North's final conclusion is much the same as that of Nyberg; indeed he closes his book with a quotation of the sentences in which Nyberg summed up his own conclusions, adding to them an expression of his agreement therewith. Nyberg's words are as follows: 'The spiritual development among the Greeks describes a curve which can be expressed in the formula "from *mythos* to *logos*": the world of myth succeeded by the world of reason, the thought-forms of myth by abstract thought-forms, and the mythical associations of ideas by systematized knowledge. The Semitic development presents a completely different curve, for which we may suitably employ the formula, "The word became flesh": what was once conceived in the words and thought-forms of myth is taken up into a living man, in whom it takes manhood and becomes a reality in and through him'. North's concurrence is couched in these terms: 'This, together with Nyberg's handling of the category of myth, is substantially the conclusion reached in the present study' (p. 222).

So far as the book of Jeremiah is concerned, we have investigations into its composition, and the provenance of the individual 'sources' or 'strata' to be discerned in it, from the hands of the following very different scholars: B. Duhm, *Jeremia* (K.H.C. 1901); S. Mowinckel, *Zur Komposition des Buches Jeremia*, 1914; and T. H. Robinson, 'Baruch's Roll' (*Z.A.W.* xlii, 1924, pp. 209–21). The discussion begun and stimulated by them has been carried still farther. General agreement has been accorded to their conclusion that in fact we have to reckon with *three* 'sources': (1) sayings and poems; (2) narratives about Jeremiah; (3) speeches by Jeremiah, with actual or apparent echoes of Deuteronomic diction. Mowinckel designates these three classes, *A*, *B*, and *C*, respectively. W. Rudolph, *Jeremia* (H.A.T. i, 12, 1947) declares himself in favour of this classification, though he certainly introduces many new suggestions in matters of detail. It does now appear that here we have reached a fairly permanent verdict. H. G. May, 'Towards an Objective Approach to the Book of Jeremiah: the Biographer' (*J.B.L.* lxi, 1942, pp. 139–55), appears to be of another opinion, however. He would put forward a quite different key to the understanding of the composition of the book of Jeremiah. His opinion is that the book as we have it is the work of a 'Biographer' living at the very earliest during the first half of the fifth century B.C. In spite of being influenced by *D* (the redactor of Deuteronomy), Deutero-Isaiah, and other outstanding notables of the Old Testament, this Biographer displays a quite independent diction and ideology. His 'biography' is made up of sayings and recollections of Jeremiah, and other material ascribed to him, to which he has not scrupled to add long speeches or oracles, altogether or largely of his own creation, which he puts into the mouth of Jeremiah. But this thesis needs to be much more thoroughly proved before it can be regarded as seriously threatening the hitherto dominant view of the composition of the book of Jeremiah. By this we do not mean that this latter view should be accorded the rank of dogma. How much is still in dispute, even among its supporters, may be seen in the fact that there is still no unanimity as to the nature of the original roll; did it consist of *A*, the Sayings, or of *C*, the Speeches?—the *B* section, the narratives about Jeremiah in the third person, does not come into the question at all. Whereas T. H. Robinson, in his above-mentioned article 'Baruch's Roll', and O. Eissfeldt, in his *Einleitung in das Alte Testament*, 1934 (pp. 393–7), believed that Mowinckel's preference for *A*-material in the reconstruction of the original roll was unsound, and themselves prefer to find it in *C*, Rudolph, in his commentary, goes back in a large degree to Mowinckel's view.

Of the other important points raised by a study of the book of Jeremiah, we have no room to consider more than two; one of comparatively recent emergence, the second, one which has exercised the minds of scholars for generations or even centuries. Firstly, then, the connexion between Jeremiah and the prophet mentioned in the Lachish ostraca discovered in 1935. According to Henri Michaud, 'Le Témoignage des Ostraca de Tell Douweir concernant le prophète Jérémie' (*R.E.S.-B.*, 1941, pp. 42–60), the end of Letter III and Letter VI. 5–7 may with confidence be brought into connexion with the political activity of Jeremiah, and specifically with his pro-Babylonian proclivities. D. Winton Thomas, '*The Prophet*' in the Lachish Ostraca, 1946, on the contrary, can find no reference to Jeremiah in these letters, and considers it altogether impossible to identify any more closely the prophet therein mentioned (III. 26). In view of the defective and ambiguous nature of the evidence, we are scarcely likely to get beyond a plain confession of ignorance, unless and until other, more productive, material comes to light.

The second point is the relationship of Jeremiah to Deuteronomy. Nowadays, as previously, voices are heard denying any dependence of Jeremiah on Deuteronomy. J. N. Schofield, 'The Significance of the Prophets for Dating Deuteronomy' (*Studies in History and Religion*, ed. by E. A. Payne, 1942, pp. 44–60), makes Deuteronomy dependent on Jeremiah and not vice versa. J. P. Hyatt, 'Jeremiah and Deuteronomy' (*J.N.E.S.* i, 1942, pp. 156–73), thinks that Jeremiah first began his ministry in 615 B.C., and so could not have been a promoter of the Josianic reform already put through six years earlier. But all such arguments fall to the ground in face of the case made out by H. H. Rowley, 'The Prophet Jeremiah and the Book of Deuteronomy' (*Studies in Old Testament Prophecy*, ed. by H. H. Rowley, 1950, pp. 157–74). Rowley subjects Jer. xliv, xxxiv, iii. 1, and xi. 1–14 to a new scrutiny which leads him to support the view that Jeremiah at first welcomed the Josianic reform instigated by the book of Deuteronomy, and supported it, but that later he took exception to its dangerous developments.

Turning to the studies on the book of Ezekiel which characterize the first half of our period, it is the minority who follow W. Kessler, *Die innere Einheitlichkeit des Buches Ezechiel*, 1927, and G. A. Cooke, *Ezekiel* (I.C.C. 1936)—both scholars who ascribe the greater part at least of the book that bears his name to Ezekiel himself, and, in accordance with the indications within that book, make his ministry wholly exilic. The majority of scholars would restrict Ezekiel's share in his book to a minimum, and represent him as prophesying either solely or additionally in Jerusalem. Some indeed would proclaim the whole book of Ezekiel to be a third century B.C. pseudepigraphon. The most noteworthy contributions are: G. Hölscher, *Hesekiel: der Dichter und das Buch*, 1924; C. C. Torrey, *Pseudo-Ezekiel and the Original Prophecy*, 1930; J. Smith, *The Book of the Prophet*

Ezekiel, 1931; V. Herntrich, *Ezechielprobleme*, 1932; J. Battersby Harford, *Studies in the Book of Ezekiel*, 1935; A. Bertholet, *Hesekiel* (H.A.T. i, 13, 1936). According to Hölscher, only the poetic portions of the book—less than half of the whole—are from Ezekiel; the larger portion, which is in prose, has been added by a redactor flourishing in the fifth century B.C. Torrey disputes the existence of any form of the book going back to a sixth-century prophet; he explains it as a pseudepigraphon which was written in 230 B.C. and dated back to the thirtieth year (i. 1) of Manasseh, i.e. 640 B.C. The purpose of the book was to hold up before the eyes of the reprobate king his unrighteousness and coming punishment. Torrey further holds that this book was edited shortly after 230 B.C. so as to transfer the activity of the prophet to the exilic period, with a consequent dating of the individual happenings and sayings from the year of Jehoiachin's deportation, 597 B.C. The postulation of some such double scene of action is to be found also in Smith, Herntrich, Battersby Harford, and Bertholet, with the difference that these scholars do admit that there really was a prophet active towards the end of the eighth century and the beginning of the seventh (Smith only), or the beginning of the sixth century B.C. Smith holds Ezekiel to have been a native of the Northern Kingdom who was deported in 734 B.C., began his prophetic activity in exile, and having returned home in 691, thirty years (i. 1) after the fall of Samaria, continued his ministry in his homeland. Herntrich and Battersby Harford, however, reckon with a prophet Ezekiel who appeared on the scene in Jerusalem shortly before 586 B.C. They believe that the book which issued from this prophet, and which forms the groundwork of our present book of Ezekiel, was remodelled about 573 B.C. (xl. 1) by an exilic redactor, so that the prophet's activity was transferred to the exilic community, thereby establishing as determinative the hypothesis that the forces which motivated the re-founding of the Jewish nation and worship all derived from the exiles. Bertholet has his own position in the matter, in that he thinks that there is an historical basis for a Jerusalem or Judean, as well as an exilic, period in the career of Ezekiel. The prophet's call in the vision of the Book-roll

(ii. 3–iii. 9) he considers to belong to the year 593 and the Jerusalem period; whereas his call to prophesy among the exiles, which took place in 585 B.C., is to be found in the vision of the Throne-chariot (i. 4–ii. 2).

As a contrast, the type of scholarship symbolized by the names of Kessler and G. A. Cooke certainly admits secondary additions to the original book, though it ascribes the main portion of our present book of Ezekiel to the prophet of that name who was active in the exile at the beginning of the sixth century B.C. There are scholars during the second half of our period, too, who have signified their agreement, as may be indicated by reference to one or two recent works, for which alone we have space, namely M. A. Schmidt, *Prophet und Tempel: eine Studie zum Problem der Gottesnähe im Alten Testament*, 1948 (pp. 109–71), and his 'Zur Komposition des Buches Hesekiel' (*T.Z.* vi, 1950, pp. 81–98), and Jack Finegan, 'The Chronology of Ezekiel' (*J.B.L.* lxix. 1950, pp. 61–6). Finegan's article starts off from the Accadian clay tablets discovered before the First World War on the site of Babylon and published by E. F. Weidner in the *Mélanges syriens offerts à Monsieur René Dussaud*, ii, 1939, pp. 923–35. These texts give dates ranging from the tenth to the thirty-fifth years of Nebuchadnezzar's reign, i.e. 594–569 B.C., and name Jehoiachin the king of the land of Judah. Starting here, Finegan tries to prove that the system of dating presented in the book of Ezekiel is both understandable and historical, when allowed its obvious source in the recognition of the deported Jehoiachin as the legitimate king.

It may well happen that if this track is followed still further, the study of the book of Ezekiel will again take a direction determined more decisively than hitherto by the statements of the book itself. For the present, however, those scholars who whittle down most severely the part Ezekiel himself played in the formation of his book, are still in possession of most of the field, with their supposition of either an actual, or a fictitious, double scene of activity. G. R. Berry, 'The Composition of the Book of Ezekiel' (*J.B.L.* lviii, 1939, pp. 163–75), ascribes a substantial kernel of the book to Ezekiel, who was active in or near Jerusalem between 597 and 586 B.C., and supposes an amplification of this original plan by a later editor to bring in promises for the chosen people, and threats against foreign nations, and then a revision of the whole in the third century B.C. with the addition of chapters xl–xlviii and other passages which locate the prophet amongst the exilic community. W. A. Irwin, *The Problem of Ezekiel*, 1943, seeks to solve the riddle of the book of Ezekiel by means of the supposition that the Ezekiel who worked in Jerusalem until 586 B.C. and was then probably exiled to Babylon and who was a man of healthy mind, composed only certain poetic passages amounting to about one-fifth of the present book; later commentators, editors, and glossators have enlarged this original nucleus. This editing and enlargement of the Ezekelian nucleus in numerous stages has many similarities, according to Irwin, with the process which R. E. Wolfe, 'The Editing of the Book of the Twelve' (Z.*A.W.* liii, 1935, pp. 90–129), thought he could demonstrate in the case of the Minor Prophets, namely, that there, also, editing in a number of clearly distinguishable stages has taken place. N. Messel, *Ezechielfragen*, 1945, makes Ezekiel active towards the end of the fifth century B.C. in Jerusalem among the Gola returned from the Babylonian exile, and ascribes to him the body of chapters i–xxiv and xl–xlviii; while xxv–xxxii are attributed to the redactor. About 350 B.C.—so Messel believes—a redactor collected the genuine sayings of Ezekiel, edited and augmented them, and in so doing preserved and further developed the background of Babylonian exile—a time and place that had been invented by Ezekiel himself.

These two problems characterized above come into view again in A. van den Born, *De historische situatie van Ezechiels prophetie*, 1947, and in H. Wheeler Robinson, *Two Hebrew Prophets*, 1948, pp. 63–125, 'The Visions of Ezekiel'; but here they are in a form which keeps much closer to the content of the book as preserved than is the case in the works of Berry, Irwin, and Messel. According to van den Born, Ezekiel was active in Jerusalem until 586 B.C. and then in Babylon. The hands of redactors have certainly left their traces in the book which bears his name, yet they are only slight. The main part of the book comes from Ezekiel, but some transpositions must be made. The Call Vision in chapter i originally stood before chapter xxxiii, and is therefore intended quite clearly to begin the Babylonian period of the author's ministry. Wheeler Robinson, too, accepts a ministry of Ezekiel divided between two fields ; down to 586 B.C. he puts him in Jerusalem, from then on in Babylon. This means that the first half of the book of Ezekiel is the record of his Jerusalem ministry and the second records his activity in the exile. Accepting this interpretation of events, as Robinson remarks, 'we have no need to raise difficult psychical theories as to Ezekiel's telepathy and clairvoyance' (p. 78) in order to explain the fact that the prophet, who is supposedly living in exile, occupies himself almost exclusively in the narratives and sayings preserved in i–xxiv with Jerusalem and Judah. At the same time, we must reckon with secondary additions to what actually goes back to Ezekiel himself.

It seems significant that to avoid 'difficult psychical theories' Robinson prefers the view that Ezekiel first worked in Jerusalem, and that the main part of the material in chapters i–xxiv contains the record of his ministry there, rather than the picture plainly drawn in the tradition that he participated in the events in Judah and Jerusalem from Babylon. Consequently the question may well be asked whether Robinson has not given in too easily to the great difficulty actually lying in the tradition. May not Widengren be nearer the mark when, as we saw above (pp. 143 f.), he seeks to explain on psychological lines what is at any rate the traditional fact, that Ezekiel did live in exile in the body, but in spirit as good as remained in Judah and Jerusalem? Much the same could be said of Messel's book. Messel does not start out actually, in his book, from literary observations occasioned by the book of Ezekiel, but from an historical inquiry—the question what historical situation will most exactly correspond to what Ezekiel himself tells us and what is put in his mouth. From this he comes to the conclusion that only the situation which existed in Judah around 400 B.C. can be considered. But it is as true of the book of Ezekiel as of the whole of the Old Testament, that in its interpretation the second step must not be taken before the first. The literary questions must be settled first as such, and only after their solution can we form an historical reconstruction; not contrariwise, so that the literary points are elaborated only after shaping the historical picture—which, in such circumstances, is one simply drawn out of the air.[1]

V. SUMMARY AND CONCLUSION

If we take one more glimpse at what has been suggested in the foregoing pages as significant in the modern study of Israelite prophetism, we come to this conclusion: the setting of the prophets, including the writing prophets, in cult associations goes along with a general trend of present-day study of the Old Testament. Owing to the wealth of monuments and documents of every sort regained during the last half-century from the Near East and Egypt, the figures and happenings recorded in the Old Testament may now be viewed in a much more vivid and clear prospect than was open to the preceding generation. That this new way of thinking has taken in the great prophets too, is something which we may welcome. For beyond doubt it has served to give us a better understanding of several of their traits, and we may with certainty expect that the evaluation of the passages in the eighteenth century B.C. Mari texts dealing with 'prophets' will considerably further and strengthen our understanding of Old Testament prophetism. In this connexion, we may refer to the beginning already made by F. M. Th. de Liagre Böhl, 'Voorloopers der profeten sedert 1700 v. Chr.', *Ned.T.T.* iv, 1949–50, pp. 81–91; A. Lods, 'Une Tablette inédite de Mari, intéressante pour l'histoire ancienne du prophétisme sémitique', *Studies in Old Testament Prophecy*, ed. by H. H. Rowley, 1950, pp. 103–10; and M. Noth, 'History and the Word of God in the Old Testament', *B.J.R.L.* xxxii, 2, 1950, pp. 194–206.[2] On the

---

[1] [On Ezekiel cf. now C. G. Howie, *The Date and Composition of Ezekiel*, 1950, where conservative positions are defended, and a ministry exercised wholly in Babylonia is attributed to the prophet. H. H. R.]

[2] See now also W. von Soden, 'Verkündung des Gotteswillens durch prophetisches Wort in den altbabylonischen Briefen aus Mâri', in *Die Welt des Orients*, i, 1950, pp. 397–403.

other hand, as has been shown by one or two scholars, the new point of view has taken much too much upon itself, in regarding all the prophets without exception as cult prophets, and explaining as many as possible of their sayings and acts accordingly. Such exaggeration is doubly dangerous where recourse is had to methods which depend on general ancient oriental cult-myth 'patterns'. Lindblom's solemn warning against pursuing this false path farther, which was expressed in his contribution to the Bertholet Festschrift already referred to (see p. 137), has been only too fully justified. And in the same way, the remarks of Erik Sjöberg in his article 'De förexiliska profeternas förkunnelse' (*S.E.Å.* xiv, 1949, pp. 7–42) deserve the most careful attention. He points out (pp. 15 ff.) that in referring to the Ugaritic *nḳd* as the title of some member of the cultic personnel in connexion with the *nōḳēd* of Am. i. 1, we can at most show the possibility of a similar interpretation, but in no wise prove that Amos belonged to a cultic band.

By these new lines of approach we have clarified and filled in the details of our picture of the origin and transmission of the prophetic books to a much greater extent than before. For it is certainly to be counted a gain to have brought about a consideration of the possibility that the circles of disciples that gathered round the prophet and continued to exist after his death, and which may be thought of at least partially as a cultic association, not only had a decisive part in the creation of the basic editions of the prophetic books, but of later editions too, which were probably put together out of smaller collections, and in which the basic material was adapted to current circumstances. No doubt, too, with the best intentions, extraneous matter was brought into the book that bore the master's name during the process. Oral transmission undoubtedly played a great part in this process, but it is as certain that from an early period, fixed written forms were usual, and that the prophets that gave their names to our books themselves began the writing down of their own sayings, and that this may apply to many more sayings than is generally agreed today. The view that right down into post-exilic times only oral transmission need seriously be considered is certainly to be rejected, as also that our prophetic books were only then written down, after the hitherto exclusively oral tradition had petrified. In this connexion, Mowinckel, Widengren, and Lindblom in their above-mentioned publications (pp. 130, 137, 139) are right when they point out that the name 'literary criticism' to many is like a red rag to a bull, and that in their antipathy to it, some scholars are led on to assertions of which it may be said that the sooner they are forgotten the better. In short, like all literature—since they are such—the prophetic books must needs be examined along literary-critical lines, but—and this has not always happened—this literary criticism must bear in mind its own limits. It may be reckoned to the credit of the traditio-historical school that they have reminded us once more of these limits.

With regard to the psychology of the prophets, opinions still differ widely whether, and in what degree, supranormal—or to give the usual adjective, 'ecstatic'—qualities, experiences, and acts are to be thought of. Yet all are at one in the view that the religious and ethical value of these figures does not depend on the answer given to this question, but that they have an enduring meaning for mankind in any case, and that there lies their true significance. The clearer it is seen and admitted that the affirmation of the prophets' claim to be the messengers of the living God can neither be propped up nor overthrown by our accepting or denying certain particular mental capacities, the fewer fetters will hinder study of their mysterious experiences, and the more confidently may we hope that the future will advance our studies in this field yet another step.[1]   O. EISSFELDT

BIBLIOGRAPHY

(Works mentioned in the body of the essay are not listed here)

BÖHL, F. M. Th. de Liagre. 'De substituut-koning en de lijdende Knecht des Heren' (*Ned.T.T.* iv, 1949–50, pp. 161–76).

VAN DEN BORN, A. *De symbolische Handelingen der Oud-Testamentische Profeten*, 1935.

[1] This chapter has been translated from the German text of Professor Eissfeldt by Mr. D. R. Ap-Thomas, of Bangor.

BROCKINGTON, L. H. ' "The Lord shewed me": the Correlation of Natural and Spiritual in Prophetic Experience' (*Studies in History and Religion* [H. Wheeler Robinson Festschrift], ed. by E. A. Payne, 1942, pp. 30–43).

EISSFELDT, O. 'Das Berufungsbewusstsein der Propheten als theologisches Gegenwartsproblem' (*T.S.K.* cvi, 1934, pp. 124–56).

GRAHAM, W. C. *The Prophets and Israel's Culture*, 1934.

GUILLAUME, A. *Prophecy and Divination among the Hebrews and other Semites*, 1938.

HÄNEL, J. *Das Erkennen Gottes bei den Schriftpropheten*, 1923.

HÄUSSERMANN, Fr. *Wortempfang und Symbol in der alttestamentlichen Prophetie*, 1932.

HEMPEL, J. *Worte der Propheten in neuer Übertragung und mit Erläuterungen*, 1949.

HERTZBERG, H. W. *Prophet und Gott: eine Studie zur Religiosität des vorexilischen Prophetentums*, 1923.

HUMBERT, P. 'Les Prophètes d'Israël ou les Tragiques de la Bible' (*R.Th.Ph.*, N.S. xxiv, 1936, pp. 209–51).

HYATT, J. P. *Prophetic Religion*, 1947.

JACOBI, W. *Die Extase der alttestamentlichen Propheten*, 1923.

LINDHAGEN, C. *The Servant Motif in the Old Testament: a Preliminary Study to the 'Ebed-Yahweh-Problem' in Deutero-Isaiah*, 1950.

LODS, Ad. 'Recherches récentes sur le prophétisme israélite' (*R.H.R.* civ, 1931, pp. 279–316).

LOFTHOUSE, W. F. "Thus hath Jahveh said" (*A.J.S.L.* xl, 1924, pp. 231–51).

MICKLEM, N. *Prophecy and Eschatology*, 1926.

PEAKE, A. S. *The Servant of Yahweh and Other Lectures*, 1931.

PORTEOUS, N. W. 'Prophet and Priest in Israel' (*E.T.* lxii, 1950–1, pp. 4–9).

PUUKKO, A. F. 'Ekstatische Propheten mit besonderer Berücksichtigung der finnisch-ugrischen Parallelen' (*Z.A.W.* liii, 1935, pp. 35–54).

SCOTT, R. B. Y. *The Relevance of the Prophets*, 1944.

SISTER, M. 'Die Typen der prophetischen Visionen in der Bibel' (*M.G.W.J.* lxxviii, 1934, pp. 399–430).

SMITH, J. M. P. *The Prophets and Their Times* (1925), revised by W. A. Irwin, 1941.

VOLZ, P. *Prophetengestalten des Alten Testaments: Sendung und Botschaft der alttestamentlichen Gotteszeugen*, 1938.

VI

THE PSALMS[1]

I

IN so far as the study of the Psalter has made any progress
during the generation which has passed since the foundation
of the Society for Old Testament Study, it is largely due to
the influence of one man—Hermann Gunkel. Accordingly any
satisfactory understanding of the developments which have taken
place during the period under review must be based upon a survey
of the conclusions which he reached. At the same time it must
be borne in mind that his work on the psalms is no isolated
phenomenon so far as the religious literature of ancient Israel
is concerned; for his treatment of the Psalter, like his famous
commentary on Genesis,[2] may be regarded as no more than an
outstanding example of what has proved to be an epoch-making
approach to the study of the Old Testament as a whole.[3] In
making this approach he maintained that in the ancient world
the power of custom was much greater than it is today, and
that this was particularly true of religious literature, for religious
faith and practice are notoriously conservative. Accordingly he
held that the personal contributions of individuals to the religious
literature of ancient Israel can only be rightly understood against
the more conventional background furnished by an examination
of the different 'categories' or 'types' (Gattungen) which it presents and, what is more, the recognition in each case of the
general 'situation in life' (Sitz im Leben) which brought it into

[1] An asterisk prefixed to the title of any work indicates that this is one to which the
writer has not had access.

[2] Genesis, H.K., 3rd ed. rev., 1910.

[3] See esp. 'Die Israelitische Literatur', in Die Kultur der Gegenwart, ed. P. Hinne-
berg, i, 7, 1906, pp. 51–102 (2nd ed. rev., 1925): also 'Die Grundprobleme der
israelitischen Literaturgeschichte', *D.L.Z., xxvii, 1906, cols. 1797–1800, 1861–6,
reprinted in Reden und Aufsätze, 1913, pp. 29–38, E.Tr. by A. K. Dallas in What
Remains of the Old Testament and Other Essays, 1928, pp. 57–68; and the articles
'Bibelwissenschaft: I.C. Literaturgeschichte Israels', R.G.G.[1], i, 1909, and 'Literaturgeschichte, biblische', R.G.G.[2], iii, 1929.

existence and indeed kept it in being. That is to say, if one would write a history of Israel's religious literature, it must begin as a history of its forms (*Formgeschichte*); and, what is equally important, these must be studied in the light of the similar material which has come down to us from the early civilizations of Mesopotamia and Egypt. In this way and with the aid of a sympathetic imagination Gunkel sought to share the religious experiences of this ancient people and to recapture as a still living issue the faith of which this literature is, in many respects, so stirring an expression; and in his work upon the Psalter he made a contribution to this end which cannot fail to exert a direct influence upon its study for many years to come.

His conclusions in this field are presented for the most part in an attractive little volume, *Ausgewählte Psalmen*,[1] his article 'Psalmen' in *Die Religion in Geschichte und Gegenwart*,[2] and, finally, his elaborate commentary *Die Psalmen*[3] and its companion volume, carried to completion after his death by his pupil J. Begrich, *Einleitung in die Psalmen*.[4] From the first he insisted that the Psalter, as a collection of religious lyrics, must be studied within the context offered by the existence of other literary compositions of the same general pattern not only in Israel and Judaism but also in the earlier or contemporary cultures of Mesopotamia and Egypt. The narrative portions of the Old Testament, for example, have preserved several outstanding examples of just such religious lyrics in the Song of the Red Sea (*or* of Miriam),[5] the Song of Moses,[6] the Prayer of Hannah,[7] the

[1] 1904, 4th ed. rev., 1917.

[2] iv. 1913, cols. 1927–49, 2nd ed. rev., 1930, cols. 1609–27.

[3] H.K., 1926.

[4] 1933. For a fairly comprehensive list of Gunkel's shorter studies in the Psalter and allied subjects, see *Einleitung in die Psalmen*, pp. 20 f. Three of these will be found in an English translation in *What Remains of the Old Testament*, i.e. 'Fundamental Problems of Hebrew Literary History', pp. 57–68 (as referred to above, p. 162, n. 3), 'The Religion of the Psalms', pp. 69–114, and 'The Close of Micah: A Prophetical Liturgy', pp. 115–49. See also 'The Poetry of the Psalms: Its Literary History and its application to the Dating of the Psalms', in *Old Testament Essays*, with a Foreword by D. C. Simpson, 1927, pp. 118–42.

[5] Exod. xv. 1–18, 21.

[6] Deut. xxxii. 1–43.

[7] 1 Sam. ii. 1–10.

Psalm of Hezekiah[1] and the Prayer of Jonah,[2] all of which are somewhat different in type from, say, the Song of Deborah[3] or, more clearly, David's dirge over Saul and Jonathan.[4] Similarly, the utterances of the canonical prophets are often couched in poetical forms which, even on a cursory reading, are reminiscent of corresponding features in the Psalter. Their exultant predictions of Yahweh's coming intervention in power to deliver His people from their afflictions occasionally share the hymnal qualities which are to be found in many of the psalms;[5] and much the same may be said of the expression which they sometimes give to a deep and widespread longing for such deliverance, for these passages, too, have features in common with several psalms which echo the sound of public lamentation and express a like concern for the well-being of the nation.[6] Even more striking in this connexion are the haunting poems in which Jeremiah pours out his grief; for their plaintive terms have very close parallels in the intimate revelations of some of the more personal psalms.[7] Moreover, so far as the Palestinian Canon is concerned, similar compositions of both a private and a public kind are clearly to be found in Lamentations, a book which was for so long ascribed to Jeremiah, while a number of passages, whose lyrical qualities may be felt even in translation, are scattered throughout the additional sections of the Alexandrian Canon, for example in the psalm of Judith,[8] and in the corresponding parts of Baruch,[9] Ecclesiasticus[10] and 1 Maccabees.[11] Similarly, in the extra-canonical literature account must at least be taken of the collection of hymns known as the Psalms of Solomon.[12] Moreover, it may now

---

[1] Isa. xxxviii. 10–20.
[2] Jonah ii. 3–10 (EVV. 2–9).
[3] Judges v.
[4] 2 Sam. i. 19–27.
[5] Cf., for example, Isa. xii. 1 f., 3–6, xxv. 1–5, 9, xxvi. 1 ff., xlii. 10–12, lii. 9 f.; Mic. vii. 18–20: and see below, p. 166.
[6] Cf., for example, Isa. lix. 9 ff., lxiii. 11–lxiv. 11; Jer. iii. 22 *b*–25, x. 19–21, 23–5, xiv. (2–6), 7–9, 19–22: and see below, pp. 166 f.
[7] Cf., for example, Jer. xi. 18 ff., xii. 1 ff., xv. 15 ff., xvii. 12 ff., xviii. 18 ff., xx. 7 ff.: and see below, pp. 168 ff.
[8] xvi. 2–17.
[9] iii. 9–v. 9.
[10] i.e. for the most part in xlii. 15–li. 30.
[11] e.g. i. 25–8, 36–40, ii. 7–13.
[12] See now with regard to this later literature H. L. Jansen, *Die spätjüdische Psalmendichtung, ihr Entstehungskreis und ihr 'Sitz im Leben'* (Videnskapsselskapets Skrifter II. Hist.-Filos. Klasse 1937, No. 3), 1937.

prove necessary to add to these the small group of hymns which has come to light among the Dead Sea Scrolls, although the question of their date remains highly controversial and in any case they do not appear to be of any great literary merit.[1] As for the comparative material from the ancient Near East, Gunkel had no hesitation in claiming that the recovery of such data from the early civilizations of Babylonia and Egypt was the most important occurrence of the whole of the nineteenth century so far as the study of the Psalter is concerned, and he early expressed surprise that hitherto so little use had been made of these texts by Old Testament scholars both in the preparation of their commentaries and in the publication of special studies in the psalms.[2] Something of the change in attitude which has since been manifested by students of the Psalter may be gauged by noting the rapidity with which similar material, provided by the Canaanite religious texts from Ras Shamra (Ugarit), has already been used successfully to illumine its contents from the standpoint of language, form, and thought.[3]

With a view to introducing some sort of order into the study of these literary remains, which are not only varied in character but are spread in origin over so many centuries, Gunkel broke with what we may call the more personal approach to the study of the Psalter, and, following the example of Linnaeus in the botanical realm,[4] sought as a first step to classify the psalms according to their types (*Gattungen*) and then, only secondarily and on the basis of this, to deal with the question of their authorship and date. This is not to say that there had not been an earlier awareness of the existence of these types; but we now have a deliberate attempt to study them in a systematic way on the basis of a certain recognizable uniformity of style. As already indicated, the principle governing his approach is that of discovering for each psalm its 'setting in life' (*Sitz im Leben*), i.e. the kind of situation for which each was composed or the sort

---

[1] See E. L. Sukenik, מגילות גנוזות i, 1948, pp. 29–33, ii, 1950, pp. 32–49.

[2] *R.G.G.*[1] iv, col. 1929 : cf. *Ausgewählte Psalmen*[4], p. vii.

[3] See below, pp. 188 f.

[4] *R.G.G.*[1] iv, col. 1930 : cf. S. Mowinckel, *Kongesalmerne i det Gamle Testaments*, 1916, pp. 4 f.

of occasion on which each was used. Operating from this standpoint Gunkel ultimately distinguished five main classes or types,
all cultic in origin and each having features which are duly noted
as reappearing in the wider context of Israel's religious literature
as a whole, so that the reader is continually confronted with
the important question of interrelationship and mutual dependence.[1]

The first of these five main types is the 'Hymn' (*Hymnus*),[2]
which was originally intended for use either chorally or as a solo
in connexion with the normal round of worship,[3] although in
the course of time it was freed in part from its cultic associations
and might be composed simply as a means of expressing the
author's own personal adoration and devotion. The examples
which fall completely within this category (i.e. as distinct from
those in other categories which merely contain hymnal elements
or features) are Pss. viii, xix, xxix, xxxiii, lxv, lxviii, xcvi, xcviii,
c, ciii, civ, cv, cxi, cxiii, cxiv, cxv, cxvii, cxxxv, cxxxvi, cxlv,
cxlvi, cxlvii, cxlviii, cxlix, and cl. To these Gunkel added (*a*)
Pss. xlvi, xlviii, lxxvi, and lxxxvii, which have sufficient in common to be classified as 'Songs of Zion' (*Zionslieder*); (*b*) Pss. xlvii,
xciii, xcvii, xcix and, annexed to these, Pss. xcvi. 10ff. and xcviii
(already included in the main group), all of which are classed
as 'Enthronement Songs' (*Thronbesteigungslieder*), because they
appear to have been composed in celebration of the enthronement of Yahweh as the universal King, and, as such,
form a special eschatological type of hymn which, like a
number of others, reveals the influence of the canonical prophets; and (*c*) the Song of the Red Sea and the so-called Prayer
of Hannah.[4]

The second of the five main types is the class which Gunkel
finally described as 'Communal Laments' (*Klagelieder des*

---

[1] The references in the following pages are confined for the most part to Gunkel's
article in *R.G.G.*[1,2] and his *Einleitung in die Psalmen*; but it should be noted that his
findings were already established along more or less permanent lines in the first
edition of *Ausgewählte Psalmen*.

[2] *R.G.G.*[1,2] iv, 'Psalmen' 3, 12; *Einleitung*, §§ 2, 3.

[3] Cf. Amos v. 21 ff.

[4] See also *Ausgewählte Psalmen*[4], pp. 204–9.

Volkes);[1] and its setting is furnished by the occurrence of some calamity which threatens the well-being of society as a whole and is not peculiar therefore to any one individual, for example the menace of famine or the perils of foreign invasion. On such occasions it was evidently the practice to assemble, if possible in the sanctuary, and with a spectacular display of grief such as the donning of sackcloth and ashes, loud wailing and beating of the breast, the self-discipline of fasting and the offering of sacrifice, to plead with Yahweh for deliverance from this dangerous threat to the communal life.[2] Within the Psalter, Gunkel found, this type with its deep emotional content is represented by Pss. xliv, lxxiv, lxxix, lxxx, lxxxiii, and, in somewhat freer fashion, Pss. lviii, cvi, and cxxv, although here again a number of psalms which are included in other categories contain elements or features of a corresponding kind.

It is a measure of the growing recognition of the importance to be attached to the next class to be considered, i.e. the so-called 'Royal Psalms' (*Königspsalmen*), that they were ultimately advanced by Gunkel from their original position among the lesser groups of psalms to a prominent place as one of his five main classes.[3] In thus assigning Pss. ii, xviii, xx, xxi, xlv, lxxii, ci, cx, and cxxxii to a special category of this kind,[4] Gunkel emphasized as their distinguishing feature the fact that they deal with a king who must be regarded as a native Israelite monarch of the pre-exilic period. As he pointed out, there is evidence enough elsewhere in the Old Testament to show that in ancient Israel the reigning monarch was regarded as standing in a peculiarly intimate relationship to Yahweh and, accordingly, playing a leading

---

[1] *R.G.G.*[1,2] iv, 'Psalmen' 4, 13; *Einleitung*, § 4.

[2] Cf. Joshua vii. 6; Judges xx. 23, 26 ff., xxi. 2 ff.; 1 Sam. vii. 6; 1 Kings viii. 33–6, 44 ff.; 2 Chron. xx. 3 ff.; Ezra viii. 21; Neh. ix. 1 ff.; Esther iv. 3, 16; Isa. xxii. 12, xxxii. 11 f., lviii. 3 ff.; Jer. ii. 27, iii. 21–5, iv. 8, vi. 26, xiv. 2, 12, xxxvi. 6 f., 9; Hos. vii. 14; Joel i. 1–ii. 27; Zech. vii. 1–7 : also Isa. xvi. 6–12; Jonah iii. 5 ff.

[3] *R.G.G.*[1,2] iv, 'Psalmen', 9; *Einleitung*, § 5. There is also a more popular treatment of the subject in *'Die Königspsalmen', Pr.J.B.*, clviii, 1914, pp. 42–68.

[4] Add Ps. cxliv. 1–11 from the category referred to below, p. 180.; also 2 Sam. xxiii. 1–7. Note, too, that, in so far as these psalms form a separate class, they do so in a different way from that of the other literary types which Gunkel recognized, for most of them may also be distributed amongst these other groups.

part in Israelite worship;[1] and, this being the case, it is but
reasonable that outstanding events in the life of such a reigning
monarch, whether actually attested or only conceivable, should
be borne in mind as a possible setting for psalms which are clearly
concerned with a royal figure. What is more, this is made all the
more likely by the fact that in both the Assyro-Babylonian and
the Egyptian fields archaeological investigation has brought to
light numerous examples of religious or cultic texts which were
obviously used in just such a connexion. Accordingly Gunkel
assigned the psalms in this category to the following occasions in
the pre-exilic period: the anniversary of the founding of the
Davidic dynasty and its royal sanctuary on Mount Zion (Ps.
cxxxii), a king's enthronement (Pss. ii, ci, cx) or some such
anniversary (Pss. xxi, lxxii), a royal wedding (Ps. xlv), the fateful
period just prior to the king's departure for the battlefield (Ps.
xx),[2] and, finally, the celebration of his victorious return (Ps.
xviii). This is not to say that such an interpretation was not
already current when Gunkel began his work upon the Psalter;
but on the whole his treatment certainly represents a vigorous
and healthy reaction against the tendency, which had been much
to the fore during the latter half of the nineteenth century, to
date these psalms, like most of the psalms in fact, to the post-
exilic period and to see in the kingly figure which they portray
one of the Maccabaean princes[3] or a foreign but friendly ruler[4]
or, indeed, in some cases a personification of the people of Israel.[5]

The last two out of the five main types of psalm which Gunkel
distinguished are somewhat similar in principle to the first two,

[1] Cf., for example, 1 Sam. xxvi. 11; 2 Sam. vi. 12–19, xxiv. 18–25; 1 Kings iii. 4,
viii; 2 Chron. xiv. 8 ff. (EVV. 9 ff.), xx. 1–30: and see further, in addition to the
works cited above, p. 167, n. 3, *R.G.G.*[1] iii, 1912. 'Königtum in Israel' 3.

[2] Similarly, Ps. cxliv. 1–11.

[3] e.g. J. Olshausen, *Die Psalmen*, K.e.H., 1853, on Pss. cx, cxxxii, cxliv; F. Hitzig,
Die Psalmen, 1863, on Pss. ii, ci, cx, cxxxii, cxliv. 1–11; J. Wellhausen, *The Book of
Psalms*, S.B.O.N.T., 1898, on Pss. ci, cx; B.Duhm, *Die Psalmen*, K.H.C., 2nd ed.
rev., 1922, on Pss. ii, xviii, xx, xxi, xlv, lxxii, ci, cx, cxxxii, cxliv; E. Kautzsch and
A. Bertholet, *H.S.A.T.*, 4th ed. rev., 1922–3, on Pss. ii, xviii, xx, xxi, lxxii, ci, cx.

[4] e.g. Olshausen, Hitzig, and Wellhausen on Ps. lxxii, Kautzsch-Bertholet on
Ps. xlv.

[5] e.g. F. Baethgen, *Die Psalmen*, H.K., 2nd ed. rev., 1897 (*3rd ed., 1904), on
Pss. ci, cxliv; and Wellhausen on Pss. ii, cxxxii.

namely, the hymns and laments which possess a congregational character; but they differ from these essentially in that they are psalms which appear to have been, in origin at least, the immediate concern of individual worshippers rather than the congregation as a whole. In making this broad distinction Gunkel agreed with E. Balla[1] in decisively rejecting the view, which had secured considerable acceptance through the work of R. Smend,[2] that the 'I' who speaks in so many of the psalms is not an individual but a personification of the community. In fact, he was prepared to admit such personification only where the psalmist is quite explicit on the point.[3] Accordingly his fourth main type is the 'Individual Lament' (*Klagelied des Einzelnen*),[4] and it is comparatively numerous in that it embraces Pss. iii, v, vi, vii, xiii, xvii, xxii, xxv, xxvi, xxvii.7–14, xxviii, xxxi, xxxv, xxxviii, xxxix, xlii–xliii, li, liv, lv, lvi, lvii, lix, lxi, lxiii, lxiv, lxix, lxx, lxxi, lxxxvi, lxxxviii, cii, cix, cxx, cxxx, cxl, cxli, cxlii, and cxliii. Indeed, this type may be said to form the backbone of the Psalter, the more so that, in addition to the somewhat freer example in Ps. lii, Gunkel recognized elements of the same kind in the psalms which he placed in other categories. In making this classification Gunkel noted that the psalms in question have a common theme which is characterized by the same or similar modes of expression and intensity of feeling, the worshipper obviously being in some form of distress and frequently bewailing the enemy or enemies by whom he is continually persecuted or slandered. While Gunkel listed a number of features which he regarded as normative for this class, there is one which, although not without parallels in the communal laments and the so-called 'Prophetic Liturgies' of which these sometimes form a part,[5] is particularly common in the psalms of this type and is so important as to require special mention, i.e. that which is known as 'The

---

[1] *Das Ich der Psalmen*, F.R.L.A.N.T. xvi, 1912.

[2] 'Über das Ich der Psalmen', *Z.A.W.* viii, 1888, pp. 49–147.

[3] Cf. Ps. cxxix. 1. In *R.G.G.*[2] iv, col. 1615, and in *Einleitung* § 6, 3 Gunkel admits that occasionally the sense may also require it, but he cites only Mic. vii. 7 ff., Isa. xxi. 10, Ps. of Sol. i, and offers no instance from the Psalter.

[4] *R.G.G.*[1,2] iv, 'Psalmen' 7, 15; *Einleitung*, § 6.

[5] See below, pp. 178 ff.

Certainty of a Hearing' (*Die Gewissheit der Erhörung*).[1] It is by
no means always present; and even where it occurs there is occasionally a marked rise and fall in the psalmist's mood, as at one
moment he gives expression to such an assurance only to sink
back awhile into renewed lamentation and supplication before
reaching a final conviction that his prayer will indeed be heard
and accepted.[2] It sometimes happens that the psalm is brought
to a close with no more than a simple expression of such assurance.[3] On the other hand, the transition in mood may be accompanied by another element, described by Gunkel as a 'Vow'
(*Gelübde*),[4] in which the psalmist eagerly anticipates his ultimate
expression of gratitude to Yahweh in words which occasionally
imply the offering of a sacrifice[5] but usually refer only to a song
of thanksgiving, whether actually on the lips or merely in the
heart;[6] and at the same time the theme of such thanksgiving may
even be introduced into the text either in summary fashion or,
occasionally, in an expanded form.[7]

Gunkel also drew particular attention to the description which
the psalmist gives of his sufferings, noting that as a rule it is
expressed in very general terms and highly figurative language,
so that when one seeks to analyse the situation it is usually difficult to determine just what the immediate cause of the psalmist's
trouble may be. In fact, the language points to a wide range of
misfortune from bodily sickness[8] to sheer anguish of thought at

[1] See esp. *Einleitung*, § 6, 23.

[2] Cf. Pss. xxxi, xxxv, lxxi, and lxxxvi.

[3] Pss. iii. 8 f. (EVV. 7 f.), v. 13 (EVV. 12), vi. 9–11 (EVV. 8–10), lv. 24 (EVV.
23), lxiii. 10–12 (EVV. 9–11), cxl. 13 f. (EVV. 12 f.); also xxxvi. 13 (EVV. 12).

[4] See esp. *Einleitung*, § 6, 24.

[5] Pss. xxii. 23 ff. (EVV. 22 ff.), liv. 8 (EVV. 6), lvi. 13 (EVV. 12). Cf. Ps. xxvii.
6, as referred to below in the text in connexion with 'Psalms of Confidence', and
Ps. lxi. 9 (EVV. 8).

[6] Pss. vii. 18 (EVV. 17), xiii. 6 (EVV. 5 f.), xxvi. 12, xxviii. 6 f., xxxi. 8 f. (EVV.
7 f.), xxxv. 9 f., 27 f., xlii. 6 f. (EVV. 5 f.), xliii. 4 f., li. 15–17 (EVV. 13–15),
lvii. 8 f. (EVV. 7 f.), lix. 17 (EVV. 16), lxi. 9 (EVV. 8), lxiii. 5 f. (EVV. 4 f.),
lxix. 31 ff. (EVV. 30 ff.), lxxi. 8, 14–16, 18 ff., lxxxvi. 12 f., cix. 30, cxl. 14 (EVV.
13), cxlii. 8 (EVV. 7): cf., among the royal psalms, xxi. 14 (EVV. 13), cxliv. 9–10.

[7] Pss. xiii. 6 (EVV. 5 f.), xxii. 23 ff. (EVV. 22 ff.), xxviii. 6 f., xxxi. 22 ff.
(EVV. 21 ff.), liv. 8 f. (EVV. 6 f.), lvi. 13 f. (EVV. 12 f.), lix. 17 (EVV. 16), lxix.
31 ff. (EVV. 30 ff.), lxxi. 14–16, 18 ff., lxxxvi. 12 f.: cf., among the royal psalms,
cxliv. 9–10.　　　　　[8] e.g. Pss. vi, xxii, xxviii, xxxviii, lxix, lxxi, lxxxviii, and cii.

one's enforced absence from the familiar haunts and scenes on Mount Zion.[1] In many cases the most striking aspect of the psalm is the expression which it gives to the worshipper's fear of death and his vivid sense of already being engulfed by the waters of the Underworld as he descends captive to the realm of the dead.[2] Moreover, whatever the immediate cause of the psalmist's trouble may be, expression is commonly given to the thought that, if Yahweh Himself is not directly responsible, He has at least permitted it; and as a result the sufferer may be found either confessing his sin[3] or affirming his innocence,[4] and, in any case, pleading with Yahweh in the language of the law-court to manifest the divine justice by delivering the suppliant from his straits or freeing him, as it were, from prison.[5] This figurative language becomes most varied where the sufferer refers to the enemy or enemies with whom he is forced to contend; for, while they are sometimes referred to in simple, straightforward terms as gathering triumphantly about him, whispering and plotting, talking slander and telling lies,[6] the psalmist may feel that he is beset by a body of troops or brigands, armed with sword, bow and arrows,[7]

[1] e.g. Pss. xlii–xliii.

[2] e.g. Pss. xxviii. 1, lxix. 2 f., 15 f. (EVV. 1 f., 14 f.), lxxxviii. 4 ff. (EVV. 3 ff.), cxliii. 7; Jonah ii. 4 ff. (EVV. 3 ff.).

[3] i.e. particularly in Gunkel's so-called 'Psalms *or* Songs of Penitence' (*Busspsalmen, Busslieder*), e.g. Pss. li and cxxx. Cf. *R.G.G.*[1], iv, 'Psalmen' 7, 15 : *Einleitung*, § 6, 21, 26.

[4] i.e. particularly in Gunkel's so-called 'Psalms *or* Songs of Innocence' (*Unschulds-psalmen, Unschuldslieder*), e.g. Pss. v, vii, xvii, and xxvi. Cf. *R.G.G.*[1], loc. cit.; *Ein-leitung*, loc. cit.

[5] e.g. Pss. vii. 5 ff. (EVV. 4 ff.), xvii. 2, xxvi. 1, xxvii. 12, xxxv. 1, 11, xliii. 1, lxxxviii. 9 (EVV. 8), cxli. 8 (EVV. 7).

[6] e.g. Pss. iii. 3 (EVV. 2), v. 9 ff. (EVV. 8 ff.), xiii. 5 (EVV. 4), xvii. 8 ff., xxii. 8 f., 17 ff. (EVV. 7 f., 16 ff.), xxv. 19, xxvii. 11 f., xxviii. 3 ff., xxxi. 12 ff. (EVV. 11 ff.), xxxv. 4, 11 f., 15, 19 ff., 24 ff., xxxviii. 12 f., 17, 20 (EVV. 11 f., 16, 19), xlii. 4, 11 (EVV. 3, 10), lv. 4, 13, 22 (EVV. 3, 12, 21), lxiv. 6 f. (EVV. 5 f.), lxix. 5, 8, 20 ff. (EVV. 4, 7, 19 ff.), lxxi. 10 f., lxxxviii. 9, 19 (EVV. 8, 18), cii. 9 (EVV. 8), cix. 25. Cf., as referred to below in the text s.v. 'Psalms of Confidence', Ps. iv. 3 ff. (EVV. 2 ff.); also Pss. x. 4 ff., xxxvi. 4 f. (EVV. 3 f.), xl. 15 f. (EVV. 14 f.), xli. 6 ff. (EVV. 5 ff.).

[7] e.g. Pss. xvii. 9, xxxv. 10, lv. 19 (EVV. 18), lvi. 2 f., 7 (EVV. 1 f., 6), lvii. 5 (EVV. 4), lix. 4 f., 8 (EVV. 3 f., 7), lxiv. 2 ff. (EVV. 1 ff.), cix. 3, cxx. 7, cxl. 3, 8 (EVV. 2, 7). Cf., as referred to below in the text s.v. 'Psalms of Confidence', Pss. xi. 2, xxvii. 3, lxii. 4 (EVV. 3); also Pss. x. 8 ff., xxxvii. 14.

or that they are hunting him like a wild beast, spreading their nets and digging pits to trap and kill him,[1] or, indeed, that he himself is being attacked by savage beasts who lust for his blood.[2]

This raises the long debated question as to who exactly are the enemies to whom reference is made in this way; and here Gunkel accepted the view that for the most part two interpretations must be admitted. In some cases the psalmist's enemies are self-righteous neighbours and even erstwhile friends who see in his sufferings the clear evidence of retribution for sin.[3] In others, however, the psalmist contrasts himself with his enemies in terms of one who is poor, afflicted, humble, or downtrodden in opposition to those who are rich, powerful, arrogant, and oppressive, the latter taking what they regard as a more realistic view of life and pouring scorn on the simple believer with his acceptance of the foregoing dogma of retribution and its implication that in the ultimate it is only the righteous who prosper.[4] Beyond this Gunkel was not prepared to go; that is to say, he explicitly rejected the attempts which have been made to see in these psalms a reflection of the party strife of post-exilic Judaism;[5] it is a cleavage which may well have occurred during the period of the monarchy.

To understand this type of psalm, Gunkel maintained, we have to bear in mind that in ancient Israel such a misfortune as that of bodily sickness was regarded as having been brought about, directly or indirectly, by Yahweh; so that we must expect to find definite cultic measures for recovering the divine favour and thus securing relief for the sufferer.[6] This inference is also supported by the fact that, as we have seen in discussing the communal laments, such measures were regularly adopted in time of public peril. It is also reinforced to a considerable degree by the fact that the Babylonian religious literature contains many examples of just such lamentations of the individual, which offer

[1] e.g. Pss. vii. 16 (EVV. 15), xxxi. 5 (EVV. 4), xxxv. 7 f., lvii. 7 (EVV. 6), cxl. 6 (EVV. 5). Cf. Ps. ix. 16 (EVV. 15).

[2] e.g. Pss. iii. 8 (EVV. 7), vii. 3 (EVV. 2), xvii. 12, xxii. 13 f., 17 (EVV. 12 f., 16), xxxv. 16 f., 21. Cf., as referred to below in the text s.v. 'Psalms of Confidence', Ps. xxvii. 2; also Pss. x. 9, xxxvii. 12, lviii. 7 (EVV. 6).

[3] Cf. *Einleitung*, pp. 207 f.　　[4] Cf. ibid., pp. 208 ff.　　[5] See below, pp. 197 ff.

[6] Cf. *R.G.G.*[1] iii, 1912, 'Leiden (biblisch)'; *R.G.G.*[2] iii. 1929, 'Leiden: II. Im AT.'

close parallels in general construction and in points of detail to those of the Psalter and are explicitly associated with different forms of penitential ritual. At the same time Gunkel found two major points of difference between the Babylonian penitential psalms and those which have survived from ancient Israel. In the first place the former have an obviously polytheistic background, while the latter show knowledge only of Yahweh; and in the second place the former have a pronounced magical content which is almost totally lacking in the Psalter, although such features are also to be expected in any cultic compositions of this type which may have been in use amongst the Israelites. Accordingly, while Gunkel found echoes of cultic language and practice in some of these psalms, he regarded them on the whole as freed from such a magical or quasi-magical content and, therefore, as more spiritual in quality. That is to say, he regarded them rather as imitations of a cultic prototype; and while he was prepared to admit the possibility that the vagueness of reference to the psalmist's situation is to be traced to the fact that in course of time these psalms were adapted for congregational use, he tended to think that such vagueness was really due to their being based on the models furnished by the cultus. Thus many of them deal with quite other circumstances than those of actual bodily sickness; but the old familiar language appropriate to such a situation is still used in a metaphorical sense, and what was normally a priestly rite of absolution now gives place to the psalmist's own spontaneous expression of confidence in a favourable response.[1] It is true that in course of time he modified his views slightly and admitted evidence of a somewhat closer connexion with the cultus; but, as we shall have occasion to notice more fully in due course, he was led to this in part by other and subsequent research in this field. Finally, before we leave this question of a cultic prototype, we need to note Gunkel's passing remark that the vivid similes from the battlefield, which are sometimes used of the psalmist's enemies, are really a legacy from an age when the psalms of this type came within the category of royal psalms, and that it was only in the course of time that their use was no

---

[1] See also J. Begrich, 'Das priesterliche Heilsorakel', *Z.A.W.* lii, 1934, pp. 81–92.

longer restricted to a king but was extended to ordinary individuals.[1] It should also be noted that Gunkel added as an appendix to this class a small group which he described as 'Psalms of Confidence' (*Vertrauenspsalmen*) and regarded as a development of this type on the ground that here all complaint has disappeared and confidence alone finds expression, i.e. Pss. iv, xi, xvi, xxiii, xxvii. 1–6, lxii and cxxxi.[2]

The last of the five main types of psalm which Gunkel recognized, i.e. the 'Individual Songs of Thanksgiving' (*Danklieder des Einzelnen*), may be regarded as the correlative to that which has just been discussed; in other words, it is 'the obverse of the coin'.[3] So far as the Psalter itself is concerned, there are comparatively few examples of this class, i.e. Ps. xviii, already included in the royal psalms, and Pss. xxx, xxxii, xxxiv, xli, lxvi, xcii, cxvi, cxviii, cxxxviii; but within the Palestinian Canon we also have the Psalm of Hezekiah (Isa. xxxviii.10–20)[4] and the Prayer of Jonah (Jonah ii. 3–10 (EVV.2–9)),[5] both of which must obviously be included in the list. Gunkel again drew attention to similar features in psalms of other categories; but the only class of outstanding importance, other than the royal psalms which we have seen to be represented by Ps. xviii, is that of the foregoing individual laments, in which one often finds that such thanksgiving is either promised or actually introduced in connexion with the feature known as 'The Certainty of a Hearing'.[6] There is also a close connexion between these two classes in the general terms and figurative language used to describe the misfortunes from which the worshipper has been delivered; and here again we have to note the picturesque conception of his deliverance from the waters of the Underworld[7] and the problem raised by the occasional references to the psalmists'

[1] *Einleitung*, p. 200, n. 5 : cf. pp. 147 ff.

[2] *R.G.G.*[1,2] iv, 'Psalmen' 15; *Einleitung*, § 6, 27.

[3] *What Remains of the Old Testament*, p. 111. See in general *R.G.G.*[1,2] iv, 'Psalmen' 6, 14; *Einleitung*, § 7.

[4] Cf. J. Begrich, *Der Psalm des Hiskia*, F.R.L.A.N.T., N.F. xxv, 1926.

[5] See *Ausgewählte Psalmen*,[4] pp. 209–15.

[6] See above, p. 170, nn. 5, 6, 7.

[7] Cf. Pss. xxx. 4, 10 (EVV. 3, 9), cxvi. 3; Isa. xxxviii. 10 f.; Jonah ii. 3–7 (EVV. 2–6); also Pss. ix. 14 (EVV. 13), ciii. 4, cvii. 18.

enemies,[1] which, as one would expect, Gunkel sought to interpret along the lines already mentioned.

From the first Gunkel recognized that this type of psalm had a close connexion with the cultus in more than origin, and he rightly thought in terms of an offering or sacrifice whereby the worshipper made payment of whatever he had vowed to Yahweh in virtue of his being delivered from some misfortune of the kind which we have already discussed in connexion with the individual laments. As is clear from the actual language of several of these poems, the offering or sacrifice was accompanied by a psalm which not only made the thanksgiving more explicit but also gave the worshipper, as he stood by the altar in the presence of fellow-worshippers and guests with the 'cup of salvation'[2] in his hand, an opportunity of bearing witness to Yahweh's readiness and power to save those who call upon His Name;[3] and it is well-known, of course, that the same term *tôdāh* is applicable to both sacrifice and psalm as an expression of 'thanksgiving'. In short, Gunkel recognized that in this case, if not in that of the individual laments, the internal evidence was sufficient to prevent one's thinking merely in terms of a derivative from a cultic prototype.

Nevertheless, while it is true that several of these psalms and the corresponding elements in the individual laments give a clear indication of an accompanying sacrifice, they do not all do so; and, this being the case, it must not be assumed without more ado that the latter also presuppose such a background. In Gunkel's opinion it may well be that the psalm came to be regarded as intrinsically of more value than the sacrifice itself in that it gave clearer expression to the worshipper's mood and, therefore, greater scope for the development of man's spiritual life. In any case, there are several instances in which such ritual is clearly rejected;[4] and here Gunkel followed familiar lines and insisted

[1] e.g. Pss. xxx. 2 (EVV. 1), xcii. 12 (EVV. 11), cxviii. 10–12, 22, cxxxviii. 7; also Ps. ix. 4 (EVV. 3). [2] Cf. Ps. cxvi. 13 f.
[3] Pss. lxvi. 13 ff., cxvi. 17; Jonah ii. 10 (EVV. 9): cf. Ps. cvii. 22. See also p. 170, n. 5.
[4] Cf., in the corresponding elements in the individual laments, Pss. li. 17 f. (EVV. 15 f.), lxix. 31 f. (EVV. 30 f.); also Pss. xl. 7 (EVV. 6) and l. 14, as cited below, p. 180.

that, where this occurs, we must recognize the influence of the canonical prophets from whom the psalmists in question had learnt to renounce sacrifice and to worship God freed from the trappings and trammels of the cultus.

Finally, the example afforded by Ps. xviii and the exaggerated language which is employed elsewhere in these psalms and really appears suitable only in the mouth of a king,[1] taken in conjunction with parallels from the earlier and contemporary cultures of the ancient Near East,[2] were all held by Gunkel to indicate that this type of psalm, like the individual lament, was in origin a royal psalm, and that it was only in the course of time, however early, that its use was extended to others besides the king before it was freed in the way described from its continued association with the cultus.[3]

Of the other categories recognized by Gunkel there are only four which merit serious consideration as being clearly defined types, each with its own distinct representatives amongst the individual compositions of the Psalter. The first is a very small class, and is that which he labelled 'Songs of Pilgrimage' (*Wallfahrtslieder*) on the ground that Pss. lxxxiv and cxxii point to the existence of a type of psalm which was composed for the use of pilgrims to one or another of the annual festivals, and, as such, might be sung by them on their way to the holy city, for example while they were assembling for the road or when they had reached their journey's end.[4] The second group is equally small, for it includes only Pss. lxvii and cxxiv as full examples of the class, which he designated 'Communal Songs of Thanksgiving' (*Danklieder des Volkes*), inasmuch as they appear to be hymns for special rather than regular occasions of thanksgiving, i.e. psalms which express gratitude to Yahweh for some outstanding manifestation of His favour.[5]

---

[1] e.g. Pss. cxviii. 10–12, cxxxviii. 1, 4.

[2] Cf. now, in addition to the examples offered by Gunkel, *Einleitung*, pp. 285–90, the short but important article by H. L. Ginsberg, 'Psalms and Inscriptions of Petition and Acknowledgement', in *Louis Ginzberg Jubilee Volume: English Section*, 1945, pp. 159–71.   [3] *Einleitung*, p. 281, esp. n. 4: cf. pp. 147 ff.

[4] Ibid., § 8, 20–2.

[5] Ibid. 28–39, i.e. s.v. 'Das Danklied Israels'.

The third of these minor types is that of the 'Wisdom Poetry' (*Weisheitsdichtung*), which is a little stronger numerically than either of the preceding and is of special importance in that it needs to be studied in the wider context of the general wisdom-literature of ancient Israel and indeed the whole of the Near East.[1] The total picture is that of a comprehensive literary *genre* which makes its appearance in the form of proverbs, longer poems, and even whole books; but in the nature of the case only the first and second of these may be traced in the Psalter, the simple proverbial type being discovered in Pss. cxxvii and cxxxiii, while the more developed class of poem is represented by Pss. i, xxxvii, xlix, lxxiii, cxii, and cxxviii. Naturally the latter, as a class, are found to yield a wider scope for the individuality of the writer, two outstanding examples being Pss. xxxvii and lxxiii with their differing attempts to stem a rising tide of doubt, whether one's own or another's, concerning the orthodox doctrine of God's requital of the righteous and His punishment of the wicked. Finally, the presence of such works amongst the other, remarkably different literary types of the Psalter, regarded as an anthology from the devotional life of post-exilic Judaism, is explained as being due to their popularity with the laity.

The last clearly defined type to which Gunkel drew attention was regarded by him as a logical development from the antiphonal element in Hebrew psalmody, which is not only attested by a number of passages in the Old Testament[2] but appears to be implied by the presence of a refrain in several psalms which are either cultic in origin or clearly have a cultic background.[3] That is to say, in his opinion it was an extension of this principle which led to the combination of different literary types in such a way as to form a new but complex whole for which he proposed to use the term 'Liturgy' (*Liturgie*).[4] Moreover, apart from the development of such antiphonal elements within a particular type, for example a hymn[5] or the case of a choral introduction

---

[1] *R.G.G.*[1,2] iv, 'Psalmen' 16; *Einleitung*, § 10.

[2] Exod. xv. 20 f.; 1 Chron. xvi. 36; Ezra iii. 11; Neh. xii. 27 ff.; Pss. xix. 3 (EVV. 2), xlii. 8 (EVV. 7), cxv. 9–11, cxviii. 1–4, cxxxv. 19 f.; Isa. vi. 3: also Judith xv. 14.

[3] Pss. viii, xlii–xliii, xlvi, lxvii, lxxx, xcix, cxxxvi.

[4] *R.G.G.*[1,2] iv, 'Psalmen' 16; *Einleitung*, § 11, 8–21. [5] Ps. cxv.

to an individual song of thanksgiving,[1] there were various occasions in the religious life of the community when an opportunity must have occurred for the growth of the dialogue form: for example, the need for priestly direction (*tôrāh*) on a matter of cultic procedure;[2] the desire for some kind of oracular guidance in times of crisis;[3] and the longing for a divine response to prayer at a time of misfortune, i.e. such as might lead in favourable circumstances to the feature known as 'The Certainty of a Hearing'.[4]

From this point of view Gunkel found that Ps. xv appears to be a type of liturgy in which the worshipper attending one of Israel's festivals is given priestly direction, not to say a warning, concerning the personal integrity required of anyone who seeks admission to the sanctuary; and Ps. xxiv seems to presuppose a similar situation on the occasion of what is probably an annual festival, at which the ark is borne in procession up the slopes of Mount Zion to the Temple. Gunkel therefore described these as 'Torah Liturgies' (*Tora-Liturgien*), and, what is more, advanced evidence for the view that imitations of this style, like that of the simpler types under discussion,[5] may even be found in the works of the canonical prophets.[6] Another liturgy of an exceptionally brief but not altogether unrelated character may be found in Ps. cxxxiv, which Gunkel explained as a combination of hymn and priestly blessing appropriate to the close of worship at one of Israel's festivals.

Other psalms which fall within this category have a more obviously oracular element; and as a rule Gunkel attributed this feature either to an individual priest or to a soloist in one of the Temple choirs. He found that the earliest examples of these oracular forms occur among the royal psalms: namely Pss. ii

---

[1] Pss. lxvi and cxviii: cf. Ps. cvii, as cited below, p. 180.

[2] Cf. Hag. ii. 10 ff.; Zech. vii. 1 ff.

[3] Cf. 1 Sam. xxiii. 2, 4, 10 f., 12, xxx, 7 f.; 2 Sam. v. 19, xxi. 1 ff.

[4] See above, pp. 169 f.

[5] Cf. H. Gunkel, 'Die Propheten als Schriftsteller und Dichter', in the introduction to H. Schmidt, *Die grossen Propheten*, S.A.T. ii, 2, 2nd ed. rev., 1923, esp. pp. lvi ff.

[6] Isa. xxxiii. 14–16; Mic. vi. 6–8. Cf. *R.G.G.*[1,2] iv, 'Psalmen' 8; *Einleitung*, § 11, 14. See also 'Jesaia 33, eine prophetische Liturgie', *Z.A.W.* xlii, 1924, pp. 177–208, esp. p. 193.

and cx, which, as we have seen, he assigned to the occasion of a king's enthronement; Ps. cxxxii, which he thought to have been composed for the anniversary of the founding of the Davidic dynasty and the establishment of the royal sanctuary on Mount Zion; and Ps. xx, which obviously reflects an attempt to secure Yahweh's assurance of success prior to a king's departure for the battlefield. The last example has something of a parallel in Ps. cxxi, which Gunkel construed as a dialogue between a suppliant and a priest, regarding it as an instance of the blending of the lament of an individual with an oracular address of the type which is to be found in Ps. xci; but the question appears to have been left open as to whether it was composed for actual use in this way or is no more than an imitation of a cultic prototype. Accordingly the only oracular element of this kind outside the royal psalms which Gunkel was clearly prepared to assign to the pre-exilic period is that which occurs in Ps. lx, i.e. a communal lament, incorporating for its steadying influence an earlier oracle on the nation's ultimate triumph, which he was inclined to associate as a whole with a flight to Edom following a disastrous defeat at the hands of some enemy from the north. For the rest, Gunkel maintained that the blending of a lament with an oracular response, which is presupposed elsewhere in the Old Testament,[1] and is supported by parallels from both Babylonia and Egypt, was a device which, like other liturgical forms,[2] came to be adopted by the canonical prophets,[3] and that in Pss. xii, lxxv, lxxxv, and cxxvi we have examples of the way in which such 'Prophetic Liturgies' (*Prophetische Liturgien*) ultimately exercised a reverse influence upon genuine cultic productions of a similar kind. Gunkel also held that the influence

---

[1] Cf. Joshua vii. 6 ff.; Judges xx. 23, 27 f.; 2 Kings xix. 14 ff.; 2 Chron. xx. 3 ff.; Jer. xxxvi.

[2] See above, p. 178, nn. 5, 6, also 'Der Micha-Schluss', *Z.S.* ii, 1924, pp. 145–78, E.Tr. in *What Remains of the Old Testament*, pp. 115–49.

[3] Isa. xxvi. 8–14 a, 14 b f.; xxvi. 16–18, 19–21; xxxii. 2, 3–6; xxxiii. 7–9, 10–12; xlix. 14, 15 ff.; xlix. 24, 25 f.; lix. 9–15 b, 15 c–20, lxiii. 7–lxiv. 11 (EVV. 12), lxv; Jer. iii. 22 b–5, iv. 1 f.; xiv. 2–9, 10; xiv. 19–22, xv. 1 f.; xxxi. 18 f., 20; li. 34 f., 36 ff.; Hosea vi. 1–3, 4–6; xiv. 3 f., 5–9 (EVV. 2 f., 4–8); Joel i. 5–ii. 11, ii. 12–14; ii. 15–17, 18–27; Mic. vii. 7–10, 11–13; vii. 14–17, 18–20; Hab. i. 2–4, 5 ff.; i. 12–17, ii. 1 ff.

of the canonical prophets is again to be seen in the blending of hymn and oracle in Pss. lxxxi and xcv, which he explained as introducing in true prophetic style a priestly warning against the danger of overlooking the serious import of Yahweh's claims amid all the glamour and excitement of a public festival; and in Pss. xiv (liii), l, and lxxxii he recognized similar but somewhat freer imitations of the oracular style of the canonical prophets, in which judgement is pronounced respectively upon a corrupt priesthood, a purely formal worship, and the irresponsible behaviour of the gods of the Gentiles.

Finally, Gunkel had to make allowance for the fact that a number of psalms cannot be classified along any of the foregoing lines but represent, rather, a mixture of different types, i.e. what he called 'Mixed Poems' (*Mischungen* or *Mischgedichte*).[1] We have already had occasion to note that, apart from the blending of types which was to be found as the mark of a liturgy, the characteristic features of one type may make their appearance in psalms assigned to another class; and Gunkel explained this as being due to the attempt to enrich one form by drawing upon the distinctive features of another. In such a case, however, the predominance of one type was found to be unmistakable, so that such conscious borrowing was treated as something different from the almost indiscriminate fusion which became possible, when once the majority had been freed from their original connexion with the cultus. Such a mixture of forms might take place, Gunkel thought, either through the adaptation of earlier material as in the case of Pss. xl, lxxxix, xc, cvii, cviii, and cxliv and the possible examples of Pss. xxxvi and lxxvii, or through free composition as in the case of Pss. ix–x, lxxviii (cf. Deut. xxxii.1–43), xciv, cxix, cxxiii, cxxix, cxxxvii, and cxxxix.

Despite a certain arbitrariness in the delineation of the subsidiary types and the assignment of some of the psalms to the different classes, there should be no question about the value of this approach. As the following pages will show, it has already brought increased life to the study of the Psalter, which is now one of the most fascinating fields of research for students of the

---

[1] *R.G.G.*[1,2] iv, 'Psalmen' 16; *Einleitung*, § 11, 1–7.

Old Testament. On the other hand, Gunkel's attempt to trace the inner history of these types must be regarded as much more arbitrary, and it need not detain us long in view of the generally unsettled condition of Old Testament studies which this volume cannot fail to make clear. In short, when he seeks to distinguish a development from short and simple forms to longer and more complex styles, and when he thinks to trace in the thought of the psalms the influence of the great canonical prophets and the emergence of a more spiritual kind of faith, one cannot but feel that he is still under the spell of a school of thought whose attempted reconstruction of the history of Israel's religion in terms of a simple unilinear development is proving more and more untenable. Accordingly, so far as his dating of the Psalter is concerned, it will suffice to note that, with the obvious exception of the royal psalms and those which were thought to contain allusions to a reigning king,[1] he assigned its contents, for the most part, to the sixth and fifth centuries B.C.[2] Finally, it remains to be said that even Gunkel's most ardent admirer can hardly acquit him of a supreme manifestation of arbitrariness in his attempted emendations of the text, which are on such a scale that they would have made the work of a lesser man appear almost ridiculous.

II

All the more important introductions to the literature of the Old Testament which were published for the first time during the period under review already bear marks of Gunkel's influence both in their general approach to the subject and in their treatment of the Psalter. This is particularly true of the works by J. Hempel,[3] O. Eissfeldt,[4] A. Weiser,[5] A. Bentzen,[6] and

[1] i.e. Pss. xxviii, lxi, lxiii, lxxxiv, and lxxxix. 2, 3, 6–19 (EVV. 1, 2, 5–18); but with regard to these psalms see also p. 195, n. 4.   [2] *R.G.G.*[2] iv, col. 1629.

[3] *Die althebräische Literatur und ihr hellenistisch-jüdisches Nachleben*, in the collection *Handbuch der Literaturwissenschaft*, ed. O. Walzel, 1930, esp. pp. 30–44.

[4] *Einleitung in das Alte Testament*, 1934, esp. pp. 114–37.

[5] *Einleitung in das Alte Testament*, 1939, esp. pp. 22–3, 2nd ed. rev., 1949, pp. 26–36.

[6] *Indledning til det Gamle Testamente*, 1941, esp. pp. 258–71, and, in a revised form, *Introduction to the Old Testament*, i, 1948, ii, 1949, esp. i, pp. 146–67.

I. Engnell;[1] but the influence is also discernible in the joint work of W. O. E. Oesterley and T. H. Robinson[2] and in the massive volumes by R. H. Pfeiffer[3] and A. Lods,[4] although the former of these looks askance at Gunkel's acceptance of a pre-exilic date for even a small proportion of the psalms, and clings resolutely to the view that the royal psalms, with the exception of Ps. xlv, are all post-exilic and in the case of Pss. ii and cx are even so late as the Hasmonaean period. Further, this new approach to the study of the Psalter is the underlying factor in several more or less popular works by A. C. Welch,[5] A. Causse,[6] I. Hylander,[7] F. James,[8] and J. Paterson.[9]

What is more important is the fact that a similar situation is revealed by a glance at the most important commentaries on the Psalter which have been written since Gunkel first advocated the study of these poems from the standpoint of their literary types.[10] To be sure, some Protestant scholars, notably E. König,[11] W. E. Barnes,[12] and B. D. Eerdmans,[13] as well as such representative Roman Catholic scholars as H. Herkenne[14] and J. Calès,[15] have continued to pursue the old atomistic approach, labelling the psalms, if at all, according to their subject-matter and dealing in a purely individual way with any question of date. Moreover,

[1] *Gamla Testamentet. En traditionshistorisk Inledning*, i, 1945, esp. pp. 52–63.

[2] *An Introduction to the Books of the Old Testament*, 1934, pp. 191–4.

[3] *Introduction to the Old Testament*, 1941, 2nd ed. rev., 1948, esp. pp. 629 ff.

[4] *Histoire de la littérature hébraïque et juive*, with a preface by A. Parrot, 1950, esp. pp. 725–41.

[5] *The Psalter in Life, Worship and History*, 1926.

[6] *Les Plus Vieux Chants de la Bible*, E.H.P.R. xiv, 1926, esp. pp. 79–172.

[7] *Gamla Testamentets Psalmbok*, 1937.

[8] *Thirty Psalmists* (with sub-title *A Study in Personalities of the Psalter as seen against the Background of Gunkel's Type-study of the Psalms*), 1938.

[9] *The Praises of Israel* (with sub-title *Studies literary and religious in the Psalms*), 1950.

[10] In the ensuing discussion no reference is made to F. Wutz, *Die Psalmen text-kritisch untersucht*, 1925, which is less a commentary on the psalms than a critical study of the text, and is based upon the highly questionable view that the translators of the LXX worked from a Hebrew text which had been transcribed into Greek letters.

[11] *Die Psalmen*, 1927.

[12] *The Psalms*, W.C., 1931.

[13] *The Hebrew Book of Psalms*, O.T.S. iv, 1947.

[14] *Das Buch der Psalmen*, H.S.A. Tes., 1936.

[15] *Le Livre des psaumes*, 1936.

it is of interest to note that this ranges from a refusal to deny the Mosaic authorship of Ps. xc[1] and a willingness in every case to accept the Davidic authorship of certain psalms to an admission that in Ps. lxxiv we may have one solitary product of the Maccabaean period.[2] Similarly, the liberal Jewish scholar M. Buttenwieser[3] ignored any such classification of the psalms, and offered instead an attempt on the grand scale to treat them in their historical sequence, doing so, for the most part, with an exactness of dating which, as is usual in cases of this kind, fails to carry conviction because of the general terms in which the thought of each psalm tends to be expressed and the fact that history is full of repetition in the lives of both nations and individuals. The result is that the work is mainly of interest here for the view that many of the psalms are pre-exilic and even reach back to the period of the Judges, while none may be dated so late as the Maccabaean age. Nevertheless, while all of these commentaries are of service for the detailed study of the individual psalms, particularly those of Calès and Buttenwieser, one is left with the realization that the full value of the Psalter, not only as an expression of the devotional life of ancient Israel or Judaism but also as a source-book for the study of the religious faith which gave it birth, is insufficiently brought out by the simple adoption of this atomistic approach. In other words these are not the commentaries which are most successful in enabling the reader to live imaginatively in that ancient world and to share in a realistic fashion the living faith which these psalms so clearly reflect.

These must be sought, rather, amongst the works which have obviously been influenced by Gunkel in his attempt to arrive at a common denominator, not merely in terms of the literary types into which the Psalter may broadly be divided, but also in terms of these types in so far as they reflect the different situations in life which through successive generations of believers brought it into being. This is not to say that the works in question all

---

[1] König, Herkenne. [2] König.
[3] *The Psalms* (with sub-title *Chronologically Treated with a New Translation*), 1938.

slavishly follow Gunkel in his attempted classification, but it does mean that in varying degree they have accepted the principle underlying his approach and, what is more, show in most cases a large measure of agreement in the delineation of at least the main types. As is indicated by the general introductions and more popular studies already cited, the acceptance of this point of view has naturally been most rapid in the liberal Protestant circles of Germany and its more immediate neighbours. Within Germany it already appears in the elaborate attempt at such a classification which was made with somewhat too strong a sense of being definitive by W. Staerk[1] and, on more moderate lines, in the deservedly successful commentary of R. Kittel;[2] and in the period under review it dominates the slighter but colourful work by H. Schmidt[3] and, even more so, the sympathetic theological exposition of a selection of the psalms by A. Weiser.[4] Indeed it is now meeting with cautious acceptance in Roman Catholic circles, for it occurs to some degree in the simple, but frankly critical, commentary by F. Nötscher.[5] Outside Germany this point of view governs the detailed and important Danish introduction and commentary by A. Bentzen,[6] and is viewed favourably in the smaller but thoroughly up-to-date and, within its limits, excellent little commentary in Dutch which is the joint production of F. M. Th. Böhl and B. Gemser,[7] while it is again of interest to note that, apparently, Gunkel has not been without influence upon the elaborate, thoroughly critical and valuable commentary which is in course of publication by the

---

[1] *Lyrik (Psalmen, Hoheslied und Verwandtes)*, S.A.T. iii, 1, 2nd ed. rev., 1920.

[2] *Die Psalmen*, K.A.T., 5th and 6th eds., with an appendix, 1929. Cf. the work of Balla, as cited above, p. 169, n. 1. Cf., too, the cautious acceptance of the principle by A. Bertholet, *H.S.A.T.*, 4th ed. rev., 1922–3, ii, p. 114, and by M. Löhr, *Psalmenstudien*, B.W.A.T., N.F. iii, 1922, pp. 1 ff.

[3] *Die Psalmen*, H.A.T., 1934. Cf. the same writer's earlier and popular study, *Die religiöse Lyrik im Alten Testament* (= *Religionsgeschichtliche Volksbücher*, ed. F. M. Schiele, ii, 13), 1912.

[4] *Die Psalmen ausgewählt, übersetzt und erklärt*, 1935, 2nd enlarged ed. under the title *Die Psalmen übersetzt und erklärt*, i, 1939, as a volume in the series A.T.D.

[5] *Die Psalmen*, Echt. B., 1947.

[6] *Forelæsninger over Indledning til de gammeltestamentlige Salmer*, 1932; *Fortolkning til de gammeltestamentlige Salmer*, 1939.

[7] *De Psalmen*, T.U., i (Böhl), 1946, ii (Böhl), 1947, iii (Gemser), 1949.

French Roman Catholic scholar E. Podechard.[1] So far as the English-speaking world is concerned, this influence has been somewhat slower to make itself felt; but in Britain it is discernible in the work of W. O. E. Oesterley,[2] and as regards America it is enthusiastically acknowledged in the somewhat popular exposition by E. A. Leslie.[3] Finally it is to be observed that all these scholars are prepared to assign some and indeed, in the case of Bentzen and Böhl, a considerable number of psalms (including, of course, the royal psalms) to the pre-exilic period, the latter going so far as to think in terms, not merely of Davidic authorship, but of a pre-Davidic date in at least half a dozen instances. Moreover, while Staerk and Kittel are confident enough that at least Pss. xliv, lx, lxxiv, lxxix, and lxxxiii should be assigned to the Maccabaean period, all the subsequent commentators (with the exception of Nötscher who is non-committal) definitely reject the view that the Psalter contains any Maccabaean psalms. All this is significant, and marks the turn of the tide which Pfeiffer, for example, seeks vainly to stop.[4]

At this point it is appropriate to note the argument, advanced independently by J. P. Peters as a result of some forty years' study of the Psalter,[5] that the psalms are not to be regarded as

---

[1] *Le Psautier* (with sub-title *Traduction littérale et explication historique*), i, 1949; id. (with sub-title *Notes critiques*), i, 1949. In referring to this valuable work it seems appropriate to add that the more enlightened attitude to Old Testament studies, which is being increasingly manifested in Roman Catholic circles and points to a growing recognition by the Vatican that it has little to lose and perhaps much to gain by giving its Old Testament scholars a freer rein, may be seen in the authorization by the Pope of a new Latin translation of the Psalter made direct from the Hebrew. Cf., for example, A. Bea, *Le Nouveau Psautier latin*, 1947.

[2] *The Psalms*, 1939: cf. *A Fresh Approach to the Psalms*, 1937.

[3] *The Psalms* (with sub-title *Translated and Interpreted in the Light of Hebrew Life and Worship*), 1949.

[4] At the same time it is interesting to note that the Maccabaean dating of the psalms is found in its most extreme form in a work which falls within the period under review, i.e. R. H. Kennett, 'The Historical Background of the Psalms', in *Old Testament Essays*, 1928, pp. 119–218, where the theory is advanced that the Psalter as a whole was composed during the Maccabaean period and reflects many of the events which took place during those years. Kennett's work reproduces in lavish measure all the weaknesses of these repeated attempts to date the psalms on the basis of supposed historical allusions, and, frankly, it is difficult to discover any good reason for taking it seriously.

[5] *The Psalms as Liturgies*, 1922. Cf. J. A. Montgomery, *A.T.R.* xvi, 1934, p. 192,

'occasional poems' but as 'hymns composed or used for liturgical purposes'. Briefly his view is that Book I of the Psalter, i.e. the first of the Yahwistic Books, corresponds to the J element in the Pentateuch and emanates from Jerusalem; that Books II and III, i.e. the Elohistic Books, correspond to the E strand in the Pentateuch and are to be traced to northern sanctuaries, specifically Bethel, Shechem, and Dan, although in their final form they have been adapted for use in the Jerusalem Temple; and that Books IV and V, i.e. the remaining Yahwistic Books, reflect the conditions of the Second Temple and correspond to the P strand in the Pentateuch, no psalm being so late as the Maccabaean period. Superficially this theory appears plausible, or, at least, it may do so to the orthodox adherent of the Wellhausen School; but on examination the argument proves somewhat strained (for example in the supposed topographical allusions to Dan in Pss. xlii and xlvi), and it is not surprising to find that Peters has gained no following. Nevertheless, despite its vagaries, this work may be regarded as a healthy reaction which was not altogether out of keeping with the modern trend, initiated by Gunkel, in the direction of a more balanced appraisal of the part played by the pre-exilic cultus in the formation of the Psalter.

Turning now to Gunkel's early expression of surprise that so little use had been made of the rich field of comparative material available from the early cultures of Mesopotamia and Egypt,[1] we have to note that when the second edition of *Die Religion in Geschichte und Gegenwart* came to be published a couple of decades later, this had been withdrawn; and with good reason, for a glance at the commentaries under review (not to mention some of the special studies which have yet to be considered) is sufficient to show that the lack of balance was soon redressed. Indeed, there was now a danger of going too far in the other direction. F. Stummer[2] had already made a detailed comparison of the formal similarities between the Sumerian and Accadian

where it is stated that Peters was already working along these lines in the 80's of the last century.   [1] See above, p. 165, n. 2.

  [2] *Sumerisch-akkadische Parallelen zum Aufbau alttestamentlicher Psalmen*, 1922.

hymns and the Hebrew psalms, and had drawn the conclusion
that, although the latter showed considerable freedom in their
development, they must be regarded as dependent in origin upon
the former either directly or indirectly through the culture of
Canaan. Similarly H. Gressmann, who was an enthusiastic
worker along similar lines to those of Gunkel, had sought to
show (in his contribution to an important volume of essays published under the editorship of D. C. Simpson)[1] that the Psalter
offers clear parallels in both language and thought to similar
compositions from both Babylonia and Egypt, and that this
points to a dependence, direct and indirect, upon the older
psalmody of the ancient Near East. In this he was supported in
the same volume, so far as Egypt is concerned, by A. M. Black-
man,[2] who went far beyond the familiar reference to Ps. civ and
its supposed dependence upon the famous Hymn of Ikhnaton in
his citation of parallels from the two fields, but nevertheless found
the question complicated by the likelihood of a certain amount
of cross-fertilization between the Semitic and Egyptian cultures
in the second millennium B.C. On the other hand, G. R. Driver,
who contributed to the same volume a long and particularly
interesting survey of the more important parallels, not only in
language and form but also superficially in thought, between
the Hebrew psalms and their Babylonian counterparts,[3] wisely
maintained that the discovery of such analogies does not in itself
constitute proof of direct dependence. In fact he held that they
may well be due to a quite independent functioning of the human
mind or even to a common heritage, and that, if there was any
Babylonian influence, this must have been conveyed through
Canaanite channels.

The last judgement is now offered confirmation through more

[1] 'The Development of Hebrew Psalmody', in *The Psalmists*, ed. D. C. Simpson,
1926, pp. 1–21. The remaining essays in this volume (other than those which are
cited in the following notes) are by H. W. Robinson and T. H. Robinson, and deal in
broad general terms with the social background and religious ideas of the psalmists.
Like the popular study by J. M. P. Smith, *The Religion of the Psalms*, 1922, they
break little new ground, and therefore call for no special comment in this survey of
current trends in the study of the Psalter.

[2] 'The Psalms in the Light of Egyptian Research', ibid., pp. 177–97.

[3] 'The Psalms in the Light of Babylonian Research', ibid., pp. 109–75.

recent and more systematic studies in this field. Thus C. G.
Cumming, in his comparison of the Accadian and Hebrew
hymns,[1] thinks somewhat vaguely in terms of direct dependence,
while presenting a better case for indirect dependence mediated
through earlier contacts of Canaan with the Tigris–Euphrates
valley; and G. Widengren, in his exhaustive survey of the individual psalms of lamentation from these two fields,[2] gives it as
his considered judgement that the Accadian psalms must have
exerted an indirect influence upon the Hebrew Psalter through
the medium of the earlier cultic literature of Canaan. Finally
R. G. Castellino, who has gone over the field again in a careful
comparative study of both these literary types,[3] allows that,
while there is no evidence of direct dependence, there *may* have
been a little indirect influence by way of Canaan. All this is
particularly interesting inasmuch as the possible dependence of
the Hebrew Psalter upon the earlier cultic literature of Canaan
had already been stressed by F. M. Th. Böhl,[4] who had sought
to show that in the letters of the petty kings of Canaan to their
Egyptian overlord, which are to be found in the Tell el-Amarna
tablets, the somewhat extravagant language which is occasionally
used in addressing the Pharaoh may be derived from Canaanite
hymnology, and so may point to the existence of Canaanite
prototypes for the Hebrew psalms; and, as J. H. Patton has
shown quite clearly,[5] this is now confirmed by the remarkable
discoveries from Ras Shamra (Ugarit), which have shed a flood
of light upon the language, the poetical forms, and the general
mythology of the Psalter.[6] Indeed, the parallels with Pss. xviii,

---

[1] *The Assyrian and Hebrew Hymns of Praise*, 1934.

[2] *The Accadian and Hebrew Psalms of Lamentation as Religious Documents*, 1937.

[3] *Le lamentazioni individuali e gli inni in Babilonia e in Israele*, 1939.

[4] 'Hymnisches und Rhythmisches in den Amarnabriefen aus Kanaan', *T.L.B.*
xxxv, 1914, cols. 337 ff.; cf. *De Psalmen*, i, pp. 25 ff. See also A. Jirku, 'Kana'anäische
Psalmenfragmente in der vorisraelitischen Zeit Palästinas und Syriens', *J.B.L.* lii,
1933, pp. 108–20.

[5] *Canaanite Parallels in the Book of Psalms*, 1944.

[6] The forms of Hebrew poetry as illustrated by the Psalter belong to a much wider
question, which cannot be dealt with satisfactorily here; but they have been the subject
of special publications, particularly from the standpoint of the vexed question of
strophic structure, by A. Bruno, *Der Rhythmus der alttestamentlichen Dichtung. Eine
Untersuchung über die Psalmen I–LXXII*, 1930; H. Möller, *Strophenbau der*

xxix, xlv, and lxviii are thought to be so close that they have
been assigned provisionally to the tenth century B.C., while Pss.
lxxxviii, lxxxix, and xcii–xcvi (like Ps. xxix) have been described
as 'swarming with Canaanitisms'.[1]

The powerful effect of such comparative study of the Psalter
is to be seen most clearly in the work of the Norwegian scholar
S. Mowinckel, who, next to Gunkel, may be safely regarded as
the most stimulating influence in this field.[2] This is due in some
degree to the influence of H. Zimmern and his special studies in
the realm of Babylonian religious literature, but it is also due
in part to the fact that, like the equally influential Danish scholar
J. Pedersen,[3] he came under the spell of the famous Danish
anthropologist V. Grønbech and enlarged the horizon of his
comparative studies so as to include the social customs and general
outlook upon life of the so-called 'primitive' peoples of the world.
Mowinckel freely acknowledges that his study of the Psalter is
based upon that of Gunkel, and he admits that he is greatly
indebted to him for the stimulus of his approach to the subject;
but he also insists that this still remains to be freed from earlier
obsessions and older untenable views. As we have seen, Gunkel
took the view that, although the different types of psalm had
their origin, for the most part, in cultic circles, the majority of
the compositions in the existing Psalter have been freed from
such an association and are correspondingly more spiritual in
outlook. Mowinckel reacts strongly against this, and asserts

Psalmen, 1931 (cf. *Z.A.W.* l, 1932, pp. 240–56); A. Condamin, *Poèmes de la Bible
avec une introduction sur la strophique hébraïque*, 1933; L. Desnoyers, *Les Psaumes.
Traduction rythmée d'après l'hébreu*, 1935; and C. F. Kraft, *The Strophic Structure of
Hebrew Poetry as illustrated in the first Book of the Psalter*, 1938; but, as in other
aspects of the study of the Psalter, some suggestive and important work, like that of
Nils W. Lund (e.g. 'The Presence of Chiasmus in the Old Testament', *A.J.S.L.* xlvi,
1929–30, pp. 104–26, 'Chiasmus in the Psalms', *A.J.S.L.* xlix, 1932–3, pp.
281–312) lies buried in the learned periodicals.

[1] Cf. W. F. Albright, *A.R.I.*, 2nd ed., 1946, pp. 128 f.; also 'The Psalm of Habakkuk', in *Studies in Old Testament Prophecy* (Theodore H. Robinson Festschrift), ed.
H. H. Rowley, 1950, pp. 6 f.

[2] See especially *Psalmenstudien I–VI* (Videnskapsselskapets Skrifter II. Hist.-
Filos. Klasse 1921, No. 4; 1921, No. 6; 1922, No. 1; 1922, No. 2; 1923, No. 3;
1924, No. 1), 1921–4.

[3] *Israel: Its Life and Culture I–II*, 1926; *III–IV*, 1940.

that such a point of view is due to an inherited failure to appreciate the constructive part played by the cultus in the life of society and an over-emphasis upon the opposition between what is regarded as purely formal religion and that which appears to be a more personal type. Accordingly he rejects Gunkel's views at this point and, by contrast, would explain the psalms as being wholly, or almost wholly, cultic in both origin and intention.

His most important contribution to our understanding of the Psalter is probably to be found in his argument that in ancient Israel there existed, in association with the Jerusalem Temple, an autumnal New Year Festival, at which Yahweh's enthronement as the universal King was celebrated and indeed enacted as an annual event of epoch-making significance.[1] Starting from Pss. xlvii, xciii, and xcv-c, which embrace, for example, Gunkel's 'Enthronement Psalms', he emphasizes that on the analogy of the accession to the throne of the earthly king the recurrent expression *yahweh mālak* must be rendered as 'Yahweh *has become* King'.[2] He then rejects the earlier attempts to interpret these psalms against an historical background or in purely eschatological terms, and, following the lead offered by the celebration of the New Year Festival in Babylon with Marduk in the leading role, insists that they can only be understood aright against a cultic background of a similar kind. Working partly from the analogy of the Babylonian festival and its counterparts elsewhere, partly from a comparison with the rabbinical traditions concerning the celebration of the New Year Festival in post-exilic Judaism, and partly along simple inductive lines, he finds no difficulty in developing his thesis so as to include not merely Gunkel's 'Songs of Zion' (Pss. xlvi, xlviii, lxxvi, and lxxxvii) and the familiar 'Songs of Ascent' (Pss. cxx–cxxxiv), but a grand total of over forty psalms.[3] With due allowance for certain modifica-

---

[1] *Psalmenstudien II. Das Thronbesteigungsfest Jahwäs und der Ursprung der Eschatologie*, 1922. Cf. *R.G.G.*[2], i, 1927, 'Drama, religionsgeschichtlich'. Unknown to Mowinckel until his investigations in this field were well advanced, he had been anticipated in part by P. Volz, *Das Neujahrsfest Jahwes (Laubhüttenfest)*, 1912.

[2] Pss. xciii. 1, xcvi. 10, xcvii. 1, xcix. 1 ; cf. xlvii. 9 (EVV. 8).

[3] i.e. in addition to those already mentioned Pss. viii, xv, xxiv, xxix, xxxiii, l, lxv, lxvi. 1–12, lxvii, lxxv, lxxxi, lxxxii, lxxxiv, lxxxv, cxviii, cxlix; also Exod. xv. 1–18.

tions in the festival during the passage of time, his conclusions may be said to be that this is the great occasion on which, year by year, Yahweh makes all things new, repeating His original triumph over the primeval chaos and His work in creation. All this is expressed in a ritual drama in which He triumphs over the kings and nations of the earth, who are the allies of the primeval chaos, and in a procession at which the Ark as the symbol of His presence is borne in triumph to the sanctuary, where He is acclaimed afresh as the proven, universal King. In this way He vindicates the faith of His chosen people, sees that, as we might say, they are put right ($\sqrt{sdk}$) once again, and, renewing His covenant with them and with the house of David as represented by the reigning king,[1] shows Himself prepared to restore their fortunes for the coming year. What is more, Mowinckel finds that Israel's eschatological hopes, as presented so graphically in the works of the canonical prophets, are to be traced to this source and regarded in a measure as the fruit of disillusionment. That is to say, the 'Day of Yahweh', which was originally the cultic 'day' of His enthronement, is now projected into the future as the true day of enthronement, when Yahweh will indeed come with power to prove Himself the universal King. Finally, it is to be observed that in Mowinckel's opinion, as originally presented, this festival reaches back beyond the time of Isaiah, for whose 'call' it provides the appropriate background,[2] to the years of the early monarchy; and, while still laying emphasis upon a Babylonian prototype, he recognizes that this has been mediated through Canaanite channels, and even hazards the suggestion that the festival under discussion may be rooted in the pre-Davidic worship of '*ēl ʿelyôn* (A.V. 'the most high God', R.V. 'God Most High').[3]

Mowinckel's theory has been accepted in principle by several Old Testament scholars who have published commentaries on

[1] Cf. the development of this point by Mowinckel in *Le Décalogue*, E.H.P.R. xvi, 1927.

[2] Cf. Isa. vi. 5.

[3] Cf. Gen. xiv. 18 f. See *Psalmenstudien II*, p. 204, but note that Mowinckel later withdrew his view of so early a date in the monarchy, *Z.A.W.* xlviii, 1930, p. 267, n. 3.

the Psalter, specifically Schmidt,[1] Böhl,[2] Bentzen, and Leslie, while others, such as Gunkel, Oesterley, and Weiser, seek to combine the older eschatological interpretation of the so-called enthronement psalms with the newer cultic one of Mowinckel and to see the development of an eschatological type of psalm from the hymns in use at some such festival as Mowinckel has sought to reconstruct.[3] At the same time the theory is far from having received general acceptance; and there can be no reasonable doubt that, while it is not so easily overthrown as some of its critics suggest, Mowinckel's treatment requires considerable modification and a more cautious restatement. Thus O. Eissfeldt[4] early gathered together in characteristically thorough fashion the material which was then available in order to show what an important place the conception of a divine 'King' (*melek*) must have had in West-Semitic thought, and he is undoubtedly right in emphasizing the importance of this background, rather than the comparative data from, say, Babylon, for the solution of the problem as to how Yahweh came to be worshipped in this way. On the other hand, when he objects that the earliest application of this term to Yahweh, which can be dated with certainty, is Isaiah's famous utterance on the occasion of his 'call',[5] one may justifiably protest that it is much more credible that this scene should be explained in terms of Isaiah's sudden realization of the ultimate significance of a characteristic feature in the formal worship of the royal Temple on Mount Zion than that he should have been uniquely inspired to apply to Yahweh a widespread divine epithet which had never been used previously in this way with reference to the God of Israel. As for the argument that the first certain use of the term *melek* in a personal name with direct reference to Yahweh does not occur until the

---

[1] See also *Die Thronfahrt Jahves am Fest der Jahreswende im Alten Israel*, 1927, as cited below, p. 196, n. 4.

[2] See also *Nieuwjaarsfeest en Koningsdag in Babylon en in Israël*, 1927.

[3] Cf., too, the modified acceptance of Mowinckel's theory by C. C. Keet, *A Liturgical Study of the Psalter*, 1928, in which the author examines the use of the psalms in the worship of post-exilic Judaism.

[4] 'Jahwe als König', *Z.A.W.* xlvi, 1928, pp. 81–105.

[5] Isa. vi. 5.

time of Jeremiah,[1] this has the characteristic weakness of every
argument from silence which is based upon a comparative paucity
of material, and seems to be all the weaker when it is borne in
mind that during the monarchy the Temple of Solomon (where,
Mowinckel argues, the festival under discussion took place) was
but one of a number of important sanctuaries at which Yahweh
was worshipped. The fact is that we are far too prone to think
in terms of a unilinear development in our treatment of the
religion of ancient Israel. Another important attempt to refute
Mowinckel's theory is that of L. I. Pap,[2] who argues at length
that there is nothing to prove the existence of a New Year
Festival in pre-exilic Israel. At the same time he criticizes
Mowinckel's use of the supposed biblical evidence on the ground
that the passages in question either have nothing to do with a
New Year Festival or yield no case for the existence of such
a festival as Mowinckel envisages, and emphasizes that the data
advanced from rabbinical sources must be regarded as too late to
be valid for the pre-exilic period. Accordingly he reiterates the
view that the enthronement psalms are of late date, and are to
be interpreted, for the most part,[3] along purely eschatological
lines. There can be no reasonable doubt that Mowinckel overstates his case in the use which he makes of the data from the
Old Testament and the Mishnah; but, as it happens, the first
part of Pap's argument is now sufficiently met by yet another
critic of Mowinckel's theory in the person of N. H. Snaith, who,
in an able discussion of the Jewish New Year Festival,[4] marshals
the evidence for the existence of such a feast in the pre-exilic
period.

So far as Snaith's own criticism of Mowinckel's theory is concerned, his most important contribution to the discussion is his
treatment of the supposed evidence from rabbinical sources; for
he here reinforces Pap's argument by offering cogent reasons for
the view that in Palestinian Judaism the association of the Kingdom of God with the New Year Festival, while undoubtedly

---

[1] Jer. xxxviii. 6. [2] *Das israelitische Neujahrsfest*, 1933.
[3] i.e. in the case of Pss. xlvii and xcvi–xcix.
[4] *The Jewish New Year Festival: Its Origins and Development*, 1947.

prominent in later thought and practice, is not earlier than the
second century A.D., and, therefore, is not valid as evidence
for the presence of such a feature in any corresponding festival
of the pre-exilic period. Nevertheless Snaith's work, valuable and
important as it is, must be read with caution. Thus it comes with
something of a shock to be told that Mowinckel 'made no
attempt to fix the date of his "Coronation Psalms", xciii, xcv–
xcix, xlvii, with diverse others, but assumed without discussion
that they could be used for any period of Israelite-Judahite
history.'[1] The truth is that Mowinckel devotes a whole section
of his book to just this question, and seeks to show that not a few
of these psalms are pre-exilic, and, what is more, that the
enthronement psalms (specifically Pss. xlvii, xciii, and xcv–c)
have influenced both the style and the thought of Deutero-
Isaiah.[2] This is the exactly contrary thesis to that of Snaith, who
argues that in the Jewish liturgies these psalms (with the exception of Ps. xlvii) are psalms for the Sabbath, not the New Year,
and that all of them are post-exilic in origin, the instances of
direct dependence upon Deutero-Isaiah being too numerous to
be refuted. In support of his claim Snaith cites the list of parallels
between Pss. xciii, xcvi–xcviii and Isaiah xl–lv, which he gives
in an earlier work along similar lines,[3] and overlooks the fact
that such a list may prove to be a two-edged sword, and that as
a result quite the opposite conclusion is possible. In other words,

---

[1] Op. cit., p. 36.

[2] *Psalmenstudien II*, pp. 190–202, 'Das Alter der verschiedenen Thronbesteigungs-
psalmen'.

[3] *Studies in the Psalter*, 1934, pp. 66–9. The earlier part of this work is an attempt
to show that the whole of the 'Elohist Psalter' (Pss. xlii–lxxxiii), with the exception
of Pss. xlv–xlix, is to be linked in origin with the events of the period *c.* 530–420 B.C.,
and that the 'Jehovist Supplement' (Pss. lxxxiv–lxxxix), with certain exceptions
which also belong to the closing years of this period, is to be dated, preferably, to the
early years of the period *c.* 420–400 B.C. and in any case not later than 397 B.C. This
is no more convincing than other attempts to arrive at a precise dating of the psalms,
and the reader will find it instructive to compare the arguments advanced by Snaith
for assigning the psalms in question to the early post-exilic period with those advanced
by Kennett for a Maccabaean date. See above, p. 185, n. 4. Incidentally a simple
and on the whole cautious survey of the unmistakable references to history in the
psalms will be found in A. Lauha, *Die Geschichtsmotive in den alttestamentlichen
Psalmen*, A.A.S.F., B LVI, 1, 1945.

the evidence which he cites may be used, rather, to support the view that the dependence is really on the side of Deutero-Isaiah. Further, if the enthronement psalms were really dependent upon Deutero-Isaiah, one would expect to find in them some reference to Yahweh's role as the 'Redeemer' (*gô'ēl*) of His people, a conception which dominates the thought of Deutero-Isaiah from end to end;[1] but in fact there is none. Moreover, we know from Ps. cxxxvii that 'the songs of Zion' must have been in the minds of the exiles, even though they had not the heart to sing them; so we may well expect to find such songs exerting an influence upon the thought and indeed the style of the great prophet of the Exile, when the time of deliverance seemed near. Finally, if these psalms are thus pre-exilic (and the evidence from Ugarit appears to lend additional support to this view),[2] their employment as Sabbath psalms in the changed conditions of post-exilic Judaism need have no bearing upon their use during the period of the monarchy. All in all, therefore, while there can be no question that Mowinckel overstates his case in that (*a*) he makes somewhat uncritical use of the data from both the Old Testament and late rabbinical sources, (*b*) lays much too great a weight upon the Babylonian counterpart and its supposed influence upon the Israelite festival, and (*c*) drags in far too many psalms (seeing, as Gunkel puts it, 'Helena in jedem Weibe'),[3] his basic theory is far from having been overthrown.

At the same time it is interesting to note that, although Mowinckel early appreciated the importance of Gunkel's treatment of the royal psalms against the background of the somewhat similar texts from Mesopotamia and Egypt,[4] and, like H. Gress-

---

[1] xli. 14, xliii. 1, 14, &c., esp. xliv. 6.

[2] See above, p. 189, n. 1. It is true that Albright recognizes two main periods of outstanding Canaanite influence upon the Psalter, i.e. (*a*) the eleventh and tenth centuries B.C., and (*b*) the sixth to the fourth centuries B.C. (*A.R.I.*, pp. 128 f.); but in the light of, say, Ps. xxix and in view of what is said above the evidence appears to be in favour of the earlier period for the psalms under discussion.

[3] *Einleitung*, p. 104.

[4] *Kongesalmerna i det Gamle Testamente*, 1916, in which the number of royal psalms is extended so as to include Pss. ii, xviii, xx, xxi, xxviii, xliv, xlv, lx, lxi, lxiii, lxvi, lxviii, lxxii, lxxx, lxxxiii, lxxxiv, lxxxix, ci, cx, cxviii, cxxxii, cxliv, and 1 Sam. ii. 1–10, 2 Sam. xxiii. 1–7. Cf. *Psalmenstudien III*, pp. 78 ff., *VI*, pp. 72 ff.

mann,[1] used them in his own way but with a stronger emphasis upon their cultic background in order to illustrate the social and religious importance of the Israelite conception of kingship, he made comparatively little use in this connexion of the many royal psalms which he himself had already sought to recognize.[2] This is the more surprising in that he rightly drew attention to the important role which the king appears to have played in the social life of ancient Israel as a uniquely powerful mediator between Yahweh and His chosen people;[3] and to the present writer it seems that a better case can be made for the incorporation of several psalms of this type than for many and indeed the majority of those which Mowinckel actually presses into the service of his theory. An early attempt to make good this apparent omission is to be found in the work of H. Schmidt, who, prior to the publication of his commentary, had already accepted enthusiastically the basic theory of such a festival as Mowinckel describes, and had restated it with certain modifications which included a slightly greater emphasis upon the part played in the ritual by the human king;[4] and later the present writer, who likewise accepts the theory in principle, attempted to show and would still maintain that, as Mowinckel surmised, the festival was indeed rooted in the pre-Davidic worship of *'ēl 'elyôn* (R.V. 'God Most High'), and that the Davidic king played a much more important part in it than either Mowinckel or Schmidt had realized.[5] Here the argument is that in the ritual drama the kings or nations of the earth, representing the forces of darkness and

[1] *Der Messias*, F.R.L.A.N.T., N.F. xxvi, 1929, pp. 1–64, on 'Der israelitische Hofstil', with special reference to Pss. ii, lxxii, and cx. For a Roman Catholic attempt to refute this approach in terms of the older Messianism, see R. E. Murphy, *A Study of Psalm 72(71)*, 1948.

[2] *Psalmenstudien II*, pp. 112 ff. and 177 f., with special reference in each case to Ps. cxxxii.

[3] Op. cit., pp. 299 ff., which offer an interesting, if sometimes questionable, account of the Israelite conception of kingship in the light of the original Danish edition of Pedersen's *Israel: Its Life and Culture I–II*.

[4] *Die Thronfahrt Jahves*, pp. 36 ff., incorporating (in addition to Ps. cxxxii) Pss. ii, xx, xxi, lxxxix. 1–3, 6–19 (EVV. 1–2, 5–18), cx, and 1 Sam. ii. 1–10.

[5] 'The Rôle of the King in the Jerusalem Cultus', in *The Labyrinth*, ed. S. H. Hooke, 1935, pp. 71–111, incorporating (in addition to Ps. cxxxii) Pss. ii, xviii, lxxxix, cx, and cxviii.

death as opposed to those of light and life, unite in an attempt to destroy Yahweh's chosen people by attacking the Davidic king upon whom its vitality as a social body is peculiarly dependent. At first the king, who is referred to from time to time as the Son, the Servant, and the Messiah of Yahweh, suffers humiliation and defeat, and is nearly swallowed up by the chaos of waters which lead to the underworld of Sheol; but ultimately, in virtue of his protestation of devotion and his claim to righteousness, he is delivered by Yahweh from this threat of death. Such a renewal of life on the part of the king, however, is nothing less than a ritual re-birth; it is an indication that the suffering Servant and duly humble Messiah has been adopted once more as the Son of the Most High or, to express this mediatory role in different terms, that he has been renewed in office as priest 'after the order of Melchizedek'. In this way the life or well-being of the nation, for which the king is directly responsible, receives provisional guarantee for another year. The reader should be warned, however, against exaggerating the degree to which this theory fits into that of a general myth and ritual pattern common to the ancient Near East, which is advocated by S. H. Hooke, the founder of the so-called Myth and Ritual School. There is certainly no suggestion in all this that Yahweh was ever thought of as a dying and rising god or that the reigning member of the house of David played the role of the High God or indeed of any god in this ritual as a type of divine king.[1]

Mowinckel's attempt to interpret the Psalter, not only in the light of the general psalmody of the ancient Near East but also by reference to the point of view of the so-called 'primitive' peoples of our own day, is to be seen again in his treatment of the type of psalm known as the individual lament.[2] In this case he is primarily concerned with the question of the *pôᶜᵃlê 'āwen* or, to use the familiar rendering of the standard English versions, the 'workers of iniquity'. He advances the view that in the terms

[1] Cf., for example, G. Widengren, 'Konungens vistelse i dödsriket. En studie till Psalm 88', *S.E.Å.* x, 1945, pp. 78 f.; A. Haldar, *Studies in the Book of Nahum* (U.U.Å., 1946:7), 1947, p. 154.

[2] *Psalmenstudien I. Áwän und die individuellen Klagepsalmen*, 1921; also *Z.A.W.* xliii. 1925, pp. 260-2.

'*ôn* ('vigour', 'wealth') and '*āwen* ('trouble', 'iniquity') we have
a kind of semantic polarization, both words having been differentiated from an original form '*aun* with the simple meaning of
'power', and the latter being opposed to the former by its restriction to forms of power which were devoted to evil or anti-social
ends. However, in the ancient world in which Israel had its part,
as also in the so-called 'primitive' societies of today, such anti-
social power, says Mowinckel, is first and foremost the magical
power of the sorcerer; and the very language used of the words,
gestures, and general behaviour of the *pô'ªlê* '*āwen* in the psalms
is found to point to the fact that they are to be explained in such a
way. This has wider repercussions in that it serves to place the
general problem of the 'enemies' in these psalms (as also in the
individual songs of thanksgiving) in quite a new light; for on this
theory they are the sorcerers and their demonic allies, and the
language employed to describe the psalmists' sufferings, far from
being used figuratively, is to be taken literally as having reference
to actual forms of sickness which their opponents have succeeded
in bringing about through the effective use of their occult power.
Correspondingly the terms '*ānî* and '*ānāw*, which are so commonly used to describe the psalmist and his fellows as 'afflicted'
or 'humble', are not to be regarded as having developed a common
religious emphasis in virtue of the party strife of post-exilic
Judaism,[1] but denote from the first both the condition of one
who suffers from some form of social oppression and the characteristic humility of the pious Semite which may be expected to
come to the fore in time of need. Hence the individual laments,
like the songs of thanksgiving (for some of which Gunkel himself had recognized a close cultic connexion), are not the lyrical

---

[1] The most influential work in this respect was the detailed study by A. Rahlfs,
עָנִי *und* עָנָו *in den Psalmen*, 1892; but an attractive exposition of much the same
point of view (although more general in character and with greater emphasis upon
social and economic factors) appeared at the beginning of the period under review in
the work of A. Causse, *Les 'Pauvres' d'Israël* (Prophètes, psalmistes et messianistes),
E.H.P.R. iii, 1922, pp. 81–135. Subsequently, however, Causse recorded his qualified
acceptance of Mowinckel's theory and the necessity of making certain modifications
in the argument of the foregoing work. See *Les Plus Vieux Chants de la Bible*, pp. 115,
n. 5, and 119, n. 2.

outpourings of pious individuals who expressed their feelings in a
style derived from cultic sources, but are themselves wholly cultic
in origin, their authors being the professional poets of the temple
personnel, who could enter sympathetically and imaginatively
into the experience of the worshipper and compose pieces suitable
for use by or on behalf of the believer in connexion with some
form of purificatory rite whereby the sufferer was restored to that
right relationship with Yahweh which would ensure the latter's
active intervention on his behalf. Accordingly the striking change
of tone from one of supplication to one of certainty as to Yahweh's support or one of glad thanksgiving for answered prayer,
each of which is so marked a feature of some of these psalms,[1]
is to be explained, along the lines already suggested by F.
Küchler,[2] in terms of an intervening priestly oracle which gave
the desired assurance or positive answer to the suppliant's prayer.

Mowinckel's argument with regard to the derivation of the
term *'āwen* is attractive and has found a measure of recognition;[3]
but his attempt to limit its scope so as to see in the *pōʿᵃlê 'āwen*
the activities of those who exercised magical powers has rightly
found little support. It is conceivable that certain *pōʿᵃlê 'āwen*
were 'workers of magic', and, indeed, repeated efforts have been
made to trace magical terminology in the Psalter;[4] but Mowinckel offers no convincing evidence to support his view that
the term *'āwen*, as used of a power which was abused for anti-
social ends and therefore issued in evil, was at any time restricted
to forms of magic, however widely one may choose to understand this term.[5] In short, there is no sufficient reason for aban-

---

[1] See above, pp. 169 f.

[2] 'Das priesterliche Orakel in Israel und Juda', in *Abhandlungen zur semitischen Religionskunde und Sprachwissenschaft* (Baudissin Festschrift), B.Z.A.W. xxxiii, 1918, pp. 299 f.

[3] Cf. Pedersen, *Israel: Its Life and Culture I–II*, p. 539 (p. 431, n. 1); A. Hjelt, 'Die Bedeutung des 'āwen im AT', *Studia Orientalia* (Societas Orientalis Fennica), i (Tallqvist Festschrift), 1925, pp. 67 f.; K.-B., p. 20.

[4] Cf., for example, N. Nicolsky, *Spuren magischer Formeln in den Psalmen*, B.Z.A.W. xlvi, 1927 (with special reference to Pss. vii, xxxv, lviii, lix, lxix, xci, cix, and cxli), and the more general discussion by A. Guillaume, *Prophecy and Divination among the Hebrews and other Semites*, 1938, pp. 272 ff.

[5] Cf. Mowinckel's rejoinder to critics of his theory in *Psalmenstudien VI*, p. 17, n. 3, with its special appeal to the original Danish edition of Pedersen's *Israel: Its*

doning the view that the *pōʿᵃlê ʾāwen* were 'evil-doers' in a quite general sense. Indeed Mowinckel's theory has been sufficiently refuted by Gunkel himself[1] (although the latter concedes that in a few cases the individual laments offer more evidence of close cultic associations than he had previously allowed)[2] and by N. H. Ridderbos, who made a comprehensive and detailed examination of the whole question in an admirably thorough way.[3]

Another approach to the problem of the 'enemies' in the individual laments has been made by H. Schmidt, who likewise recognizes a close connexion with the cultus and seeks to show that many of these psalms are really the prayers of those who have been accused of some breach of the law but, possibly for want of evidence, cannot have their case decided by ordinary judicial procedure.[4] In such an event provision was made for the accused to be brought before the priests, upon whom rested the responsibility of obtaining a clear verdict on the matter direct from Yahweh Himself.[5] The procedure on such an occasion is unknown; it may have involved some form of divination,[6] or, as one piece of legislation suggests, it may have been through some form of trial by ordeal.[7] Be that as it may, Schmidt would explain a number of the individual laments in the light of this practice,[8] taking them to be prayers in which the accused protests his innocence by an oath of purgation and, occasionally using the appropriate language of the law-courts (which is not to be taken figuratively, as Gunkel, for example, maintained), pleads with

---

Life and Culture I–II, pp. 411–52, where the same interpretation of the term *ʾāwen* is presented in the context of a general study of Israelite psychology (pp. 430 ff. and 448).

[1] *Einleitung*, pp. 196 ff.　　　　　　　　　　[2] Op. cit., pp. 175 ff.

[3] *De 'Werkers der Ongerechtighed' in de individueele Psalmen*, 1939, with a summary in German.

[4] *Das Gebet der Angeklagten im Alten Testament*, B.Z.A.W. xlix, 1928: cf. the more summary form which appears in *Old Testament Essays*, pp. 143–55.

[5] Cf. Deut. xvii. 8 ff., 1 Kings viii. 31 f.; also the cultic aspect of the procedure described in Exod. xxii. 6 ff. (EVV. 7 ff.), Num. v. 11 ff., and Deut. xxi. 1 ff.

[6] Cf. 1 Kings viii. 31, *ad fin.*

[7] Cf. Num. v. 11 ff.

[8] i.e. primarily Pss. iv, v, vii, xvii, xxvi, xxvii. 1–6, 7–14, xxxi. 1–9 (EVV. 1–8), lvii (cix), cxlii; also perhaps Pss. xi, xiii, liv, lv. 1–19 (EVV. 1–18), lvi, lix, xciv. 16–23, cxl.

Yahweh for justice and deliverance.[1] On this view the 'enemies' of whom the psalmist is so afraid are his false accusers; and the two parts into which some of these psalms so clearly fall, as lamentation and appeal give place to thanksgiving and praise, represent an occasion upon which the suppliant has been accorded a favourable response. Further, this theory is extended so as to offer yet another explanation of certain of the psalms in which the speaker, while apparently suffering from sickness of some kind, also laments that he is beset by enemies who persistently plot against him and even set him in peril of his life. Here Schmidt argues (against Mowinckel) that there is no evidence that the enemies are in any way the cause of the psalmist's malady. Yahweh Himself must be the primary cause, and, this being the case, the obvious inference for the ancient Israelite was that the psalmist was suffering for some form of sin.[2] It would then be an easy step to go on to infer that it was he who was guilty of a particular crime for which no likely perpetrator could otherwise be found. Here again, therefore, the 'enemies' of whom the psalmist complains are to be regarded as those who seek his harm by their false accusations.[3] The theory, besides appearing in Schmidt's own commentary, has been accepted in part by Bentzen[4] and, one fears, somewhat too enthusiastically by Leslie. Its ingenuity can hardly be denied, and it should certainly be taken seriously as at least a possible explanation of some of these psalms.[5]

Somewhat later the problem of the 'enemies' in the individual laments and songs of thanksgiving, like that of the terms 'ānî and 'ānāw, was attacked again by H. Birkeland in two important studies. In the former of these,[6] which was begun when, as a pupil of Mowinckel, he still found the latter's theory of the origin and purpose of the individual laments to be the only one

---

[1] e.g. Pss. xxvi. 1, xxxi. 8 f. (EVV. 7 f.), cxlii. 8 (EVV. 7).

[2] Cf. Pss. xxxviii and xli.

[3] i.e. primarily Pss. xxxi. 10–25 (EVV. 9–24), xxxv, lxix, (cix); also perhaps Pss. xxv, xxviii, lxxxvi, and cii.   [4] See below, p. 204, n. 3.

[5] Cf. Eissfeldt, *Einleitung in das Alte Testament*, pp. 131 ff.

[6] '*ānî und* '*ānāw in den Psalmen* (Videnskapsselskapets Skrifter II. Hist.-Filos. Klasse 1932, No. 4), 1933.

which offered a satisfactory solution of the problem, he under-
took a careful re-examination of the use of the terms '*ānî* and
'*ānāw* in the Psalter; and, while regarding the latter as probably
no more than a corruption of the former and rejecting the view
that '*ānî* had a religious connotation from the first, he agreed that
Mowinckel had succeeded in refuting the theory that the use of
these terms in the Psalter reflects the party strife which came to
a head in post-exilic Judaism. Before this work could be issued
from the press, however, he had abandoned Mowinckel's main
thesis in favour of another and, in part at least, much more
attractive theory, which actually appeared in print the same year.[1]
An examination of the descriptions of the 'enemies' in both the
communal and the royal psalms, where their foreign character is
clearly to the fore,[2] led Birkeland to the conclusion that, for the
most part, the 'enemies' in the individual laments and songs of
thanksgiving, as well as a number of psalms from other categories,
must also be regarded as foreigners, and that the 'I' who speaks
is really a king or, sometimes perhaps, the leader of the armed
forces and, in the case of psalms from the post-exilic period,
a governor of Jewish blood or a high priest. Only in Pss.
xxxviii and xli is there any clear indication of physical sickness,[3]
and here the 'enemies' are to be regarded as fellow-countrymen
whose actions are to be seen, perhaps, against a background of
court intrigue. Normally, however, the background is either one
of actual war or that of permanent subjection to a foreign overlord; and, this being the case, the accusers now stand revealed as
political rivals who would create mischief between, say, the king
and his overlord in much the same way as that which is suggested
by the protests of the petty kings of Canaan in their correspondence with the Pharaoh as revealed by the Tell el-Amarna
tablets. Thus, for the most part, it is the Israelites or Jews as a

---

[1] *Die Feinde des Individuums in der israelitischen Psalmenliteratur*, 1933.

[2] i.e. (*a*) Pss. xliv, lx, lxxiv, lxxix, lxxx, lxxxiii, cxxiv, cxxv; (*b*) Pss. xviii, xx, xxi,
lxxxix, cxliv (as above, p. 195, n. 4).

[3] Birkeland regards it as doubtful that Pss. vi, xxx, and cii, which also refer to the
psalmist's enemies, really have anything to do with actual sickness, while Ps. lxxxviii,
which is certainly to be interpreted in this way, makes no such reference to enemies
and therefore is not discussed.

whole who are the 'afflicted' or 'humble'; and this is really just another aspect of the way in which, as the 'righteous' (*ṣaddîḳîm*) or the 'pious' (*ḥᵃsîḏîm*), they see themselves opposed to the nation's enemies, who by contrast are the 'evil-doers' (*pōᶜᵃlê 'āwen*), the 'wicked' (*rᵉšāᶜîm*) and the like. In this way justice also appears to be done (*a*) to the language which Gunkel himself regarded as so often unsuitable for an ordinary individual, and therefore sought to explain in terms of the democratization of terminology which was originally peculiar to royal psalms;[1] and (*b*) to that corporate consciousness which comes to the fore so clearly in some of these psalms and earlier gave rise to the view that the 'I' who speaks is the community.[2] There can be no reasonable doubt that, as Mowinckel himself agrees in a long and dignified reply to Birkeland's argument,[3] we have here another suggestive line of approach, even though the latter clearly presses his case too far and with too little regard for the possibility that the 'enemies' may be other than foreigners. The fact is that, as Mowinckel himself finally admits, the problem as to who are meant by the 'enemies' in these psalms is not likely to be solved by resort to any one formula.[4]

With all this developing interest in the role which the king

---

[1] See above, pp. 173 f. and 176.

[2] As H. W. Robinson points out in his important paper on 'The Hebrew Conception of Corporate Personality', in *Werden und Wesen des Alten Testaments*, ed. J. Hempel, B.Z.A.W. lxvi, 1936, pp. 57 f., the sharp antithesis between the collective view of Smend and the individualistic standpoint of Balla is largely removed when one recognizes the fluidity of movement from the individual to the community and vice versa which was so marked a feature of the Israelite conception of society. At the same time, as the psalms under discussion are primarily those of an individual, Birkeland's suggestion that the speaker's position in society was a more leading one than we have been wont to recognize may make this fluidity of movement all the more intelligible.

[3] 'Fiendene i de individuelle klagesalmer', *Nor. T. T.* xxxv, 1934, pp. 1–39. Cf., too, Ridderbos, op. cit., p. 354.

[4] A less rigid treatment of the problem so far as Book I of the Psalter is concerned is apparently to be found in G. Marschall, *Die 'Gottlosen' des ersten Psalmenbuches*, 1929. Cf., for example, Birkeland, *Die Feinde des Individuums*, p. 14. Further, the problem of the terms 'ānî and 'ānāw, as it affects the whole of the O.T., has recently been examined with care by J. Van der Ploeg, 'Les Pauvres d'Israël et leur piété', *O.T.S.* vii, 1950, pp. 236–70. His conclusion is that ''ānî, which was employed originally to denote the poor (in the economic sense), came to be used along with what may have been the secondary formation ''ānāw to connote the humble (i.e. in a strictly religious sense and without regard to economic conditions), because the poor, unlike the rich,

may have played in Israelite worship it is not surprising to find that the energetic leaders of the so-called Uppsala School, G. Widengren and I. Engnell, have also begun to study the problem in the light of the supposed general culture pattern of the ancient Near East with its focus in the dying and rising god. They are working along similar lines to those laid down by S. H. Hooke, but are trying to pursue the subject more exhaustively. As yet, however, they have offered no systematic study of this important aspect of the Psalter, although one has been promised by both Engnell[1] and Widengren;[2] and in the meantime A. Bentzen has examined the question from the Scandinavian side and pointed out in what is on the whole a balanced and cautious way the line along which he thinks that progress is likely to be made.[3] To the present writer, however, one thing is clear, namely that the problem must be examined, not merely against the general background of the ritual and mythology of the ancient Near East, but also in the light furnished by a careful study from the standpoint of Israelite psychology of the actual forms of thought revealed by the psalms themselves.[4] Something of the importance of this approach is brought out in an examination by Mowinckel of the cultic ideas associated with the thought of 'blessing' and 'curse' and their possible bearing upon the Psalter, which is closely akin to the work of Pedersen; but while suggestive and valuable, this must be read with caution as being too highly coloured by what is known of the views of 'primitive' peoples.[5] It also comes to the fore in an excellent survey by C. Barth of the passages in the

---

were not tempted to commit the greatest sin known to the O.T., i.e. that of pride, and so were more ready to adopt the proper attitude of a man in the presence of his Maker.

[1] *Studies in Divine Kingship in the Ancient Near East*, 1943, pp. 174–7.

[2] *S.E.Å.* x, 1945, p. 69, and the preface to *Mesopotamian Elements in Manichaeism = King and Saviour II* (U.U.Å., 1946: 3), 1946.

[3] *Det sakrale kongedømme, Bemærkninger i en løbende diskussion om de gammeltestamentlige Salmer*, 1945. Bentzen admits the possibility of royal psalms in more cases than we have been wont to think, but still regards Schmidt's theory of prayers of the accused to be the most likely explanation in the case of Pss. v, vii, xxvi, xxxi (?), xxxv (?), cix, cxx, and cxlii.

[4] Cf. A. R. Johnson, 'Divine Kingship and the Old Testament', in *E.T.* lxii, 1950–1, pp. 36–42, esp. 41 f.

[5] *Psalmenstudien V. Segen und Fluch in Israels Kult und Psalmdichtung*, 1924.

individual laments and songs of thanksgiving which, as Gunkel pointed out,[1] deal in strikingly pictorial language with the psalmist's descent to Sheol;[2] for it is clear that these can only be understood properly in the light of normal Israelite thought concerning 'life' and 'death', and the fact that, just as death itself in the strict sense was a weak form of life, so any weakness in life, and not merely physical sickness, was regarded as a degree of death in which one was brought dangerously close to the Underworld.[3]

The emphasis upon the close cultic connexion of the psalms, which is thus the distinguishing feature of Mowinckel's work as opposed to that of Gunkel,[4] is continued in three other studies which are designed (*a*) to reinforce this view by an examination of the technical terms employed in the headings of the psalms,[5] and (*b*) to throw light upon the question of their authorship.[6] Here Mowinckel is mainly concerned to show that the majority of the psalms, far from having been composed by individuals who in many cases had escaped from the formalism of the cultus, were composed by members of the temple personnel, specifically poets belonging to the temple singers.[7] Moreover, closely related to

---

[1] See above, pp. 171 and 174.

[2] *Die Errettung vom Tode in den individuellen Klage- und Dankliedern des Alten Testamentes*, 1947.

[3] Cf. Pedersen, *Israel: Its Life and Culture I–II*, pp. 460 ff.; A. R. Johnson, *The Vitality of the Individual in the Thought of Ancient Israel*, 1949. Note, too, the treatment of the ideas of 'light' and 'darkness' in the Psalter by A. M. Gierlich, *Der Lichtgedanke in den Psalmen*, 1940, which is a useful collection of material by a Roman Catholic scholar, but suffers from a failure to make proper use of the general cultural background to the psalms.

[4] For an attempt to solve the problem posed by the conflicting opinions of Gunkel and Mowinckel, see G. Quell, *Das kultische Problem der Psalmen*, B.W.A.T., N.F. xi, 1926, where emphasis is laid upon tracing the religious experience which comes to the fore in the different types. Incidentally it is to be observed that Mowinckel has at least this in common with the work of the Roman Catholic writer, V. Schönbächler, *Die Stellung der Psalmen zum alttestamentlichen Opferkult*, 1941, that he would hold that such supposedly anti-cultic works as Pss. xl, l, li, and lxix are not really so but are concerned only with a truer appraisal of what Yahweh most requires in worship.

[5] *Psalmenstudien IV. Die technischen Termini in den Psalmenüberschriften*, 1923.

[6] *Psalmenstudien III. Kultprophetie und prophetische Psalmen*, 1923; *Psalmenstudien VI. Die Psalmdichter*, 1924. Cf. A. R. Johnson, 'The Prophet in Israelite Worship', *E.T.* xlvii, 1935–6, pp. 312–19.

[7] Cf., in addition to the relevant passages on p. 206, n. 2, Ps. lxviii. 26 (EVV. 25); and see above, pp. 188 f.

this point is the question of the oracular element in so many of
the psalms, which, as we have seen, Gunkel attributed to the
influence of the canonical prophets;[1] for there is ample evidence
outside the Psalter to prove that during the monarchy and until
well into the post-exilic period there were prophets who had as
close a connexion with the formal religion of Israel as the priests
themselves and were only quite late in this period absorbed, like
the singers, into the Levitical orders.[2] This being the case, the
question arises as to whether or not the oracular element in the
Psalter and indeed some of the prayers themselves should not be
ascribed to such cultic prophets, who from the first show themselves to have been subject to the inspirational power of music.[3]
The question is important and deserves careful consideration;
for its implications for the study of the canonical prophets are
obvious. Indeed attempts have already been made, following the
lead offered by Mowinckel himself, to see, not only in the obvious
cases of Haggai and Zechariah but also in the books of Joel,[4]
Nahum,[5] Habakkuk,[6] and Zephaniah,[7] close ties with such a
cultic background. To say as much, however, is to begin to
trespass upon other ground so far as this volume is concerned; so
here our survey of trends in the study of the Psalter must be
brought to an end.

If, therefore, one may close this discussion with a simile, it is
to say that, while on the older critical view which is rapidly
passing away the Psalter was like a reservoir whose resources
were deep but well-fathomed, the tendency now is to regard this
reservoir as fed by a river, equally deep but far more mysterious,

[1] Mowinckel includes here Pss. ii, xii, xiv, xx, xxi, xlv, l, lx, lxii, lxxii, lxxv, lxxxi,
lxxxii, lxxxv, lxxxvii, lxxxix. 20–38 (EVV. 19–37), xci, xcv, cx, cxxxii.

[2] e.g. (*a*) Num. xi. 24 *b*–30 (E?); 1 Kings xviii. 30 ff., xix. 10, 14, xxii (cf. 2 Chron.
xviii); 2 Kings iv. 23; Jer. v. 30 f., xxiii. 11, xxxv. 4; Lam. ii. 20: (*b*) 1 Chron. xxv.
1–6; 2 Chron. xx. 1–30, xxxiv. 30 (as compared with 2 Kings xxiii. 2). Cf. now
A. R. Johnson, *The Cultic Prophet in Ancient Israel*, 1944; also, for an attempt to
examine the problem on a much wider basis, A. Haldar, *Associations of Cult Prophets
among the Ancient Semites*, 1945.

[3] Cf. 1 Sam. x. 5–13; 2 Kings iii. 15.

[4] e.g. A. S. Kapelrud, *Joel Studies*, 1948.

[5] e.g. A. Haldar, *Studies in the Book of Nahum* (U.U.Å. 1946: 7), 1947.

[6] e.g. P. Humbert, *Problèmes du livre d'Habacuc*, 1944.

[7] G. Gerleman, *Zephanja textkritisch und literarisch untersucht*, 1942.

whose course still remains to be charted but the exploring of which promises to open up far wider and richer territories in the realm of Israel's faith and worship than had hitherto been suspected. All in all, therefore, it was with good reason that Gunkel modestly prefixed to his commentary the well-known words, 'Bin ich zu Ende, beginne ich'. A. R. JOHNSON

BIBLIOGRAPHY

Commentaries and General Introductions

BARNES, W. E. *The Psalms*, W.C., 1931.

BENTZEN, A. *Forelæsninger over Indledning til de gammeltestamentlige Salmer*, 1932.

— *Fortolkning til de gammeltestamentlige Salmer*, 1932.

BÖHL, F. M. Th., and GEMSER, B. *De Psalmen*, T.U., i, 1946; ii, 1947; iii, 1949.

BUTTENWIESER, M. *The Psalms*, 1938.

CALÈS, J. *Le Livre des psaumes*, 1936.

EERDMANS, B. D. *The Hebrew Book of Psalms*, O.T.S. iv, 1947.

GUNKEL, H. *Die Psalmen*, H.K., 1926.

— and BEGRICH, J. *Einleitung in die Psalmen*, H.K., 1933.

HERKENNE, H. *Das Buch der Psalmen*, H.S.A.Tes., 1936.

KÖNIG, E. *Die Psalmen*, 1927.

LESLIE, E. A. *The Psalms*, 1949.

NÖTSCHER, F. *Die Psalmen*, Echt.B., 1947.

OESTERLEY, W. O. E. *The Psalms*, 1939.

PETERS, N. **Das Buch der Psalmen*, 1930.

PODECHARD, E. *Le Psautier. Traduction littérale et explication*, i, 1949; id., *Notes critiques* i, 1949.

SCHMIDT, H. *Die Psalmen*, H.A.T., 1934.

WEISER, A. *Die Psalmen ausgewählt, übersetzt und erklärt*, 1935, 2nd ed. enlarged as *Die Psalmen übersetzt und erklärt*, i, 1939.

Special Studies

BARTH, C. *Die Errettung vom Tode in den individuellen Klage- und Dankliedern des Alten Testamentes*, 1947.

BENTZEN, A. *Det sakrale kongedømme. Bemærkninger i en løbende diskussion om de gammeltestamentlige Salmer*, 1945.

BIRKELAND, H. *'anî und 'anāw in den Psalmen* (Videnskapsselskapets Skrifter II. Hist.-Filos. Klasse 1932, No. 4), 1933.

— *Die Feinde des Individuums in der israelitischen Psalmenliteratur*, 1933.

BRUNO, A. *Der Rhythmus der alttestamentlichen Dichtung. Eine Untersuchung über die Psalmen I–LXXII*, 1930.

CASTELLINO, R. G. *Le lamentazioni individuali e gli inni in Babilonia e in Israele*, 1939.

CAUSSE, A. *Les 'Pauvres' d'Israël* (Prophètes, psalmistes et messianistes), E.H.P.R. iii, 1922.

— *Les Plus Vieux Chants de la Bible*, E.H.P.R. xiv, 1926.

CONDAMIN, A. *Poèmes de la Bible avec une introduction sur la strophique hébraïque*, 1933.

CUMMING, C. G. *The Assyrian and Hebrew Hymns of Praise*, 1934.

DESNOYERS, L. **Les Psaumes. Traduction rythmée d'après l'hébreu*, 1935.

GIERLICH, A. M. *Der Lichtgedanke in den Psalmen*, 1940.

HALLER, M. ***'Ein Jahrzehnt Psalmenforschung', *T.R.*, N.F. i, 1929, pp. 377–402.

HYLANDER, I. *Gamla Testamentets Psalmbok*, 1937.

JAMES, F. *Thirty Psalmists*, 1938.

JOHNSON, A. R. 'The Rôle of the King in the Jerusalem Cultus', in *The Labyrinth*, ed. S. H. Hooke, 1935, pp. 71–111.

KEET, C. C. *A Liturgical Study of the Psalter*, 1928.

KENNETT, R. H. 'The Historical Background of the Psalms', in *Old Testament Essays*, 1928, pp. 119–218.

KRAFT, C. F. *The Strophic Structure of Hebrew Poetry as illustrated in the first book of the Psalter*, 1938.

LAUHA, A. *Die Geschichtsmotive in den alttestamentlichen Psalmen*, A.A.S.F., B LVI, 1, 1945.

LÖHR, M. *Psalmenstudien*, B.W.A.T., N.F. iii, 1922.

MARSCHALL, G. **Die 'Gottlosen' des ersten Psalmenbuches*, 1929.

MÖLLER, H. **Strophenbau der Psalmen*, 1931.

MOWINCKEL, S. *Kongesalmerne i det Gamle Testamente*, 1916.

— *Psalmenstudien I–VI* (Videnskapsselskapets Skrifter II. Hist.-Filos. Klasse, 1921, No. 4; 1921, No. 6; 1922, No. 1; 1922, No. 2; 1923, No. 3; 1924, No. 1), 1921–4.

NICOLSKY, N. *Spuren magischer Formeln in den Psalmen*, B.Z.A.W. xlvi, 1927.

OESTERLEY, W. O. E. *A Fresh Approach to the Psalms*, 1937.

PATERSON, J. *The Praises of Israel. Studies literary and religious in the Psalms*, 1950.

PATTON, J. H. *Canaanite Parallels in the Book of Psalms*, 1944.

PETERS, J. P. *The Psalms as Liturgies*, 1922.

QUELL, G. *Das kultische Problem der Psalmen*, B.W.A.T., N.F. xi, 1926.

RIDDERBOS, N. H. *De 'Werkers der Ongerechtighed' in de individueele Psalmen*, 1939.

SCHMIDT, H. *Die Thronfahrt Jahves am Fest der Jahreswende im alten Israel*, 1927.

SCHMIDT, H. *Das Gebet der Angeklagten im Alten Testament*, B.Z.A.W. xlix, 1928.

SCHÖNBÄCHLER, V. *Die Stellung der Psalmen zum alttestamentlichen Opferkult*, 1941.

SCHULZ, A. *Kritisches zum Psalter*, A.A. xii, 1, 1932.

— *Psalmen-Fragen*, A.A. xiv, 1, 1940.

SIMPSON, D. C. (ed.). *The Psalmists*, 1926.

SMITH, J. M. P. *The Religion of the Psalms*, 1922.

SNAITH, N. H. *Studies in the Psalter*, 1934.

STUMMER, F. *Sumerisch-akkadische Parallelen zum Aufbau alttestamentlicher Psalmen*, 1922.

WELCH, A. C. *The Psalter in Life, Worship and History*, 1926.

WIDENGREN, G. *The Accadian and Hebrew Psalms of Lamentation as Religious Documents*, 1937.

WUTZ, F. *Die Psalmen textkritisch untersucht*, 1925.

VII

THE WISDOM LITERATURE

I. INTRODUCTORY

APART from Job and Ecclesiastes, it is only within recent years that the books which belong to the Wisdom Literature, or Hokmah, have come under close scrutiny, to be examined against their proper background. According to the methodical type-analysis (*Gattungsforschung*) of Gunkel, the single *māšāl* developed into groups of aphorisms, extended maxims, and didactic poems of still greater length, ending up on the one hand with the collection of aphorisms, and, on the other, with a considerable didactic poem, such as Job. The Old Testament itself often compares Israelite Hokmah with its counterpart among its neighbours, the Edomites, Arabs and Egyptians, and now scholars have learnt to see it, too, against the background of the Wisdom of the ancient east. From Egypt have come a round dozen of such Wisdom books[1] extending from the third to the end of the first millennium B.C., and, with the exception of the latest, all proffering the class ethics of a feudal aristocracy. The dependence of Israelite Wisdom on that of Egypt, which had already been recognized by Gunkel, was proved when Erman recognized the original of Prov. xxii. 17–xxiii. 11 in the Wisdom book of Amenemope. Our knowledge of Babylonian and Assyrian Wisdom[2] is not so complete, but it was certainly not less significant in either extent or importance. We know how it enriched Greek literature,[3] and that it reached back into Sumerian times.[4] The Aramaic Aḥiḳar, which was

[1] In addition to the texts edited by Humbert, we must now add those mentioned in *J.E.O.L.* ii, 7, 1940, pp. 298 ff., 8, 1942, pp. 587 ff.

[2] With B. Meissner, *Die babylonisch-assyrische Literatur*, 1927, pp. 79 ff., cf. now Du Toit, although his work suffers somewhat from dogmatic narrowness.

[3] Cf. E. Ebeling, *Die babylonische Fabel und ihre Bedeutung für die Literaturgeschichte*, M.A.O.G. ii, 3, 1927.

[4] S. N. Kramer, *Sumerian Literary Texts from Nippur* (*A.A.S.O.R.* xxiii), 1944, pp. 35 ff.; C. J. Gadd, *Ideas of Divine Rule in the Ancient East*, 1948, pp. 81 ff.

known to the Jews of Elephantine and which shows many points of contact with Proverbs, can serve as an example of Assyrian Wisdom. These connexions between Israelite and ancient oriental Hokmah are often so close that a verse of the one may quite easily be exchanged for a verse of the other, without any noticeable drop in moral quality. It is this relationship that explains what separates the Israelite Wisdom Books so completely from the rest of the Old Testament, namely, that its piety scarcely mentions the election of Israel or its history. The opposite question, whether Israel's Wisdom might not in turn have contributed something to the lore of the ancient east, is raised by Kittel, Oesterley and Robinson, and Du Toit; the last-named would point to Aḥiḳar in this connexion. The results attained by type-analysis have a bearing on questions of date. The tradition that ascribed Proverbs, Ecclesiastes, and the Book of Wisdom to Solomon has long been disposed of with little difficulty; it was replaced by the view that the individual books were of quite late date, since this literature was strongly to the fore in the Apocrypha, continuing on into Jewish literature in Pirke Aboth, and into early Christian literature in one element in the Synoptic tradition, the Epistle of James, and the Didache. Now, however, they would appear to be parts of a long development in literary history, so that the latest collection in Proverbs, on literary grounds, must be slightly older than Jesus Sirach. Amos (iii. 3–6, vi. 12), and Isaiah (v. 1–7, x. 15, xxix. 14) testify to the presence of wisdom poetry in the middle of the monarchic period, while the fable of Jotham (Judges ix) carries it back to the time of the Judges. Since it cannot, therefore, have just sprung up in post-exilic times as the successor of Law and Prophecy, such late datings call for careful re-examination.

This change in circumstances has led also to a more detailed study of the contents of these books; the general results may be found in the following works. Ranston gives an interesting appreciation of Hokmah as a whole, tracing, amongst other things, its relationship to the prophetic literature, but his statement of the case makes it appear simpler and more uniform than it really was. Rankin traces a few fundamental ideas right through the literature: God as creator, divine and human responsibility, divine providence, reward and punishment, belief in a future life. Zimmerli examines the peculiar religious structure of Hokmah: on the main point of what profits man and how he may 'become satisfied', Hokmah approaches the question entirely from the human side, without reference to membership among the covenant people; it frames its answer on grounds of purely human experience and sagacity, and makes the riddle of life into a question of longevity; the writers of Job and Ecclesiastes, each in his own way, point out the weakness of this system. Rylaarsdam poses the question, in what way the authors of these books conceived 'that God and his ways became known to them'; he finds different, indeed opposing, answers, which, however, find their meeting-point in the question of authority, and the problem: 'Nature or Grace?' Along these lines Rylaarsdam then discusses the nationalization of Hokmah, its hopes, transcendence, and the relation of wisdom and spirit.

II. PROVERBS

The previously mentioned theory that Amenemope is the original of Prov. xxii. 17–xxiii. 11 has now been generally accepted. The attempt to dispute this historical connexion between the two texts, or to trace both back to an earlier Hebrew collection of proverbs has been given up. Amenemope cannot be torn out of its place in the succession of Egyptian wisdom books, and Ptahhotep and Merikare already bear a religious tint. On the other hand, it is just as old-fashioned to suppose that the borrowing was a purely mechanical process; the translator treated his original with considerable freedom, adapting it to suit the rhythm of Hebrew, the land of Palestine, and the religion of Israel.

The deduction has been previously drawn from language and subject-matter that, of the nine collections which go to make up the book of Proverbs, the first (i–ix) was the youngest. This has been confirmed by type-analysis, which finds here larger units, and indeed also traces of other literary types. The earliest possible attribution of the whole book would be to the fourth century B.C.; the lower limit is given by Jesus Sirach, i.e. *c.* 200. It is more difficult to assign a date to the other collections. The most simple forms are to be found in the second (x. 1–xxii. 16) and fifth (xxv–xxix). There is now again more disposition to treat seriously the ascription of both to Solomon who, according to 1 Kings v. 9–14 and x. 1–10, was himself a 'sage' and composer of proverbs; this is also true of the statement in xxv. 1 that 'the men of Hezekiah' had a hand in compiling that collection. The existence of a school of wisdom poetry is thus confirmed for the period of the monarchy, and the previously mentioned passages in the prophets describe the profession of the sages and give an imitation of their poetic style. It has been customary to take the royal proverbs in this sense. In the same way, we now know that the idea of retribution and the sense of indifference towards the cultus are not primarily sequels to prophetic teaching; further, Torah, in Proverbs, does not mean the written law, but the instruction of the sages themselves. Consequently the second to the fourth collections (x–xxix) are nowadays attributed to the pre-exilic period even by many thoroughly critical scholars. That the practice of wisdom found a home at Solomon's court is made the more likely by the latter's strong leaning towards the Egyptian monarchy, and it must on other counts have been a centre of literary culture.

Yet it is surprising that animal and plant proverbs, such as are referred to in 1 Kings v. 12–13, scarcely occur at all in the above-mentioned collections, with the exception of xxx. 15–33 (xxx. 1–xxxi. 9 appearing to be of non-Israelite origin). In the same way the curse, as preserved in Jer. xvii. 5, to form the counterpart of the blessing, is lacking. Wisdom, in fact, appears both tamer and less harmful than the contemporary prophetical polemic would lead us to expect. Nor can the presence of such material at so early a period be proved from other literary parallels, since the date assigned to Amenemope oscillates between the tenth and sixth centuries, and Aḥiḳar is no older. It is therefore understandable if many scholars, in spite of this newer point of view, still assign the oldest collections, and therewith the golden age of wisdom poetry, to post-exilic times.[1] In that case

---

[1] So Kittel, pp. 721 f., 725; Hempel, pp. 51 f., 55; Causse, pp. 164 ff.; Hamp,

the titles in x. 1 and xxv. 4 will have remained the same, while the content of these collections was renovated as time went on.

We can describe the development of Israelite Hokmah only in broad outline. Simple proverbial sayings, which occur universally, the Hebrews may have brought with them from the wilderness. The elaboration of a developed stylistic wisdom first took place, however, on Canaanite soil, in dependence on the developed styles from East and West that they found there. Presumably it was Egyptian wisdom that was chiefly followed at Solomon's court. By Hezekiah's time the hitherto purely oral transmission may have been changed to writing (Bentzen). Quite possibly this occupation was still for a time bound up with the office of *sōpēr* (Ps. xlv. 2), as the passages referred to in the prophets suggest (Duesberg, Vriezen). But, more and more it lost the character of a class-ethic and catered for all who were concerned to pass through life with honour and as free from hurt as possible. Oesterley and Robinson describe in a short and telling way how it was adapted to Israelite circumstances and became more and more imbued with the spirit of Israelite religion. Fichtner illustrates at greater length its differentiation from its ancient oriental basis; how the rules of mere worldly wisdom diminish, eudaemonistic motives are replaced by moral and religious ones, and instead of having success in life or office as the norm, we have the divine will, and later also the written law; woman is more highly regarded, adultery more strongly condemned, moral exhortations are more frequent, and religious injunctions of a fundamental type. Such a change can be traced down into the later wisdom books, and so too may it be observed in the Septuagint.[1]

Gunkel considered that Israelite wisdom was itself at first purely this-worldly and eudaemonistic and opportunist; but this has been questioned by Rylaarsdam and Vriezen, for ancient oriental wisdom also rested in part on a religious basis. That the

p. 6. Hylmö, p. 305, regards collections III–V as pre-exilic, the second he brings into close connexion with the first. Albright too, who particularly emphasized the Canaanite element in chapters viii, ix, does not put the collecting of the material before the fifth century, the final redaction taking place in the third (*J.B.L.* lxi, 1942, p. 123).

[1] Cf. G. Bertram, *Z.A.W.* liv, 1936, pp. 153 ff.

central ideas of Israelite religion first come into view surprisingly late is of course hardly to be denied, but it may quite well be that Gunkel has painted too simple and innocuous a picture of the older wisdom. Many passages represent the Sages as possessing and putting to full use all the 'knowledge' of their times (Bentzen, i, p. 172); furthermore the pre-history of the *mašāl* may be a good deal more complex than is there recognized (Boström). Yet, in my view, there still seems to be insufficient evidence for making wisdom an offshoot of the cultus, and bringing it into connexion with the psalms, as is suggested by Bentzen, though admittedly with much greater reserve than by Engnell.

The hypostatization of wisdom,[1] which appears in Prov. viii. 22–31, Job xxviii, Sir. xxiv, Wisd. vii, &c., as a Heavenly Being by the side of God, and which was the forerunner of the Sophia of the gnostic systems, is still a vexed question. Some (Kittel, Sellin) have tried to derive it from the Greek Nous or Logos; but the conception can be traced back on West-Semitic soil far beyond the times of Greek influence. Others (Gemser, Humbert) have brought in comparisons with Babylonian and Egyptian divinities who have wisdom as an attribute; but that is not quite the same thing, and there is often a disagreement in sex. The nearest parallels are those hypostases which are just as commonly found in the ancient orient, namely, personified attributes or abstractions such as Righteousness, Truth, &c., and these have received a thorough investigation by Ringgren. A 'wisdom' of this sort is exemplified in Aḥiḳar and in Ugaritic.[2] But now the question becomes still more involved by the problem of the seven-pillared house built by Wisdom (ix. 1). Archaeology failed to provide evidence of any such house-style, and this appeared to support Reitzenstein's theory of a cosmic interpretation, wherein the world rests on the seven planets, a conception of which we have evidence for a later period (Boström, pp. 1 ff.; Rankin,

---

[1] Cf. P. Heinisch, *Personifikationen und Hypostasen im Alten Testament*, 1921, *Die persönliche Weisheit des Alten Testaments*, 1926; Humbert, *R.G.G.*[2] v, 180 ff., *T.R.*, 1933, pp. 286 ff.; Rankin, pp. 222 ff.; J. Arvedson, *Das Mysterium Christi*, 1937, pp. 158 ff.; and now particularly Ringgren.

[2] According to D. Nielsen, *Z.D.M.G.* xcii, 1938, pp. 510 ff., 550 ff., in South-Arabic also; against this see Ringgren, pp. 186 ff.

pp. 251 f.[1]). But Gemser has now discovered the seven pillars in Sennacherib's New Year Festival house, so that the cosmic significance here is not uncircumventable. But there remains the problem of the warning against the 'strange woman' (v, vi. 20–35, vii). Reitzenstein and Kittel again both take it allegorically, as referring to a foreign (Greek?) religion. Others, however, interpret it concretely as referring to the foreign harlot or the adulterous Jewess. Boström makes a good case against the allegorical interpretation by remarking that the straightforward warning against harlots is common enough in both Israelite and Egyptian wisdom. But then he goes half-way towards re-accepting it when he sees in this 'stranger' the 'lady' of foreign traders who practise a foreign cult of a strongly sexual hue which is therefore dangerous. She it is, whether indeed she be Astarte the goddess of love, or Siduri-Sabitu,[2] that stands behind the figure of 'Lady Foolishness' (ix. 7 ff.); but she also provided the paint that colours the picture of wisdom as bride (ix. 1–6). Rankin (pp. 103 ff.) and Ringgren (pp. 132 ff.) accept Boström's acute and often penetrating observations, but Gemser and Humbert[3] still maintain that an Israelite woman is meant. We may at least say that some traits derive from that other, cult-mythical, milieu.

III. JOB

It is hardly accidental that interest in the book of Job has become particularly keen during the last decades. The literature on the subject has been both prolific and exceedingly helpful, if we think of the commentaries by Dhorme, Peters, Szczygiel, and Hölscher, among others, or the monographs of Kraeling, Lindblom, and Stevenson.

It is quite generally accepted today that the author of the poetic dialogue took over an ancient, possibly Edomite, tale of the afflictions and trials of a righteous man, and used it as the

---

[1] Cf. also W. Staerk, *Z.N.W.* xxxv, 1936, pp. 232 ff.

[2] Cf. in this connexion W. F. Albright, *F.S.A.C.*, pp. 282 ff. = pp. 365 ff. of the German edition (1949).

[3] *R.E.S.*, 1937, pp. 49 ff.; *Mélanges Syriens*, 1939, pp. 259 ff.

framework of his story.[1] But over against the view that i. 1–10 and xlii. 10–17 were taken over word for word from any such popular 'story book', the common opinion inclines to a more complicated previous history. Further possibilities in the way of reconstruction are opened up if we include ii. 11–13 and xlii. 7–9 in the discussion. Alt supposes a primary form of the story in which only the loss of possessions and their restoration occurred, i.e. what corresponds roughly to i, and xlii. 11–17. Lindblom is able to wrest out of xlii. 7 an original version, ending with xlii. 10 f., in which it was Job's friends, not his wife, that incited him against God, his wife and the Satan being added only after the story had been adopted by Israel. Kraeling distinguishes the following: an older form located in Aramaean terrain (i. 1–ii. 10) ending with the spoliation of Job, a later version sited in Edom (ii. 11–13 and xlii. 7–9) and then xlii. 10–17, the editor's 'make-shift conclusion'.

In the midst of such divergent views, to date the tale itself is naturally difficult. Kraeling together with Oesterley and Robinson would make it pre-exilic, but a distinction is now normally made between the old material and its present developed form which, with its Aramaisms, points clearly to the post-exilic period (Pfeiffer, Albright, Lods). But in that case we are approaching the time of the very author of Job himself, and consequently Eissfeldt, Hölscher and Bentzen, make the author himself responsible for a free handling of the traditional stuff, in which case, of course, we must face up to the presence of any inconsistencies. According to Stevenson, the framework was only put in, for the first time, by a later hand who missed all reference to a happy ending in the dialogue; but how is one to conceive of the dialogue without the framework?

A separate problem concerns the source of this dialogue style which is unique in the Old Testament. L. Koehler[2] finds its prototype in judicial speech that also seeks to carry through an absolutely rigid point of view with the same passion and the same

---

[1] Eerdmans believes the framework of the story to be later than the dialogue, because of its supposedly later conception of God.

[2] *Die hebräische Rechtsgemeinde*, 1931, pp. 10 ff.

lack of development in thought. The jurist van Proosdij will not allow any place to the problem of pain or theodicy—nothing beyond a plain, concrete, passage-at-law. But in fact, wisdom poetry itself does show a tendency to develop the dialogue form; Egyptian wisdom has examples of fairly lengthy dialogues,[1] and so has the Babylonian too.[2] Bentzen sees here a dramatized form of the psalm of lament, whose connexion with Job has been long recognized; some such conversational form could then easily develop with the bringing in of the friends as comforters. These various factors may also have interacted upon one another. Type-analysis shows us in how masterly a manner the author of Job handles the most varied materials.

The authenticity of the Elihu speeches within the dialogue (xxxii–xxxvii) is now denied even by König, and the Roman Catholic scholars, Dhorme and Goettsberger. When they do still find champions (Thilo, Peters, Szczygiel), it is above all because in them alone in the whole book do we find offered us a rational solution of the problem; so that it may appear that by cutting them out, we are depriving the book of its point also. But did the author wish to give this solution? That, in fact, is just the question. It was precisely the lack of such a solution that must have led to their insertion to begin with. There are, however, today fewer who judge Elihu as unfavourably as Duhm did.

Almost as unanimously, chapter xxviii, the hymn to wisdom, is treated as secondary; if transferred to follow xlii. 6 (Szczygiel) it ceases to anticipate the speech of Yahweh, but it is impossible there on other grounds. The originality of the Yahweh speeches is attacked by Hempel and Kraeling, who would have the dialogue end with the passionate lament and accusation (xxix–xxxi). But how are we to get from there to the happy ending

---

[1] Cf. the dispute of the man weary of life with his soul, *A.O.T.*, pp. 25 ff.; the conversation of two vultures concerning retribution, G. Roeder, *Altägyptische Erzählungen und Märchen*, 1927, pp. 304 ff.; the conversation between cat and jackal concerning the power that rules the underworld, A. Wiedemann, *Der Alte Orient*, iii, 4, 1903, pp. 11 f.

[2] Cf. the dialogue of a nobleman and his slave, *A.O.T.*, pp. 287 ff., *Z.A.* xliii, 1936, pp. 32 ff.; the conversation of a scholar with his disciples concerning the value of secretarial ability, *M.D.O.G.* lviii, 1917, pp. 38 ff.

which is presupposed by the framework and the book as a whole? The reasons brought forward for their deletion are not compelling. The encounter with Yahweh does turn out differently from what Job had expected, even if the author has to take pains to make the difference apparent. Consequently these speeches represent an answer to the problem, and as such they are indispensable. Whether or not the description of the ostrich, the hippopotamus and the crocodile are to be deleted, as most modern writers hold, and the two speeches to be then condensed into one (Eissfeldt, Hölscher, Lindblom), is a minor point. Finally, the baldness and disorder of the third cycle of speeches (xxii–xxvii) needs some attention.

Some individuals have gone a good deal farther than this in breaking down the dialogue. The most important attempt of this kind is that of Baumgärtel, with which Kraeling's complicated analysis partly coincides. Baumgärtel leaves the poet only one single cycle of speeches and bits of one monologue of Job's. But he never really succeeds in justifying these numerous deletions; and the fact that it is just those sections that do not belong to the Wisdom category and those portions that do not treat of Job's individual case upon which the axe falls, betrays a *petitio principii*. A hymn-like note is found in *The Wisdom of Ben Sira* and in the Egyptian *Insinger Papyrus*. Consequently Baumgärtel has found little acceptance for his view.

The opposite tendency has also appeared, namely, that of emphasizing the existing inner unity more strongly in all critical discussions. Hertzberg, for example, considers the Elihu speeches to be so closely in line with the theological position of the book as a whole, that he thinks it must be traced back to collaborative work between the author and a fellow worker. Sellin, again, would make the author himself responsible for inserting at a later period the suspected portions. But his parallel from Goethe's lifelong preoccupation with the Faust theme is not so easily carried over. Even in the case of chapter xxviii, where others too deem identity of authorship possible, we may be content to recognize a certain affinity of spirit. That those preoccupied with the problem fastened directly on this material, and that this led to continual new additions to the book is evident without any further ado.

The home of the author has been sought in Egypt (Humbert) or Edom, possibly Arabia. But Edom is simply the background for the story, and in other points the grounds adduced in its favour cancel each other out. This region could have become just as familiar to him from travelling. His psychology is actually not Arabian but Israelite (Pedersen).

The date of the book can be given only very approximately. Goettsberger, Pfeiffer, and Szczygiel would give *c*. 600 B.C. as its date of composition. But we must recognize in it an acquaintance with Jeremiah, Ezekiel, and the Priestly Code. The highly developed and complex poetic form, too, is more easily to be understood at a later time. Consequently the usual dating between 400 and 200 B.C. has most to be said for it. Pedersen and Bentzen refrain from giving any date.

With what conclusions are we left? After all deletions we have left a work of literature that, even on the score of its size—Stevenson reckons it at a minimum of 800 lines without the framework—and the skill of its portrayal, stands out as 'one of the greatest riddles and marvels of literary history' (Hempel). Baumgärtel rejects the usual description of it as 'didactic poetry' as making it altogether too academic. He has a certain amount of justification in so far as the poem has certainly grown out of the poet's own hard experience, and that 'Job' may be more or less equated with the poet himself. That he only wished to entertain his readers (Kraeling), or to pose a problem in all its magnitude without any attempt of his own at solving it (Pedersen), is scarcely credible. The poet does, however, often go beyond his own particular case to the more general problem, and a certain academic note is imparted by the very forms of the wisdom poetry that he utilizes. Foreign, particularly Babylonian, literary influence has often been assumed. The name 'the Babylonian Job' has been given to the poem of thanksgiving beginning 'I will praise the Lord of Wisdom' (*A.O.T.*, 273 ff.); but the view has now been generally accepted that this poem, with the laments and doubts of its first part, is simply an independent Babylonian

counterpart. The same is true also of the above-mentioned Babylonian dialogues; these grew up out of the same soil of ancient
oriental wisdom, though now standing partly in opposition to it.
A more detailed comparison with the spiritual position of Job
and Ecclesiastes is to be found in Stamm.

Unfortunately we have no room here to discuss the sequence
and development of thought in the book when treated on this
critical basis. We must be satisfied with referring to the relevant
literature, particularly to Hempel's article and Stevenson's study,
that contains so much that is new. To show how the interpretation of important passages is still in a state of dispute even today,
we may mention xix. 25–7, once the *locus classicus* for the
resurrection. Opinions still differ as to whether Job is to 'see God'
in this or in a future, life. Not only Lindblom and Hertzberg,
but also Dhorme, Peters and Szczygiel support the first view.
Those who support the *post mortem* interpretation however are not
showing a mere return to tradition as may be seen by the varying
ways in which it is treated by Ranston, Hölscher, Humbert, and
Rankin. These general points seem to me to be clear: (1) The
rendering of *gō'alī* by 'my Redeemer', which goes back to Jerome
and Luther, does not rightly express his legal function; (2)
'Vindication, not the vindicator is the essential requirement of
the situation' (Stevenson); since the person is not defined, must it
inevitably be God? (3) The setting of these verses in a connexion
where this confidence bears no fruit, tells against according to
these verses a central significance in the old sense. In the same
way the parallel with the cultic cry of the Ugaritic myth: 'I
know that Aliyn Baal is alive' is purely fortuitous, since both
times it occurs in entirely different situations.

IV. ECCLESIASTES

The difficulties with which the would-be exegete of this book
has to contend are indicated by the fact that this work, which
shows a peculiar and independent by-formation of wisdom, is
described by Heine as 'the quintessence of scepticism', but by
Franz Delitzsch as 'the quintessence of piety'. The matter at
issue is, whether this diversity is to be explained by the vicissitudes

of the book's history, or whether the dichotomy is in the character of the author himself. Though the question is still in dispute, we have advanced a certain distance, as may be gathered from reading Galling's review of recent investigations.

The riddle of the author's name, *Ḳôhelet*, is usually explained now by analogy with those masculine names which have a feminine termination, either with or without the article, and which originally denoted a man's calling. That the author represents himself as King Solomon (i. 1, 12, 16) is unmistakable, though not explicitly stated; this, however, is not a later addition, but a literary disguise taken over from Egyptian practice. Although the impersonation is one of position rather than of personal identity, no other king of Israel will fit the case so well. Egyptian wisdom again provides the explanation for the 'I was king' (i. 12), which are the words of the dying, or—as the words occur in Egyptian tomb inscriptions—already dead, monarch; they are his last testament (Torczyner, Galling).

The most important question concerns the structure of the book. Allgeier, Kuhn, Odeberg, Thilo are at pains to establish the presence of a self-consistent system of thought throughout the book. But on the whole, the impression makes itself felt that such is not in fact the case, any more than in the other wisdom books—Job is an exception. Ecclesiastes is a collection of separate sayings from 2 to 15 lines long, just strung together. Where to draw the line between one saying and the next is not always clear, and so their number varies; Gemser makes them 32; Galling 37.[1] A distinction is to be made between the editor of the separate sayings, the sage and poet Ecclesiastes himself, and whoever published the final version, whether or not they are one and the same person. What Ecclesiastes thought and felt may be gathered from the separate sayings alone, since they are the original units. Their collocation and consequent development into book form is not the result of pure chance, however, but is determined by subject matter and formal association, especially in the first

---

[1] Hertzberg distinguishes 34 sub-divisions, which he groups in 12 longer poems, these latter, though not co-terminous with the traditional chapters, are somehow related to them and have also some interconnexion between themselves.

chapter. But the position is not much different from that in Proverbs, and so is of no great importance for our understanding. For this reason, and in consequence of a somewhat changed outlook on the matter of inner contradictions, the earlier attempts to explain the problem have been largely laid aside; these attempted to infuse into the book an appreciably better arrangement and a more consistent standpoint by radical transpositions and deletions. Today, some few glosses, such as iii. 17, vii. 18 b, viii. 5, xii. 12–14, are normally regarded as intended to render harmless certain heresies on the part of the author and to support traditional piety; but apart from these—Hertzberg and Gemser would admit the last of them only—the book is regarded as essentially authentic.

It is recognized on all sides that this book cannot have been written either by, or in the time of, Solomon. Language considerations would forbid it by reason of the presence of Aramaic elements even if Greek influence is disputed. It may be assigned to the latter part of the third century B.C. The lower limit is marked by Ben Sira, if he really was acquainted with Ecclesiastes, and the Maccabean period with its entirely different spirit. The attempt to fix the date of composition more nearly by means of supposed references to historical events has not led to any useful result. Sellin's attempt to make ix. 13–16 refer to Archimedes and the siege of Syracuse, or Dornseiff's preference for the battle of Marathon, are no improvement on the Jewish attempts to link it up with events in biblical history. As in iv. 13–16, viii. 2, x. 6, &c., we are dealing with stock illustrations.

Owing to the wide range covered, and the acquaintance with Egyptian wisdom that is displayed, Sellin and Humbert regard the place of origin of Ecclesiastes as probably Alexandria. But such considerations are scarcely more cogent than in the case of Job; it appears sufficient to predicate a school of thought influenced by Egypt (Galling).

The determination and type-analytical classification of the separate sayings is most satisfactorily carried out in the commentaries of Galling and Gemser. For the most part the literary forms are those in normal use. There is a more frequent use of the appeal to personal experience (i. 12 ff., iv. 7 f., vii. 25–8, viii. 10), which gives to the whole book its personal tone, though this cannot be interpreted autobiographically, for its use of the mode of direct address is simply to make the statement of a general truth more concrete. The maxims in vii, ix, and x, particularly, have close parallels in the book of Proverbs and in Sirach; and there is a close approximation in themes. But often enough where we have a positively expressed maxim we find a limiting clause or even a contrary expression appended to it (v. 9, ix. 16 a, 18, 16 b), or the sense of it may be the opposite of the usual (vii. 1–4). Here again attempts have been made to distinguish between the authentic Ecclesiastes and the hand of a later corrector (Lods and others). But this unevenness shows itself throughout the book, as well as in many individual sayings. It is not simply the sign of a 'dialectic' mode of thought; it indicates rather Ecclesiastes' alternating attitude to tradition: now with it, now standing against it. This half and half reaction has roots that go deeper: he does not know what to make of the doctrine of retribution, but does not quite like to break with ancestral belief. This fact sets us the task of ascertaining where and to what extent he is just passing on the wisdom of the schools, and where his own divergent standpoint comes in.

Scholars have tried to explain this peculiar attitude of Ecclesiastes from various angles. Pedersen starts with the particular psychological presuppositions of the early Israelites: the conception of 'Righteousness', which denotes a harmony between human and divine activity, is the decisive one for ethics, but it was strongly shaken by the prophetic development of the notion of God's sovereign power. This latter conception modified the relative position of man, and carries us very near to scepticism. Even Hertzberg finds the sovereignty of God, depersonalized and fatalistically construed, to be one of Ecclesiastes' main ideas. Galling, however, produces well-founded arguments against his assumption that Ecclesiastes was strongly influenced by Gen. i–iii. In my estimation, Zimmerli's suggestions, which are supported in the main by Galling, have most to be said for them. These are as follows: Ecclesiastes starts along the normal wisdom-school lines, but is not so easily satisfied; he pursues certain trends of thought to their extreme end and so to conclusions quite unexpected by himself. His positive assertions are merely second-hand declarations useful for the practical business of life, but built on shaky foundations. He has gradually grown out of the old wisdom, but does not feel any joy on that account and ends up with a sorry theory, quite divorced from historical fact, of Nature as the field of caprice and irregularity.

This view is definitive as regards our all-round estimate of him. There are still those who will try to credit him with a more positive assessment, e.g. Thilo, Hertzberg, and Eichrodt. K. Barth, too, sees in him a philosopher whose views on civilization and society bring him near to a Christian standpoint, while W. Vischer has indeed expounded him along these lines. But anything that Ecclesiastes has in common with Christian belief is purely negative. It is true enough that the transitoriness of man and the uncertainty of his existence can hardly be more impressively or vehemently described than by him; but he goes no farther. The reaction against wisdom leads him to no new and better solution. His spiritual perception carries him as far as criticism and scepticism, but not to the building up of a new and perfected doctrine on this basis. So that, for him, 'to fear God' (iii. 14, &c.) means merely to have sufficiency and freedom from want (Galling); or again, the common phrases 'gift of God', and 'from the hand of God' (ii. 24, iii. 12 f., v. 18), are an indication of the chanciness and caprice of his gift (Bentzen). Consequently Galling and Zimmerli quite rightly warn us against over-estimating his ideas. Other scholars too are forced to admit how lukewarm his faith really is, and how far he falls below the higher peaks of Old Testament piety. One has only to compare his faith with the wrestlings of a Job or the assurance expressed in Psalm lxxiii, to see that no artifices of exegesis will serve to explain this away. Kuhn holds the view that Ecclesiastes represents the wisdom which is to be preached to the people, as distinguished from its esoteric form as it appears in Canticles; but the supposition of such a relationship to Canticles is just as arbitrary as the mystical allegorization of the latter. Odeberg would have us see in the frequent phrase 'under the sun' (i. 3, &c.) only a preliminary attitude, in comparison with which the book itself in viii. 15 f., ix. 10. &c., recommends a better and a higher life; but he is placing far too much weight on that expression, which is to be found in both Phoenician and Egyptian sources. So Zimmerli may be right in saying: 'We must guard against making Ecclesiastes into a pious soul who treads the path of the biblical believer. He is not. But perhaps just in his strange piety . . . he becomes a dependable witness, in his way, to the inescapable bankruptcy of a wisdom philosophy that concerns itself only with man's earthly needs.'

The question of foreign influences naturally arose in connexion with a mode of thought so unusual within the Old Testament. Greek philosophy sprang first to mind, particularly Heraclitus' πάντα ῥεῖ, the Stoa and Epicurus, or the cynic-stoic diatribe. But Pedersen has shown that in spite of superficial similarities the estimate of mankind is entirely different on the two sides. Galling holds similar views, and he regards the matter of literary dependence on Theognis and the Greek gnomists, which Ranston asserts, as, for the most part, just superficial resemblance. In a few cases of closer correspondence the Greek saying itself may be suspected of being of oriental extraction (Dornseiff). Consequently Greek influence may be reduced to the role of helping to bring about the condition under which an Ecclesiastes could arise (Pedersen); or, with Hempel, be the source of his logically consistent thought; or again, with Zimmerli, provide the idea of an unchanging natural law. But much that is considered to be Greek is equally to be found in old oriental sources too. The exhortation to taste the pleasures of life in view of death's onset is an old motif in Egyptian and Babylonian drinking songs. Scepticism, too, is found there from of old, as an undercurrent of their wisdom—in Babylon, in the Dialogue between Lord and Slave, in Egypt, in the Harpist's Song and other texts dealt with by Humbert, while Galling has a comparison with the Insinger papyrus, which stands nearest in point of time. But no one has been able to adduce a direct connexion, comparable with the case of Amenemope and Proverbs anywhere. All these parallel instances accompany Ecclesiastes on his road but a very short way. They lack the personal vehemence which is here added to what is really a quite respectable intellectual product, and last but not least, the background of that ever recurring Israelite faith in God. Ecclesiastes therefore takes up his own particular position even within the field of oriental scepticism. Pedersen describes him as a typical example of the transitional period in the spiritual development of hellenistic Judaism, which was then swept away by the rising tide of the Maccabean period and the growth of apocalyptic.

V. WISDOM IN THE OLD TESTAMENT APOCRYPHA

In order to obtain a complete picture it is necessary to include this section. In addition to the various commentaries, mostly Roman Catholic, useful service is rendered by the Introductions of Torrey and Pfeiffer.

The Wisdom of Ben Sira, which was composed *c.* 180 B.C., still bears many traces of the simple wisdom book about it, and stands right in line with the school tradition, but it is both more uniform and more personal. This is particularly to be seen in its inclusion of discrete types (hymns, laments and thanksgiving songs, prophetic passages), which make up almost a quarter of the whole, and add much to its vividness. At the same time, the national religious heritage, which has been hitherto missing from literature of this type, finds a place; moreover, we do get here sacred history and appreciation of the cultus, while the Law is found side by side with wisdom with which, indeed, it is identified. In fact, Ben Sira is the first scribe (*sōpēr*). The book deals only in an indirect fashion with the influx of Hellenism, which was the great danger of the day, especially since the annexation of Palestine by the Seleucids; it merely sets forth, as a contrast to Greek culture, the values of that wisdom which was indis-severably linked with their own past.

A more original and noteworthy work is the *Wisdom of Solomon*, written about 100 years later, in Alexandria. Its unity, and the originality of the Greek version, have been successfully defended by Fichtner and Pfeiffer, as against those who have suggested a Hebrew original for at least the first part of the book, and attributed the two sections to different authors. The author certainly utilized very heterogeneous material, gathered out of both Palestinian and Hellenistic Jewry, and indeed from Greek philosophy, and he has worked it up in very different ways; so that wisdom wears rather a different look here. The book bears Solomon's name, and continues the tradition of the wisdom school; but it no longer speaks to individuals as such, addressing itself, after the manner of the Greek diatribe, to a wide, mixed, Jewish-cum-Gentile, audience; while it seeks to strengthen them in the old faith, or lead them back to it, or incline them towards it for the first time. Here, too, wisdom is identical with the Law, the eschatological and apocalyptic element is more skilfully interwoven than in Sirach, and Greek forms and ideas intermingle with the purely Jewish. This commingling is characteristic of both the place and the time of the book's origin, though hardly advantageous to clarity of thought with respect to the future of either individual or people. Yet at bottom it is, in spite of that, a genuinely Jewish book, which unequivocally rejects both heathen philosophy and heathen religion.

In the book of *Tobit*, which appeared *c.* 200 B.C., in the Diaspora, we have 'one of the best extant examples of an ancient Semitic short story' (Pfeiffer). The paternal admonitions to Tobias in view of his journey, which are recorded in chapter iv together with xii. 6–10, reflect a wisdom still in touch with the situations of everyday life and not yet developed into a professional literary form; at the same time they do show the tendency to build up a framework, i.e. to put groups of such sayings within the run of a story.

The book of *Baruch* was perhaps the liturgy for a day of repentance (Ringgren). The didactic poem (iii. 9–iv. 4) identifies Wisdom with the Law and regards it as an independent, though not clearly personified, entity.

In 1 *Esdras* three pages lay a wager as to what is the greatest power in the world—'a fine bit of oriental wisdom' (Torrey).

The third page is identified with Zerubbabel and the reward has reference to the Jewish situation, which affords strong evidence of its Jewish origin. The introduction of Truth as the greatest power contradicts the first answer given by the third page, and is often attributed to a Jewish redaction, but may well be older.[1]

4 Maccabees deals with the theme of whether Reason is mistress of the emotions. It follows the pattern of a diatribe, and that with a knowledge of Greek philosophy which almost certainly presupposes attendance at Greek schools (Pfeiffer). But the illustrative material he uses is culled from Jewish history of the Maccabean period.

The *Letter of Aristeas* in its second half (*vv.* 187–300) provides an example of somewhat monotonous table-talk, after the manner of Greek deipnosophistic, in which the Jewish scholars must needs show how, for every question the king asks, they have a good answer ready.

Finally, *Pseudo-Phocylides*, which is the work of an Alexandrian Jew,[2] combines elementary wisdom sayings with borrowings from the Pentateuch and Greek philosophers.

In conclusion, it must be stated that during the last generation no revolutionary innovations have appeared in the field of wisdom literature. On the whole, what we find is the systematic development of the new material and views that came to light in the first twenty years of this century. But those works on literary critical lines that were written during the last century have stood the test of time wonderfully well on the whole, where studies of the complete books are concerned. It is only in questions of individual sections within the books, the early history and the actual classification according to type, that they must be revised in the light of more recent knowledge. The view that all the books of the Old Testament first came into being, or were first

[1] Cf. W. Rudolph, *Esra und Nehemia*, H.A.T. i, 20, 1949, pp. 5 f., who suggests a Greek origin; but a Persian tale would be more probable (Pfeiffer).

[2] Franz Dornseiff, *Echtheitsfragen antik-griechischer Literatur*, 1939, pp. 37 ff., once more upholds its composition by the old Phocylides of Miletus (*c.* 540 B.C.). The fact that this requires the Pentateuch to have been already completed and in circulation at Miletus in a Greek translation by that time, causes him no uneasiness.

completed, in the Jewish period, i.e. in post-exilic times, is to be taken as true of these also. A really important point is that, in contrast to the earlier position, we have learnt to see the development of this whole literature as a type very much more plainly and distinctly. Though in origin non-Israelite and international, in Proverbs and Sirach it becomes more Israelitish and Yahwistic. This means an enrichment and a deepening, but at the same time a nationalistic narrowing down. Possession of wisdom, once the alluring prize of any honourable endeavour, is now reserved for the members of God's Chosen People. Only in Ecclesiastes does it appear once more de-nationalized, where the author sees and attacks the weaknesses in its system, as does Job in another way. Expressing the tenor of the age, it associated itself in ever closer sympathy with the Greek spirit, though without surrendering its own Jewish character. Our theological understanding of these books, too, has advanced, though not altogether—particularly in the case of Ecclesiastes—along traditional lines.

VI. CANTICLES

Since the 'Song of Songs', i.e. the 'finest of Solomon's songs', goes under Solomon's name, it is usually reckoned among the wisdom literature, and Ranston defends that custom. In its literary type, it has nothing whatever to do therewith, or with any didactic purpose. The exclusive theme is love between man and woman, which is celebrated in glowing colours and passionate words, and in close connexion with the world of Nature also (ii. 11–13). No wonder that the history of its interpretation shows a motley pattern, and is moreover a wearisome story (cf. the historical reviews of Kuhl and Rowley).

We must say one word on the problem of form. Although long refuted, the view that it is a completely worked out drama still finds supporters. But this view can only be maintained by doing violence to the text; even in the introduction (i. 2–4, 9–17) the lovers are tasting the bliss of full union. Further, when dealing with Job, it has been already pointed out that the Hebrews had no acquaintance whatsoever with the drama, since dialogue alone is no proof to the contrary. Far more probably we have to do with a bundle of separate songs,[1] of which some 25–30 have been counted. This song theory is mostly bound up with the interpretation of them as wedding songs after the manner of songs sung in connexion with the Syrian 'King's week'. This explanation, of course, goes back to Wetzstein and Budde. Such customs, however, are only faintly attested in Palestine itself, and only a small number of the songs are suited to it, since often enough it is quite plain that we are dealing with love before marriage (iii. 1–4, v. 3, viii. 1 f.). It is better to think of a collection of love songs in general. How far the erotic interpretation is to be carried in individual cases has not yet found unanimity of opinion. Allusions to the recognized images and symbolic language of all love poetry are frequent and unmistakable. The form of the songs, too, supports this, as may be further studied in Horst as well as Hylmö and Bentzen.

The collection will have come about in much the same way as with Proverbs: it is a matter of association, according to both form and content, with keywords, &c. Gemser predicates conscious composition. Whether the frequent recurrence of individual songlets is a mark of refrains (Gemser), or of the combination of smaller collections (Eissfeldt, Bentzen), is a difficult point to decide; likewise whether we are dealing with an anthology of popular songs (Hylmö), or whether, in view of a certain unity in matter and style, we should not see a single author behind them (Rowley, Fischer). In any case, Solomon's name was only subsequently attached to this work owing to the mention of him in vi. 8, viii. 11 f. and the reference in 1 Kings v. 12, as well as the general tendency to attribute all possible lyric poetry to that golden age of Israel.

When the collection was made cannot be decided exactly. The occurrence of a Persian, and a Greek, loan word takes us down at least into the fourth or third century. It is just feasible that these words have later ousted the original Hebrew (Dorn-

---

[1] Thilo alone finds a finished cycle of songs leading on from first love to bridal and marriage songs, thereby, too, documenting the development of Israelite marriage from polygamy to monogamy. This is as unsatisfactory from the exegetical as from the historical side; cf. Sir. xxxvii. 11.

seiff, Rudolph), but the whole character of the language of the book is late. Of course, it remains quite possible that much older material has been included, as in Proverbs. The mention of Tirzah (vi. 4), Omri's capital in northern Israel, which is so often adduced, may only have been introduced, however, because of its literal meaning 'Charm'. The city was almost certainly known in later times through tradition. Consequently, the derivation of the collection from a north-Israelite source (Haller) remains quite uncertain.

When all is said and done, the presence of this book within the canon remains a problem, for this cannot be explained simply by its circulation under Solomon's name. It is well known how an allegorical interpretation passed over from Judaism into Christianity, and maintained its hold there very tenaciously. Such an interpretation, or a closely related typological one, has been retained in the Roman Catholic Church, though certainly nowadays, for the most part, alongside of a realistic appreciation of the book as consisting of love and wedding songs. Miller and Fischer carry this double interpretation right through, though giving the former one only in broad outline, with just a few more detailed passages. According to Fischer, the allegorical sense was first introduced by the redactor. On the Protestant side, the allegorical interpretation was of course adopted by the Reformers and is still maintained by Kuhn, who links it up with his exegesis of Ecclesiastes. In a milder form its influence is to be found wherever, in line with Eph. v. 25–33, Canticles is understood as an admonition to a married couple to love one another as Christ loved the Church, from which passage earthly love also may be justified.[1] Such an interpretation not only brings in the reference to Christ and the restriction of love to the married; it also, as Rudolph states quite correctly, redirects the love which, in contradistinction to Prov. xxxi. 10 ff., Sir. vii. 19, xxv. 8, xxvi. 1–4, is here bound up exclusively with the physical aspect.

Recently, the theory that it was the allegorical interpretation which first made possible the inclusion of Canticles in the canon

[1] So W. Bieder, *In Extremis*, 1941, pp. 179 ff.

has been challenged. According to this theory it first entrenched itself in the national estimation owing to its popularity, and the allegorical meaning followed afterwards (Gemser). According to Vriezen it found its way in as an appendix to Proverbs—a difficult hypothesis to prove. Rudolph takes it to consist of wedding songs; he quotes the well-known saying of Rabbi Akiba against those that sing it in the *bêt mišteh*, and understands this to mean the house where the marriage takes place. But the normal translation 'inn' or 'banquet' does not need to be linguistically justified, and the very severity of the threat appears to me to indicate a more secular situation.[1] Secondary, spiritual, re-interpretation of love-songs is a general phenomenon, and in no wise bound up with the question of canonicity.[2] On the other hand, mysticism in all ages and climes has borrowed a goodly portion of its imagery from the sphere of earthly love; in Israel, too, passages in the prophets, such as Hos. i–iii, Jer. ii. 2, Ezek. xvi, &c., had prepared the ground for it.

The hitherto mentioned interpretations have now had to meet the competition of another one, the cult-mythical. This finds in the songs the ritual of a divine marriage. The theory arose in H. Winckler's school, and after the publication of a cuneiform catalogue giving the first lines of hymns from the Ištar-Tammuz cult, it was developed in various ways, and took up Canticles as the liturgy of a pre-Israelite cult which, after being slightly camouflaged, was taken over into the Yahweh cult. Somewhat similarly, Haller explains it as a collection of hymns and songs anciently connected with the Canaanite *maṣṣôt* festival, but which was later made eligible for inclusion in the canon by being referred to Solomon and the marriage of Yahweh and Israel. Such a thesis falls in well with the present-day tendency to find in the Old Testament in large measure the residue of cultic customs and texts; it has this much to be said for it, too, that it

---

[1] The words used and their parallels in the Talmud are given by Rowley in *J.R.A.S.*, 1938, p. 268, n. 3.

[2] It is found, for example, with Chinese love-songs (cf. Rowley, ibid., pp. 274 f.); with the love scene of Krishna and the Shepherdess (cf. R. Garbe, *Indien und das Christentum*, 1914, pp. 226 f.); with a Georgian heroic poem (cf. Fr. Bodenstedt, *Tausend und ein Tag im Orient*, 1865, iii, p. 33).

raises Canticles from the purely secular into the religious sphere, even though it be in connexion with a false and, at bottom, foreign cult. The significance of the vegetation god's cult in the ancient orient has become more and more apparent in the past twenty or thirty years, particularly through the Ugaritic texts. It is now generally recognized that the Israelite cultus was strongly Canaanite in character, and that the Old Testament is riddled with traces of Canaanite customs and conceptions, together with traces of Adonis worship. But this theory above mentioned goes a good deal farther than that, and needs to be convincingly proved if it is to be accepted. That, however, has not yet happened, as may be gathered from Eissfeldt, Rowley (*J.R.A.S.*), and Bentzen (i, pp. 129 ff.). The connexion of Canticles with the *maṣṣôt* festival appears to be late (cf. Kuhl, p. 143). The allegedly mythical references are often sought out as if there were no such thing as ordinary love-making and love-words, or are obtained by doubtful textual emendations, &c. Another counter-indication may be seen in the similarities it shows with old Egyptian and modern Arabic love-songs. The most that can be admitted is that such cultic love-poems have provided all kinds of images and motifs (Hempel). The greatest difficulty is to see how this inter-pretation would make the inclusion of Canticles within the canon any easier to understand; since, in view of the deeply rooted repugnance to any sexual association with the deity which we find in Israelite religion, the slightest hint of anything in this direc-tion would have the exactly opposite effect. I find it as difficult to follow Kuhl when he says that future study must investigate whether there is not something higher in Canticles than wedding songs, namely, speculation concerning life and the dominant position of life as an absolute. Such speculations fit in with the mental climate of the Mandaeans and other gnostic religions, but they are entirely foreign to Hebrew thought and religion.

On the whole, therefore, the love poems of Canticles may be allowed to retain their secular character (Hylmö); Bentzen, too, restricts the validity of their cultic interpretation to the very early stages in the songs' history. This brings us back very nearly to the view put forward by Theodore of Mopsuestia, which was condemned by the Council of Constantinople in 553, called down the anathema of Calvin on Castellio in 1545, and brought Luis de Leon into the hands of the Inquisition in 1567. We certainly owe our thanks to the allegorical interpretation for the preservation of these songs. We may still find an innocent delight in them, particularly if we slough off any theological justification, which would only do violence to their meaning. Here it is, indeed, that we have borne in upon us the conclusion that the composition of the canon can only be understood historically.[1]

W. BAUMGARTNER

BIBLIOGRAPHY

ALLGEIER, A. *Das Buch des Predigers*, H.S.A.Tes. vi, 2, 1925.

ALT, A. 'Zur Vorgeschichte des Buches Hiob', *Z.A.W.* lv, 1937, pp. 265–8.

BAUMGÄRTEL, F. *Der Hiobdialog*, B.W.A.N.T. iv, 9, 1933.

BAUMGARTNER, W. *Israelitische und altorientalische Weisheit*, 1933.

— 'Die israelitische Weisheitsliteratur', *T.R.* v, 1933, pp. 259–88.

BENTZEN, A. *Introduction to the Old Testament*, i, 1948; ii, 1949.

BOSTRÖM, G. *Paronomasi i den äldere Hebreiska Maschal-litteraturen*, L.U.Å. xxiii, 8, 1928.

— *Proverbiastudien*, ibid. xxx, 3, 1935.

CAUSSE, A. 'Sagesse égyptienne et sagesse juive', *R.H.P.R.* ix, 1929, pp. 149–69.

DHORME, P. *Le Livre de Job*, 1926.

DORNSEIFF, F. 'Das Buch Prediger', *Z.D.M.G.* lxxxix, 1935, pp. 243–9.

DÜRR, L. *Das Erziehungswesen im Alten Testament und im Alten Orient*, M.V.A.G. xxxvi, 2, 1932.

DUESBERG, H. *Les Scribes inspirés*, i, 1938; ii, 1939.

EERDMANS, B. D. *Studies in Job*, 1939.

EICHRODT, W. 'Vorsehungsglaube und Theodizee im Alten Testament', *Festschrift O. Procksch*, 1934, pp. 45–70.

EISSFELDT, O. *Einleitung in das Alte Testament*, 1934.

FICHTNER, J. *Die altorientalische Weisheit in ihrer israelitisch-jüdischen Ausprägung*, B.Z.A.W. lxii, 1933.

FISCHER, J. *Hohes Lied und Das Buch der Weisheit*, Echt. B. x, 1950.

GALLING, K. 'Kohelet-Studien', *Z.A.W.* l, 1932, pp. 276–99.

— 'Stand und Aufgabe der Kohelet-Forschung', *T.R.* vi, 1934, pp. 355–73.

— 'Der Prediger', in *Die fünf Megilloth*, H.A.T. i, 18, 1940, pp. 47–90.

---

[1] This chapter has been translated from the German text of Professor Baumgartner by Mr. D. R. Ap-Thomas, of Bangor.

GEMSER, B. *De Spreuken van Salomo, Prediker en Hooglied*, T.U. i, 1929; ii, 1931.

— *Sprüche Salomos*, H.A.T. i, 16, 1937.

GOETTSBERGER, J. *Einleitung in das Alte Testament*, 1928.

GRESSMANN, H. *Israels Spruchweisheit im Zusammenhang der Weltliteratur*, 1925.

HALLER, M. 'Das Hohe Lied', in *Die fünf Megilloth*, H.A.T. i, 18, 1940, pp. 21–46.

HAMP, V. *Sprüche*, Echt. B. viii, 1949.

HEMPEL, J. 'Das theologische Problem des Hiob', *Z.S.T.* vi, 1929, pp. 621–89.

— *Die althebräische Literatur und ihr hellenistisch-jüdisches Nachleben*, 1930.

HERTZBERG, H. W. *Der Prediger*, K.A.T. xv–xvi, 4, 1932.

— 'Der Aufbau des Buches Hiob', *Festschrift A. Bertholet*, 1950, pp. 233–58.

HORST, F. 'Die Formen des althebräischen Liebesliedes', *Festschrift E. Littmann*, 1935, pp. 43–54.

HUMBERT, P. *Recherches sur les sources égyptiennes de la littérature sapientiale d'Israël*, 1929.

HYLMÖ, G. *Gamla Testamentets Litteraturhistoria*, 1938.

KITTEL, R. *Geschichte des Volkes Israel*, iii, 1927, § 73.

KÖNIG, E. *Hiob*, 1929.

KRAELING, E. G. *The Book of the Ways of God*, 1938.

KUHL, C. 'Das Hohelied und seine Deutung', *T.R.* ix, 1937, pp. 137–67.

KUHN, G. *Erklärung des Buches Koheleth*, B.Z.A.W. xliii, 1926.

— *Erklärung des Hohen Liedes*, 1926.

LINDBLOM, J. *Boken om Job och hans lidande*, 1940.

— 'La Composition du livre de Job', *Bull. de la Soc. Royale des Lettres de Lund* (1944–5, iii), 1945.

MILLER, A. *Das Hohe Lied*, H.S.A.Tes. vi, 3, 1927.

ODEBERG, H. *Qohæleth*, 1929.

OESTERLEY, W. O. E. *The Book of Proverbs*, W.C., 1929.

— and ROBINSON, T. H. *An Introduction to the Books of the Old Testament*, 1934.

PEDERSEN, J. *Israel I–II*, 1926.

— 'Scepticisme israélite', *R.H.P.R.* x, 1930, pp. 317–70.

PFEIFFER, R. H. *Introduction to the Old Testament*, 1941.

— *History of New Testament Times with an Introduction to the Apocrypha*, 1949.

VAN PROOSDIJ, A. C. G. *Het Boek Job*, 1948.

RANKIN, O. S. *Israel's Wisdom Literature*, 1936.

RANSTON, H. *Ecclesiastes and the Early Greek Wisdom*, 1925.

— *The Old Testament Wisdom Books and their Teaching*, 1930.

RINGGREN, H. *Word and Wisdom*, 1947.

ROWLEY, H. H. 'The Interpretation of the Song of Songs', *J.T.S.* xxxviii, 1937, pp. 337–63.

— 'The Song of Songs: an Examination of Recent Theory', *J.R.A.S.*, 1938, pp. 251–76.

RUDOLPH, W. 'Das Hohe Lied im Kanon', *Z.A.W.* lix, 1942–3, pp. 189–99.

SCHMIDT, H. *Hiob, das Buch vom Sinn des Leidens*, 1926.

SCHMIDT, J. *Studien zur Stilistik der alttestamentlichen Spruchliteratur*, A.A. xii, 1, 1936.

SELLIN, E. *Geschichte des israelitischen Volkes*, ii, 1932.

— *Einleitung in das Alte Testament⁷*, 1935.

STAMM, J. J. *Das Leiden des Unschuldigen in Babylon und Israel*, 1946.

STEVENSON, W. B. *The Poem of Job*, 1946.

SZCZYGIEL, P. *Das Buch Job*, H.S.A.Tes. v, 1, 1931.

THILO, M. *Das Hohe Lied*, 1921.

— *Der Prediger Salomo*, 1923.

— *Das Buch Hiob*, 1925.

DU TOIT, S. *Bybelse en Babilonies-Assiriese Spreuken*, 1942.

TORREY, C. C. *The Apocryphal Literature*, 1945.

TORCZYNER, H. 'Hiobdichtung und Hiobsage', in M. Soloweitschik, *Vom Buch das 1000 Jahre wuchs*, 1932, pp. 147–68.

VISCHER, W. *Der Prediger Salomo*, 1926.

VRIEZEN, Th. C. *Oud-Israëlietische Geschriften*, 1948.

WEISER, A. *Einleitung in das Alte Testament²*, 1949.

WITTEKINDT, W. *Das Hohe Lied und seine Beziehungen zum Istarkult*, 1926.

ZIMMERLI, W. 'Zur Struktur der alttestamentlichen Weisheit', *Z.A.W.* li, 1933, pp. 177–204.

Die Weisheit des Predigers Salomo, 1936.

ADDENDUM

GINSBERG, H. L. *Studies in Koheleth*, 1950 (distinguishes four sections, variations of the programme i. 2–ii. 26, and xi. 8–xii. 8 as a grand finale; Ecclesiastes does not describe himself as a king, but as a property holder, *mōlēḳ*; the Hebrew text is the translation of an Aramaic original composed in the third century: not in every respect convincing, but very stimulating and suggestive).

SELLIN, E. *Einleitung in das Alte Testament⁸* (revised by L. Rost), 1950 (does not bring in substantial variations, but brings the bibliography up to date).

VIII

THE TEXTUAL CRITICISM OF
THE OLD TESTAMENT

IN the last generation the search for the original text of the
Hebrew Bible has been carried on with rare intensity, and
much significant work bearing upon the textual criticism of
the Old Testament has appeared. In this chapter an attempt is
made to give a survey of it. In the first part of the chapter we shall
consider work which relates to the Hebrew Bible. Three matters
especially will claim our attention here. First, epigraphic and
manuscript discoveries have been made which have made available valuable new sources of knowledge. Secondly, the study of comparative Semitic philology has been carried on with a notable bearing
upon the problems of textual criticism. And thirdly, much study
has gone into the problems presented by the Massoretic text itself
—more especially the theory of the archetype, the vocalization
of the Hebrew text, both pre-Massoretic and Massoretic, and the
recovery of the Ben Asher text. On all these matters something
will be said. In the second part of the chapter, important work
which has been done on the Greek Old Testament will be
surveyed. The matters here which will call for our notice are the
manuscripts and papyri which have recently come to light; the
problem of the recovery of the original text of the Septuagint (in
this connexion reference will be made to recent editions of the
Septuagint); and the question of the alphabet in which the
Septuagint-*Vorlage*, i.e. the text from which the Greek translators worked, was written. In the third part of the chapter
recent work on the other chief ancient versions[1] will be referred
to briefly, and this will be followed by some concluding remarks.

---

[1] Considerations of space do not allow any treatment of the secondary versions.

I. THE HEBREW BIBLE

(i) *New Sources of Knowledge*

Two new sources of knowledge, each in its different way of outstanding significance for the textual criticism of the Hebrew Bible, have become available in the last fifteen years. The first are the ostraca, bearing Hebrew inscriptions, discovered at Tell ed-Duweir, the ancient Lachish.[1] They may be dated 589–8 B.C. The textual critic of the Hebrew Bible may learn much from them. For example, the irregularity with which the use of a dot as a word divider is employed is a reminder of a type of error which has arisen in the text of the Old Testament through words being wrongly divided, or wrongly read together. Further, words are often split at the end of a line and continued into the next, a source of error which later Hebrew scribes sought to avoid by the employment of the so-called *litterae dilatabiles*. Scribal errors too, for example, the omission of a letter, occur. There is again frequent use of *scriptio defectiva*—a phenomenon which should warn us against the supposition that the Massoretic text reflects the orthography of its prototype; allowance must be made for the modernization of it by the scribes.[2] The divine name YHWH, moreover, is always written out in full, whereas in the Massoretic text it is sometimes abbreviated.[3] More important than all this for textual criticism, however, are two other features of the ostraca. First, they provide us for the first time with definite proof as to the script that was being commonly used in Judah in the period of Jeremiah. The script is a cursive form of the ancient Hebrew script known to us from the Siloam and other inscriptions. It is the script which Jeremiah himself will have used (Jer. xxxii, 10; cp. verse 12), and Baruch also (Jer. xxxvi). We are now thus able to see much more clearly how parts of the Old Testament, for example, the historical books and a large part of the prophetical writings, will have looked, written originally, as

[1] The most important literature upon them may be found in the present writer's *'The Prophet' in the Lachish Ostraca*, 1946, p. 24.

[2] Cp. W. F. Albright, *F.S.A.C.*, 1940, p. 46. Further, W. Baumgartner, *Anthropos*, xxxv–vi, 1940–1, p. 609.

[3] See F. Perles, *Analekten zur Textkritik des A.T.*, 1922, pp. 2 ff.

they will have been, in this same script, on leather or papyrus. That this was probably the case has, of course, long been suspected. But the proof that was lacking is now forthcoming, with the result that 'at least in his mind the scholar must visualize the Biblical text recopied in this original form'.[1] In the second place, the language of the ostraca is of importance for the textual criticism of the Hebrew Bible. It is in all essentials the same classical Hebrew which we know from the Old Testament, with particular contacts with the book of Jeremiah and the writings of the Deuteronomists. That the Massoretic text reflects the southern, Judaean, dialect of Hebrew in use round about 600 B.C. was long ago thought to be probable. Certainty on this point is now achieved, and with it the case for the general trustworthiness of the Massoretic text receives additional support.

The second new important source of knowledge is provided by the Biblical manuscripts discovered, with other Hebrew manuscripts, in 1947 in a cave at the north-western end of the Dead Sea. Among them is an all but complete scroll of the book of Isaiah, which has recently been published in its entirety.[2] The orthography of the scroll, with its profusion of *matres lectionis*, differs in a striking way from that of the Massoretic text. The scroll-text contains numerous variant readings,[3] which are of different kinds, some being due merely to scribal errors, others being of a more substantial character. Often the latter are supported by the Septuagint and by the other ancient versions. On the other hand, the scroll-text sometimes supports the Massoretic text against the versions. It is interesting to observe that, while it sometimes supports emendations which have been proposed, it shows at other times that such emendations are unjustified. The important fact is that, when all due allowance has been made for the divergencies between the scroll-text and the Massoretic text, the two texts show remarkable agreement—

---

[1] H. Torczyner, *The Lachish Letters*, 1938, p. 15.

[2] By the American Schools of Oriental Research, with the title *The Dead Sea Scrolls of St. Mark's Monastery, i: The Isaiah Manuscript and the Habakkuk Commentary*, 1950, ed. by M. Burrows, with the assistance of J. C. Trever and W. H. Brownlee.

[3] A useful, but by no means exhaustive, list of them has been made by M. Burrows, *B.A.S.O.R.*, No. 111, 1948, pp. 16 ff.; No. 113, 1949, pp. 24 ff.

but, it should be added, not identity.[1] The scroll-text brings, therefore, its own independent witness to the tradition which lies behind the Massoretic text form. How far back we may carry its witness is uncertain, since there is as yet no unanimity of opinion as to the date of this scroll, some scholars holding that it is of pre-Christian origin (second or first century B.C.), others believing that it belongs to the early centuries of the Christian era. The debate will doubtless long continue. In the meantime it may be said that if, as may well be, the scroll-text is older by several centuries than the earliest Hebrew manuscripts of the Hebrew Bible hitherto known (ninth to tenth centuries A.D.), we may by means of it trace the Massoretic text form considerably farther back than has been possible previously. If the scroll-text is to be dated in the early centuries of the Christian era, it will take its place beside the versions of the time—Aquila, Symmachus, Theodotion, the Targums, the Peshitta, and the Vulgate—all of which testify to essentially the same text as that of the Massoretic text. Unlike them, however, the scroll-text is in Hebrew, the original language of the Old Testament, and is not a version, and in this respect its witness to the Massoretic tradition has a significance of a kind different from that of the versions just mentioned. If again the scroll is pre-Christian in origin, its witness can, of course, be carried still farther back. In any case, the scroll-text shows that the Massoretic text, if, as seems probable, it is junior to it, has been carefully transmitted from an earlier period, and that in the pre-Massoretic period it was essentially the same as we have it today.[2]

It should be emphasized that, at this early stage of the discus-

---

[1] The citations from Habakkuk in the Habakkuk Commentary, and the Leviticus fragments, written in ancient Hebrew script, which were also found in the cave, likewise agree in the main with the Massoretic text. A noteworthy variant in the latter is the reading *hī'* for *hū'* in xx. 21, thus supporting the Qere. See R. de Vaux, *R.B.* lvi, 1949, pp. 597 ff.; D. Diringer, *P.E.Q.*, 1950, pp. 20 ff.

[2] On the relationship between the scroll-text, if it dates from pre-Christian times, and the Septuagint text of Isaiah, see B. J. Roberts, *E.T.* lx, 1949, p. 306; *The Listener*, 8 Sept. 1949, p. 405. G. R. Driver, *J.Q.R.* xl, 1950, p. 361, writes—'If the Scrolls were contemporary with the LXX, the abundant *scriptio plena* would have been unnecessary and would be inexplicable'; the text of the scroll of Isaiah is, he thinks, 'certainly not a Septuagintal text' (p. 367).

sion of the scroll-text, our remarks must be regarded as tentative only.[1]

(ii) *Comparative Semitic Philology*

It has been pointed out that both the Lachish ostraca and the Dead Sea scroll-text of Isaiah give cause for increased confidence in the general trustworthiness of the Massoretic text. The study of comparative Semitic philology, which has been carried on steadily in the last generation, tends in the same direction. A great deal of textual work on the Massoretic text in the past has been characterized by excessive emendation of the text. Many of the emendations which have been proposed, and perpetuated, are now seen to be groundless, and a welcome, and necessary, reaction has set in. What were at one time thought to be corrupt or impossible Hebrew forms are today often seen to be patient of explanation from some other Semitic language.[2] And a more searching study of the ancient versions, especially of the Septuagint, has shown that many supposed divergencies from the Massoretic text are not in reality divergencies at all, but, on the contrary, reflect a text identical with the Massoretic text. The meanings which the translators of the ancient versions sometimes give to Hebrew words, and which suggest that they had a divergent text before them, can often be recovered from some other Semitic language or languages, in which the meaning which the translators knew belonged by tradition to the Hebrew

---

[1] How far we are from certainty on some essential points may be illustrated by reference to two recent articles. First, G. R. Driver, op. cit., states the case for a date as late as A.D. 650–800—the scroll-text is one of the *Vulgärtexte* 'which survived the closing of the canon *c.* 100 C.E. and were current until the M.T. was finally standardized, when they were eliminated' (p. 367). Secondly, H. M. Orlinsky, *J.B.L.* lxix ,1950, pp. 149 ff., thinks that, whatever the date of the scroll-text may be, it is not likely to have much value for the textual critic—'except insofar as it will help to convince more biblical scholars that the traditionally preserved text of the Hebrew Bible should be treated with far greater respect than it has been' (p. 152). The scroll derives, he believes, from a manuscript which was copied from memory—it is 'an unreliable oral variation on the theme of what came to be known as the masoretic text of Isaiah' (p. 165), and under no circumstances is its Hebrew text to be given any independent value.

[2] See further the present writer in *Record and Revelation*, ed. by H. Wheeler Robinson, 1938, p. 400.

word can be traced. An example in illustration may be given. In Prov. xxx. 17 the rendering of the word *lik̲eḥaṯ* in the Septuagint by γῆρας has led to a general acceptance of the emendation *ziḵnaṯ* 'old age'.[1] In Ethiopic, however, the root *leḥḵa* means 'was old'—in Arabic it means 'was white' (e.g. of hair)—and so we may regard *lik̲eḥaṯ* as a corruption of *leḥīḵaṯ* or *liḥeḵaṯ* (construct state of *leḥīḵāh* or *leḥāḵāh* old age).[2] It may be concluded, therefore, that the Septuagint translators had this Hebrew word before them, and not *ziḵnaṯ*. The proposed emendation is accordingly without justification. In such a way do comparative Semitic philology and the study of the versions combine to sustain the identity of the text used by the Septuagint translators with the Massoretic text. It would be absurd, of course, to deny that divergencies between the Massoretic text and the Septuagint, and other ancient versions, exist. Nor is it to be denied that sometimes a version may preserve a reading superior to the Massoretic text. It may be admitted, moreover, that conjectural emendation, when it is methodically carried out,[3] has a legitimate place in the textual criticism of the Hebrew Bible. Yet the verdict of comparative Semitic philological research, combined with the study of the ancient versions, is today wholly in favour of the view that 'the reputation of the Massoretic text stands deservedly high, and that for the serious study of the Old Testament it must, in spite of its imperfections, constitute the proper starting-point'.[4]

(iii) *The Massoretic Text*

(a) *The Theory of the Archetype.* The theory, generally associated with the name of Paul de Lagarde,[5] that the Jews had, from the early part of the second century A.D., a standard, authoritative

---

[1] So BH³ ad loc. This is only one of the many cases in which an emendation for which there is no justification is perpetuated in BH³.

[2] See the present writer in *J.T.S.* xlii, 1941, pp. 154 f.

[3] As, for example, in F. Delitzsch, *Die Lese- und Schreibfehler im A.T.*, 2nd ed., 1920, and F. Perles, op. cit. J. Kennedy's *An Aid to the Textual Amendment of the O.T.*, ed. N. Levison, 1928, is useful, but needs careful handling.

[4] So the present writer in *The Recovery of the Ancient Hebrew Language*, 1939, p. 37.

[5] He had, however, predecessors; see W. Robertson Smith, *The Old Testament in the Jewish Church*, 1892, p. 57, n. 2.

text of the Hebrew Bible, based on a single manuscript, and that this text was thereafter transmitted with scrupulous exactness, even to the reproduction of errors, and is the text to which all our manuscripts of the Hebrew Bible go back, has enjoyed wide support. It appeared to be well grounded. The work of Kennicott and de Rossi in the eighteenth century had seemed to show that the many manuscripts which they examined presented no really important variants. The quotations from the Old Testament in rabbinical literature, moreover, were thought to reflect the Massoretic text, as did also the versions of Aquila, Symmachus, and Theodotion in the second century A.D. Later work,[1] however, was to show that a more extensive examination of Hebrew manuscripts revealed a far greater number of variants than had been suggested by the investigations of Kennicott and de Rossi; that down to the eighth century, and later still, Old Testament quotations in rabbinical literature do not always show verbal agreement with the Massoretic text; and that in Aquila variants from the Massoretic text are frequent. The doubts which have been thus thrown upon the tenability of the theory of the archetype have of late been reinforced by the work of Paul Kahle and his school on Hebrew manuscripts found in the Genizah of the synagogue in Old Cairo. This material, some of it dating, according to Kahle, before A.D. 700,[2] reveals the activity of different schools of Massoretes, working in Babylon (third to ninth centuries A.D.), in the Jewish schools of Sura, Nehardea, and Pumbeditha, and in Palestine (eighth to ninth centuries A.D.) at Tiberias. These eastern and western schools differed in their systems of vocalization, as well as in the consonantal text they preserved.[3] It is evident, therefore, that Hebrew manuscripts were not transmitted with the scrupulous exactness which the theory of the archetype implies. Though there can still be found

---

[1] For the relevant literature see A. Bentzen, *Introduction to the Old Testament*, i, 1948, p. 51.

[2] J. L. Teicher, *J.J.S.* i, 1949, pp. 156 ff., argues, however, that no manuscript found in the Cairo Genizah should be presumed to be older than about the middle of the ninth century, unless there are strong reasons for assigning it to an earlier period.

[3] As is well known, the text, both consonantal and vocalic, as fixed by the Tiberian Massoretes, in time prevailed and became authoritative.

defenders of the theory today, for example, H. M. Orlinsky[1] and
R. Gordis,[2] it has been abandoned by a large number of scholars.
There has been, however, at the same time a disposition to
recognize the truth that lies behind the theory. Due stress is
laid, for example, upon the fact that *c.* A.D. 100 a uniform
Hebrew text seems to have begun to assert itself—this may be
inferred from the Greek versions of the second century A.D.
which, as has been said, reflect the Hebrew text in approximately
the same form as we have it today—and that, since that time, the
uniformity of the Hebrew text which has been handed down is,
despite textual divergencies, as solid as it is remarkable. In so far
as the theory compels recognition of such considerations as these,
it still merits attention.[3]

(*b*) *Vocalization: Pre-Massoretic and Massoretic.* It is well
known that the Septuagint and other ancient versions testify to
the fact that the vocalization of the Hebrew text which they
suppose—which was as yet without vowel signs—is often
different from that of the Massoretic text. The recovery of the
pre-Massoretic vocalization of the Hebrew text has been carried
a long way farther by recent important investigations of a number of scholars into the transcriptions of Hebrew (in the Septuagint, in the second column of Origen's Hexapla, and in Jerome),
into the vocalization of early Palestinian and Babylonian manuscripts, and into the pronunciation of Hebrew by the Samaritans.[4]

---

[1] See *J.A.O.S.* lxi, 1941, pp. 84 ff.

[2] *The Biblical Text in the Making: A Study of the Kethib-Qere*, 1937, pp. 44 ff.
The archetype was, according to him, adopted not later than A.D. 70. For criticism of
his work see Orlinsky, *J.A.O.S.* lx, 1940, pp. 30 ff.

[3] See further B. J. Roberts, 'Divergencies in the pre-Tiberian Massoretic Text',
J.J.S. i, 1949, pp. 147 ff.

[4] F. X. Wutz, *Die Transkriptionen von der Septuaginta bis zu Hieronymus*, 1925 f.;
E. Brønno, *Studien über hebräische Morphologie und Vokalismus*, 1943 (on this see
Kahle, *The Cairo Geniza*, 1947, pp. 231 ff.); A. Sperber, 'Hebrew based upon Greek
and Latin Transliterations', *H.U.C.A.* xii–xiii, 1937–8, pp. 103 ff. (on this see
Brønno, op. cit., pp. 464 ff.); B. J. Roberts, *J.J.S.*, loc. cit.; G. Mercati, 'Il Pro-
blema della Colonna II dell' Esaplo', *Biblica*, xxviii, 1947, pp. 1 ff., 173 ff.; E. A.
Speiser, 'The pronunciation of Hebrew according to the transliterations in the
Hexapla', *J.Q.R.* xvi, 1925–6, pp. 343 ff., xxiii, 1932–3,.pp. 233 ff., xxiv, 1933–4,
pp. 9 ff.; W. E. Staples, 'The Hebrew of the Septuagint', *A.J.S.L.* xliv, 1927–8,
pp. 6 ff. (strongly criticized by Brønno, *Classica et Mediaevalia*, iii, 1940, pp. 194 ff.),
and 'The Second Column of Origen's Hexapla', *J.A.O.S.* lix, 1939, pp. 71 ff.;

Their work has made it possible to penetrate farther behind the vocalization of the Massoretic text to an earlier stage of Hebrew pronunciation. There has been a notable tendency to emphasize the importance of sound method in the use of this material, which is by its very nature difficult to handle. Thus, for example, in the case of the Septuagint, it has been shown by Wutz that different strata in the transcriptions of Hebrew are to be recognized, which point perhaps to changes in the pronunciation of Hebrew which came in in the course of time. Septuagint transcriptions call, therefore, for thorough sifting. Results in this field are bound, at any rate for the present, to be tentative, and inferences which are drawn from the evidence need careful scrutiny. Kahle's view, for example, that the Massoretes tried to create an ideal pronunciation of Hebrew (under Arab and Syrian influences)[1] has been judged to be questionable on the ground that it takes too little account of the strength of the Massoretic adherence to tradition;[2] and again, it has been questioned whether such a conclusion from the evidence of the Genizah material is justifiable.[3] Differences of dialect, and way of recitation, too, may have to be allowed for. One fact, however, stands out clearly, viz. that the Massoretic vocalization cannot any longer be regarded as wholly authoritative. The degree of its authority will only be properly estimated when the true tradition it retains has been more closely distinguished from those elements in it which owe their origin to the Massoretes themselves. This is the essential task, and it must be carried out on a basis of sound study of all the pre-Massoretic material available.[4] To the

Kahle, op. cit., pp. 86 ff., and 'Die Lesezeichen bei den Samaritanern', *Paul Haupt Commemoration Volume*, ed. C. Adler and A. Ember, 1926, pp. 425 ff.; F. Diening, *Das Hebräische bei den Samaritanern*, 1938; G. Lisowsky, *Die Transkription der hebräischen Eigennamen des Pentateuch in der Septuaginta*, 1940; E. F. Sutcliffe, 'St. Jerome's pronunciation of Hebrew', *Biblica*, xxix, 1948, pp. 112 ff.

[1] *The Cairo Geniza*, pp. 78 ff.

[2] See G. Bergsträsser, *O.L.Z.* xxvii, 1924, cols. 582 ff., and Kahle's reply, *The Cairo Geniza*, pp. 109 f.

[3] I. Engnell, *The Call of Isaiah*, 1949, pp. 55, 61 ff.

[4] The importance of this material for the historical study of Hebrew grammar has been shown by Brønno, Sperber, and others. See Sperber also in *J.B.L.* lxii, 1943, pp. 137 ff. (criticized by Kahle, *The Cairo Geniza*, p. 109, n. 1). Further, K. Levy, *Zur masoretischen Grammatik*, 1936.

successful carrying out of it, scholarship in the last generation has made a large and noteworthy contribution.

(c) *The Ben Asher Text.* The publication of the third edition of *Biblia Hebraica*[1] in 1937 was an event of outstanding importance in the history of the textual criticism of the Hebrew Bible, for it represented a definite break with the past. The two earlier editions of 1905 and 1912 were based—as indeed were all previous critical editions—on the edition of Jacob ben Chayyim as published in 1524-5 in the second Rabbinical Bible. The manuscripts which were at Jacob ben Chayyim's disposal were, however, late and not altogether trustworthy. The new *Biblia Hebraica* is no longer based upon this unsatisfactory text, but on the older tradition of Ben Asher, whose family, with that of Ben Naphtali,[2] formed the two great schools of Tiberian Massoretes in the tenth century A.D. A manuscript of the whole of the Old Testament, dated by Kahle A.D. 929, attributed to Aaron ben Moshe ben Asher, is preserved in the Sephardic synagogue at Aleppo. This manuscript was not available for publication in *Biblia Hebraica*, but another one, from the Public Library of Leningrad (MS. B 19 A), dated A.D. 1008, was put at Kahle's disposal. This latter manuscript, Kahle thinks, is the best Ben Asher text available, and it is the text printed in the third edition.[3] This edition is thus based, not on a printed text, but on a manuscript. Noteworthy features of it are the inclusion of many readings of Babylonian manuscripts; the addition of the *Massora*

---

[1] Ed. by R. Kittel, A. Alt, and O. Eissfeldt; Kahle edited the Massoretic material (see his preface, pp. vi ff.).

[2] There is no complete manuscript which truly represents the Ben Naphtali recension. The differences in readings between the two Massoretic schools can now be more easily studied since the publication of a manuscript written by Misha'el ben 'Uzziel. It has been edited by L. Lipschütz (*Ben Ascher–Ben Naftali. Der Bibeltext der tiberischen Masoreten. Eine Abhandlung des Mischael b. Uzziel, veröffentlicht und untersucht*, 1937. See Kahle, *The Cairo Geniza*, p. 67, n. 1). See further B. J. Roberts, 'The Emergence of the Tiberian Massoretic Text', *J.T.S.* xlix, 1948, pp. 8 ff.

[3] J. L. Teicher, *J.J.S.* ii, 1950, pp. 17 ff., believes that the Leningrad manuscript was not copied from a text of the Old Testament corrected by Aaron ben Asher, but that it represents, not a genuine Ben Asher, but an eclectic, text. He further thinks that the Cairo Ben Asher Codex of the Prophets (Siglum C in BH³), which Kahle dates A.D. 895, is not earlier than the eleventh or twelfth century. If Kahle's date is correct, this Codex will be the oldest dated Hebrew manuscript.

parva, which was not printed in the earlier editions; and the utilization of some of the recently discovered manuscripts and papyri of the Greek Old Testament, such as the Freer manuscripts and the Chester Beatty papyri[1] (see next section).

II. THE GREEK BIBLE

(i) *New Sources of Knowledge*

In the last generation new material—manuscripts and papyri —of great importance for the textual criticism of the Greek Old Testament has come to light. In 1917 a manuscript of the Psalms (i. 1–cxlii. 8—all the leaves are, however, imperfect), belonging to the fifth or sixth century A.D., was edited by H. A. Sanders.[2] In 1927 the same editor published a manuscript, probably to be dated in the third century A.D., containing portions of the Minor Prophets (Hos. xiv. 7 to the end of Malachi, with a few fragments of the earlier chapters of Hosea).[3] In the same volume appeared the text of a papyrus of Genesis i. 16–xxxv. 8, belonging to the third or fourth century A.D.[4] During the years 1934–8 all the Biblical texts in the Chester Beatty papyri were edited by Sir Frederic Kenyon.[5] The Old Testament portions cover Genesis, Numbers, Deuteronomy, Isaiah, Jeremiah, Ezekiel, Daniel, and Esther, and date variously from the first half of the

---

[1] As has already been pointed out (p. 243, n. 1), the critical apparatus of BH³ calls for careful use; see Orlinsky's warning against accepting at its face value any variant or emendation in it (*B.A.* ix, 1946, p. 25, n. 5), and Sperber's criticism, *P.A.A.J.R.* xviii, 1948–9, pp. 303 ff.

[2] *The Old Testament Manuscripts in the Freer Collection, Part II, The Washington Manuscript of the Psalms.* Further, 'A newly discovered leaf of the Freer Psalter', *H.T.R.* xxii, 1929, pp. 391 ff., by the same editor.

[3] *The Minor Prophets in the Freer Collection.* In 1910 Sanders published *The Old Testament Manuscripts in the Freer Collection; Part I, The Washington Manuscript of Deuteronomy and Joshua.*

[4] Known as the Berlin Genesis. It was edited by C. Schmidt and H. A. Sanders.

[5] *The Chester Beatty Biblical Papyri.* Fasc. i, General Introduction, 1933; fasc. iv, Genesis, 1934–6; fasc. v, Numbers and Deuteronomy, 1935; fasc. vi, Isaiah, Jeremiah, Ecclesiasticus, 1937; fasc. vii, Ezekiel, Daniel, Esther, 1937–8. See the same writer's *Recent Developments in the Textual Criticism of the Greek Bible* (Schweich Lectures, 1932), pp. 51 ff. Further, A. Allgeier, *Die Chester Beatty-Papyri zum Pentateuch,* 1938 (on this see H. M. Orlinsky, *J.Q.R.* xxxii, 1941–2, pp. 89 ff.), and H. I. Bell, *Recent Discoveries of Biblical Papyri,* 1937.

second century A.D. to the fourth century A.D. In 1936 C. H. Roberts[1] published a papyrus containing fragments of Deuteronomy—xxiii. 24(26)–xxiv. 3, xxv. 1–3, xxvi. 12, 17–19, xxviii. 31–3—belonging to the middle of the second century B.C. And lastly in 1938 came the publication of the Scheide papyri, probably early third century A.D., containing Ezekiel xix. 12–xxxix. 29, edited by A. C. Johnson, H. S. Gehman, and E. H. Kase.[2]

The significance of these new finds can, of course, be illustrated here only very briefly. A few points may be singled out for special mention. First, it will be observed that some of the material antedates the fourth century A.D.—the period to which the Codex Vaticanus and the Codex Sinaiticus belong—and thus makes it possible to trace the text tradition of the Greek Old Testament back beyond these codices. The period prior to them has been one of great obscurity in the history of the Greek Old Testament. Now, thanks to these new sources, this obscurity is to an appreciable degree dispelled. The Chester Beatty papyri are in this respect outstandingly important, for five of the seven manuscripts containing portions of the Old Testament belong to the third century A.D., while the Numbers–Deuteronomy papyrus belongs probably to the first half of the second century A.D. This latter manuscript was, at the time of its discovery, the earliest known manuscript of any part of the Greek Old Testament. The Rylands fragments of Deuteronomy are, however,

---

[1] *Two Biblical Papyri in the John Rylands Library, Manchester* (see P. Katz's review, *T.L.Z.*, 1936, cols. 34 f.). See further J. Hempel, 'Zum griechischen Deuteronomiumtext des II. Jahrhunderts a. C.', *Z.A.W.* lv, 1937, pp. 115 ff.; A. Allgeier, 'Dt. 25¹⁻³ im Manchester-Papyrus (PRG 458)', *Biblica*, xix, 1938, pp. 1 ff. The Fouad Papyrus which contains part of Deut. xxxi and xxxii may be dated in the second or first century B.C;. see W. G. Waddell, *J.T.S.* xlv, 1944, pp. 159 f. This and the Rylands fragments are the oldest pieces of the Septuagint in existence.

[2] *The John H. Scheide Biblical Papyri: Ezekiel.* These papyri and the Chester Beatty papyri of Ezekiel are parts of a single manuscript. See further H. S. Gehman, 'The Relations between the Hebrew Text of Ezekiel and that of the John H. Scheide Papyri', *J.A.O.S.* lviii, 1938, pp. 92 ff., and 'The Relations between the Text of the John H. Scheide Papyri and that of the other Greek Manuscripts of Ezekiel', *J.B.L.* lvii, 1938, pp. 281 ff.; J. Ziegler, 'Die Bedeutung des Chester Beatty-Scheide Papyrus 967 für die Textüberlieferung der Ezechiel-Septuaginta', *Z.A.W.* lxi, 1945–8, pp. 76 ff.; and J. B. Payne, 'The Relationship of the Chester Beatty Papyri of Ezekiel to Codex Vaticanus', *J.B.L.* lxviii, 1949, pp. 251 ff.

some three hundred years older,[1] and so we are enabled now to trace the Greek text of part of this book back to within a century or so after the original translation was made. These fragments, and the Numbers–Deuteronomy papyrus, have, by reason of their early date, a special importance for the recovery of the pre-Origenian form of the Septuagint text. It is of great interest that the Rylands fragments and the Chester Beatty papyrus of Deuteronomy appear to agree rather with the Codex Alexandrinus than with the Codex Vaticanus,[2] thus presenting a challenge to the authority of the latter. Secondly, the Chester Beatty papyrus containing Daniel ii. 20–viii. 6, which belongs to the first half of the third century A.D., is especially important, for it represents the original Septuagint text, and not that of Theodotion, which is found in all available manuscripts except one, the Chigi manuscript, a minuscule of the ninth century A.D. or later. The new discovery, older by centuries, confirms in the main the accuracy of the later manuscript. Thirdly, a valuable contribution is made by the two Chester Beatty papyri containing substantial portions of Genesis, for only a few verses of this book are preserved in the two great codices of the fourth century. And lastly, this new material compels us to recognize even more forcibly that the text of the Greek Old Testament cannot be treated as a whole. The various books, translated at different times by different persons, have each their own textual problems which call for careful and minute investigation.[3]

(ii) *The Recovery of the Original Greek Text of the Septuagint*

Lagarde's ultimate aim in his work on the textual criticism of the Septuagint was, as is well known, the establishment of the original Septuagint text—the text from which, he argued,

---

[1] They would be roughly contemporary with the Dead Sea scroll of Isaiah, if the latter does in fact belong to the second century B.C. If it does, the Rylands fragments are no longer 'earlier by some three hundred years than any other manuscript of any part of the Bible' (C. H. Roberts, op. cit., p. 11).

[2] Ibid., pp. 34 f. See, however, J. A. Montgomery, *J.B.L.* lv, 1936, pp. 309 ff.

[3] See, for example, H. St. John Thackeray on the translators of the books of Sam., Kings, Jer., and Ezek., *The Septuagint and Jewish Worship* (Schweich Lectures, 1920), pp. 16 ff.

all existing manuscripts of the Greek Old Testament derive. Septuagint manuscripts could, he believed, be identified as belonging to one or other of the recensions of Origen, Hesychius, or Lucian, and the task is, therefore, first to recover the text of the three recensions, and then, once they have been recovered, to reduce them to a basic text which would represent as nearly as possible the original Greek text of the Septuagint. In this way should we be led nearer to the Hebrew prototype from which the Septuagint translation was made. The possibility or otherwise of the recovery of the original Greek text of the Septuagint—called by some scholars the *Urtext*, by others the Proto-Septuagint— has come greatly into prominence in recent years. Scholars who have worked along Lagardian lines are A. Rahlfs, M. Margolis, J. A. Montgomery, H. M. Orlinsky, J. Ziegler, P. Katz, and A. Allgeier.[1] Lagarde's principles have, however, been challenged by Kahle,[2] and more especially by A. Sperber.[3] They regard the attempt to reconstruct the oldest form of the Septuagint text as misguided, for Septuagint manuscripts go back, they believe, not to a variety of recensions of a single translation, but to a variety of independent translations. We can do no more than indicate how the debate appears to stand at present. If we may judge from the work of Orlinsky,[4] who has exposed some of the weaknesses in Sperber's position, and of Katz,[5] who has replied effectively to Kahle, we may conclude that the fundamentals of the Lagardian thesis are not yet in real danger of being overthrown. The new material, to which reference has been made, allows us, as has been said, to trace the Septuagint text back to a time nearer to the composition of the Septuagint. It does not, however, alter the essential nature of the problem under discussion.

It will be convenient to refer here to editions of the Septuagint

---

[1] References to their work are made in the footnotes and in the Bibliography.

[2] See *The Cairo Geniza*, pp. 174 ff.

[3] *Septuagintaprobleme* (B.W.A.N.T. xlix, 1929); *J.B.L.* liv, 1935, pp. 73 ff.; *Studien zur Geschichte und Kultur des Nahen und Fernen Ostens, Paul Kahle zum 60. Geburtstage überreicht* . . . ed. W. Heffening and W. Kirfel, 1935, pp. 39 ff.

[4] 'On the present state of Proto-Septuagint studies', *J.A.O.S.* lxi, 1941, pp. 81 ff.; cp. H. H. Rowley, 'The Proto-Septuagint Question', *J.Q.R.* xxxiii, 1942–3, pp. 497 ff.

[5] 'Das Problem des Urtextes der Septuaginta', *T.Z.*, 1949, pp. 1 ff.

which have appeared recently. The larger Cambridge Septuagint,[1] of which Genesis–Deuteronomy had been published in 1906–11, was continued with the publication of Joshua–Judges–Ruth in 1917, 1–4 Kingdoms and 1, 2 Chronicles in 1932, and Ezra and Nehemiah in 1935. In this edition, as in Swete's smaller edition, the text of the Codex Vaticanus is printed, but with a much enlarged critical apparatus, which includes the readings of the papyri and uncials, of a considerable selection of minuscules, and of the chief versions and patristic writings. This edition thus provides all the material, presented with exactness and objectivity, necessary for a reconstruction of the original text. Rahlfs's edition of the whole Septuagint,[2] published in 1935, presents, on the contrary, a reconstructed text, based in the main upon the Codices Vaticanus, Alexandrinus, and Sinaiticus, with a short critical apparatus. It presents, that is to say, the oldest form of the Septuagint which, in the editor's view, it is possible to achieve. It is the first attempt ever made to produce in a handy form a critical text of the whole of the Septuagint. Such a text cannot, of course, claim finality. And indeed, Rahlfs's edition already calls for revision.[3] Of the Göttingen edition,[4] planned to be issued in sixteen parts under the direction of Rahlfs, and again presenting an eclectic text, with a succinct critical apparatus, Psalms (together with Exod. xv, Deut. xxxii, and other canticles),[5] Isaiah,[6] and the Minor Prophets[7] have so far appeared.

[1] *The O.T. in Greek*, ed. A. E. Brooke, N. McLean, and H. St. John Thackeray.

[2] *Septuaginta id est Vetus Testamentum Graece iuxta LXX Interpretes.*

[3] Cp. Katz, *T.L.Z.*, 1936, cols. 265 ff.

[4] *Septuaginta: Vetus Testamentum Graecum auctoritate Societatis Litterarum Gottingensis editum.*

[5] *Psalmi cum Odis*, ed. A. Rahlfs, 1931 (on this see P. L. Hedley, *H.T.R.* xxvi, 1933, pp. 61 ff.). In 1922 Rahlfs published, simultaneously with *Studie über den griechischen Text des Buches Ruth*, his *Das Buch Ruth griechisch als Probe einer kritischen Handausgabe der Septuaginta*. In 1926 appeared, as Part 1 of the edition itself, but on a reduced scale, *Septuaginta ed. A. Rahlfs: I. Genesis.*

[6] *Isaias*, ed. J. Ziegler, 1939. In his *Textkritische Notizen zu den jüngeren griechischen Übersetzungen des Buches Isaias* (Nachrichten von der Ges. der Wiss. zu Göttingen, 1939) he justifies the readings of Aquila, Symmachus, and Theodotion which he has admitted into his edition. The same writer's *Untersuchungen zur Septuaginta des Buches Isaias*, 1934, is very valuable.

[7] *Duodecim Prophetae*, ed. J. Ziegler, 1943. See further on these editions G. Bertram, *T.R.*, N.F. iii, 1931, pp. 282 ff.

(iii) *The Alphabet of the Septuagint-Vorlage*

A problem of fundamental importance for the textual criticism of the Hebrew Bible, which has come much into prominence recently, is the question of the alphabet in which the Septuagint-*Vorlage*, that is, the text from which the Septuagint translators worked, was written. That it was a Hebrew alphabet of some kind has been universally assumed, and the view of S. R. Driver that, except perhaps in the case of the Pentateuch, the manuscripts used by the translators were written in an alphabet which represented a transitional stage between the ancient Hebrew alphabet, known to us from the Lachish ostraca and other early Hebrew inscriptions, and the Hebrew square character,[1] has gained wide currency. It is not surprising, therefore, that the transcription theory advocated by F. X. Wutz[2] has attracted the attention of a large number of scholars. It is, however, still comparatively little known in this country. Briefly stated, his theory is that the Septuagint translation was made from texts transcribed from Hebrew into Greek characters.[3] That instances of transliterated words occur sporadically throughout the Septuagint is, of course, well known. It is on these transliterations, regarded as relics of a complete text similar to the second column of Origen's Hexapla, that Wutz's theory is to a large extent based. The translators thus had no manuscripts written in Hebrew characters before them. The Pentateuch, however, may have been revised later on the basis of texts written in Hebrew characters. Thus, prior to translation, there was, so the theory runs, a process of transliteration, and Wutz's aim is to work back, through Greek transliteration, to the pre-Massoretic Hebrew text which underlies the Septuagint translation. Wutz's theory has been carefully

---

[1] *Notes on the Hebrew Text and the Topography of the Books of Samuel*[2], 1913, p. lxiv.

[2] Besides *Die Transkriptionen*, etc., already referred to, his chief works are, *Die Psalmen textkritisch untersucht*, 1925, and *Systemätische Wege von der Septuaginta zum hebräischen Urtext*, I. Teil, 1937.

[3] O. G. Tychsen in 1772 had put forward a similar theory in *Tentamen de variis codicum Hebraicorum Vet. Test. MSS. generibus a Judaeis et non-Judaeis descriptis*, pp. 59 ff. Further, H. M. Orlinsky, *The Bible Today and Tomorrow*, ed. H. R. Willoughby, 1947, pp. 155 ff.

investigated by J. Fischer,[1] who has successfully shown that, so far as the Pentateuch and Isaiah, at any rate, are concerned, Wutz's theory is untenable.[2] As for the Pentateuch, the evidence shows that the manuscripts used by the Septuagint translators were written in a neo-Aramaic alphabet which approximated to square script. The same is true in the case of Isaiah, the tendency to square script being, however, more pronounced.[3] Two considerations which argue strongly against Wutz's theory may be briefly mentioned. In the first place, the confusion between certain letters, for example, *daleth* and *resh*, in the Septuagint translation is well known. Surely such confusion must prove direct contact with a Hebrew, and not a Greek, alphabet. It is significant that Fischer has found in Isaiah only two examples—and they are both doubtful—of confusion between *delta* and *lambda*, two letters which, in Greek capitals, could easily be confused. And secondly, Wutz himself regards the Septuagint translators as good Hebraists, who drew upon the contemporary Aramaic at need. They could, therefore, read Hebrew texts written in an Aramaic-Hebrew alphabet. What need then for them to resort to Greek transcription texts? The presence of Aramaisms in the Septuagint text of Isaiah, where they are especially frequent, and elsewhere, is in itself an argument against the use of Greek transcription texts by the translators. That a translator may sometimes have transcribed a word or expression which he did not understand, and placed his transcription over

[1] *Das Alphabet der LXX-Vorlage im Pentateuch*, 1924; *Zur Septuaginta-Vorlage im Pentateuch* (B.Z.A.W. xlii, 1926); *In welcher Schrift lag das Buch Isaias den LXX vor?* (B.Z.A.W. lvi, 1930).

[2] This is the view of almost all scholars. See, for example, H. St. John Thackeray, *Some Aspects of the Greek Old Testament*, 1927, p. 34; W. Rudolph, *Z.A.W.* xlviii, 1930, p. 274; Kahle, *Z.D.M.G.* xcii, 1938, pp. 282 ff.; M. L. Margolis, *J.Q.R.* xvi, 1925–6, pp. 117 ff.; A. Barrois, *R.B.* xxxix, 1930, pp. 332 ff., *et al.*

[3] H. M. Orlinsky, *B.A.* ix, 1946, p. 31, thinks that the alphabet used was somewhere between that of the Lachish ostraca (early sixth century B.C.) and that of the Nash papyrus, which, like some other scholars, he dates in the second or first century B.C. If the Dead Sea Scrolls are as early as the second century B.C., the square script in which they are written, except for the Leviticus fragments (see p. 241, n. 1), becomes relevant here. See further M. Plessner, 'Neue Arbeiten zur Septuaginta-Forschung', *M.G.W.J.* lxx, 1926, pp. 237 ff.; A. Sperber, 'Das Alphabet der Septuaginta-Vorlage', *O.L.Z.* xxxii, 1929, cols. 533 ff.

the line or in the margin, and that such glosses may ultimately have found their way into the text is intelligible. So much truth there may well be in Wutz's theory. That entire books of the Septuagint were translated from Greek transcription texts, there is, however, as yet no proof.[1]

Despite the untenability of Wutz's main thesis, his work is not without importance for textual criticism, for he has drawn attention to some facts which have not been sufficiently appreciated by Septuagint scholars hitherto.[2] Mention has been made of the different strata which, he believes, are to be distinguished in the transcriptions of Hebrew words in the Septuagint. Again, he has carried further the study of 'Graecised' transcriptions in the Septuagint, that is, Greek-Hebrew forms which, not being at once clear, were adapted to the nearest Greek form.[3] His attempts at the restoration of the original Hebrew text, on the other hand, must be regarded with great suspicion, for they frequently result in a travesty of the Hebrew language and a consequent distortion of the thought of the Biblical writer.[4] His method of research has proved fruitful in the sphere of Hebrew lexicography, but here again his own results need to be carefully checked. His writings, some of them very bulky, contain a great deal of material which will repay study by the Hebrew lexicographer. The importance of this sphere of study for the textual criticism of the Hebrew Bible has already been touched upon.

[1] On the question whether Old Testament texts, transcribed from Hebrew into Greek characters, were in circulation before the second column of Origen's Hexapla, see Kahle, *The Cairo Geniza*, p. 87, who thinks they were. *Contra* G. Mercati, op. cit., loc. cit. See further I. L. Seeligmann, *The Septuagint Version of Isaiah*, 1948, p. 58, n. 29, and Katz, *T.Z.*, 1949, p. 21, n. 23.

[2] See, for example, G. Bertram, *T.R.*, N.F. x, 1938, pp. 69 ff., 133 ff.; R. Kittel, *D.L.Z.* xlvi, 1925, cols. 657 ff.; H. St. John Thackeray, *Some Aspects of the Greek Old Testament*, 1927, p. 32; I. L. Seeligmann, op. cit., loc. cit.; J. Fischer, *In welcher Schrift . . . Isaias . . .*, p. 89, *et al.*

[3] *Die Transkriptionen, etc.* ii, 1925, pp. 47 ff. H. St. John Thackeray lists many examples in *Grammar of Old Testament Greek*, 1909, pp. 34 ff.

[4] See the present writer's review of his *Das Buch Job*, in *J.T.S.* xli, 1940, pp. 288 f. W. F. Albright (*B.A.S.O.R.*, No. 82, 1941, p. 49) regards Wutz's revision of Ps. xxix as absurd in the light of Ugaritic parallels.

III. OTHER CHIEF ANCIENT VERSIONS

In his search for the original text of the Hebrew Bible, the textual critic who would, as, of course, he must, appeal to the witness of the other chief ancient versions—the Samaritan Pentateuch, the Targums, the Peshitta, and the Vulgate—has to labour under a serious handicap which results from the lack of critical editions of these versions. All these versions have their own problems, which should ideally be solved before they can be used. In the last generation considerable contributions have been made which have gone some way towards easing the difficulty in which the textual critic finds himself. It will be possible here to do no more than indicate briefly how some of the gaps have been filled.[1]

So far as the Samaritan Pentateuch is concerned, the outstanding event has been the appearance of A. von Gall's critical edition.[2] Very welcome though it is, its reliability is impaired by reason of the fact that the editor did not make exhaustive use of all the manuscript material available.[3] Further critical work has been done by Sperber[4]—whose lists of variants in the Samaritan Pentateuch as compared with the Massoretic text show how difficult it is to determine which text is original—and by J. Hempel, whose examination of the variants in the two texts in the book of Deuteronomy well illustrates how complex this kind of study can become.[5] It is an interesting suggestion of Sperber that some of the grammatical differences between the two texts may be explained on the supposition that the Samaritan text preserves northern dialectical peculiarities, whereas the Massoretic text reflects the southern dialect of Judah.[6]

---

[1] A mass of information on these versions will be found in Kahle, *The Cairo Geniza*.

[2] *Der hebräische Pentateuch der Samaritaner*, 1914–18.

[3] See E. Robertson, *Catalogue of the Samaritan Manuscripts in the John Rylands Library, Manchester*, 1938, p. xv. See further Kahle, *Z.D.M.G.* xcii, 1938, pp. 682 ff.

[4] *H.U.C.A.* xiv, 1939, pp. 161 ff.   [5] *Z.A.W.* lii, 1934, pp. 254 ff.

[6] *H.U.C.A.* xii–xiii, 1937–8, pp. 151 f. The peculiarities of the Samaritan dialect as a source of divergencies in the Samaritan Pentateuch is a point made also by Ch. Heller, *The Samaritan Pentateuch: An Adaptation of the Massoretic Text*, 1923, pp. 186 ff. In this book he attempts to show that the Samaritan Pentateuch cannot be regarded as an independent witness to the Massoretic text. He has collected some useful material, but his treatment of his theme is not impressive.

Critical editions of the Targum of Onkelos to the Pentateuch and of the Targum of Jonathan to the former prophets, which were intended to take the place of the editions of Berliner (1884) and of Lagarde (1872), had been prepared by Sperber prior to 1931, but they were never published. An introductory chapter dealing with the variant readings of the Targum of Onkelos has, however, appeared,[1] as well as some preliminary results of his examination of the Targum to the former prophets.[2] How Lagarde's edition needs to be supplemented has been shown also by W. E. Barnes, who has examined thirteen chapters of the Targum of Ezekiel as preserved in Yemenite manuscripts;[3] and by R. H. Melamed, who has compared Lagarde's text of the Song of Songs with six Yemenite manuscripts.[4] J. F. Stenning's recent edition of the Targum of Isaiah,[5] based upon a Yemenite manuscript in the British Museum (Or. 2211), with collations from ten other manuscripts, marks a considerable advance in the study of the Targum of this prophetical book. It too, however, requires supplementation, and needs to be checked before it can be cited as authoritative.[6]

No critical edition of the Peshitta as a whole yet exists. Critical studies of some of the books of the Old Testament in Syriac have, however, recently been made—of Ezra,[7] the Song of Songs,[8] and 2 Samuel;[9] and the Syriac text of the book of Psalms

---

[1] *P.A.A.J.R.* vi, 1934-5, pp. 309 ff.

[2] *Z.A.W.* xliv, 1926, pp. 175 f.; xlv, 1927, pp. 267 ff. Much interesting material —not always very clearly presented, however—on the historical background of the Targum, the textual variations, exegetical principles, &c., will be found in P. Churgin, *Targum Jonathan to the Prophets* (Yale Oriental Series—Researches xiv, 1927—not 1907, as printed on the title-page).

[3] *J.T.S.* xxviii, 1927, pp. 283 ff.

[4] *J.Q.R.* x, 1919-20, pp. 377 ff.; xi, 1920-1, pp. 1 ff.; xii, 1921-2, pp. 57 ff.

[5] *The Targum of Isaiah*, 1949. 'The Hebrew text presupposed by the Targum differs very slightly from the Massoretic text, and the Targum therefore is an early and valuable witness to the fidelity with which the Massoretic text has been preserved' (p. xi).

[6] See H. H. Rowley, *Bi. Or.* vi, No. 5, Sept. 1949, pp. 159 f.; W. D. McHardy, *H.J.* xlviii, 1950, pp. 190 ff.

[7] C. A. Hawley, *A Critical Examination of the Peshitta Version of the Book of Ezra*, 1922.

[8] J. Bloch, *A.J.S.L.* xxxviii, 1922, pp. 103 ff.

[9] D. M. C. Englert, *The Peshitto of Second Samuel*, 1949.

has also been investigated in part.[1] Very valuable for the textual criticism of the Peshitta is the edition of Barhebraeus's *Scholia* on Genesis–2 Samuel prepared by M. Sprengling and W. C. Graham.[2] A great deal of useful information—on the chief manuscripts, the printed texts, the character of the Peshitta in different parts of the Old Testament, and suchlike—is contained in L. Haefeli's introduction to the study of the Peshitta.[3]

An important contribution to the textual criticism of the Hebrew Bible is the edition of the Vulgate, with full critical apparatus, which is being undertaken by the Benedictine Order.[4] Of individual books of the Latin Old Testament the Psalter has especially attracted the attention of scholars in recent years.[5]

Our survey of some of the more important work which has been done in the last generation in the sphere of the textual criticism of the Old Testament will, it is hoped, have given the reader some idea of its scope and significance. We may conclude by asking to what extent it has brought us nearer to the attain-

[1] F. Zimmermann, *J.T.S.* xli, 1940, pp. 44 ff.; E. R. Rowlands, ibid. xlii, 1941, pp. 65 ff.

[2] *Barhebraeus' Scholia on the Old Testament, Part I. Gen.–II Sam.* (Univ. of Chicago Oriental Institute Publications, xiii, 1931).

[3] *Die Peschitta des A.T.*, 1927. See also J. Bloch, *A.J.S.L.* xxxv, 1919, pp. 215 ff. (on the authorship of the version); xxxvii, 1920–1, pp. 136 ff. (on printed texts).

[4] *Biblia sacra iuxta latinam Vulgatam versionem ad codicum fidem iussu Pii PP. XII cura et studio monachorum Abbatiae Pontificiae Sancti Hieronymi in urbe Ordinis Sancti Benedicti edita.* For an explanation of the critical principles adopted, see Dom H. Quentin, *Mémoire sur l'établissement du texte de la Vulgate* (Collectanea Biblica Latina, vi, 1922). Genesis appeared in 1926; Exodus and Leviticus in 1929; Numbers and Deuteronomy in 1937; Joshua, Judges and Ruth in 1939; Samuel in 1944; Kings in 1945; Chronicles in 1948; and Ezra, Tobit, and Judith in 1950. For further literature, see R. H. Pfeiffer, *Introduction to the Old Testament*[2], 1948, p. 126.

[5] e.g. J. M. Harden, *Psalterium iuxta Hebraeos Hieronymi*, 1922; A. Allgeier, 'Die Hexapla in den Psalmenübersetzungen des heiligen Hieronymus', *Biblica*, viii, 1927, pp. 450 ff., and 'Die erste Psalmenübersetzungen des h. Hieronymus und das Psalterium Romanum', ibid. xii, 1931, pp. 447 ff. Mention may be made here of the new Latin translation of the Psalter, made from a Hebrew text established critically, which has been made by a Commission of professors of the Pontifical Institute, with the title *Liber Psalmorum cum Canticis Breviarii Romani: Nova e textibus primigeniis interpretatio latina cum notis criticis et exegeticis*, 1945. See A. Bea, *Le Nouveau Psautier latin*, 1947, especially pp. 71 ff., where the principles and methods which the translators applied in the critical reconstruction of the text are expounded.

ment of the avowed aim of textual criticism, which is the recovery
of the original Hebrew text. This aim, it should never be forgotten, is an ideal one, and will ever remain so. It is impossible
of complete attainment. There is indeed a sense in which it is
true to say that we are as far off from its attainment today as we
ever were. The work of the last generation has made us aware
of this fact. It has, however, also made it clear that the accession
of new material, the application of new methods, and a greater
understanding of the complexity of the problems involved, have
opened up new possibilities of advance towards the attainment of
the ideal aim which the textual critic has set for himself. It is no
exaggeration to say that the last generation has been one of very
considerable achievement in the sphere of textual criticism. This
achievement, however, only throws into higher relief the im-
mensity of the problems which it has bequeathed to this, and
future, generations.[1] It is much to be hoped that there may not
be wanting scholars who will be willing to undertake research
in this sphere of work, which, if it is not among the more exciting
aspects of Old Testament study, is yet fundamental to them all.

D. WINTON THOMAS

BIBLIOGRAPHY

(The literature included is additional to that cited in the notes accompanying the essay)

AP-THOMAS, D. R. *A Primer of Old Testament Text Criticism*, 1947.

BAAB, O. J. 'A Theory of Two Translators for the Greek Genesis', *J.B.L.* lii, 1933, pp. 239 ff.

BARNES, W. E. 'The Recovery of the "Septuagint" ', *J.T.S.* xxxvi, 1935, pp. 123 ff.

BAUMSTARK, A. *Geschichte der syrischen Literatur*, 1922, pp. 18 f., 23 f.

BERTRAM, G. 'Zur Septuaginta-Forschung', *T.R.*, N.F. v, 1933, pp. 173 ff.

— *Das Problem der Umschrift und die religionsgeschichtliche Erforschung der LXX*, B.Z.A.W. lxvi, 1936, pp. 97 ff.

BILLEN, A. V. 'The Hexaplaric Element in the LXX Version of Judges', *J.T.S.* xliii, 1942, pp. 12 ff.

---

[1] See P. Volz, 'Ein Arbeitsplan für die Textkritik des A.T.', *Z.A.W.* liv, 1936, pp. 100 ff.

BLOCH, J. 'The Influence of the Greek Bible on the Peshitta', *A.J.S.L.* xxxvi, 1920, pp. 161 ff.

DE BOER, P. A. H. *Research into the Text of 1 Samuel·i–xvi: a Contribution to the Study of the Books of Samuel,* 1938.

—— '1 Samuel xvii: Notes on the Text and the Ancient Versions', *O.T.S.* i, 1941–2, pp. 79 ff.

—— 'Research into the Text of 1 Samuel xviii–xxxi', *O.T.S.* vi, 1949, pp. 1 ff.

CANNON, W. W. 'Jerome and Symmachus: Some Points in the Vulgate Translation of Koheleth', *Z.A.W.* xlv, 1927, pp. 191 ff.

CHOMSKY, W. 'The History of our Vowel-System in Hebrew', *J.Q.R.* xxxii, 1941–2, pp. 27 ff.

CHURGIN, P. 'The Targum and the Septuagint', *A.J.S.L.* l, 1933, pp. 41 ff.

DEBRUNNER, A. *Zur Übersetzungstechnik der Septuaginta,* B.Z.A.W. xli, 1925, pp. 69 ff.

EISSFELDT, O. *Einleitung in das Alte Testament,* 1934, pp. 693 ff.

FISCHER, J. 'Die hebräischen Bibelzitate des Scholastikers Odo', *Biblica,* xv, 1934, pp. 50 ff.

—— *Einige Proben aus den hebräischen Bibelzitaten des Scholastikers Odo,* B.Z.A.W. lxvi, 1936, pp. 198 ff.

FRITSCH, C. T. *The Anti-anthropomorphisms of the Greek Pentateuch,* 1943.

GERLEMAN, G. *Studies in the Septuagint (i) Book of Job (ii) Chronicles,* 1946.

HAUPERT, R. S. 'The Transcription-theory of the Septuagint', *J.B.L.* liii, 1934, pp. 251 ff.

HEMPEL, J. 'Innermasoretische Bestätigungen des Samaritanus', *Z.A.W.* lii, 1934, pp. 254 ff.

HERRMANN, J. and BAUMGÄRTEL, F. *Beiträge zur Entstehungsgeschichte der Septuaginta,* B.W.A.T., N.F. v, 1923.

JANSMA, T. 'Inquiry into the Hebrew and the Ancient Versions of Zechariah ix–xiv', *O.T.S.* vii, 1950, pp. 1 ff.

KAHLE, P. *Masoreten des Ostens,* 1913.

—— *Aus der Geschichte der ältesten hebräischen Bibelhandschrift,* B.Z.A.W. xxxiii, 1918, pp. 247 ff.

—— Sections 6–9 in H. Bauer and P. Leander, *Historische Grammatik der Hebräischen Sprache,* 1922, pp. 71 ff.

—— *Die Punktation der Masoreten,* B.Z.A.W. xli, 1925, pp. 167 ff.

—— 'Die hebräischen Bibelhandschriften aus Babylonien', *Z.A.W.* xlvi, 1928, pp. 113 ff.

—— *Masoreten des Westens I,* 1927, II, 1930.

—— 'Der alttestamentliche Bibeltext', *T.R.,* N.F. v, 1933, pp. 227 ff.

—— 'Die Septuaginta: Prinzipielle Erwägungen', *Festschrift O. Eissfeldt,* ed. J. Fück, 1947, pp. 161 ff.

KAMINKA, A. 'Studien zur Septuaginta an der Hand der zwölf kleinen Prophetenbücher', *M.G.W.J.* lxxii, 1928, pp. 49 ff., 242 ff.

KAMINKA, A. 'Septuaginta und Targum zu Proverbia', *H.U.C.A.* viii–ix, 1931–2, pp. 169 ff.

KATZ, P. 'Notes on the Septuagint', i, ii, *J.T.S.* xlvii, 1946, pp. 30 ff.; iii, iv, pp. 166 ff.; v, vi, xlviii, 1947, pp. 194 ff.

— *Philo's Bible. The Aberrant Text of Bible Quotations in some Philonic Writings and its Place in the Textual History of the Greek Bible*, 1950.

KENYON, F. G. *The Text of the Greek Bible*, 1937.

— *Our Bible and the Ancient Manuscripts*, 1948.

LEANDER, P. 'Bemerkungen zur palästinischen Überlieferung des Hebräischen', *Z.A.W.* liv, 1936, pp. 91 ff.

LIEBREICH, L. J. 'Notes on the Greek Version of Symmachus', *J.B.L.* lxiii, 1944, pp. 397 ff.

MARGOLIS, M. L. 'Textual Criticism of the Greek Old Testament', *P.A.P.S.* lxvii, 1928, pp. 187 ff.

— 'Corrections in the Apparatus of the Book of Joshua in the Larger Cambridge Septuagint', *J.B.L.* xlix, 1930, pp. 234 ff.

— *The Book of Joshua in Greek* (Parts i–iv), 1931–8.

MEECHAM, H. G. *The Oldest Version of the Bible: 'Aristeas' on its traditional origin. A study in early apologetic* (Hartley Lecture, 32), 1932.

— *The Letter of Aristeas: a linguistic study with special reference to the Greek Bible*, 1935.

MÖHLE, A. 'Ein neuer Fund zahlreicher Stücke aus den Jesaiaübersetzungen des Akylas, Symmachos und Theodotion', *Z.A.W.* lii, 1934, pp. 176 ff.

MONTGOMERY, J. A. 'The Hexaplaric Strata in the Greek Texts of Daniel', *J.B.L.* xliv, 1925, pp. 289 ff.

— *The Book of Daniel* (I.C.C.), 1927, pp. 24 ff.

MORDELL, P. 'The Beginning and Development of Hebrew Punctuation', *J.Q.R.* xxiv, 1933–4, pp. 137 ff.

NESTLE, E. *Das Buch Jeremia griechisch und hebräisch (Nach dem Tode des Herausgebers besorgt von Johannes Dahse und Erwin Nestle)*, 1924.

NYBERG, H. S. 'Das textkritische Problem des Alten Testaments am Hoseabuche demonstriert', *Z.A.W.* lii, 1934, pp. 241 ff.

— *Studien zum Hoseabuche: Zugleich ein Beitrag zur Klärung der alttestamentlichen Textkritik*, 1935.

OLMSTEAD, A. T. 'The Greek Genesis', *A.J.S.L.* xxxiv, 1917, pp. 145 ff.

ORLINSKY, H. M. 'The Columnar Order of the Hexapla', *J.Q.R.* xxvii, 1936–7, pp. 137 ff.

— 'The Kings–Isaiah Recensions of the Hezekiah Story', *J.Q.R.* xxx, 1939–40, pp. 33 ff.

— 'The Septuagint—Its Use in Textual Criticism', *B.A.* ix, 1946, pp. 22 ff.

— *The Septuagint. The Oldest Translation of the Bible* (Union Anniversary Series. Union of American Hebrew Congregations, Cincinnati, 1949).

OTTLEY, R. R. *A Handbook to the Septuagint*, 1920.

PRETZL, O. 'Septuagintaprobleme im Buch der Richter. Die griechischen

Handschriftengruppen im Buch der Richter untersucht nach ihrem Verhältnis zu einander', *Biblica*, vii, 1926, pp. 233 ff., 353 ff.

PRETZL, O. 'Die griechischen Handschriftengruppen im Buche Josue untersucht nach ihrer Eigenart und ihrem Verhältnis zu einander', *Biblica*, ix, 1928, pp. 377 ff.

PRICE, I. M. *The Ancestry of Our English Bible* (2nd revised ed. by W. A. Irwin and A. P. Wickgren, 1949).

PRIJS, L. *Jüdische Tradition in der Septuaginta*, 1948.

PROCKSCH, O. 'Tetraplarische Studien', *Z.A.W.* liii, 1935, pp. 240 ff.; liv, 1936, pp. 61 ff.

RAHLFS, A. *Verzeichnis der griechischen Handschriften des Alten Testaments, für das Septuaginta-Unternehmens* (Nachrichten d. k. Ges. d. Wiss. zu Göttingen. Philol.-hist. Kl., 1914).

— *Paul de Lagardes wissenschaftliches Lebenswerk im Rahmen einer Geschichte seines Lebens dargestellt* (Mitteil. d. Septuaginta-Unternehmens d. Ges. d. Wiss. zu Göttingen, 4, i, 1928).

REIDER, J. *Prolegomena to a Greek-Hebrew and Hebrew-Greek Index to Aquila*, 1916.

— 'The Present State of Textual Criticism of the Old Testament', *H.U.C.A.* vii, 1930, pp. 285 ff.

ROBERTSON, E. *The Text of the O.T. and the Methods of Textual Criticism* (Lectiones in vetere testamento et in rebus judaicis, No. 1, published by Shapiro, Vallentine and Co., London; n.d.)

— 'Points of Interest in the Massoretic Text', *J.N.E.S.* ii, 1943, pp. 35 ff.

ROBINSON, H. WHEELER (ed.). *The Bible in its Ancient and English Versions*, 1940.

SILVERSTONE, A. E. *Aquila and Onkelos*, 1931.

SPERBER, A. 'Zur Sprache des Prophetentargums', *Z.A.W.* xlv, 1927, pp. 267 ff.

— 'Peschitta und Onkelos', *Jewish Studies in Memory of George A. Kohut*, ed. S. W. Baron and A. Marx, 1935, pp. 554 ff.

— 'The Targum Onkelos in its Relation to the Masoretic Hebrew Text', *P.A.A.J.R.* vi, 1935, pp. 309 ff.

STUMMER, F. *Einführung in die lateinische Bibel*, 1928.

— 'Einige Beobachtungen über die Arbeitsweise des Hieronymus bei der Übersetzung des Alten Testaments aus der hebraica veritas', *Biblica*, x, 1929, pp. 3 ff.

— *Hauptprobleme der Erforschung der alttestamentlichen Vulgata*, B.Z.A.W. lxvi, 1936, pp. 233 ff.

— 'Beiträge zu dem Problem "Hieronymus und die Targumim" ', *Biblica*, xviii, 1937, pp. 174 ff.

SUTCLIFFE, E. F. 'St. Jerome's Hebrew Manuscripts', *Biblica*, xxix, 1948, pp. 195 ff.

WEISER, A. *Einleitung in das Alte Testament*[2], 1949, pp. 257 ff.

WEVERS, J. W. 'A Study in the Hebrew Variants in the Book of Kings', *Z.A.W.* lxi, 1949, pp. 43 ff.

ZIEGLER, J. 'Der textkritische Wert der Septuaginta des Buches Job', *Miscellanea Biblica edita a Pontificio Instituto Biblico ad celebrandum annum XXV ex quo conditum est Institutum 1909–vii Maii–1934*, ii, pp. 277 ff.

— *Beiträge zum griechischen Dodekapropheton* (Nachrichten der Akad. d. Wiss. in Göttingen, 1943, pp. 345 ff.).

— 'Der griechische Dodekapropheton-Text der Complutenser Polyglotte', *Biblica*, xxv, 1944, pp. 297 ff.

— 'Studien zur Verwertung der Septuaginta im Zwölfprophetenbuch', *Z.A.W.* lx, 1944, pp. 107 ff.

— 'Der Text der Aldina im Dodekapropheton', *Biblica*, xxvi, 1945, pp. 37 ff.

ZIMMERMANN, F. 'The Perpetuation of Variants in the Massoretic Text', *J.Q.R.* xxxiv, 1943–4, pp. 459 ff.

IX

SEMITIC EPIGRAPHY AND HEBREW PHILOLOGY

IN the second half of the nineteenth century the dominant factor in the development of studies ancillary to the interpretation of the Hebrew Bible was the rise and progress of Assyriology. In the thirty years since The Society for Old Testament Study came into existence a like role has been played by the uncovering and publication of antiquities from Syria and Palestine and of a remarkable and in part unexpected succession of epigraphs in Aramaic and Canaanite dialects.

The founders of the Society can hardly have foreseen this development in North-west Semitic studies, yet it is no accident that it began with the close of the First World War. The dissolution of the Ottoman Empire opened new territories and committed the rule and development of large tracts of the Near East to European powers. The fresh and differing opportunities presented under the new dispensation and secured by enlightened legislation for the safeguard of antiquities and the proper conduct of antiquitarian research were put to good use by various archaeological undertakings, and it is with one part of the results of such investigation that we are here in the first place concerned. None of the archaeological campaigns had as a primary objective the recovery of specific or putative documents, yet almost all the documents here referred to emerged in the course of systematic excavation.

Passing over the older cuneiform material from various parts of Syria which is dealt with by W. F. Albright in another chapter, we may appropriately begin with the Phoenician inscription on the sarcophagus of King Ahiram of Byblus and the minatory graffito on the side of the vertical shaft giving access to the tomb. Both were found in 1923 in the course of the excavation of ancient Byblus by P. Montet, and were manifestly older than the Moabite inscription of Mesha, which, from his synchronism with Omri and Ahab of Israel in the middle of the ninth century, had since its discovery in 1868 provided the earliest certain date in the North-west Semitic epigraphic record. A more positive indication of date appeared to be given by fragments of alabaster vases from the debris of the tomb bearing the name and title of Ramses II (*c.* 1301–1234). A difficulty in the way of this dating was the close resemblance of the script of the Ahiram texts to that of the imperfectly understood Abibaal inscription from the same city, which, being incised on a portion of a statue of Shishak, the first Pharaoh of the XXIInd Dynasty, could hardly be earlier than the third quarter of the tenth century. It was not until 1946 that M. Dunand was able to show, in an insert to his *Byblia Grammata*, that the pottery found in the debris was Iron I ware and so dated the Ahiram sarcophagus to the period about 1000 B.C. Meanwhile other inscriptions from the same city and from the same general period came to light, and we now have a series of half a dozen inscriptions concerning the same number of rulers of Byblus in the tenth century. From the same excavations a missing fragment of the fifth-century inscription of Yehawmilk (*C.I.S.* i, 1) was recovered, enabling a partial restoration of the beginnings of the last six lines.[1] The later cities of Tyre and Sidon were not subjected to any systematic excavation in the period under review, and no major epigraphic finds were made there. But across the water in Cyprus T. B. Mitford brought to light a tomb-inscription, unfortunately badly eroded, which must be dated to the ninth century,[2] thus attesting the presence of Phoenicians in Cyprus a full century before the inscribed fragments from Limasol (*C.I.S.* i, 5) dedicated to Baal Lebanon by 'Hiram king of the Sidonians'. But the priority as the oldest colonial Phoenician document is perhaps to be conceded to the Nora inscription from Sardinia (*C.I.S.* i, 144), for while the textual reconstructions of W. F. Albright and A. Dupont-Sommer are somewhat conjectural, the re-examination of the script shows that it must be placed in the ninth century. From farther west the new evidences of early Phoenician colonization

---

[1] M. Dunand in *B.M.B.* v, 1944, pp. 71–85.
[2] *Iraq*, vi, 1939, pp. 106–8.

are archaeological rather than epigraphic, and while in Carthage itself inscriptions of the familiar type have continued to accumulate they belong without exception to the period after she ceased to be a Tyrian colony. In the east Phoenician inscriptions have been found in places so far apart as the island of Rhodes, Ur in Iraq, and Karatepe in Cilicia; Egypt has contributed the first two examples of Phoenician writing on papyrus. The Ur ivory lid, which belongs to the seventh century, may be an imported item.

The Karatepe inscriptions are not only the longest Phoenician documents ever discovered, but are of great historical importance for the information they give about the kingdom of the Danunians and its chief city Azitawaddaya, situated about twenty-four miles west-north-west of Zenjirli. They demonstrate the use of Phoenician as an official language in a region where hitherto its employment had barely been suspected, and that too at a time when in inland northern Syria it was giving place to Aramaic. They date from the latter half of the eighth century and the language is pure Phoenician. The Kilamuwa inscription of the ninth century at Zenjirli is in the same tongue, but Aramaic had become the language of public epigraphy there before the time of the conquests of Tiglath-Pileser III, as we see from the Hadad statue from Zenjirli, belonging to the first half of the eighth century and from the rather older inscription from Afis near Aleppo, in which Zakir, king of Hamath and Laash, uses an Aramaic contaminated with Canaanite. From the early ninth century and from the same region we have an Aramaic dedication to Melqart by Bar Hadad of Damascus, who aided Asa of Judah against Israel.[1] A small votive altar of the ninth century found, along with some seventh-century ostraca, at Tell Khalaf (Gozan) in Iraq has a short Aramaic inscription.[2] One of the Arslan Tash ivories bears the name of Hazael of Damascus and is to be counted in the booty removed from Syria by Shalmaneser III (859–824). But for the next century the Assyrian hold on the west was at best precarious, and in 1931 an important piece of evidence as to the political situation appeared in the form of a long but frag-

[1] M. Dunand in *B.M.B.* iii, 1941, pp. 65–76.
[2] J. Friedrich, *Die Inschriften von Tell Halaf*, 1940, pp. 69–78.

mentary Aramaic inscription from Sujin, which lies one mile north-west of Sefire, fifteen miles from Aleppo towards the Euphrates. The text, which is none too certain in parts, is a treaty between Bar-Ga'yah, king of Katka, and Mati''el, king of Arpad. The terms of the treaty and the curses invoked upon Mati''el in the event of his non-fulfilment of its terms have similarities in form to those of the treaty of Aššur-nirari V (753–746) of Assyria with Mati'ilu of Bit-Agusi, and while Katka cannot be identified with certainty it is clear that Arpad at this period was the centre of an active Aramaean coalition. These documents constitute a valuable addition to the previously known Old Aramaic group from Zenjirli.[1]

From Achaemenid times there may be singled out for mention the oldest dated papyrus, an agricultural contract of let from the seventh year of Darius I (515),[2] two Lydian bilinguals dated in the tenth and sixteenth years 'of Artaxerxes' and a cuneiform conjuration text from Warka (Uruk).[3] And several larger collections are at present being prepared for publication—the remainder of the Clermont-Ganneau collection of ostraca from Elephantine, some fourteen leather administrative letters formerly in the possession of L. Borchardt and connected with the Achaemenid official Aršama/Arsames, a collection said to have been in the United States for over half a century, about five hundred ostraca lettered in paint from Persepolis and various other lots, mainly from Egypt. Arsames is already known as governor at Elephantine in the latter part of the reign of Artaxerxes I from the Elephantine papyri which were definitively edited, along with the words of Aḥiḳar and the Aramaic version of the Behistun trilingual of Darius I, by A. Cowley in *Aramaic Papyri of the Fifth Century B.C.*, published in 1923.

When we turn to Palestine itself and to Hebrew epigraphy

---

[1] For French translations of selected parts of all these documents, with historical elucidation and some original interpretations, see Dupont-Sommer's excellent *œuvre de vulgarisation*, *Les Araméens* (= *L'Ancien Orient illustré*, 2), 1949.

[2] H. Bauer and B. Meissner in *S.P.A.W.* 1936, pp. 414–24.

[3] The lesser items, as well as those in Nabataean and Palmyrene, are listed down to 1939 in E. Rosenthal, *Die aramaistische Forschung seit Theodor Nöldeke's Veröffentlichungen*, 1939, pp. 295–301.

the yields of the last thirty years are by contrast exceedingly meagre. Inscribed seals, jar-stamps, graffiti, ostraca, and the like have come in small quantities from almost every modern excavation in Palestine, from Beisan (Beth Shean) and Tell el-Mutesellim (Megiddo) in the north to Tell el-Kheleifeh (Elath) on the shores of Gulf of Aḳaba. But until the sensational discoveries at the cave near 'Ayn Feshkhah above the Dead Sea, which, in so far as they have been published, belong mainly to the chapter on textual criticism, only two sites yielded epigraphic material of any great extent. The joint excavations at Samaria produced a series of ostraca of the early eighth century, which illustrate Israelite administration about the time of Jeroboam II, the majority of the sherds being invoices to accompany tributes of oil and wine paid over to the royal collector; some Aramaic ostraca of the fifth century were also found.

Still more important results came from the third season's work of the Wellcome Archaeological Research Expedition at Tell el-Duweir (Lachish) in 1935 under the direction of the late J. L. Starkey. In a chamber between the outer and the inner gateways of the city and below the foundation level of a Persian structure there came to light some hundreds of jar fragments blackened by a conflagration which could be dated from the results of earlier excavation to the time of the destruction of the city at the end of the Judaean monarchic period, i.e. just before the fall of Jerusalem in 586. About a score of the fragments bore legible writing; other pieces were found in a later campaign, and it is possible that new techniques will increase the legibility of some pieces. The ostraca are written in a carbon and iron ink and in a cursive hand. The language is a good and free Biblical Hebrew, with interesting idiomatic and orthographic features. Some of the documents are letters sent by one Hoshaiah in some outlying station to his superior Jaush in Lachish; others are business documents and lists of personal names. Their historical importance is increased by the fact that they form a homogeneous and datable corpus.

Other finds have contributed in various ways to the elucidation of Hebrew history and Biblical exegesis. Thus the ostraca from

Ezion Geber show, by the forms of the personal names, that the town was occupied by Edomites in the sixth century but had Arabs among its population in the Persian period. A brief epigraph from Tell el-Qasileh near Tell Aviv testifies that 'gold of Ophir' was not simply a literary phrase but a commercial article in the eighth century. Among the many inscribed seals[1] of Phoenician workmanship there is one belonging to 'Shema' the liegeman[2] of Jeroboam', i.e. Jeroboam II, and another of 'Ushna, liegeman of Ahaz' of Judah, one 'of Jotham', very possibly the king of that name, and one which not only attests familiarity with the domestic cock in the Levant in the sixth century but contains the name Jaazaniah which is known from that period from one of Jeremiah's contemporaries. Our knowledge of Hebrew and Jewish names has similarly been enriched by the discovery of inscribed ossuaries. Lastly, in the field of Samaritan epigraphy we may take note of the discovery of an abbreviated decalogue of the third century of our era and the re-discovery, after nearly seventy years, of the Leeds decalogue inscription, with the possibility of improved readings and interpretation.

It is a curious circumstance that throughout this very productive period there has been no text-book to take the place of Cooke[3] and Lidzbarski[4] and no periodical publication devoted exclusively or primarily to epigraphic studies. Lidzbarski's *Ephemeris*[5] was a casualty of the First World War, and its place has not been filled by any similar review, with the result that epigraphic publications remain scattered over a variety of archaeological and philological journals. It is therefore a cause for satisfaction that the commission charged by the Académie des Inscriptions et Belles-Lettres with the production of the *Corpus Inscriptionum Semiticarum* has since the war accelerated its

---

[1] Cf. K. Galling in *Z.D.P.V.* lxiv, 1941, 121–202.

[2] On '*bd* as 'the class designation of royal officials' see Albright in *J.B.L.* li, 1932, pp. 77–106.

[3] G. A. Cooke, *A Text-Book of North Semitic Inscriptions*, 1903.

[4] M. Lidzbarski, *Handbuch der nordsemitischen Epigraphik*, 1898, and *Altsemitische Texte; Erstes Heft* (no more published) *Kanaanäische Inschriften*, 1907.

[5] *Ephemeris für semitische Epigraphik*, i, 1900–2; ii, 1903–7; iii, 1909–15.

programme of publication.[1] Fascicules of Punic and of Palmyrene inscriptions were issued in 1926 and 1947; with the appearance of a third fascicule, to contain further Punic inscriptions from Carthage, Utica, and Numidia, the third volume and with it the whole of the First Part of the *Corpus* will be complete. In the Himyaritic series the second volume was completed and a third volume issued in the first dozen years of the Society's life, and a new Pars Quinta has been projected to cover the Safaitic, Lihyanite, and Thamudic material. Meanwhile the *Répertoire d'Épigraphie sémitique*,[2] under the same auspices, offers convenient interim presentation of material awaiting definitive publication in the Corpus. A third and last fascicule of vol. vii will complete the third volume of South Semitic inscriptions, all under the general editorship of G. Ryckmans, and a second fascicule of vol. iv will cover all Phoenician inscriptions from 1919 on.[3]

The epigraphic discoveries just surveyed have greatly elucidated the art of writing as practised in Asia. Thus such a document as the Greek-Aramaic bilingual inscription from Armazi, near Tiflis in Georgia,[4] illustrates by its ungrammatical use of Aramaic the evolution of the Pehlevi *huzvaresh* forms from Aramaic words used ideogrammatically, a feature now known to occur also in the derivative Buddhist Sogdian script. And the occurrence of Aramaic inscriptions in the third century B.C. at Pul-i-Darunteh, east of Kabul,[5] and at Taxila near Rawalpindi

[1] Pars I (Phoenician and Punic), tom. i, 1881–7; ii, 1890–1911; iii, fasc. 1, 1926, 2, 1947; pars II (Aramaic), tom. 1, 1881–1902; ii (Nabataean), fasc. 1, 1907; iii (Palmyrene), fasc. 1, 1926, 2, 1947; pars III (Hebrew), in preparation; pars IV (Himyaritic), tom. i, 1889–1908; ii, 1911–20; iii, 1925–30. Atlases of plates provide separate reproductions of the inscriptions.

[2] Tome i (1–500), 1900–5; ii (501–1200), 1907–14; iii (1201–2000), 1916–18; iv, fasc. 1 (2001–2221), 1919; v (2624–3052), 1928–9; vi (3053–3946), 1933–5; vii, fasc. 1 (3947–4207), 1936, 2 (4208–4664), 1938. Apart from a few items in vols. i–ii, vols. i–iv are concerned with North Semitic and v–vii exclusively with South Semitic inscriptions. Vols. i–iii are fully indexed, and vol. v has a bibliography of 841 items on South Arabian epigraphy down to 1928. No illustrations are given.

[3] See also *L'Académie des Inscriptions et Belles-Lettres. Les Travaux, Histoire et Inventaire des Publications; notices rédigées par* A. Blanchet, R. Dussaud, F. Lot, A. Merlin, C. Picard, &c., 1947.

[4] H. W. Bailey in *J.R.A.S.*, 1943, pp. 1–3.

[5] i.e. in ancient Lampaka, on the frontier of the Maurya empire; the inscription itself appears to be an abbreviated version of the edicts of Asoka, with the authority

not only illustrates the use of Aramaic in the eastern satrapies but helps to explain the origin of the Brahmi and Kharoṣṭhi scripts.

Equally instructive is the light cast upon the history of writing in its early phases. It is now clear that before the development of the Phoenician alphabet there was considerable experimentation along the shores of the eastern Mediterranean with a view to producing a simpler system of signs than the hieroglyphic script of Egypt or the cuneiform script of Mesopotamia. One such experiment is to be seen in the series of inscriptions, some on stone and some on bronze tablets and spatulae, discovered in the course of the excavations at Byblus and published by M. Dunand in his *Byblia Grammata* (1945). The documents, whose archaeological context is indecisive, probably date from the first half of the second millennium, and are inscribed in a script comprising some 114 separate signs which have some external resemblances to the Egyptian hieroglyphs and to the Cypriote syllabary. Decipherment is rendered more difficult by the absence of word-dividers, the relatively large number of different signs, the lack of a bilingual, and uncertainty as to the language of the texts.[1] The most probable language is Canaanite, and working on this hypothesis and starting from the group of numerical signs preceded by a group of four other signs at the end of one of the longer texts the distinguished French savant E. Dhorme made a valiant effort at decipherment.[2] He read two of the texts as pure Phoenician with frequent *matres lectionis* and with a plurality of signs to represent the same sound value. Polysemy, i.e. redundancy of signs in a system of writing, of which Accadian cuneiform and the Hittite hieroglyphic[3] afford examples, may be due to various factors. A complete series of signs may have been borrowed for a tongue for whose phonemic system a smaller series would suffice; or the

for each added in Middle Indian; see Henning's interpretation in *B.S.O.A.S.* xiii, 1949, pp. 80–88.

[1] Cf. P. Aalto's 'Notes on Methods of Decipherment of Unknown Writings and Languages', in *Studia Orientalia*, xi, 1945.

[2] *C.R.A.I.*, 1946, pp. 360–5 and 472–9, and *Syria*, xxv, 1946–8, pp. 1–35; cf. De Langhe in *Bi. Or.* v, 1948, pp. 73–83.

[3] This appears to be established by Bossert's reading of the royal name in the Karatepe bilinguals; see *Belleten*, xii, 1948, p. 527, and cf. infra.

language for which the sign-system is employed may itself have developed a simpler phonemic basis, as happened in North-West-Semitic at certain stages; or the signification of the signs themselves may be modified, as when a syllabary becomes an alphabet without the shedding of otiose features. In each case the presence of polysemy is an indication that the system of signs in which it occurs has an earlier history. We must then presume the existence of an earlier stage, not as yet attested by the survival of documents, in which the Byblus script had a full range of values for the various signs and may have been used for a non-Semitic language. On the other hand, if the Byblus documents represent the original use of the system then unless the invention is an exceedingly maladroit one some other basis of interpretation must be found. The number of signs strongly suggests a syllabic system in which each of the separate sounds of second millennium Canaanite—in which, for example, h and $\d{h}$, $\underline{d}$ and z had not yet coincided in sound—is represented as pronounced by itself or in conjunction with one of the three primary sounds a, i, u. The example of Accadian would readily account for the syllabic principle, which reappears in the Ugaritic representation of the glottal stop ('alef). But attempts to decipher the script on this basis have not so far yielded satisfactory results.

More positive assertions are possible in regard to the cuneiform script of the numerous tablets recovered from Ras Shamra (Ugarit) from 1929 onwards. Decipherment of this system of thirty signs, without the aid of any external clue or key, is due to the efforts of H. Bauer, E. Dhorme, and other Semitists. With the exception mentioned above the system is entirely alphabetic, and it was adapted for writing Hurrian as well as Ugaritic. Despite fortuitous resemblances to the Phoenician alphabet it is only the alphabetic principle and the general order of signs that is common to both, and the system was produced by taking the simplest arrangements of cuneiform signs and attaching agreed values to them. The direction of writing is from left to right, as is natural in horizontal writing for a right-handed cuneiform scribe.[1] The Ugaritic documents date from the

---

[1] Driver, *Semitic Writing*, 1948, pp. 33 ff.

fourteenth century, and variant examples of the same script from the same period have been found at Beth Shemesh and Mount Tabor as well as in Ugarit itself. But the script was suitable only for writing on the clay tablet which was not a native writing medium in Palestine, and the Ugaritic alphabet died out, probably quite soon after. Yet it survived long enough to transmit to its successors the conventional order of signs employed by users of the Phoenician alphabet and its descendants, for a truncated tablet from Ras Shamra published in the spring of 1950 has the Ugaritic alphabet of thirty signs in an order[1] which, apart from the additional signs, conforms exactly to the Phoenician order.

Other abortive attempts to evolve a new script can be seen in various isolated documents of uncertain relationship, all discovered in the last twenty years—the Baluah stele from Transjordan, the 'proto-Sabaean' inscriptions from Ur, and others from the Iron Age.

One system developed at this time was destined to play a greater role. This was the script of the fifteenth-century inscriptions found in 1905 by (Sir) Flinders Petrie at the old turquoise mines of Serabiṭ el-Khadim in the peninsula of Sinai. The basis for a sound interpretation was laid by (Sir) Alan Gardiner, who in 1915 propounded his solution. Reading a recurring sequence as Semitic (*l*–)*b*–ʿ–*l*–*t* ʿ(to) Baalat, the Lady', he associated the shape of the characters with the objects designated by the corresponding letter-names in Hebrew-Phoenician and so divined the relationship of the Sinaitic script to the Hebrew alphabet and its acrophonic and alphabetic character, i.e. while the forms of some of the signs may have been borrowed from Egyptian, the signs were named in Semitic after the objects they were held to depict and the alphabetic value of the sign was that of the first element in the name of the object depicted.[2] Further contributions advanced the decipherment but little until in 1948 W. F.

---

[1] Viz.—*a, b, g, ḥ, d, h, w, z, ḥ, ṭ, y, k, š, l, m, š, n, ẓ, s, ʿ, p, ṣ, q, r, t, ġ, ṭ, i, u, š.* The last three signs may be secondary, and the position of those other signs which have no direct counterpart in the Phoenician alphabet shows that the convention was not borrowed from that quarter.

[2] *J.E.A.* iii, 1916, pp. 1–16; cf. Cowley, ibid., pp. 17 ff.

Albright, after a personal examination of the inscriptions *in situ*, was able to offer intelligible interpretations of several continuous passages. His success was due to his assumption of a consonantal system essentially similar to that of contemporary Ugaritic rather than of later Canaanite and to his happy adducing of linguistic analogies from cognate sources of the same period. In all some nineteen signs, or two-thirds of the total, have been identified. But while the Sinaitic descent of the Phoenician-Hebrew-Greek-Latin alphabet is generally admitted, the intermediate stages remain obscure, and it is not yet certain, for example, what is the relationship, if any, of the Lachish and other epigraphs of the Middle and Late Bronze Ages, nor from what type of script the South-Arabian alphabet derived.

Continued efforts to decipher the Minoan scripts[1] have not so far had any measurable success, although with the publication of the Evans corpus and the discovery of some hundreds of tablets at Pylos and of Cypro-Minoan items at Enkomi the available material is on the increase. On the other hand the Phoenician bilingual inscriptions from Karatepe are likely to force the Hittite hieroglyphic texts[2] to yield their secrets, and while there is no solid ground for the sanguine predictions that have been expressed that the decipherment of Lydian and Etruscan must surely follow, the decipherment of any further portion of the Anatolian records must appreciably improve our very imperfect knowledge of the languages and history of that region.[3]

The recovery of these various systems of writing and interest in the history and techniques of the art have called forth a number of works surveying various aspects of the subject. The Schweich

---

[1] A review of those efforts and of the factors involved is given by Alice E. Kober under the title 'The Minoan Scripts: Fact and Theory' in *A.J.A.* lii, 1948, pp. 82–103. For a general survey of the lost tongues of antiquity the reader may consult J. Friedrich, 'Verschollene Sprachen des Altertums und ihre Wiedererschliessung' in *N.J.D.W.* xii, 1937, pp. 354–69, 438–53.

[2] Bibliography in I. Gelb, *The Hittite Hieroglyphs*, i, 1931; ii, 1935; iii, 1942.

[3] The non-Hittite sources are conveniently presented in J. Friedrich, *Kleinasiatische Sprachdenkmäler* (= H. Lietzmann's *Kleine Texte*, no. 163), 1932. For further literature the reader should consult the bibliographies by B. Schwartz on *The Hittites*, 1939, and by D. C. Swanson on *The Anatolian Languages*, 1948, reprinted separately from *B.N.Y.P.L.* for Aug.–Oct. 1938 and May–June 1948 respectively.

Lectures of G. R. Driver deal with *Semitic Writing* (1948).
J. G. Février's *Histoire de l'Écriture*, published in the same year,
and H. Jensen, *Die Schrift in Vergangenheit und Gegenwart*
(1935), have a more general scope, and D. Diringer's *The Alphabet* (1948), being a revision of his *L'Alfabeto nella Storia della
Civiltà*, covers a wider range of topics than the main title indicates.

The second major development in connexion with the history
of scripts has been in the department of North-west Semitic
palaeography. It is true that by comparison, e.g. with the palaeography of Greek or Latin documents on stone or vellum or
papyrus, the material at the disposal of the ancient Semitic
palaeographer is still exiguous to a degree, and where a period or
category of writing is known only from one or two examples
there can be no perfect confidence that they are thoroughly
characteristic of their class. Uniformity of development is a
postulate that is confuted by such facts as the aberrant retroverted
base-line in the *beth* of some of the Byblus inscriptions or the
long curving tail that is characteristic of *kaf*, *mem*, and *nun* at
Siloam. Difference of medium affects the form of a script, and
the conservatism and formalism of the stone-cutter's work is in
contrast to the flexibility and cursive tendency that marks the
professional scribe.[1] Local and personal mannerisms, the time-
lag in the diffusion of a new form or style or in the obsolescence
of an old one, the differences between Phoenician, Aramaic, and
Hebraeo-Jewish forms of the alphabet are factors that must be
reckoned with. A further factor can be seen in recent discussion
of the Dead Sea leather fragments of Leviticus; the early style
of the lettering is indisputable, but while R. de Vaux regards the
script as an example of archaizing in a scriptural text, D. Diringer
sees in the script evidence of a standardized early Hebrew book-
hand. On either interpretation the existence of this type of
script complicates the account of the Hebrew palaeographic
development, and caution is required in using evidence of this
sort to settle chronological questions. Nevertheless when one

---

[1] The features of the Siloam inscription just mentioned represent the transference
to stone by amateurs of cursive tendencies familiar to them in contemporary ink
writings.

considers that down to 1924 the archaic *kaf* of the Abibaal inscription was mistaken for a *šin* and that twenty years later the improved knowledge of Hebrew palaeography was so much taken for granted that the notion that the Mesha stone was a forgery required to be refuted afresh, it will be seen how great the advances have been, and the palaeographical charts given in the works of Driver and Rosenthal and from time to time in the pages of *B.A.S.O.R.* and *P.E.Q.* show the increasingly detailed knowledge of the evolution of the North-west Semitic script. The significance of this knowledge for the textual criticism of the Hebrew Bible is examined in the preceding chapter.

The philological importance of the accumulation of new material has been considerable in several directions; while it has upset some long-held dogmas and at times has complicated or temporarily obscured what had been a clear picture, the net result is that the scholar to-day has at his disposal a much broader and more detailed conspectus of the linguistic milieu of the Biblical records. The situation is least satisfactory in the matter of lexicography. For the mass of South Arabian inscriptions, which are of importance in themselves and for the sometimes remarkable parallels they provide to data from the north, there is as yet no dictionary. The glossary of Lidzbarski's *Handbuch* and S. A. Cook's *Glossary of the Aramaic Inscriptions*, both published in 1898, have long been out of date but have not been superseded, and for the Elephantine papyri the index to Cowley's edition is the best tool available. For the Old Testament itself until recently the most modern work was the edition of Gesenius's *Hebräisches und Aramäisches Handwörterbuch über das Alte Testament* which F. Buhl published in 1915. As a result the ordinary student has sometimes lacked the information that an up-to-date dictionary could give him, and exegetical writers have been obliged to make their own lexicographical researches, sometimes with unfortunate results through undue reliance on 'root meanings' and inadequate attention to semantic histories. Two new dictionaries are now in process of publication—the *Lexicon Hebraicum et Aramaicum Veteris Testamenti* (1940–) of F. Zorell and T. Semkowski, and the more original *Lexicon in Veteris Testamenti Libros* (1948–), of which the Hebrew part is the work of L. Köhler and the Aramaic of W. Baumgartner. The work is provided with English as well as German renderings. It may also be mentioned here that the English-reading student has now a comparative grammar in the *Introduction to Semitic Comparative Linguistics* of L. H. Gray (1934), which is provided with a good general bibliography and has the advantage for the Biblical student of taking Hebrew as the starting-point.

In Aramaic philology the outstanding achievement of the last generation is the closer identification and description of the Imperial Aramaic of the Assyrian and Achaemenid chancelleries. Ginsberg, with characteristic ingenuity, has plausibly suggested that in the Zenjirli inscriptions we can trace the transition from the local dialect to this official *koine*, and it has been shown that Nabataean and Palmyrene are in effect descendants therefrom. Grammars now exist for all the main bodies of material except the Old Aramaic; special mention may be made of the *Grammatik des Biblisch-Aramäischen* (1927) of H. Bauer and P. Leander and the latter's *Laut- und Formenlehre des Ägyptisch-Aramäischen* published in the following year. What is now required is a comprehensive historical and comparative study of the language.

Discussion of the vernacular in use in Palestine in New Testament times has been given a new turn as a result of closer study of the Aramaic dialects. The Targum of Onkelos is now appreciated to be a Babylonian redaction, and it is seen that the Palestinian Targum and the Aramaic portions of the Palestinian Talmud are more nearly representative of Palestinian vernacular idiom. At the same time there has been considerable, but inconclusive, discussion of the question of the use of Aramaic by Jesus and the probability of an Aramaic gospel. It is noteworthy that the case for an Aramaic gospel has found its strongest supporters among Semitists, and that its opponents have directed their attention less to presenting the positive case for an original Greek gospel than to attacking the weaknesses of arguments based on alleged translational features.

Study of the relations of the Aramaic to the Canaanite group of tongues in the light of the increased comparative material has shown that many of the alleged Aramaisms of the Hebrew Bible, on which occasionally far-reaching critical conclusions have been based, are in fact pure Canaanitisms or common North-west Semitic, and that the question of the 'Hebrewisms' of Imperial Aramaic is a very involved one, since in addition to the factors just mentioned we have to reckon with the use of Aramaic by Jews and with the fact that Aramaic overlay an earlier stratum of Canaanite, not only in Palestine but at an earlier date also in Syria, as we see from the inscriptions and from a study of place-names recorded at Ugarit. For these, as for so many other questions in Aramaic philology, Rosenthal's manual gives the most convenient *mise au point*, with its appraisal of the literature down almost to the outbreak of the last war.

Interest in the history of the Hebrew language in its earlier phases may be said to have been quickened by the discovery of Canaanite glosses in the Amarna letters[1] from about 1375 B.C. These and other cuneiform representations have the important advantage of reproducing the vowels, although they cannot always present the Canaanite consonants unambiguously. The oldest external material is contained in a series of ostraca from the beginning of the second millennium onwards, on which the Egyptian rulers had written in hieratic script magical execrations of foreign foes and rebels.[2] Other Egyptian sources give accurate transliterations of place and personal names,[3] and Origen's second column, the *Poenulus* of Plautus, and single words in classical sources and in the Bible versions give Greek and Latin transcriptions from later days. Much of this material was utilized by Bauer and Leander in their uncompleted *Historische Grammatik der hebräischen Sprache* (i, 1922) and by Bergsträsser in

---

[1] The standard edition is that of Knudtzon, published thirty-five years ago; it does not exhaust the material. See also F. M. Böhl, *Die Sprache der Amarnabriefe*, 1909.

[2] K. Sethe, *Die Ächtung feindlicher Fürsten, Völker und Dinge* ... (= *A.P.A.W.*, 1926, Nr. 15), and G. Posener, *Princes et pays d'Asie et de Nubie*, 1940.

[3] See especially W. F. Albright, *The Vocalization of the Egyptian Syllabic Orthography*, 1934, and J. Simons, *Handbook for the Study of Egyptian Topographical Lists Relating to Western Asia*, 1937.

the 29th edition of Gesenius's *Hebräische Grammatik* (1918–29).
An outstanding specialized study is the work of M. Noth on
*Die israelitischen Personennamen im Rahmen der gemeinsemitischen
Namengebung* (1928), which entirely supersedes all previous
work on the subject, and by its detailed examination of formal
aspects, theophorous elements, semantic connotations, and
historical distribution of personal names provides an important
criterion for all sorts of studies. A similar service was performed
for the peripheral 'Amorite' personal names on Babylonian
tablets by T. Bauer[1] and for the toponymy of ancient Palestine
by W. Borée.[2]

It cannot be said that the interest in syntax, idiom and stylistic
has been as intense as that in *Laut-* and *Formenlehre*. Useful
specialized, and in some cases pioneering, work has been done
on the stylistic predilections of various Biblical writers, on the
fossils of conversational idiom embedded in the Hebrew Bible,
and on such features as the numerical idioms of the Bible,
chiasmus, merismus, and aspects of Hebrew prosody; but no
writer has essayed to replace the last part of König's *Lehrgebäude*,
or to complete the work of Bauer and Leander. This relative
neglect may be ascribed in part to a pre-occupation on the part of
philologists with the more basic aspects of the new cognate
materials and in part to a tendency for Biblical exegetes to employ
the versions mainly for textual and lexicographical purposes and
to pay less attention to the formal and stylistic evidences afforded
by them and by the extra-Biblical materials.

By far the greatest accession to the Canaanite linguistic corpus
has come from the alphabetic cuneiform tablets uncovered at
Ras Shamra (Ugarit), published by C. Virolleaud and studied
intensively by many scholars, of whom a considerable proportion
are in the United States. The precise linguistic affiliation of the
Ugaritic tongue was for some time the subject of keen debate,
Bauer and Goetze holding that the differences between Ugaritic
on the one hand and Hebrew and Phoenician on the other are
so pronounced that Ugaritic cannot be classed as a Canaanite

---

[1] *Die Ostkanaanäer*, 1926.
[2] *Die alten Ortsnamen Palästinas*, 1930.

dialect, while Ginsberg, Albright, and others, now followed by the majority of Semitists, regard it as diverging only to a greater degree and at an earlier date than the other Canaanite dialects. Knowledge of the language has now reached a stage at which the grammatical structure and poetical framework are in general well understood, some outstanding syntactic and stylistic features can be identified, and continuous translations are possible, though many interpretations are tentative and the lexicography progresses with less assurance than other aspects of Ugaritian studies. C. H. Gordon's *Ugaritic Handbook* (1947), which is a revised edition of his *Ugaritic Grammar* (1940), presents the assured results in regard to orthography, phonology, accidence, syntax, and prosody, together with the transliterated texts and a comprehensive glossary.[1]

In 1939 Z. S. Harris, who three years earlier had placed all Semitists in his debt for a thorough *Grammar of the Phoenician Language* with a glossary, brought out his *Development of the Canaanite Dialects*, in which he sought to synthesize the evidence available in all the material, both new and old, and by examining the linguistic changes and their distribution in time and place to trace the history and inter-relationship of the Canaanite dialects. The resultant picture, although in need of modification in detail, is not a simple one, as the isoglottal charts show; even in Ugarit the interpenetration of influence is to be seen. But while dialectal features overlapped and tended to diffuse themselves, the individual character of Jerusalem Hebrew, which became the standard language of all South Palestine at least, stands out clearly.

A few illustrations will show more clearly than description the sort of light that is cast by the kindred dialects on the fabric of Biblical Hebrew. In the matter of phonology Jerusalem Hebrew went its own way in its treatment of the sibilants. Whereas for the creators of the alphabet etymological *š* and *ś* coincided in

---

[1] Other important introductory works are C. Schaeffer's *Ugaritica*, i, 1939, and R. de Langhe, *Les Textes de Ras Shamra-Ugarit et leurs rapports avec le milieu biblique de l'Ancien Testament*, i–ii, 1945. Both have full bibliographies, and the latter gives the personal and geographical onomastic material.

sound and were represented by the penultimate letter of the 22-sign alphabet, in Jerusalem they were distinct, the latter approximating in sound to *s* (*samek*), with the result that *samek* could replace *śin* in spelling and a secondary distinction had to be made between *śin* and *śin* by means of an orthographic device; this would not have been necessary if the Hebrew alphabet had been invented in Jerusalem. In accidence we may cite the Hebrew noun and verb forms with preformative *śin* which have their immediate parallel in the Ugaritian causative of *śafel* type, or the old Phoenician and Ugaritian *Ifta'ala* stem which illustrates the three Judaean place-names of that form. The discovery of the enclitic particle -*ma* in Biblical Hebrew, as in the Canaanite of Amarna and Ugarit, renders gratuitous some conjectural emendations of apparent inconcinnities of text. In the same way some curious uses of the prepositions *le-* and *be-* are explained by their occurrence in the more northerly dialects of Canaanite. Again, doubts as to the legitimacy of the Biblical construction of the infinitive absolute before the subject to take the place of a finite verb are completely removed as a result of the detection of the same idiom at Karatepe, Sidon, and elsewhere. The metrical system of the Ugaritic poems is rich and varied, but has the same general features as Hebrew poetry, and the occurrence of different forms according to no discernible pattern should be a warning to critics not to treat Biblical poems too cavalierly on account of such freedom of structure. At the same time the occurrence of certain archaic features in the poetry of Ugarit and again in early Hebrew poetry has suggested to some critics that those Hebrew poems may be earlier than is generally allowed, but whether an improved knowledge of the vocalization and accentuation of Old Hebrew will lead to the formulation of a more rigorous system of metrical laws for Hebrew remains to be seen.

To turn in conclusion from recent achievements to future prospects, we have indicated in the preceding pages some of the outstanding tasks for Canaanite and Aramaic scholarship. As an ancillary thereto there is a clamant need for an annual bibliography of contributions to Semitic research, if not indeed for a journal in English devoted mainly or exclusively to this branch of philology. With each passing year the best of standard works decreases in bibliographical usefulness; the output meanwhile continues to grow in volume; at present it is scattered over Biblical, historical, archaeological, and even classical, as well as general Oriental and philological journals, and few workers have access to all of these. Nor is there any reason to suppose that epigraphic and archaeological research in Syria and Palestine has yet reached the stage of diminishing returns. The cities of southern Phoenicia remain virtually unexploited, and the possibility of substantial finds on Palestinian soil cannot be ruled out. The prospects of philological advance in Anatolia and the Aegean are better than ever before. And there is ample room for closer investigation of the material already known, particularly in its finer and more involved aspects. From all of those sources elucidation of the Biblical milieu may be anticipated, and to secure that elucidation the Biblical life and idiom must be viewed against their complete historical and linguistic context and at the same time used to illumine that environment.

A. M. HONEYMAN

X

HEBREW RELIGION

It has recently been said that at no time was it harder to write on the literature of the Old Testament than at present. To describe and assess the contemporary position in the study of Hebrew religion is at least as difficult. In such a field unanimity is not easily won; but if a generation ago complete unanimity had not been attained, there was nevertheless a considerably larger measure of agreement than exists today, when new answers are being given to old questions and new questions are the subject of eager debate.

One aspect of the change may be described as a revolt against Wellhausenism.[1] The brilliant achievements of the great nineteenth century critics resulted in a remarkable synthesis of literary analysis and historical reconstruction. The arguments which led to the recognition and dating of the Pentateuchal sources and to the view that the completed Pentateuch was the outcome and not the presupposition of the prophetic teaching also depicted the development of Israel's religion from the more primitive, pre-prophetic stage, through the prophetic movement, to the monotheism and legalism of the post-exilic period. Other contributions to the present volume show how varied and vigorous have been the challenges in literary criticism. At no point has the conflict been keener than in connexion with the date and nature of Deuteronomy, the keystone in the Wellhausen system of chronology. If there is serious uncertainty here, the entire structure of the theory is weakened and may collapse. In more general ways the older critical orthodoxy has been assailed. Views such as those of Professor Ivan Engnell[2] are far from commanding universal assent; but they are the radical expression of tendencies which, in their more moderate forms, blur the outlines of critical analysis and leave the main blocks of material

[1] A change of approach was already evident at the end of last century and the beginning of the present one in the work of Gunkel and Gressmann.

[2] See Professor C. R. North's contribution to the present volume.

much less sharply defined. It is clear that such modifications cannot leave the religious reconstruction entirely unaffected; and it is significant that one of the most brilliant and profound interpretations of Israelite thought, that of Professor Johannes Pedersen,[1] is the work of one who is sceptical of the methods and results of literary analysis.

The Wellhausen theory has also been criticized as based upon an erroneous view of the development of religion. It has often been observed that Hegelianism supplied its threefold framework;[2] and indeed Wellhausen admitted his great debt to the Hegelian W. Vatke. The theory is also attacked because of the evolutionary description which it gives of Hebrew religion, as developing from crude beginnings through henotheism to monotheism. This, it has been asserted, is an unjustifiable application to religious development of a concept which is in place in biology but not in the history of human culture.[3]

One of the earliest modifications of the Graf-Wellhausen position came through the work of Gunkel and Gressmann who, without jettisoning the methods and results of literary criticism, sought to show more clearly the relation of Hebrew religion to the mythology and eschatology of the ancient east. This remains a necessary undertaking, and one which can be carried through today on a much larger scale. Archaeological research has provided a vast mass of new material for the reconstruction of Israel's religious and cultural environment; but the very bulk of this material makes any attempt at assessment and appraisal a task to be undertaken with imaginative insight chastened by sobriety and caution. It ought to be remembered, too, that the interpretation of some of the material (e.g. the Ras Shamra texts) is still a matter of legitimate controversy.

[1] *Israel, I–II. Sjæleliv og Samfundsliv*[2], 1934; *Israel, III–IV. Hellighed og Guddommelighed*, 1934. E.Tr. *Israel: Its Life and Culture*, I–II, 1926; III–IV, 1940. See also his article 'Die Auffassung vom Alten Testament', in *Z.A.W.* xlix, 1931, pp. 161–81, especially pp. 174–9.

[2] *F.S.A.C.*, pp. 52 f.; *A.R.I.*, p. 3; A. Bentzen in *T.R.* xvii, 1948–9, p. 278, n. 1, pp. 327 f.; and Pedersen's article mentioned in n. 1 above.

[3] e.g. I. Engnell, *Gamla Testamentet, en traditionshistorisk inledning*, i, 1945, p. 111. Cf. E. O. James, *The Old Testament in the Light of Anthropology*, 1934, pp. 83 ff.; *Comparative Religion*, 1938, p. 11.

In some quarters there has been a change not merely of emphasis or of theory but of approach. The emergence during the past generation of a lively interest in the theology of the Old Testament and in its intimate relationship with the New Testament has had effects both good and bad. On the one hand it has led some to indulge in premature systematization or to disregard the differences between the two Testaments. On the other it has stimulated attempts to define the distinctive motif or motifs of Old Testament religion, a task which must be achieved if the relating of Israel's faith and practice to those of its neighbours is to be adequately essayed. The endeavour to discern and describe such essential characteristics should not be divorced from the study of that wider setting. Unless we constantly make the effort to see Israel against the background of the ancient orient we shall be in danger of imposing on the Old Testament concepts which are proper to the thought of later ages. On the other hand it is possible to be so engrossed in the background that it becomes foreground, to treat as central influences which were no more than peripheral, to use the non-Israelite evidence as the *basis* of our reconstruction, and then to fit the Israelite evidence, drastically altered if need be, into the superstructure. But clearly the Israelite evidence, critically and judiciously used, must be our starting point. The sequel of Hebrew religion, both in Judaism and in Christianity, makes plain that it differed decisively from that of neighbourbouring peoples. To estimate the extent and the character of that difference is a necessary part of scholarly enquiry, for the true pattern of the historical development is not likely to be adequately discerned unless the *Eigenart* of Israel's religion is appreciated. This task belongs to the ill-defined and perhaps indefinable borderland between the history of Hebrew religion and the theology of the Old Testament.

In a field where the material is so abundant and the theories so varied it is impossible to give anything like adequate treatment in a short essay to the research of a generation; and all that can be offered is a survey of selected works which are representative of recent trends. If in what follows attention is given primarily to the past twelve or fifteen years, this is not because earlier work is regarded as unimportant, but because its significance has already been indicated in the essays in *The People and the Book* and in *Record and Revelation*.

In recent discussion of the beginnings of Israel's religion no subject has received more attention than belief in God. How is the faith of the prophets related to that of Moses? At what point did a genuine monotheism emerge? What can be known of the God or gods of the patriarchal age in relation to the Canaanite pantheon and of Israelite belief in Yahweh? Though some scholars have been sceptical of the possibility of our learning much about the religion of the patriarchs,[1] others have taken a different line. In an able and stimulating monograph Alt has drawn attention to the evidence from Palmyrene and Nabataean inscriptions for the worship of a type of deity, not tied to any special locality, but associated with an individual who founded his cult, and whose name formed part of the god's title. He argues that three such gods worshipped in patriarchal times (the God or Shield of Abraham, the Fear of Isaac, and the Mighty One of Jacob) were fused into one, the God of Abraham, of Isaac, and of Jacob, and identified with Yahweh.[2] Though the inscriptional evidence comes from a period centuries later than the age of the patriarchs, it reflects the religion of former nomads who had now settled in cultivated territory; and more ancient evidence has been adduced since the publication of Alt's book.[3] Whatever difference of opinion there may be concerning the details of his thesis, the picture which it affords of a religion of personal choice has an obvious bearing on the religion of the Old Testament.

That the patriarchs were monotheists seems to be implied by the narratives in Genesis; and conservative scholars have taken their evidence at its face value.[4] In recent years, however, there has been elaborated, on general anthropological grounds, the view that there is a monotheistic tendency in primitive religion, and that this was an important factor in the religion of the

[1] W. Graf Baudissin, *Kyrios als Gottesname*, iii, 1929, pp. 152, 158 n.

[2] A. Alt, *Der Gott der Väter*, 1929 (B.W.A.N.T. iii, 12). On the rendering of these titles see *F.S.A.C.*, pp. 188 f.

[3] *F.S.A.C.*, loc. cit.

[4] e.g. L. Dennefeld, *Histoire d'Israël et de l'ancien Orient*, 1935, p. 43.

ancestors of the Hebrews. The supporting arguments are related to the work done on high gods by scholars such as Andrew Lang, Archbishop Söderblom, R. Pettazzoni, Father W. Schmidt, and G. Widengren. Belief in such a creator Deity, remote, dimly conceived, ethical in his nature, is undoubtedly widespread, though it is certainly not incompatible with belief in other gods, nor is it really similar in content to a developed monotheism. In this country Professor E. O. James has contended that through the experience and work of Moses a Supreme Being of this type became the covenant God of the Hebrew tribes. His view is advanced with caution; and he makes it clear that he neither equates belief in high gods with Hebrew monotheism nor rules out monolatrous development between Moses and post-exilic Judaism.[1]

A similar but more extreme view has been advocated by an influential group of Scandinavian scholars associated with the University of Uppsala, among whom I. Engnell may be regarded as typical.[2] Rejecting as doctrinaire the thought of an evolutionary development in religion from lower to higher, he maintains that the belief in high gods (which may exist side by side with the practice of magic, belief in demons, and the like) is the ultimate fact which confronts the inquirer into the beginnings of religion, and that polytheistic pantheons arise from an original 'monotheism' when characteristics and functions are split off from the sole or supreme Deity and hypostatized.[3] The original high god, the god of the vault of heaven, giver of fertility, decider of the fate of men and judge of their actions, can be separated from his

[1] E. O. James, *The Old Testament in the Light of Anthropology*, pp. 83 ff.; *Comparative Religion*, pp. 209 ff. James describes this 'universal monotheistic tendency' as 'the emotional evaluation of the *mysterium tremendum*'.

[2] I. Engnell, *Gamla Testamentet*, i, pp. 110 ff.; *S.B.U.* i, cols. 673 f.; *Studies in Divine Kingship in the Ancient Near East*, 1943, *passim*. Engnell's views are related, as his own references show, to the important work in the Iranian field of H. S. Nyberg (*Irans forntida religioner*, 1937) and of G. Widengren (*Hochgottglaube im alten Iran*, 1938). Cf. also Widengren's more general work, *Religionens värld*, 1945.

[3] Cf. the important and able study by H. Ringgren, *Word and Wisdom: Studies in the Hypostatization of Divine Qualities and Functions in the Ancient Near East*, 1947. Ringgren adopts an 'anti-evolutionist' standpoint, and assumes the existence of a primitive monotheism, but admits the process of *Göttervereinigung* alongside of *Götterspaltung*.

fertilizing functions and be thought of as less active, less accessible. Thus he becomes a *deus otiosus*, while the separated functions
take the form of a fertility or vegetation deity. Later, the *deus
otiosus* may be 'activated' in the experience of a man of the
prophetic type and become the object of the worship of a tribe
or group of tribes. As examples of this latter stage in the development Engnell cites the work of Muhammad, Zarathustra, and
Moses. It is held that El, the supreme Canaanite god, is a high
god of this kind, found over the entire west-Semitic area under
varying names, El Shaddai, El 'Elyon, Shalem, Ṣedek, and
Hadad,[1] and Engnell maintains that one form of this high god
was Yahweh, who before the time of Moses was 'otiose' but was
'activated' through the work of Moses. After the entry into
Canaan the fusion of Yahweh with different forms of the
Canaanite El (and, in particular, with the El 'Elyon of Jerusalem) came about the more easily since the two gods were originally
identical.[2] It is in keeping with this view that Engnell holds that
in the later syncretistic process the Israelite element was largely
overcome or transformed, and that he can describe the religion
of the Old Testament as a special form of Canaanite religion.[3]
This religion is based on a primitive monotheism, in the sense
not of speculative monotheism but of recognition of a high god,
who, in the Israelite tradition, claims the undivided allegiance
and devotion of the worshipper.[4]

Apart from the fact that this view is associated with a theory
of the development of religion which is by no means universally
accepted, the application of the term 'monotheism' to belief in
high gods is misleading. It is salutary to remind oneself that,
high god or no high god, the Canaanites were polytheists.[5]
It is, moreover, difficult to see how the identification of Israelite
and Canaanite religion can be reconciled with the persistent

[1] Cf. H. S. Nyberg, 'Studien zum Religionskampf im Alten Testament', in *A.R.W.*
xxxv, 1938, pp. 329–86, especially pp. 350 ff.
[2] I. Engnell, *Studies in Divine Kingship in the Ancient Near East*, p. 177; *Gamla
Testamentet*, i, pp. 125–30; *S.B.U.* i, cols. 673 ff.
[3] *Gamla Testamentet*, i, p. 136; *S.B.U.* i, col. 673.
[4] *Gamla Testamentet*, i, p. 133.
[5] Cf. E. Sjöberg in *S.E.Å.* xiv, 1949, p. 11; *F.S.A.C.*, p. 187.

testimony of the Old Testament that Yahweh is radically different from other gods—unless, indeed, that testimony is to be disregarded, or reinterpreted by an exegesis which makes up in ingenuity for what it lacks in cogency.

A somewhat different line is taken by W. F. Albright, one of the most vigorous of recent advocates of the view that Moses was a monotheist. More eclectic than the Uppsala group in his use of modern research on the development of religion, he emphatically rejects the notion of a simple, ascending, evolutionary development; and his survey of the relevant archaeological data shows how advanced was the religion of the Near East in the age of the Hebrew patriarchs, when deities whose functions were cosmic in scope tended to be thought of as exercising a universal sway.[1] Rejecting the view that an El monotheism existed among the early western Semites, or, in particular, among the early Hebrews, Albright maintains that the chief god of the latter was a mountain god (identified with Hadad), and that they believed in a blood relationship between clan and god, and in the right of a man (such as the founder of a clan) to choose his own god and enter into a contractual relationship with him.[2] The God of the Mosaic revelation was a creator God, unrelated to any other deity, unrestricted to any geographical area or to any specific natural phenomenon, anthropomorphically conceived yet not represented by any material form;[3] and this, Albright concludes, justifies us in applying the term 'monotheist' to Moses and in regarding 'henotheism' as an inaccurate description of pre-prophetic Israelite religion.[4]

Yet another contribution to the debate comes from H. H. Rowley, who describes the Mosaic religion as implicit or incipient

---

[1] Ibid., pp. 124–6, 130–49, 157–79. Cf. G. E. Wright in *The Study of the Bible Today and Tomorrow*, 1947, pp. 89 ff. [2] *F.S.A.C.*, pp. 187–9.

[3] Ibid., pp. 196–207. Albright maintains that there is no evidence that Yahweh was later worshipped in bull form at the northern sanctuaries: the animal figure was simply the pedestal of the invisible God.

[4] For his treatment of Judges xi. 24 (*argumentum ad hominem*) and of 1 Sam. xxvi. 19 (particularistic aberration), see ibid., p. 220; *A.R.I.*, pp. 117–19. The applicability of the term 'monotheism' to early Hebrew religion is also discussed by B. Balscheit in *Alter und Aufkommen des Monotheismus in der israelitischen Religion* (B.Z.A.W. lxix), 1938.

monotheism, coming short of speculative monotheism, but going beyond monolatry: 'though other gods may exist they are completely negligible'. In the Exodus narrative Yahweh meets with no resistance from the gods of Egypt. He is master of the situation; and all the resources of the natural order are at His disposal. Herein lie the seeds of the pure monotheism which, after the syncretism of the period following the conquest, came to flower in the teaching of the great prophets.[1]

The most important question at issue is the distinctive character of the Mosaic religion. To claim to reconstruct *in detail* the religion of the pre-Mosaic Hebrews is to claim too much. The evidence is still inadequate, though we now know enough of the period to recognize that it must have been at a relatively advanced stage of development. As has recently been said, 'We can assert with confidence that by the time of the patriarchs the religion of all parts of the Near East was a long distance removed from the animistic stage'.[2] In dealing with the religious significance of the Exodus we are on surer ground. There is, no doubt, some danger of lapsing into mere logomachy in the debate about Mosaic monotheism; and it is well to remember both that the label matters less than the contents of the packet, and also that it is inconvenient to have the same label for different things. But something more than a label is involved. Albright admittedly brings into the discussion factors which are not strictly relevant to the question; but he makes out a strong case for the distinctive and lofty character of Israel's Mosaic inheritance, a case which calls for consideration even if we reject his terminology. If we recognize (as we are surely bound to do) a difference between the monotheism of Deutero-Isaiah and what we know of Mosaic Yahwism, we may nevertheless hold that what the great prophet of the Exile made explicit for the thought of his time was already, in large measure, implicit in the older faith. The earliest Hebrew documents contain no explicit denial of the existence of gods

[1] *The Rediscovery of the Old Testament*, 1946, p. 88. Cf. the more detailed discussion of the whole question in 'The Antiquity of Israelite Monotheism', in *E.T.* lxi, 1949-50, pp. 333-8.

[2] G. E. Wright in *The Study of the Bible Today and Tomorrow* (ed. H. R. Willoughby), 1947, p. 90.

other than Yahweh; but Yahweh was a jealous Deity, claiming undivided loyalty, intolerant of rivals; and that quality of exclusiveness was of profound importance for later developments.[1] Not that Hebrew monotheism is to be traced to any one characteristic, but rather to a complex of factors present in the Mosaic religion. The significance of these factors was made plain and enriched by the subsequent crises in the life of the nation and by the teaching and experience of the great prophets. Thus, even if it seems desirable in the interests of terminological accuracy to deny the title of monotheist to Moses, the creative relationship between his faith and that of the prophets has been vindicated.

When the Israelite tribes, knit together by their faith in Yahweh, came into Canaan, they encountered a religion which is now familiar to us in considerable detail. To reconstruct its main features is easier than to estimate the extent of its influence on pre-exilic Israel. That Canaanite beliefs and practices were widely adopted by the Hebrews is, of course, shown by the Old Testament itself. How far that borrowing went, and how much of it became part of the officially recognized religious system, is one of the most strenuously debated problems of Old Testament study today. The discussion is chiefly concerned with the relation of the entire cultic system to the supposed myth and ritual pattern of the ancient Near East, with the character of the autumn festival and the existence and nature of New Year rites, with the celebration of the Kingship of Yahweh, with the relation of the king and the prophets to the cult, and with the links between cult and eschatology. Interest in these questions accounts for the space accorded in much recent writing to the pre-exilic period, and for the emphasis laid, in some quarters, on the abiding positive influence of the cult.

Of fundamental importance for the whole discussion is the work of S. Mowinckel in the second of his *Psalmenstudien*,[2] in which he argues that the enthronement psalms (i.e. primarily

---

[1] Cf. Joh. Lindblom, *Israels religion i gammaltestamentlig tid*, 1936, p. 45.

[2] *Psalmenstudien II: Das Thronbesteigungsfest Jahwäs und der Ursprung der Eschatologie*, 1922.

xlvii, xciii, xcv–c; but many others are included in the discussion)
must be interpreted neither of the contemporary historical
manifestation of Yahweh's Kingship, nor of its eschatological
realization, but purely in terms of its cultic expression. He
maintains that at the autumnal New Year festival in pre-exilic
Israel Yahweh was annually enthroned. This was the dominant
feature of a ritual in which the powers hostile to life and well-
being were repelled, and fertility, prosperity, and security were
ensured for the coming year. With the ritual were associated
both the myth of creation, in which the chaos monster was
overcome and the natural order was created, and also the
story of Israel's deliverance in which the nation was created.
The festival was one of recreation. Each year chaos was again
overcome, and Yahweh's enemies assailed and defeated; and
those who took part in the festival experienced anew Yahweh's
acts of creation, salvation, and judgement. Of prime importance for the well-being of the community was the king, who
embodied in himself the corporate life of the nation, and was
the sacramental mediator to his people of the divine life and
power.

The analogy for Mowinckel's *reconstruction* of the festival
was provided by the Babylonian *akîtu* festival. His *interpretation*
of the ritual owes much to the work of the influential Danish
savant Vilhelm Grønbech, from whom he took over the concept
of primitive cult as a creative drama (*schöpferisches Drama*) in
which ritual acts were not merely symbolic, but powerful to
achieve the results desired.[1] In the cult man comes into contact
with the divine power through which alone the factors which
make for his weal or woe may be controlled. In the cultic myth
the things which are done in the cult are projected into primeval
time; and later this myth may be linked with history, as in Israel
the myth of the overthrow of chaos at creation came to be linked
with the story of the deliverance from Egypt. In a sense, the

[1] Grønbech's most important work has been translated into English under the title
The Culture of the Teutons (1931). See also 'Primitiv Religion' in *Illustreret
Religionshistorie* (ed. by Johs. Pedersen), 1948, and Mowinckel's article 'Drama' in
R.G.G.².

early cultic experience is the antithesis of the later eschatological hope; for it is a present experience of the New Creation, and not the mere hope of its future manifestation. But Mowinckel contends that the mythological complex associated with the Enthronement Festival provided the pattern of the post-exilic eschatology.[1] As a result of the change of calendar and other factors, the festival was split up into three parts, the New Year, the Day of Atonement, and the Feast of Tabernacles, as these are known to us from the later legislation; and Passover became the chief festival.[2]

Mowinckel's study was followed by other work in the same field;[3] and further research was stimulated by the discovery and decipherment of the Ras Shamra texts, and by the formulation of the theory that there existed a myth and ritual pattern common to the entire ancient Near East. In the two volumes edited by S. H. Hooke[4] and in the same scholar's Schweich Lectures[5] it is argued that behind the seasonal rituals, coronation rituals, and initiation ceremonies of the ancient east there was a common pattern which is clearly seen in the most important Egyptian and Babylonian rituals, and notably in the *akîtu* festival in Babylonia. The chief elements in the pattern are: the drama of the death and resurrection of the god, the recapitulation in act or word of the creation myth, the mimic battle in which the god overthrew his enemies, the sacred marriage, the triumphal procession of the victorious god who was represented by the earthly king.[6] It is argued that what in Mesopotamia was a spring New Year festival of urban character was adapted on Palestinian soil to agricultural conditions, and that in the three agricultural festivals of the Old Testament (the Feasts of Unleavened Bread, Weeks, and Ingathering) there were reproduced the essential

---

[1] *Psalmenstudien II*, pp. 213–314. It is important to supplement this with the briefer discussion in *Jesaja-disiplene*, 1926, where some modifications of view are registered.

[2] Cf. H. Riesenfeld, *Jésus transfiguré*, 1947, pp. 17 f., and the references there given.

[3] e.g. H. Schmidt, *Die Thronfahrt Jahves*, 1927.

[4] *Myth and Ritual*, 1933; *The Labyrinth*, 1935.

[5] *The Origins of Early Semitic Ritual*, 1938.

[6] *Myth and Ritual*, p. 8.

elements of the ritual pattern.[1] At Ur and Erech the *akîtu* festival was celebrated in the autumn as well as in the spring;[2] and it is held that in Israel both the spring and the autumn festivals included New Year rites.

The purpose of these annual feasts, whenever and wherever they were celebrated, was the renewal of the life of the community; and the entire action of the ritual drama was focused on the person of the king. In a brilliant and striking essay in *The Labyrinth* A. R. Johnson expounds in detail a number of passages in the Old Testament (e.g. Psalms ii, xxix, xlvii, xlviii, xlix, lxviii, lxxxix, cx) which, he maintains, points to cultic usage and a conception of kingship comparable to what has been described above. The Davidic king in Jerusalem was the anointed of Yahweh, His adopted son, and His humiliated and suffering servant. As such he played a 'literally vital role' in the cultus, which may well have been that of the pre-Israelite sanctuary at Jerusalem, where the sun-god El 'Elyon was originally worshipped *in sua persona* and later identified with Yahweh. A festival such as the pre-exilic Feast of Ingathering is held to have been would renew the unity of the people with its kingly God through its divine or sacral king, and would be a powerful cohesive force when the Davidic house was establishing its power. It is significant that when Jeroboam became king of Northern Israel at the disruption, one of the factors in his religious policy, according to 1 Kings xii. 32, was the establishing of 'a feast in the eighth month, on the fifteenth day of the month, like unto the feast that is in Judah'.

The second volume of Pedersen's monumental work referred to above (cf. p. 284, n. 1) contains, *inter alia*, a detailed discussion of David's influence on religious development, and of the cultic

---

[1] In *Myth and Ritual*, p. 70, Hooke speaks of 'the breaking up on Canaanite soil of the pattern of the Babylonian *akîtu* festival'; but in *The Origins of Early Semitic Ritual*, p. 57, he says that 'the most probable inference from the close resemblance between the New Year ritual as it was practised in Mesopotamia, Canaan, and Israel is that all three represent independent developments of a common central ritual, of which the Tammuz ritual may have been the earliest form.'

[2] *Myth and Ritual*, pp. 46 f.; cf. S. A. Pallis, *The Babylonian Akîtu Festival*, 1926, pp. 27–31, where evidence is adduced to show that the month in which the festival was held varied at different periods.

significance of the reigning monarch. (It may be noted, in passing, that Pedersen, like Mowinckel, was deeply influenced by Grønbech.) Together with the priest and the prophet the king was one of the 'upholders of holiness', as the chieftain had been in earlier times. First the establishment of the Davidic house and then the building of Solomon's Temple enhanced the religious significance of the monarchy, and worship was more and more attracted to the royal sanctuary, till at last the Babylonian invasion ended the succession, leaving the priesthood to inherit many of the king's ritual functions, while in another sphere, the Messianic hope, there survived the pattern of a kingship which should yet be the channel of the divine blessing. But Pedersen cautiously reminds us that there are limits to our knowledge of ritual practice before the Exile, and that there must have been limits to what was officially borrowed from foreign sources. There were intractable and intolerant elements in Israel's religious inheritance. 'The idea of a dying and resurrected God entertained by agricultural peoples was incompatible with the nature of Yahweh. But this affects the very core of the feast. . . . The kingship was not so deeply rooted in Israel as in the great kingdoms, and Yahweh's kingship did not require such a radical renewal. Hence though the Israelite king might disappear, Yahweh's kingship would still persist. The idea might even arise that the kingship meant the stealing of some of Yahweh's royal honour.'[1]

A similar qualification is made by another Danish scholar, F. F. Hvidberg, in an important study of some of the Ras Shamra texts (I* AB, I AB, II AB) which describe the death and resurrection of Baal.[2] He treats these as cultic texts accompanying a ritual which had its climax in the enthronement of the god, presumably at the autumn festival: and he applies the results of his study to the problem of syncretism at Dan in Northern Israel. But, although he concludes that there is ground for assuming extensive Israelite borrowing, and that it is possible that in some places Yahweh was mourned as dead and then hailed as risen

---

[1] *Israel III–IV*, E.T., p. 442.
[2] *Graad og Latter i det Gamle Testamente*, 1938; cf. A. S. Kapelrud, 'Jahves tronstigningsfest og funnene i Ras Sjamra' in *Nor. T. T.* xli, 1940, pp. 38–58.

from the dead and thought of as consummating the sacred marriage, nevertheless there is in the Old Testament no evidence for this whatsoever. 'For in the Old Testament *Yahweh nowhere meets us as a dying and rising Deity.* In Israelite cultic usage it was not the resurrection or the renewal of Yahweh which was represented, but Yahweh's saving acts on behalf of Israel which were celebrated, and the covenant which was renewed.'[1]

In subsequent Scandinavian research the subject has been taken up with enthusiasm. I. Engnell has investigated the evidence for divine kingship in the ancient Near East outside Israel, and has given some indication of the views which he intends to expound in his promised volume on the Old Testament material.[2] He regards the king, in his cultic role, as identical both with the creator high god and also with the dying and rising vegetation god (of whom Tammuz is the supreme example), and, as such, playing a decisive part, both as the suffering servant of Yahweh and as the victor over the powers of chaos. On Engnell's view syncretism was carried out during the period of the monarchy to an extent which it is almost impossible to exaggerate; and he finds the old cultic and liturgical patterns recurring much later. Professor Hooke and his collaborators draw attention to the way in which the original pattern may be modified in different areas by the processes of adaptation and disintegration. Engnell lays considerable stress on 'democratization', by which there may be applied to the individual worshipper what was originally proper to the divine king.

A somewhat similar general position is adopted by the Danish scholar A. Bentzen, though in his two short studies, *Det sakrale kongedømme*, 1945, and *Messias—Moses redivivus—Menschensohn*, 1948, he criticizes Engnell and other members of the 'Uppsala school' on points of detail. He himself lays considerable stress on the influence in Israel of historical events on the cultic myths; and he argues that the idea of the *Urmensch* is prior to

[1] Op. cit., p. 118.
[2] See *Studies in Divine Kingship in the Ancient Near East*; cf. *S.B.U.* i, cols. 674, 677 ff., 1221 ff. The main ideas recur in most of the writings of the so-called Uppsala school.

that of the divine king, and that from it are derived the functions
of the king, the priest, and the prophet. This is a special development of the view that in the creation narratives and in passages
like Psalm viii the lordship of man over nature reflects the
concept of divine kingship.

This whole line of argument has not been without its critics.
Over twenty years ago Eissfeldt raised some weighty objections
in an article[1] which, so far as the present writer knows, has
never been adequately answered. He pointed out that Hebrew
proper names compounded with *melek* are very rare until the end
of the monarchy and the exilic and post-exilic periods, which is
hardly what one would expect if the Kingship of Yahweh were
being annually celebrated in so popular a festival as that of
Ingathering. The idea of Yahweh's Kingship cannot legitimately
be derived from the cult. The first occurrence which can be
clearly dated is in the account of Isaiah's vision (Isa. vi. 5), where
it is to be connected with the prophet's conception of the exalted
nature of Yahweh and not with cultic usage. Nor is there any
indubitably pre-exilic passage in which the Kingship of Yahweh
is connected with a specific act of creation. Eissfeldt also argues
that the verb *malak* in the enthronement psalms need not be
translated 'has become King', but can equally well mean 'is
King'; and he concludes that the psalms which celebrate
Yahweh's Kingship are post-exilic, and are to be interpreted
eschatologically.

N. H. Snaith, in his *Studies in the Psalter*, 1934, argues that
the enthronement psalms are post-exilic and patently dependent
on Deutero-Isaiah, that they are Sabbath psalms and unconnected with the New Year festival. In his recent study, *The
Jewish New Year Festival*, 1947, he returns to the attack in
a wide-ranging discussion of the festivals and the calendar. In
future work in these fields serious consideration will have to be
given to his contentions that when *ḥōdeš* refers to a particular
day it may mean new-month day, that before the Exile the

---

[1] 'Jahve als König', *Z.A.W.* xlvi, 1928, pp. 81–105; cf. C. R. North, 'The Old
Testament Estimate of the Monarchy', in *A.J.S.L.* xlviii, 1931, pp. 1–19; 'The
Religious Aspects of Hebrew Kingship', in *Z.A.W.* l. 1932, pp. 8–38.

month began at full moon, not new moon, and that the Sabbath was originally the new-moon day. But the main targets of his arguments are Mowinckel's theory of the *Thronbesteigungsfest*, and some of the positions of the myth-and-ritual school. He denies that there was a double New Year celebration in spring and autumn: Passover was not a New Year festival but a seasonal apotropaic ritual. In the pre-exilic period the autumnal festival included both thanksgiving for the Old Year and supplication for the New, particularly for the much-needed rains. But there is, he argues, no evidence for the association of the New Year festival with the Kingship of God before the second Christian century. The Psalms which formed the starting point of Mowinckel's argument are, as previously argued in *Studies in the Psalter*, inadmissible as evidence. Mowinckel's reconstruction of the supposed Israelite ritual in accordance with the pattern of the Babylonian *akîtu* festival is unsatisfactory, because, on the one hand, the Mesopotamian evidence is indiscriminately used regardless of its date, and, on the other, the urban culture of Mesopotamia does not offer a convincing parallel to conditions in Palestine. The agricultural fertility rites of Ras Shamra are a more likely source of influence. The fixing of the fate in the *akîtu* festival is probably astrological in character and different from the idea of a change of fortune associated with the Hebrew New Year. The Israelite kings were undoubtedly bearers of *mana*, but are unlikely to have been regarded as divine in any more exact sense, or to have taken the part of the Deity in the ritual.

Some of these contentions are open to challenge. There are those who hold that the similarity between the oracles of Deutero-Isaiah and the enthronement psalms indicates that the prophet is the borrower.[1] Moreover, although it would be generally admitted today that prototypes of Hebrew rituals are more likely to be found in Syria than in Mesopotamia, the Ras Shamra evidence is anything but an embarrassment to the most

---

[1] See *Psalmenstudien II*, pp. 49 f., 190–202; cf. A. Bentzen, *Indledning til de gammeltestamentlige Salmer*, 1932, pp. 37 f., 137; *Fortolkning til de gammeltestamentlige Salmer*, 1940, p. 506.

enthusiastic advocates of the *Thronbesteigungsfest* and divine
kingship theories.[1] Nevertheless, Snaith's original and challenging investigation will have to be taken into account in the
subsequent debate.

It seems certain that much detailed work will have to be done
before anything like definitive solutions can be reached concerning the problems raised by this discussion. Only the most general
observations can here be offered. It is established that the Feast
of Ingathering (later called Tabernacles) was the most important
of the three agricultural festivals which were taken over by the
Hebrews from the Canaanites. Before the Exile it was 'the
Feast'. It came at the end of the Old Year and the beginning of
the New. For detailed reconstruction we are dependent either
on post-exilic Jewish sources or on earlier extra-Biblical sources.
It has to be admitted that there is no indisputable, pre-exilic,
Israelite evidence for the celebration of the enthronement of
Yahweh in connexion with this feast. We are left to conjecture
to what extent the kind of ritual which we know of from Ras
Shamra and elsewhere was adopted in Israel. That syncretism
took place extensively is not denied; but in the syncretistic
process the influence was not all from the one side. As Pedersen,
Hvidberg, and others have maintained, the idea of a dying and
rising god was incompatible with the Israelite belief in Yahweh,
the living God. Pedersen's words, already quoted, are significant:
'*this affects the very core of the feast*'. Again, it can be argued that
the worship in the Jewish colony at Elephantine of Yahweh's
consort Anath among other deities points to the possibility that
the sacred marriage was not unknown in Israel. But both the
status and the interpretation of the Elephantine evidence may
be questioned. Albright maintains that what appear to be
separate deities are hypostatized aspects of Yahweh;[2] and
Hvidberg has argued that we must not too confidently draw
conclusions from Elephantine about normal Israelite practice.[3]

[1] A. S. Kapelrud says, 'Mowinckel's hypothesis of an enthronement festival in
Israel is confirmed in a striking way by the Ras Shamra texts' (*Nor. T. T.* xli, 1940,
p. 57).   [2] *A.R.I.*, pp. 168–74.

[3] *Graad og Latter i det Gamle Testamente*, p. 118; *Den israelitiske Religions Historie*,
1944, p. 70.

Israelite religion was in origin and in essence an historical religion; and although it borrowed from and was enriched by the nature religion of Canaan it remained an historical religion. Its God did not die and rise again with the changing seasons. He was the Master of the forces of nature, and not identified with them. It may be claimed that the idea of His Kingship is at least latent in the story of His deliverance of His people at the Exodus and His leading of them through the wilderness; and to this the idea of His Kingship in creation is chronologically and theologically secondary. That the institution of the monarchy brought far-reaching religious changes is clear; but there are strong general grounds for holding that in Israel the ancient oriental divine kingship lost much of its divinity. No mythical, divine origin is claimed for the Israelite monarchy; and kings and kingship are criticized freely.[1] It can, of course, be urged that later editors expunged from the records elements which to them were offensive. Within limits this may be admitted; but if our records present Hebrew religion as something of an erratic boulder among the religions of the Near East, that is precisely what the subsequent developments demand.

Other aspects of the pre-exilic cult have received attention in recent work. The relation of the prophets to the cultic system, and the interpretation of the strictures of the canonical prophet on sacrifice have both been the subject of lively debate, to which Scandinavian scholarship has made significant contributions. That prophecy was intimately connected with the cult was no new discovery. Admittedly the general tendency in the earlier phase of critical scholarship was to regard cult and ethics as antithetical, and the prophets as ethical teachers indomitably opposed to the ritual expression of religion. But the increasing recognition of the links between Israelite and non-Israelite prophecy brought a change of attitude. Already in G. Hölscher's great work the cultic connexions of prophecy are recognized.[2]

[1] Cf. A. Lauha, 'Några randanmärkningar till diskussionen om kungaideologien i Gamla Testamentet', *S.E.Å.* xii, 1947, pp. 183–91.

[2] *Die Profeten: Untersuchungen zur Religionsgeschichte Israels*, 1914, pp. 132 ff., 143 ff.

In the third of Mowinckel's *Psalmenstudien*[1] it is maintained that the prophetic element in the Psalter is to be attributed to a type of prophet who was a cultic official. More recently A. R. Johnson and A. Haldar have dealt in detail with the question.[2] Many passages in the Old Testament point to the association of prophets with priests and sanctuaries (e.g. 1 Sam. ix. 13, 22 f.; 2 Sam. vii. 1 ff.; 1 Kings xix. 10; 2 Kings x. 18 f.; Jeremiah xxiii. 11; xxvi. 7); and Johnson maintains that the prophets 'belonged to the cultic personnel of the different sanctuaries in as real a sense as did the priests'.[3] In the argument which leads up to this contention stress is laid on mechanical methods of divination, the magical or semi-magical ideas associated with the prophetic word and symbolic action, the responsibility of the prophet for the well-being of the community, and his intercessory activity. The decline of prophecy in the post-exilic age brought about the reduction of the Temple prophets to the status of Temple singers (cf. 2 Kings xxiii. 2 with 2 Chronicles xxxiv. 30).

Haldar's researches, which cover a much wider field, lead up to more sweeping claims concerning the similarity of cultic prophets in all parts of the Near East, their organization in associations derived from a mythical founder who was a sacral king, and the continuity of the canonical prophets with the cultic prophets. In spite of the great learning with which he presents his case, Haldar all too often gives the impression of fitting the evidence into a Procrustean bed, in contrast with Johnson's patient and conscientious sifting of the material.

Not unconnected with these views is the contemporary tendency to interpret passages like Amos v. 21–5; Isa. i. 11–17; Jer. vii. 21–3 as indicating only qualified hostility to the cult. It has been argued that what the prophets were attacking was not the cult as such, but cult divorced from morality, or Canaanite rites, or the cult of the Northern Kingdom. Detailed discussion is

---

[1] *Psalmenstudien III. Kultprophetie und prophetische Psalmen*, 1923.
[2] A. R. Johnson, 'The Prophet in Israelite Worship', in *E.T.* xlvii, 1935–6, pp. 312–19; *The Cultic Prophet in Ancient Israel*, 1944; A. Haldar, *Associations of Cult Prophets among the Ancient Semites*, 1945. Cf. Johs. Pedersen, *Israel III–IV*, pp. 115–17; Joh Lindblom, *Profetismen i Israel*, 1934, pp. 161 ff.
[3] *The Cultic Prophet in Ancient Israel*, p. 53.

impossible here;[1] but it seems clear that any objective consideration of the question will avoid assuming that all the prophets
held the same view (or, indeed, that any one prophet always
expressed the same type of judgement), or that the prophets were
modern enough to imagine a cultless religion, or, on the other
hand, that there was no decisive difference between the great
canonical prophets and the mass of the people or the majority of
their fellow prophets.

Yet another line of investigation which has recently received
attention is concerned with the relation of the shrines to the
law-codes. A quarter of a century ago A. C. Welch argued, in
an attack on the commonly accepted view of Deuteronomy,[2] that
the book did not legislate for worship at a single central sanctuary,
but for the use of legitimate Yahwistic sanctuaries in different
parts of the country. His reconstruction of Israel's religious
history was carried farther in subsequent publications;[3] but it
is perhaps his dating and interpretation of the Deuteronomic
material which has attracted most attention. More recently
Professor Edward Robertson has elaborated a more radical
alternative to the Graf-Wellhausen hypothesis, involving early
dating of Deuteronomy (and, indeed, of the whole Pentateuch),
and stressing the importance of provincial shrines.[4] After the
conquest Shechem was originally the central shrine; and when
conditions made necessary the establishment of others it remained
for a time the most important one. But its influence was impaired
by rivalry between the Eleazar and Ithamar branches of the
Aaronite priesthood, which led to the establishment of the
sanctuary at Shiloh. From the latter came Samuel, through whose
statesmanship the work of unifying Israel began. Presiding over
assemblies of the prophets from the different shrines, he organ-

---

[1] Cf. Joh. Lindblom, *Profetismen i Israel*, pp. 427–39; H. H. Rowley, *The Unity of the Old Testament*, 1946 (reprinted from *B.J.R.L.* xxix, 1946, No. 2).

[2] *The Code of Deuteronomy*, 1924.

[3] *Deuteronomy, the Framework to the Code*, 1932; *Post-exilic Judaism*, 1935; *Prophet and Priest in Old Israel*, 1936.

[4] In a series of lectures published in *B.J.R.L.* xx, 1936, No. 1; xxvi, 1941, No. 1; xxvi, 1942, No. 2; xxvii, 1943, No. 2; xxviii, 1944, No. 1; xxix, 1945, No. 1; xxx, 1946, No. 1; xxxii, 1949, No. 1. See also the volume by R. Brinker, *The Influence of Sanctuaries in Early Israel*, 1946.

ized the collection and recording of the traditions and codes of these shrines (as now contained in the first four books of the Pentateuch) and added Deuteronomy as the regulative supplement to them and as the code of the central sanctuary which was yet to be (Deut. xii. 5). When national unity was destroyed at the disruption, the prestige of the Temple was impaired and the Torah discarded, to be displaced, perhaps, by H (the code of Shiloh?), until it was discovered some three centuries later, only to be discarded again after Josiah's death. The return under Joshua and Zerubbabel represented a régime hostile to the Torah; but Ezra's work was the restoration of the Torah and of the old religious leadership of the pre-monarchical period, combined with rigid exclusion of the hated northerners.

Professor Robertson's dissent from 'critical orthodoxy' is wide in its range; and at many points it will evoke counter-dissent. But his emphasis on the influence of sanctuaries is timely and suggestive. The older reconstruction of Israel's religious history assumed a chronological development indicated by the different codes. It is at least possible that we should allow for contemporary strata representing local usage.[1]

Recent work on eschatology and the messianic hope is closely related to some of the theories of the cult and the divine king mentioned above. The beginnings of the discussion lie in the earliest work of Gunkel and Gressmann. The critical methods of the Wellhausen school led to the conclusion that the bulk of the eschatological sayings in the pre-exilic prophets were post-exilic interpolations; and it was held that a developed eschatology was characteristic of a relatively late stage of religious development. The first step in the new approach is represented by Gunkel's *Schöpfung und Chaos in Urzeit und Endzeit*, 1895, in which he argued that the eschatological framework was derived from the Babylonian creation myth. Primeval history is projected into the future, chaos returns, a new heaven and a new earth are created. Following on this, Gressmann contended in *Der Ursprung der israelitisch-jüdischen Eschatologie*, 1905, that

---

[1] Cf. A. R. Johnson, *The Vitality of the Individual in the Thought of Ancient Israel*, 1949, p. 3.

there was in the pre-prophetic age a real popular eschatology, and that the Day of Yahweh was an eschatological concept. The expectation entertained by the mass of the people was that a day was coming when Yahweh would manifest His power and destroy Israel's enemies in a world catastrophe.

As we have already seen, Mowinckel had discarded the eschatological interpretation of the enthronement psalms. But when he had completed his reconstruction of the *Thronbesteigungsfest* he found that the evidence compelled him to deal with the eschatology as a by-product of the festival: and in the latter part of *Psalmenstudien II* he argues at length that the postexilic eschatology had its origin in the cult. Taking into account his later work, *Jesaja-disiplene*, 1926, his view is that the ideas and motifs associated with the festival of Yahweh's enthronement were borrowed by some of the disciples of Isaiah to describe their concept of the future, a concept which had no teleological connexion with the events of their own day, but which had not yet become genuinely eschatological, for, on Mowinckel's view, eschatology emerged only after the fall of the Southern Kingdom. When it did take shape, it reproduced the main features of the New Year ritual and its associated mythology: the Kingship of Yahweh, the catastrophes in nature, deliverance from enemies as a result of the divine conflict with hostile powers, judgement, the remnant (originally all Israel), the new creation, the new covenant, the eschatological banquet (the sacrificial meal), and the Messiah, the divinely appointed ruler. Eschatology was thus a projection into the future of what had been dramatically presented in the cult. Present experience of the divine power, renewed annually in the festival, had been transformed into future hope. Israel had travelled 'vom Erlebnis zur Hoffnung'. The eschatological idea of the Day of Yahweh was derived from the day of Yahweh's enthronement in the festival. It had become the future, final, and decisive day, when, once for all, Yahweh was to assert His Kingship. As H. W. Robinson pointedly expressed it, 'Whereas Gressmann derived the day from the eschatology, Mowinckel derives the eschatology from the day'.[1]

---

[1] *Inspiration and Revelation in the Old Testament*, 1946, p. 140.

More recently J. Morgenstern has held[1] that the proximate origin of the concept of the Day of Yahweh was the annual observance of the New Year's Day at the autumnal equinox. Its ultimate origin lay in the mythological idea of the primeval struggle at creation between light and darkness, good and evil, life and death. By the time of Amos the idea had 'acquired a universal implication'; and men looked forward to the Day when Yahweh would overthrow His enemies and install Israel as the dominant nation. 'Perhaps the very next New Year's Day would be the Day of Yahweh!' It was to this attitude that Amos' announcement that the Day of Yahweh was not light but darkness came as a stern and unexpected challenge.[2] No fully eschatological sense is implied.

On the whole, it seems unnecessary to seek the origin of the expression 'the Day of Yahweh' elsewhere than in the idiomatic use of the word 'day' in the sense 'day of battle', 'day of decisive action'; and it is certainly unnecessary to assume that the expression always has an eschatological content.

It is also argued that the idea of the Messiah had its origin in the role of the divine king in the cult. Graham and May and Engnell have even applied the term 'messianic' to the king; and to this Bentzen has given a slightly qualified approval.[3] But in view of the normal associations of the words 'Messiah' and 'messianic', it can only make for confusion if they are used in any other than a future sense. To confine them to a strictly eschatological sense would involve ruling out their use in connexion with certain familiar Old Testament passages to which they are justly applied.

Mention has been made above of the attempt made to connect the idea of the *Urmensch* with that of the sacral king, and to

---

[1] *Amos Studies*, 1941, pp. 408 ff. = *H.U.C.A.* xv, 1940, pp. 284 ff.

[2] Cf. S. Mowinckel, *Jesaja-disiplene*, p. 94.

[3] W. C. Graham and H. G. May, *Culture and Conscience*, 1936, pp. 101 f.; I. Engnell, *Studies in Divine Kingship in the Ancient Near East*, p. 43, n. 3, p. 176; *Gamla Testamentet*, i, pp. 141 f.; A. Bentzen, *Det sakrale kongedømme*, 1945, pp. 113 ff.; 'Kan ordet "Messiansk" anvendes om Salmernes kongeforestillinger?' in *S.E.Å.* xii, 1947, pp. 36 ff.; *Messias—Moses redivivus—Menschensohn*, 1948, pp. 32 ff.

find in the Biblical Adam both *Urmensch* and *Urkönig*. The argument that *ben 'ādām* was a royal 'messianic' title links sacral kingship with the later figure of the Son of Man.[1] Such hypotheses must be carefully checked by the evidence. In a short but careful study E. Sjöberg has examined the occurrences of *ben 'ādām* in the Old Testament, and concluded that there is no evidence for any special use of the term as a royal title.[2] Attacking the hypothesis at another point, Mowinckel has argued strongly that the Old Testament Messiah is not divine, had originally no connexion with Paradise or with the conception of successive aeons, and should not be associated with the figure of the *Urmensch*, with which it has no contact till later.[3] A full consideration of this subject would take us outside the Old Testament field.

It will be seen that, whereas it has often been argued that Jewish eschatology owes much to late borrowing from foreign, chiefly Persian, sources, there is a strong contemporary tendency to trace it back to patterns which were widespread in the ancient east and were mediated to Israel at an early period through the cult. That the cult had an influence on eschatology may be conceded; but if the question is to be satisfactorily treated two things seem necessary. The first is that the terms used should be clearly defined and carefully used. The second is that we should recognize the importance of Israel's consciousness of election and of the consistency of the divine purpose. To find here a central and creative influence, however, is not to deny that both the cult and foreign sources provided much in the way of imagery and motif.

This essay has necessarily been confined almost exclusively to the pre-exilic stage of Israel's religion; for it is in this field that the most challenging recent work has been done. This emphasis

---

[1] A. Bentzen, *Det sakrale kongedømme*, pp. 76 f., 116 ff.; *S.E.Å.* xii, 1947, pp. 36 ff.; I. Engnell, *S.B.U.* i, cols. 14 f.

[2] 'Uttrycket "Människoson" i Gamla Testamentet' in *Svensk teologisk kvartalskrift*, xxvi, 1950, pp. 35–44.

[3] See 'Opphavet til den senjødiske forestilling om Menneskesønnen' in *Nor.T.T.* xlv, 1944, pp. 189–244; 'Urmensch und "Königsideologie"' in *Studia Theologica*, ii, 1, 1949, pp. 71–89.

is reflected in the limited space devoted to the later period in some recent histories of Hebrew religion. It must be emphasized, however, that no general treatment of the subject can be considered adequate which does not recognize the significance of the later developments. The post-exilic age has sometimes been regarded with disfavour as the period in which prophecy declined and legalism flourished. There has, however, been an increasing recognition of the significance of the period for the conservation of the great achievements of the golden age of prophecy and the highest achievements of Israelite worship.[1]

Finally, something must be said about a number of books which deal with the Old Testament as a unity or deal with specific aspects of Old Testament thought. Their importance cannot be indicated by any mere summary, for it lies less in the solutions offered to specific problems than in the way in which the reader is taken, so to speak, inside the minds of the men of the Old Testament or enabled to see certain dominant and constant themes running through the entire development of the religion.

No deep understanding of Israel's religion is possible without a study of its psychological and social background. Much has been done in recent years to extend our knowledge in these spheres. Reference has already been made to Pedersen's great work, *Israel* (cf. p. 284, n. 1). The full discussion of holiness in the second volume is intimately connected with what is said in the first about the 'totality' of the soul and of the community; and the reader is given a masterly survey of the vital organic unity of the social group and the factors which made for the maintenance of its vigour and well-being. A similar approach is represented by the work of A. R. Johnson. In a short but detailed and fully documented essay, *The One and the Many in the Israelite Conception of God*, 1942, the ideas of 'corporate personality' and 'extension of personality' are combined and applied to the Old Testament material. It is pointed out that the group, regarded as a corporate personality, is an extension of its head, as is any individual who represents him. These facts are adduced to illustrate the references in the

[1] See H. H. Rowley, *The Unity of the Old Testament*; *The Rediscovery of the Old Testament*, chapter vii; cf. G. F. Moore, *Judaism*, i, 1927, pp. 13–16.

Old Testament to the 'sons of God', and the Angel of Yahweh, and those passages where the prophet appears to be identified with Yahweh. Johnson's more recent study, *The Vitality of the Individual in the Thought of Ancient Israel*, 1949, is a careful reconsideration of the chief aspects of the Hebrew conception of man, and includes a refutation of what has been called 'the diffused consciousness theory', the view that the different parts of the body are thought of as functioning separately and independently.[1] The work is intended to form part of the prolegomena to a Biblical Theology. Such investigations make it plain that for the serious student there can be no short cut to the understanding of the Old Testament via the psychological and religious categories of today.

Most recent attempts to define the *Eigenart* of the Old Testament religion come within the sphere of theology rather than that of the history of religion, and therefore do not call for discussion in this essay. But mention may be made of three significant discussions of selected themes. J. Hempel's study of Hebrew piety[2] is a remarkable illustration of the way in which a synthetic treatment of the material can bring out the unity and distinctive character of the Old Testament religion, amid all its diversity and in spite of all its latent tensions. The God who is at once afar off and near, who manifests His power and fulfils His purpose in the events of history, and is also Lord of nature, stands over against man, requiring of him personal obedience. The nature of that obedience is considered at length in the same author's complementary study of Old Testament morals.[3] Behind the manifold precepts which affect the group and the individual, the cult and the conduct of daily life, lies the authority of God; and it is here, above all, rather than in the intrinsic character of actions or their results, that the ultimate sanction lies. On the other hand, the actual historical environment in which obedience is required is such that standards of conduct have often to be expressed negatively, in accordance with the

[1] Cf. H. W. Robinson in *The People and the Book*, pp. 362 ff.
[2] *Gott und Mensch im Alten Testament* (B.W.A.N.T. iii, 2), 1926 ([2]1936).
[3] *Das Ethos des Alten Testaments* (B.Z.A.W. lxvii), 1938.

principle of *Abgrenzung*. Both books emphasize the importance of the individual in the early period. The untenability of the older view that 'individualism emerged' in the seventh century or later is but one example of the inadequacy of neat patterns for describing the development of Israel's religion.

In a shorter and less detailed study[1] Joh. Lindblom has sought to discover the *Eigenart* of Old Testament religion. It contains a critical survey and methodological discussion of earlier attempts, which is penetrating and instructive. Selecting the idea of God as that which supremely exhibits the unity and distinctiveness of Israel's religion, Lindblom finds in the Kingship of Yahweh the characteristic Hebrew concept; and he goes on to deal with unresolved tension present in it between love and wrath, and shows how it leads to and yet is contrasted with the dominant ideas of the New Testament.

Something was said at the beginning of this essay concerning the present difficulty of writing about Hebrew religion. There is one difficulty which must always be reckoned with. Hebrew religion cannot be described in terms of a smooth, orderly, historical development. The symmetrical patterns into which we try to fit it are shattered time and again by historical crises, changes of cultural environment, and the work of great, creative personalities; and when, as we are bound to do, we have done our utmost to find in it factors which are distinctive and constant, it is of the nature of the religion that we are driven back to the actuality of history; for the Old Testament does not contain a speculative religion, but bears witness to the acts of the living God. G. W. ANDERSON

BIBLIOGRAPHY

ALBRIGHT, W. F. *From the Stone Age to Christianity*, 1940 ([2]1946).
— *Archaeology and the Religion of Israel*, 1942 ([2]1946).
BENTZEN, A. *Det sakrale kongedømme*, 1945.
— *Messias—Moses redivivus—Menschensohn*, 1948.
COOK, S. A. *The Religion of Ancient Palestine in the Light of Archaeology*, 1930.

---

[1] *Den gammaltestamentliga religionens egenart*, 1935. Cf. his contribution to *Werden und Wesen des Alten Testaments* (B.Z.A.W. lxvi), 1936.

DHORME, E. *La Religion des hébreux nomades*, 1937.

ENGNELL, I. *Studies in Divine Kingship in the Ancient Near East*, 1943.

— *Gamla Testamentet. En traditionshistorisk inledning*, i, 1945.

GRAHAM, W. C., and MAY, H. G. *Culture and Conscience*, 1936.

HALDAR, A. *Associations of Cult Prophets among the Ancient Semites*, 1945.

HEMPEL, J. *Gott und Mensch im Alten Testament* (B.W.A.N.T. iii, 2), 1926 (²1936).

— *Das Ethos des Alten Testaments* (B.Z.A.W. lxvii), 1938.

HOOKE, S. H. (ed.). *Myth and Ritual*, 1933.

— *The Labyrinth*, 1935.

— *The Origins of Early Semitic Ritual*, 1938.

HVIDBERG, F. F. *Graad og Latter i det Gamle Testamente*, 1938.

— *Den israelitiske Religions Historie*, 1944.

JOHNSON, A. R. *The One and the Many in the Israelite Conception of God*, 1942.

— *The Cultic Prophet in Ancient Israel*, 1944.

— *The Vitality of the Individual in the Thought of Ancient Israel*, 1949.

LESLIE, E. A. *Old Testament Religion in the Light of its Canaanite Background*, 1936.

LINDBLOM, JOH. *Profetismen i Israel*, 1934.

— *Den gammaltestamentliga religionens egenart*, 1935.

— *Israels religion i gammaltestamentlig tid*, 1936.

LODS, A. *Israel from its Beginnings to the Middle of the Eighth Century*, 1932. (E.Tr.)

— *The Prophets and the Rise of Judaism*, 1937. (E.Tr.)

MOWINCKEL, S. *Psalmenstudien II. Das Thronbesteigungsfest Jahwäs und der Ursprung der Eschatologie*, 1922.

— *Psalmenstudien III. Kultprophetie und prophetische Psalmen*, 1923.

— *Jesaja-disiplene. Profetien fra Jesaja til Jeremia*, 1926.

OESTERLEY, W. O. E., and ROBINSON, T. H. *Hebrew Religion, Its Origin and Development*, 1930 (²1937).

PALLIS, S. A. *The Babylonian Akîtu Festival*, 1926.

PEDERSEN, JOHS. *Israel: Its Life and Culture, I–II, III–IV*, 1926 and 1940.

ROWLEY, H. H. *The Rediscovery of the Old Testament*, 1946.

SNAITH, N. H. *Studies in the Psalter*, 1934.

— *The Jewish New Year Festival*, 1947.

XI

OLD TESTAMENT THEOLOGY

During the period of Old Testament study surveyed in the present volume there have been sundry exciting episodes. The spade of the excavator has put remarkable new material for research into our hands. Such discoveries are recalled by names like Ras Shamra, Lachish, Mari. A lucky find like that of the Dead Sea Scrolls has provided the specialists with problems for years to come. The publication of a book, such as Gunkel's *Die Psalmen* or Mowinckel's *Psalmenstudien* or Hölscher's *Die Profeten*, has diverted the course of investigation into new channels. What has been happening in the field of Old Testament theology has perhaps been less spectacular and dramatic, unless we make an exception of the appearance of Wilhelm Vischer's *Das Christuszeugnis des Alten Testaments* which has certainly caused a good deal of heart-searching. What has to be recorded in this sphere is rather a steadily growing interest and concern accompanied by a very wholesome sense of the extreme difficulty of the questions which are involved. For the Old Testament theologian the task has been the exacting one of surveying the vast collection of material relating to the religion of Israel as it is mirrored in the Old Testament and determining its theological relevance. The matter has been complicated by the fact that there is no general agreement as to what a theology of the Old Testament should aim at providing. The word 'theology' happens to be one of those ambiguous words which are susceptible of different interpretations, and so not a little of the debate about Old Testament theology has been carried on at cross-purposes. Yet the differences of opinion which have emerged have not just been a matter of words. The real question at issue concerns the degree to which a subjective element ought to be involved in the interpretation of the Old Testament. Is it possible to draw an absolute distinction between objective and normative science?

Since the publication of Gabler's famous address in 1787,[1] the correctness of the distinction which he drew between biblical and dogmatic theology has been accepted as axiomatic by the majority of scholars. If we look back now over the period of over a century and a half which has elapsed since then, it is possible to recognize how essential it was that Old Testament research should shake itself free from the control of dogmatic theology which tended to supply it with its results in advance and merely ask for corroborating evidence. If men came to the Old Testament with hard and fast assumptions as to what it ought to mean, then their eyes were inevitably blinded to a great deal that was actually there staring them in the face. The extraordinarily interesting developments which took place following upon the emancipation of Old Testament scholarship go far to justify those who made a bid for freedom.

As happens almost invariably in such cases, however, sensitiveness to presuppositions of one kind did not carry with it sensitiveness to presuppositions of another kind. It was quite essential, of course, that the presuppositions of, for example, Protestant orthodoxy should be questioned. But there were new presuppositions and it should have been realized that they too ought to have been subjected to the scrutiny of the critic. If it was wrong to assume that the Old and New Testaments stood on exactly the same level as sources of *dicta probantia* for the support of doctrinal statements, it was a naïve assumption that the biblical evidence could be fitted without distortion into a neat evolutionary scheme or that complete scientific objectivity could be obtained by ruling out the element of the supernatural. It should have been recognized that the fundamental contrast between the older and the newer way of regarding the Old Testament was a contrast between assumptions, and that, while the newer one made it possible to take into consideration a much wider range of evidence, it should not have been so readily assumed that the older one was entirely mistaken.

In so far as the change which took place was from a static

[1] Joh. Phil. Gabler: *Akademische Rede de iusto discrimine theologiae biblicae et dogmaticae.*

view of the Old Testament to a truly historical one it was thoroughly beneficial. Unfortunately dissatisfaction with what claimed to be an historical account of Israel's religion might very easily be attributed to an unscientific and subjective point of view, whereas the real ground of criticism might very well be disagreement with the principle of interpretation present in the history offered. It is regrettable that unwillingness to accept a certain view of history should sometimes have been represented as due to an unhistorical attitude. The result was that those who felt that something vital was at stake and in real danger of being lost were almost forced into non-historical ways of asserting their point of view.

If this analysis of the situation is not entirely mistaken, it throws light on the curious paralysis which for some time arrested the development of biblical theology and in particular Old Testament theology. In this country the last important book to be published on the subject of Old Testament theology before the period which has to be surveyed was the posthumous volume by A. B. Davidson entitled *The Theology of the Old Testament*, which appeared as long ago as 1904. The fact that it has had no real successor in this country on anything like the same scale makes it necessary to say something about this book before we proceed, especially as many of the things which Davidson said half a century ago still remain valid.

Davidson explains the difference between systematic and biblical theology thus. 'In Systematic Theology,' he says,[1] 'while Scripture supplies the knowledge, some mental scheme, logical or philosophical, is made the mould into which the knowledge is run, so that it comes out bearing the form of the mould. In Biblical Theology the Bible is the source of the knowledge, and also supplies the form in which the knowledge is presented. Biblical Theology is the knowledge of God's great operation in introducing His kingdom among men, presented to our view exactly as it lies presented in the Bible.' This is not the place to enter into a discussion of Davidson's definition of systematic theology. The second definition, however, must occupy our

[1] *The Theology of the Old Testament*, p. 1.

attention. Davidson claims that it means practically the same as two other definitions which he quotes, namely 'the historical and genetic presentation of the religion of the Old Testament' and 'that branch of theological science which has for its function to present the religion of Revelation in the ages of its progressive movement',[1] except that of course one of these formulations deals with the Old Testament alone. When in his own definition Davidson includes the words 'presented to our view exactly as it lies presented in the Bible', he quite clearly does not mean, as we can deduce from what he says later, that the Old Testament theologian is confined to the traditional view of the Bible and its contents. In fact he makes a full claim for scientific criticism applied to the Bible 'not pursued simply for its own sake, so to speak, but . . . used as an instrument for disposing the books of the Old Testament in their proper place so that we may correctly perceive how ideas arose and followed one another in Old Testament times, and may observe how history reacted upon the thought and life of the people'.[2]

Right at the start Davidson sets on one side the view that the Old Testament dispensation 'is a designed shadow or adumbration of the New'.[3] In his opinion the kingdom of God was not prepared for by the introduction of something which was merely a shadow of something to come. It could only be prepared for by the introduction of itself in embryonic form. 'For,' he goes on, 'as the kingdom of God in its perfect form does not lie in mere knowledge, but rather in the life which the knowledge awakens, so it could not be prepared for by the mere knowledge that it was approaching, nor even by the knowledge outwardly communicated of what it was. It could be prepared for only by bringing in, and that in ever fuller tides, the life of which it consists. That life no doubt depended on the knowledge of what the kingdom truly was; but this knowledge could be learned by men only by living within the kingdom itself.' What God sought to do by bringing in His kingdom was 'to awaken a certain religious life in His people, and to project great thoughts and hopes before

---

[1] Op. cit., p. 6.   [2] Op. cit., p. 5.
[3] Op. cit., pp. 2 ff.

their minds'.[1] Davidson argues that the task of Old Testament theology is to exhibit this religious life as it develops, not by the adding of truth to truth, but organically, as one truth arises out of the one that went before. The subject of the Old Testament is Israel, that people of God within which the kingdom of God was implanted, and 'the truths regarding the kingdom of God appearing in the Old Testament are all given in terms, so to speak, of the history, institutions, and life of the people of Israel'.[2] It is emphasized that these institutions were real institutions, the primary value of which consisted in what they were for the people whose life they controlled. Davidson leaves open the question of the extent to which Israel's institutions may have prefigured those of the Christian Church. Often enough men may not have been aware of any reference to the future, though sometimes it may have been given to the profoundest minds in Israel to foresee that the idea enshrined in the institution was destined to be yet more fully realized. At the same time Davidson, while insisting that we must neither deny all authority to the Old Testament in favour of the New nor place the Old Testament on the same level as the New, urges that the Old Testament ought to be studied in view of its climax in the New Testament, saying that 'it will be of interest to ourselves to compare the two together'.[3]

The unfortunate feature of Davidson's very great book is that it has been badly edited. This is illustrated very clearly by the fact that, when he comes to discuss the divisions of his subject,[3] he rejects the usual division into Theology, Anthropology, and Soteriology, but later in the main part of the book accepts it. What he says, however, in criticism of this division is of real importance and is mentioned here because the point he makes will come up again later. He says that the threefold theological division is 'somewhat too abstract for a subject like ours. What we meet with in the Old Testament are two concrete subjects and their relation. The two are: Jehovah, God of Israel, on the one hand, and Israel, the people of Jehovah, on the other; and

[1] Op. cit., p. 6.
[2] Op. cit., p. 8.
[3] Op. cit., p. 11.
[4] Op. cit., pp. 12 ff.

the third point, which is given in the other two, is their relation
to one another. And it is obvious that the dominating or creative
factor in the relation is Jehovah'. Davidson goes on to detail the
various ways in which the revelation about Jehovah, Israel's
God, was mediated to Israel, ethical and spiritual conceptions
being mediated by the prophets, legislative and ritual conceptions
by the priests, while personal devotion to God was expressed by
the Psalmists and personal reflections on the revelation and even
questionings on the difficulties involved in it were provided by the
Wisdom writers. Here is a possible division of his subject which
evidently appealed to Davidson but which, strangely enough, he
did not follow up himself. We do, however, find it developed in
considerable detail and most brilliantly by H. Wheeler Robinson
in his posthumous volume *Inspiration and Revelation in the Old
Testament*, which was intended to form the Prolegomena to his
projected Theology of the Old Testament. Incidentally, this
illustrates the way in which Davidson's work anticipates positions taken up by others since his time. Though standing outside
our period Davidson's book on Old Testament theology forms
an excellent introduction to it.

The first definite sign of reviving interest in Old Testament
theology was given by the publication in 1922 of Eduard
König's *Theologie des Alten Testaments*. König stands quite
firmly for what he calls a realistic interpretation of the Old
Testament based upon the use of exact grammatical and historical methods, and rejects categorically anything in the nature of
'spiritualistic', that is to say allegorical, exegesis. König, as is well
known, had a high opinion of the reliability of the Old Testament
sources and his point of view is sharply distinguished from that of
the dominant evolutionary school of interpretation. He does not,
however, give any thorough discussion of the problem of what is
involved in a theology of the Old Testament. His own method is
to give first a survey of the history of Israel's religion followed by
a systematic account of the factors and ideas which played a vital
part in that history. The systematic principle followed, however,
is not very satisfactory.

It was in a number of articles by distinguished Old Testament scholars that discussion began of the important issues involved in the production of what might justly be called a theology of the Old Testament. In 1925 Steuernagel argued in the Marti Festschrift[1] for the indispensability of Old Testament theology as a more systematic way of handling the material provided by study of the development of Israel's religion. Only so was it possible to follow up all the side lines which run out from the main line of advance and also to deal with those themes which cannot be dated at any exact point in that line of advance. Important as Steuernagel's suggestions were as a contribution to the appropriate method of historical exposition, they do not take us very far.

It was during the late twenties and especially the thirties of the century that the Church struggle in Germany began to focus attention on the Old Testament and to provoke radical thought on its nature and relevance. This grim background to the theological literature of the period should be kept in mind. The discussions which went on during these critical years were by no means purely academic. Space forbids giving here any account of the debate but readers ought to be reminded that the pamphlet literature of the period contains much that is of more than ephemeral interest.

The issues involved in our theme become very much clearer when we turn to the highly provocative and interesting article by Otto Eissfeldt which appeared in 1926.[2] It will reward somewhat careful scrutiny.

Eissfeldt begins by saying that the contemporary problem of theology is the tension between absolute and relative, transcendence and immanence, adding significantly that for biblical science this general problem has narrowed down to that of the tension between history and revelation, that is to say, to the question whether the religion of the Old Testament should be treated historically in the form of *Religionsgeschichte* or treated as the

---

[1] 'Alttestamentliche Theologie und alttestamentliche Religionsgeschichte' (B.Z.A.W. xli, 1925, pp. 266–73).

[2] 'Israelitisch-jüdische Religionsgeschichte und alttestamentliche Theologie' (*Z.A.W.* xliv, 1926, pp. 1–12).

true religion, as God's revelation, as Old Testament theology. Eissfeldt's view is that both kinds of treatment are legitimate, but that, though the one will inevitably have a considerable influence on the other, they must, so far as their method is concerned, be kept absolutely distinct.

At first glance, one might incautiously conclude that Eissfeldt had reached an ideal solution of the problem. It certainly seems to simplify things very much for the historian to be set free to look at the religion of Israel from a purely phenomenological point of view, which means that he can study all the surface relationships and interrelationships without ever being compelled to face the question of their bearing on ultimate truth. All he has to do is to determine that such and such beliefs in God and His purposes for men and His activities towards them were held at various times. No value judgement is required of him. When it is claimed, further, that such and such an element in Old Testament religion is fulfilled in Christ or otherwise in the New Testament, all the historian of Israel's religion is required to do is to record the fact that such a claim is made, if he feels that it is important that he should do so. He is under no obligation to express any opinion on the correctness of this claim. Indeed, he would be acting *ultra vires* if he did so.

It is extremely interesting to find Eissfeldt up to a certain point approving of the point of view of the promoters of the Dialectic Theology as represented by Barth and Thurneysen. He quotes with appreciation words of the latter in which it is argued that the defenders of orthodoxy had failed to realize that revelation cannot be supported by reason. The methods of the historical-critical school must be taken quite seriously, and it should be recognized that it is quite impossible to prove revelation within the sphere of historical events. Where Eissfeldt joins issue with the Dialectic theologians is where he finds them virtually equating revelation with the contents of the Canon, not only its more central portions, but even those outer boundary regions of it where it seems to be fading out into secular literature. Eissfeldt's objection to this is that the Canon is an entity that belongs within the sphere reserved for historical investigation. Barth sets the biblical principle of the Reformed Church over against that of Luther, whom he accuses of making a selection from the Bible on the basis of a highly individualized dogmatic standpoint, instead of accepting the whole Canon as he ought to have done. Eissfeldt gives his vote for Luther, claiming that what Barth regards as Luther's dogmatic standpoint was really faith, which is the proper faculty for recognizing revelation.

In forming his attitude to the Dialectic Theologians, of course, Eissfeldt was not able to take into account the views of Wilhelm Vischer, whose work *Das Christuszeugnis im Alten Testament* did not begin to appear till 1934. In the article we are considering he approves of them in so far as their theology is kept from trespassing on the field of history with its sequences of cause and effect. It would have been very interesting to have had his opinion of Vischer's Christological interpretation of history.

What we do have is Eissfeldt's opinion of the so-called *pneumatic* interpretation of the Old Testament of men like Girgensohn and Procksch. In particular he refers to a series of articles by the latter published in 1925 which unfortunately have not been available to the writer. Eissfeldt, however, makes the purport of what Procksch has to say quite clear. For the interpretation of Scripture we must, in the first instance, employ all the usual means of philology, historical criticism, and what Procksch calls *Einfühlung*, an aesthetically conditioned identification of oneself with the subject matter, literally 'feeling oneself into it'. But all this is not enough. There are mysteries and paradoxes in Scripture which cannot be apprehended in this way. The 'pneumatic' or spiritual world discloses itself to faith but withholds its secret from the ordinary faculties of cognition. Procksch goes on to say that the spiritual elements in the Old Testament are not sufficient in themselves to awaken faith capable of fully penetrating their mystery. Their full meaning is only accessible to Christian faith. That is to say, it is only the Christian who can fully understand the Old Testament.

Eissfeldt's objection to this 'pneumatic' interpretation is that it robs the historical method of its independence, making it merely ancillary to the other. He is also critical of the opposite tendency, the tendency, namely, to make the theological method dependent on the historical. He refers in this connexion to Schleiermacher and Hegel who compared the different religions and exhibited Christianity as the highest and absolute religion, or to Hermann Schultz, the author of one of the best-known books on Old Testament theology to be produced in the second half of the nineteenth century, who argued that no historical document would disclose its meaning except to someone who had an inner understanding of it and a certain affection for it and that similarly an inner understanding is necessary for the proper appreciation of the meaning of the Bible. Eissfeldt is opposed to all such tampering with historical objectivity. In his view there is no legitimate means to make the historical yield other than what is immanent and relative. Faith, on the other hand, is the faculty through which man is laid hold upon by what is absolute and transcendent. When applied to the field of history to which the religion of the Old Testament belongs it merely introduces confusion.

It is probably a consequence of Eissfeldt's Lutheran point of view that he characterizes the faculty of knowledge as activity, that of faith as passivity. Knowledge deals with what belongs to the world of space and time. Faith is man's response to the initiative of the eternal world. Knowledge asks for proofs that will compel belief. Faith is something intensely personal and involves a leap in the dark. We may approach the Old Testament with either one faculty or the other. Both are legitimate and necessary but there must be no mixture of the two. They represent, as it were, two parallel lines of understanding which will meet at infinity but not till then.

Eissfeldt holds that it is to the benefit of both faith and knowledge that they should be kept strictly apart. Faith has its changes of emphasis which suggest different fields for knowledge to investigate. Historical faith illuminates new fields, as when, for example, in the nineteenth century, it brought into the foreground of attention the Hebrew prophets as religious personalities, and faith was immeasurably enriched. Further knowledge is able to relieve faith of the burden of elements in the Old Testament which can be shown to be conditioned by what is purely limited and temporal and was indeed outlived in certain cases even within the Old Testament period itself. The rather odd argument is used that the harm that can be done by the confusion of the two methods may be illustrated from within the Old Testament itself where we find familiar examples of a pragmatic treatment of history. But surely the reason for this feature of the Old Testament is that it essentially has the form of *Heilsgeschichte*, just because faith has a relation to history as its inalienable province from which it cannot afford to be banished into some purely transcendent region.

The weakness of Eissfeldt's position is that he seems unable to get beyond that attitude of mind which is perhaps best illustrated by Kant's attempted solution of the problem of knowledge by his distinction between the phenomenal and the noumenal. Applied to the field of religion this principle means that *Religionsgeschichte* is a completely neutral discipline in which members of different Christian confessions and even members of other religious faiths can work together in harmony. Biblical theology, on the other hand, is a purely confessional matter. While its method must be scientific, it always bears the character of witness and its findings will be valid only for those who share the theologian's point of view. One might have the less hesitation in accepting this definition of the function of Old Testament theology were it not that Eissfeldt makes it very clear that, just because faith is relative to revelation, Old Testament theology, operating as it does from the standpoint of faith, cannot take the form of any kind of representation of history. Faith has nothing to do with what is past. Its object is what is timelessly present. Its method will be systematic, provided that word does not imply control by a philosophical principle. An interesting additional point is that Eissfeldt holds that there are parts of the Old Testament, some of the Psalms for example, which supplement the New Testament without requiring to be fulfilled by it.

It amounts to this, that Eissfeldt identifies revelation with the communication of timeless truths. But for the fact that he would

not call them timeless truths of reason, we are not very far from
the position of Lessing. It is curious that Eissfeldt does not seem
to realize that he can only save the autonomy of *Religionsgeschichte* at the expense of a failure to appreciate the claim of
the Old Testament itself that it was precisely in historical events
that God did reveal Himself.

The next important step in the debate was taken in an article
by Walther Eichrodt published in 1929.[1] Like Eissfeldt, Eichrodt
draws attention to the demand of the Dialectic theologians and
the advocates of pneumatic exegesis for the employment of something beyond the methods of historical research, if one is to reach
the heart of Old Testament religion. He admits frankly that,
whatever one may think in general of the Dialectic Theology, one
must recognize the service it has rendered by forcing theologians
to take seriously the reality of revelation. The problem is how
this deeper understanding of the Old Testament is to be reached.
Eissfeldt's suggested solution has been considered and found
unsatisfactory. Is the something more which is being demanded
not something which falls within the sphere of normative or
dogmatic theology and therefore entirely outside the proper
field of study of the Old Testament theologian? Would it not
be wise to hold on to the testament of Gabler and maintain that
Old Testament theology is a strictly limited historical discipline?

It is at this point that Eichrodt makes his own special contribution. He admits the truth of the contention that history
cannot make an ultimate pronouncement on the truth or falsity
of anything, on its validity or invalidity. That decision must be
left to philosophy or dogmatic theology. It does not follow,
however, that, when the Old Testament theologian wishes to
describe the nature of Old Testament religion, he is to be limited
to tracing the stages in its growth, what Eichrodt calls its
'genetic analysis'. This would be to abandon the finest task of
historical research. Eichrodt claims it as an essential part of what
the historian has to do in regard to Old Testament religion that
a great systematic task should be undertaken which will consist

[1] 'Hat die alttestamentliche Theologie noch selbständige Bedeutung innerhalb der
alttestamentlichen Wissenschaft?' (*Z.A.W.* xlvii, 1929, pp. 83–91.)

in making a cross-section through the historical process, thus laying bare the inner structure of the religion and the relationship of its various contents to each other. It will then become manifest what are the constants in Old Testament religion. All this, he claims, can be done without entrenching upon the field of the normative theologian. In fact it is high time that historians should take seriously the fact that there is inevitably a subjective element in all historical research worthy of the name. It is an entire mistake when the positivist, for example, tries for the sake of objectivity to exclude philosophy from the individual sciences. One cannot be a satisfactory historian if one ignores the philosophy of history. The historian has to be guided in his work by a principle of selection and by a goal which gives perspective to his work, but, over and above all that, there is the principle of 'congeniality'; there must be a certain affinity or relationship between the historical researcher and the subject of his research, since only so will the intellectual energy be released which will enable a man to master his subject. There is, of course, a danger in all this, but, unless one is prepared to run the risk of this danger, the achievement of genuine history will be beyond one's reach.

Eichrodt goes on to say that there is really no such thing as a history of Israel's religion which is entirely free from presuppositions. The Old Testament theologian at least must find his principle of selection and the goal which provides perspective in the New Testament. Nevertheless, Eichrodt insists, this in no way involves the use of any special technique. In every science there is a subjective element. The fact that the theologian makes an existential judgement which, in part at least, determines the subjective element to be found in his account of Old Testament religion does not imply that he uses any distinctive historical method. It is clear that at this point Eichrodt, while admitting the necessity of an existential judgement on the part of the Old Testament theologian, wishes to ensure that, by making this admission, he will not lend any countenance to the charge that Old Testament theology is unscientific in character. Generally speaking, the Old Testament theologian will be involved in making historical judgements about empirical facts and their relationships to each other and will normally leave it to the dogmatic theologian to work these relationships into the system of Christian belief. At the same time Eichrodt allows for the possibility that the Old Testament theologian may at times feel unable to keep strictly within the limits of his science and find himself obliged to make pronouncements regarding the Old Testament which properly belong to the sphere of the dogmatic theologian. What Eichrodt wishes to avoid is the claim that such value judgements should be a normal part of Old Testament theology.

This preliminary sharpshooting on the part of Old Testament scholars was followed up by the appearance in fairly rapid succession of a number of volumes on Old Testament theology. Two appeared in 1933, the first a two-volume work by Ernst Sellin entitled *Alttestamentliche Theologie auf religionsgeschichtlicher Grundlage*, the second the first volume of a very large work by Eichrodt himself with the title *Theologie des Alten Testaments*, the later volumes being published in 1935 and 1939 respectively. A third work with the same title as Eichrodt's, but on a much more modest scale, by Ludwig Köhler, came out in 1936. The year 1934 had seen the publication of the first volume of a work on Old Testament theology of a very different kind, *Das Christuszeugnis des Alten Testaments* by Wilhelm Vischer. A second volume appeared during the War in 1942 but two further volumes are still awaited. Meanwhile the first volume has been translated into English and published by the Lutterworth Press in 1949 with the title *The Witness of the Old Testament to Christ*. In 1938 a small but important contribution to the subject was made by H. Wheeler Robinson[1] in the composite volume, *Record and Revelation*, by members of the Society for Old Testament Study, edited by himself. It took the form of two essays, the first dealing with the philosophy of revelation and the second with the characteristic doctrines. After his death, the

---

[1] Years before, in 1913, Dr. Robinson had published a small book, *The Religious Ideas of the Old Testament*. Another very small manual was C. F. Burney's *Outlines of Old Testament Theology* (1923).

brilliant posthumous work, *Inspiration and Revelation in the Old Testament*, which has been already referred to, was published in 1946. Another posthumous work *Theologie des Alten Testaments* by Otto Procksch began to make its appearance in 1949 and at the moment of writing is not yet complete. In 1949 too a Dutch scholar Th. C. Vriezen entered the lists with his *Hoofdlijnen der Theologie van het Oude Testament*. Worthy of mention, though of less importance than the above-mentioned works, are *An Outline of Biblical Theology* by Millar Burrows (1946) and *The Theology of the Old Testament* by Otto J. Baab (1949). A single Old Testament doctrine has recently had a whole book devoted to it, namely H. H. Rowley's comprehensive volume *The Biblical Doctrine of Election* (1950).

Though they do not specifically claim by their titles to deal with the theology of the Old Testament, it will give a better idea of the extent of the literature with a bearing on the subject which has made its appearance in recent years if mention is made of H. H. Rowley's *The Relevance of the Bible* (1941) and *The Rediscovery of the Old Testament* (1945) and the series of books by W. J. Phythian-Adams, *The Call of Israel* (1934), *The Fulness of Israel* (1938), and *The People and the Presence* (1942). There are good things in the second section entitled 'Theology' of Harold Knight's *The Hebrew Prophetic Consciousness* (1947), which should not be overlooked because of the defects of the first section. Of quite special importance for its clarity of presentation and its suggestiveness is a small book entitled *The Bible To-day* by C. H. Dodd (1946). The above, however, is only a selection of the relevant literature.

During our period a number of books have dealt with the closely allied question of the authority of Scripture, for example C. H. Dodd's *The Authority of the Bible* (1928, rev. ed. 1938), A. G. Hebert's *The Authority of the Old Testament* (1947), in which there is a welcome emphasis on *Heilsgeschichte* and on Israel as the people of God, and H. Cunliffe-Jones's *The Authority of the Biblical Revelation* (1945), which advocates a close integration of the historical and the theological approach to Scripture. Attention should also be drawn to the unusually large number of recent books dealing with the philosophy of history in which justice has been done to the Hebrew contribution.

Another line of study which has a very important bearing on Old Testament theology is that of semantic investigation. Mention should be made of books like N. Glueck's *Das Wort ḥesed im alttestamentlichen Sprachgebrauch als menschliche und göttliche gemeinschaftsgemässe Verhaltungsweise* (B.Z.A.W. xlvii, 1927); C. H. Dodd's *The Bible and the Greeks*: Part I. The Religious vocabulary of Hellenistic Judaism (1935); Joh. Pedersen's *Israel: its Life and Culture I–II* (1926), *III–IV* (1940); N. H. Snaith's *The Distinctive Ideas of the Old Testament* (1944); A. R. Johnson's *The One and the Many in the Israelite Conception of God* (1942) and *The Vitality of the Individual in the Thought of Ancient Israel* (1949); and last but not least many of the articles in Kittel's *Theologisches Wörterbuch zum Neuen Testament*. Old Testament theology must always be kept in close touch with the study of the Old Testament religious vocabulary and the closely allied study of Hebrew psychology. At the same time a truly theological handling of the Old Testament involves a step beyond semantics and psychology.

Now, it would obviously be quite disastrous to try to say here something worthwhile about all the books which have been mentioned. Moreover, this essay is not intended in any sense to provide a compendium of Old Testament theology. What the writer proposes to do is to follow the main line of discussion about the proper nature of Old Testament theology with reference to the books which present the issues most clearly.

It will perhaps be most convenient if we first take a look at the way in which Eichrodt puts his principles into practice. In the foreword to his first volume he emphasizes the need of demonstrating the unity and enduring fundamental tendency of the Old Testament. He proposes to exhibit the fact of this unity by grouping his material round the idea of the Covenant, showing the importance of its legal and cultic regulations and of its organs, the priests and prophets. It must be admitted that Eichrodt has been singularly successful in his choice of a central idea. The unity he achieves, however, is to some extent artificial, since the

Old Testament is less amenable to system than he suggests. Moreover, he applies his principle of unity only in Volume I which has the sub-title *God and People*. It is, however, a real advantage of his method that Eichrodt refuses to operate with bloodless abstractions like ethical monotheism which belong to a non-biblical way of looking at the religion of Israel.

What Eichrodt seeks to do, then, is to reach a total picture of the Old Testament world of belief. But he does not treat the Old Testament as an isolated religious phenomenon. Bridges have to be constructed between it and the heathen religions with which it came in contact and by which it was influenced. Above all, one must not overlook the forward movement in the Old Testament, the very incompleteness of which at its different stages points towards the New Testament. Eichrodt believes that, apart from its completion in Christianity, Judaism remains a torso. The connexion between the testaments is not just an historical one. They belong together, because they are both expressions of the invasion of human life by the kingdom of God. They result from the act of the one God who in Gospel and in Law is building up His kingdom. In particular the New Testament shows how the Old Covenant at Horeb was fulfilled in the New Covenant mediated by Christ.

This relation of the Old Testament to the New Testament, however, does not involve any artificial raising of the assertions of the Old Testament to the level of those of the New Testament. That it ignored the true character of a living movement was the mistake of the old orthodoxy and, we may add, it is the mistake of the Christological exegesis advocated by Vischer. When the difference between the testaments is overlooked, it is not surprising to find Rationalism advocating the rejection of the Old Testament. The mistake of Rationalism was to occupy itself exclusively with the critical analysis of the Old Testament; it had no eyes for the living synthesis which Eichrodt seeks to delineate, exposing the nature of the permanent structure of the Old Testament and the pillars on which it is raised. His systematic treatment, however, is so planned as to exhibit the development of thought and institution within the system.

The trouble is, as Eichrodt himself frankly admits, that the Old Testament resists systematic treatment, perhaps even more than Eichrodt thinks. The spiritual values which we tend to express by means of ideas are there all right, but they are present for the most part in events of history and in institutions. Eichrodt, therefore, thinks it best in his division of his subject to avoid the customary dogmatic scheme: Theology, Anthropology, Soteriology, and recognizing that the revelation of God is made in certain concrete relationships, to take over from a suggestion of Procksch the division: God and people, God and world, God and man. It should be pointed out that this is almost the same as the division favoured by Hermann Schultz.

Sellin's view of the task of Old Testament theology is that it should present in systematic form the religious teaching and faith found in the Jewish community on the basis of the writings collected and canonized during the period from the fifth to the second century B.C. But he adds the qualification that the Old Testament Canon is significant for the Old Testament theologian only in so far as it was accepted by Jesus and his apostles. That is to say, Old Testament theology is only interested in the line which was fulfilled in the Gospel. Christianity was based on the Old Testament but added something new to it. In the same way Pharisaism and Talmudic Judaism, Sadduceeism, Essenism, and Alexandrian religious philosophy base themselves on the Old Testament and each adds to it something which it professes to find already foreshadowed in it. Christian Old Testament theology must be selective in its own way. Strictly speaking, Sellin believes, Old Testament theology should leave on one side not merely the Canaanite influence but also the whole national-cultic side of Israel's religion. It is worth noticing that recent study of the Old Testament has tended to re-emphasize the importance for Old Testament theology of the cult. Particularly relevant in this connexion are A. C. Welch's *Prophet and Priest in Old Israel* (1936) and the book by W. J. Phythian-Adams referred to above, *The People and the Presence* (1942). Sellin, however, has the insight to recognize that the cultic and prophetic sides of Israel's religion are closely intertwined, sometimes even in the same religious personality or in the same religious document. He thinks it possible that the tension between them was willed by God as helping to produce movement towards the goal, the true faith developing against the background of the popular religion. It is only from the point of view of the Gospel that we are able to distinguish between what is permanent and what is temporary. What we can say is that there is an essential unity in the stream of religion from Moses to Christ, though throughout the Old Testament period the true religion is shadowed by what is virtually a different religion.

Like Eichrodt, Sellin selects a central idea to guide him in his exposition of Old Testament theology. For him it is that of the holiness of God.[1] God is a Being who can only be understood in part by man and this explains what seem to be irrational elements in God in the Old Testament representation of Him. But His holiness does not exclude fellowship with man. He is the Holy One of Israel. Man's sin at its most serious is thought of as ὕβρις towards the Holy God. Whereas the national-cultic religion of popular belief and practice looks mainly to the past and present, the ethical and universal religion of the prophets looks to the future, to the coming of the Holy One in judgement and salvation. When God forgives He does so, not because of sacrifices which have been offered to Him, but for the sake of His holiness.

In contrast to Sellin's view, Köhler claims that Old Testament theology should contain a systematic representation of the religious views, thoughts, and conceptions which are contained in the Old Testament taken as a whole. In his work one is not so conscious of the selective control of the Christian standpoint as in Sellin's and indeed also in what Eissfeldt says. He is perhaps less conscious than Eichrodt that revelation came to Israel more in historical events and in institutions than in clearly formulated ideas. At all events it should be noticed that, unlike Eichrodt, he does not avoid the traditional division of his subject-matter under the heads of Theology, Anthropology, and Soteriology. One peculiarity of his division is that he can find within it no entirely natural place for a treatment of the cult, since it has to do with

[1] Cf. Vriezen, *Hoofdlijnen*, pp. 99 ff.

man's mistaken effort to save himself by his own works. He therefore inserts his treatment of this subject as an appendix to the section on anthropology. Köhler seems to be unaffected by the modern tendency to rehabilitate the cult. Even prayer, sacred song, and reading of the Scriptures are merely part of man's attempt to earn salvation.

Like Eichrodt and Sellin, Köhler has his own favourite central idea, namely that of God as the Lord. For him the fundamental assertion of Old Testament theology should be that God is the Lord who lays down His commands. The sphere of God's rule may vary; His character does not vary. In the Old Testament religion is thought of as consisting in a relation between command and obedience and this relation is one of will. There is a will which commands and controls and there is a will which ought to obey and be controlled. Religion is the service of God. The same thought is present in the Book of Proverbs where we are told that the fear of the Lord is the starting-point or fundamental thing in wisdom—fear before the One who has the right to obedience. Here is the cardinal point round which the whole Old Testament revolves.[1] Köhler refers with approval to Buber's recognition[2] that the thought of Yahweh's rule over Israel is fundamental for the Book of Judges and for more than that. The same significance lies in the conception of God as King. Even when the title Father is applied to God, that means that He is the One to whom respect is due. God does not forgive out of weakness but as the One before whom fear is due. His name is pronounced over those over whom He is Lord and His whole character as revealed in His name is related to His lordship. As Lord of the community He defends it against enemies without and within and in this saving activity consists His justice.

We have already in the course of this essay encountered Procksch who is criticized by Eissfeldt for his advocacy of 'pneumatic' exegesis of the Old Testament. For Eissfeldt, as we

---

[1] It is worth noting that Köhler writes (op. cit., p. 137): 'There is scarcely a word which is so central to the Old Testament as the word joy. It is Israel's task to serve its God with joy and with a glad heart.' Cf. Eichrodt, *Das Menschenverständnis des Alten Testaments*, p. 34, where Köhler's statement is quoted with approval.

[2] In *Das Kommende, I. Königtum Gottes* (1932).

saw, revelation has nothing to do with history. When we come now to consider Procksch's *Theologie des Alten Testaments* we find a very different attitude. For him all theology is Christology. Christ is the only figure in our world of experience in whom God's revelation is completely to be found, and so it is through Him that mankind and therefore the history of mankind is bound to God. Theology is therefore justified in finding in Christ the middle point of history. To use the mathematical language of which Procksch is very fond, Christ is the centre of the system of co-ordinates in history. He is related both to the Church and to the individual Christian as a personal presence. He is the centre of existence for the individual Christian, yet not in a mystical sense, and also the basis of the communion of the saints.

Now, if Christ is thus the centre of theology, it seems reasonable to ask whether the Old Testament must not lie outside a theological viewpoint, so that there would be no such thing as a theology of the Old Testament. Procksch brings forward various arguments[1] to show that this is not so. The figure of Jesus Christ has the Old Testament as its background. He is the fulfilment of the Old Testament prophecies; without Him the Old Testament is a torso. He cannot be understood without the Old Testament and the Old Testament cannot be understood without Him. He brings the Messianic Son of David, the Son of Man, and the Servant of the Lord into the same axis with Himself and claims to incorporate the New Covenant. He claims to introduce not a new God but a new knowledge of God. There is an analogy between the relation of God to the People of God in the Old Testament and His relation to the People of God in the New Testament. The history of Israel is the womb out of which Christianity was born. In both cases the Covenant rests on God's gracious choice and institutes an order which is based on faith. Christianity meant the universalizing of what was originally promised to, and asked of, man within a limited sphere. In the Old Testament Christ is already the focus, yet only partially visible, whereas in the New Testament He is always visible.

[1] *v.* esp. pp. 8 ff.

Procksch maintains that Gabler's definition of the nature of biblical theology resulted in a failure to work out a proper theology of history and the cultivation of an entirely untheological *Religionsgeschichte*, Eissfeldt's ideal. Since Christ is the centre of history for theology, a theology of history is possible only if we take seriously the revelation in Christ and recognize the part which must be played by faith in historical judgement. The word 'revelation' must not be used with the general innocuous meaning made popular as a result of the *Aufklärung*. It requires faith as its correlative.

The faith life of the Christian who comes to the Old Testament today is affected and enriched by all the biblical figures he encounters on its pages. In this way the Bible becomes normative for the life of each Christian and indeed for the whole Church which stands in an ethical relationship to the Bible as it does to no other book. This ethical or existential relationship is ignored in *Religionsgeschichte*, since it is merely able to recognize differences of value between the Bible and what other religions have to offer. *Religionsgeschichte* is not interested in revelation but only in the phenomenon of religion. In *Religionsgeschichte* there may certainly be a subjective element but it is aesthetic in character. In Procksch's view the theologian is able to make use of *Religionsgeschichte* but only in a subordinate way. God and the faith of the individual in Him must be taken quite seriously.

The general plan of Procksch's book, making allowance for the fact that it is not yet complete, is that more than half of it is devoted to an historical sketch in order that account may be taken of the places in the history where, and of the men in whom, faith in a living God arose, and then of the manner of its development and of the goal towards which the movement of faith was directed. In the second part of the book Procksch follows a very similar course to that of Eichrodt who indeed acknowledges fully his indebtedness to the older scholar. Procksch describes his procedure in two ways. He speaks of the controlling ideas on the horizon of history and he also uses the figure of the cross-section which Eichrodt adopts. The problem is, of course, to determine at what point in the process of history the cross-section should be made. Procksch suggests that the best way is to make it at different places, at any point where the idea to be exhibited theologically comes most clearly to light. In the case of faith, for example, the cross-section should be made at the point in history where Isaiah stands. The other statements about faith will be brought into relation to this central disclosure of its meaning.[1] To ensure that the ideas and relationships to be studied will not be considered in abstraction from God who gives reality to them, Procksch, followed as we have already seen by Eichrodt, though in a different order, proposes the division: God and world, God and people, God and man. It is curious, in view of his insistence on the supreme importance of the revelation of God in history, that he should adopt the order he does.

It will be interesting now to turn to the work of the English scholar whose name during the past generation has been more closely associated with the cultivation of Old Testament theology than that of any other scholar in this country—the work, that is to say, of H. Wheeler Robinson. His mature views are very clearly stated in the two essays in the volume *Record and Revelation* already mentioned. At the beginning of his first essay he refers with approval to a statement of Hempel's:[2] 'Revelation is not the communication of a system of future events, or of a system of moral or religious requirements, but the making known of God's will which is to be performed in the particular and concrete situation, and of threats and promises of divine activity which will also be realized in the particular and concrete situation.' In agreement with this Wheeler Robinson says: 'If such a people were to know God, it would be through the concrete experience of living, rather than by any intellectualistic construction.'[3] God revealed Himself to Israel in a certain series of events which were interpreted to Israel by Moses. It is characteristic of Israel's subsequent history that we find the same blending of event and prophetic interpretation. The fact that the

---

[1] This interesting suggestion does not seem to have been carried out in practice with any consistency.

[2] *Record and Revelation*, p. 67.

[3] Op. cit., p. 303.

Hebrews had a strong sense of corporate personality made it easier for them to regard history as the supreme revelation of God, since, when God chose Israel in Egypt and dealt with it at Sinai, he was in effect dealing with the whole of Israel in all its succeeding generations. If, then, God reveals Himself in Israel's history, it is important as far as possible to establish the true course of Israel's history and also the history of the ideas which were entertained in Israel. This, incidentally, will make it clear why the Old Testament contains inconsistent statements and different moral and spiritual levels of belief.

'But', says Wheeler Robinson,[1] 'that which has removed the old difficulties has created new ones, at least for those who believe that the Old Testament is a divine revelation. We can gather them up by saying that the very phrase "a historical revelation" is a paradox, according to conventional ideas of revelation. History implies dynamic movement of some kind, whether or not it can be called progress; revelation implies static and permanent truth. How can absolute truth be relative to each of a series of generations? How can human transiency express divine eternity? How can free human activity be made to serve fixed divine purpose? All such questions are different forms of the perennial problem of the philosophy of history, viz. the relation of time and eternity, of which, perhaps, the only solution is a *solvitur vivendo*.'

It is most instructive to find Wheeler Robinson tackling here the same problem which came up when we were examining Eissfeldt's views and recognizing, as Eissfeldt does not, that history and revelation are inextricably bound up together.[2] Revelation is brought right down into 'the actuality of living' which is recognized as a 'category of reality'.

The question of the Canon of Scripture is next raised. Why should this particular collection of writings with the interpretation which they provide of a certain series of events be accorded

[1] Op. cit., p. 305.

[2] It is a merit of the book by Otto J. Baab that he perceives clearly the historical character of revelation and further realizes that biblical theology cannot avoid the question of the validity of the beliefs it finds in the Bible. The weakness of the book is that too much emphasis is laid on 'religious experience'.

this unique place in the reverence of the Church? The answer which is given, so far as the Old Testament is concerned, is that the authority of the Old Testament depends, as it always has depended from the outset, 'on value-judgements made by the Synagogue and accepted by the Church'.[1] These value-judgements Wheeler Robinson seems to identify with the *testimonium Spiritus Sancti internum.*

The possibility that God should reveal Himself to men at all is grounded in the fact that man was created in the likeness of God and that there is, therefore, a relationship of analogy between the divine and the human personality. This explains and justifies the anthropomorphic way in which God is described in the Old Testament. God reveals Himself most fully in volition, in the disclosure of His purpose, and therefore in history in which His purpose works itself out.

A section is devoted to what Wheeler Robinson calls the media of revelation in the Old Testament. He shows how lower forms of mediation were taken up into higher ones until we have 'the emergence and final predominance, as an interpretative principle, of one particular type of mediation—the prophetic'.[2] He distinguishes the psychology and the metaphysic of the prophetic consciousness, arguing that though the prophetic psychology is different from ours, this need not affect the validity of what the prophets declared.[3] If God does disclose His will to man, then we might reasonably expect the revelation to be mediated through the moral consciousness of man. Such mediation we have in the prophets and history has justified their essential message. What they did was to interpret events and so God's revelation of Himself has come to us as a blended unity of the human and the divine. Wheeler Robinson goes on to point out that in the Old Testament legal ordinances and moral teaching are likewise claimed as revealing the will of God. In these two we get the same inseparable unity of the human and the divine. 'The unifying idea is that all that is essentially true is a revelation of Yahweh's will.'[4]

[1] Op. cit., p. 306.
[2] Op. cit., p. 314.
[3] Cf. supra, p. 326.
[4] Op. cit., p. 319.

In his second essay Wheeler Robinson discusses the characteristic doctrines of the Old Testament under the headings: God, Man, Sin and Grace, the Judgement of History. Once again emphasis is laid on the fact that revelation came to Israel, not through the communication of abstract terms of doctrine but through the interpretation of events of history. With this division of the material it is worth while to compare the division Wheeler Robinson adopts in his book *Inspiration and Revelation in the Old Testament*, which he planned as prolegomena to a theology of the Old Testament but which is almost itself such a theology. It falls into two main sections. The first has three parts which remind us of the arrangement favoured by Procksch and Eichrodt, namely: God and Nature, God and Man, God and History. The second main section has four parts which, as has already been pointed out, are anticipated, though not worked out, by A. B. Davidson,[1] namely the Inspiration of the Prophet, Revelation through the Priest, Revelation in Wisdom, the Psalmists. In the last part the Psalms are shown to contain a response to the revelation of God made in the realms of nature, man, and history.

In a thoughtful conclusion to the book the author deals with the nature of revelation and points out that, as it comes through personal fellowship between God and man, we need not expect it to consist 'in a series of propositions *about* God, but a disclosure of God Himself, so far as the event can disclose Him'.[2] The only way to realize what God is saying to us in the Bible is 'to learn to live in the atmosphere of the Old Testament, and of its sequel the New Testament'.[2] 'It is just as true for the piety of the Old Testament as for that of the New that the generating experience of its revelation is that of a fellowship between God and man.'[2] It seems fair to infer from these words that, in Wheeler Robinson's judgement, a theology of the Old Testament cannot be written except by one who has a personal experience of the life of faith. At the very end of the book he seems to hesitate as to whether the content of the revelation (which would have

---

[1] *v. supra*, pp. 315–16.
[2] *Inspiration and Revelation in the Old Testament*, p. 281.

constituted his second volume) should be given in the form of a *Religionsgeschichte* or in the form of a series of propositions. In either form, he feels, the statement will fail to do justice to the living, dynamic religion of Israel. To guard in some degree against this risk of desiccation he repeats the warning he has just given in the words: 'Let us constantly remind ourselves that this religion, like any other, can be understood only from within, or through a sympathy that makes us its "resident aliens" (*gērîm*).'[1]

As a contrast to Wheeler Robinson's emphasis on the interpretation of history as being absolutely central to a theology of the Old Testament, we may now turn to the work of Wilhelm Vischer who, if one is right in pressing his language to logical conclusions, advocates a timeless revelation. As showing how extremes sometimes meet, it is possible to say that on this point at least Vischer and Eissfeldt are in agreement! It is not that Vischer denies the right of the historian and the literary critic to perform their several operations on the Old Testament. Ultimately, however, he does not take their results seriously. The central dogma of the Christian Church is that Jesus is the Christ. It is this dogma which for the Christian binds the testaments together, the Old Testament telling us what the Christ is and the New Testament telling us who He is. The testaments are taken together as equally bearing witness to Jesus Christ, Who stands in the centre of a circle of prophets and apostles all pointing to Him. It is recognized, of course, that in Jesus the Word was made flesh, but, since the Christian's attitude to Him must be one of faith, it is urged that there is no essential difference between the Christian and the Old Testament believer who looked forward to Christ in faith. That is to say, Vischer scarcely does justice to the fact that Christ did come. His view is at the opposite pole to the 'realized eschatology' of C. H. Dodd. It is in line with this that Vischer fails to see that the New Testament does not only tell us who Christ is; it also tells us more fully than the Old Testament what He is. Jesus transcended all the expectations and hopes of the Old Testament. He Himself was

[1] Op. cit., pp. 281–2.

more wonderful than anything men could have looked forward to on the basis of the Old Testament. Vischer, in fact, does not take seriously the circumstance that the Old Testament is the record of a *Heilsgeschichte*, a history of salvation. This means that, if the Word truly became flesh, thus entering into the stream of history, then inevitably, whether we like it or not, there had to be a before and an after. This may mean difficulty in constructing a neat, logical theology, but then the important thing is, not whether we can get the kind of theology we want, but whether our theology really does justice to what God has done. In one place[1] Vischer declares: 'We must read the Old Testament as it stands in the best sense of the word naïvely; not as those who know before they read what they will find there.' If he had always obeyed his own injunction, it might have made him pause before, as in so many cases, he interprets the Old Testament simply by placing a New Testament passage which refers to it side by side with it. The New Testament meaning is read into the Old Testament passage and so Vischer knows beforehand what the latter must mean. One of the best examples of Vischer's procedure is to be found in his treatment of the Melchizedek pericope in Genesis.[2]

One of the most difficult points in Vischer's exegesis of the Old Testament is to determine what he really means by witness to Christ in the Old Testament. In one place,[3] for example, he declares that 'the Christ Jesus of the New Testament stands precisely at the vanishing point of Old Testament perspective', which seems to mean that Christ is the fulfilment of the Old Testament hopes and expectations. In his discussion of Jacob's wrestling with the mysterious opponent at the Jabbok, however, he states roundly with Luther: 'Without the slightest contradiction this man was not an angel, but our Lord Jesus Christ, who is the eternal God and yet was to become a man whom the Jews would crucify.'[4] This is certainly very muddled theology.

---

[1] *Das Christuszeugnis des Alten Testaments*, i, p. 36, E.Tr., p. 30.
[2] Op. cit., pp. 159 ff., E.Tr., pp. 128 ff.
[3] Op. cit., p. 33, E.Tr., p. 28.
[4] Op. cit., p. 189, E.Tr., p. 153.

Surely 'Jesus Christ' is the name of the Incarnate Word, not the name of the Pre-existent Word. Once again a dubious interpretation of certain passages in the New Testament, notably in the Fourth Gospel, has been imposed upon the Old Testament. It is difficult to see why Vischer opposes the methods of pneumatic exegesis as he explicitly does.[1] He says: 'The Author has hidden Himself in such a manner in His work that no exegetical art can bring Him forth.' Surely Vischer relies too much on his own exegetical art. In fact there is about his interpretations something of the skill of the conjuror. In this connexion it is difficult to take quite seriously the methods of an exegete who sees a connexion between the fact that under the leadership of Joshua (N.T. Jesus) the Israelites crossed the Jordan dryshod into the land of promise and the fact that John the Baptist as the forerunner of a greater Jesus baptized Israelites in the Jordan to qualify them to enter the new land of promise.[2]

Generally speaking, Vischer's wholesale use of allegory implies that he is not taking history seriously and therefore not taking biblical revelation seriously. It is true that he denies that Jesus Christ is the embodiment of a Christ-idea[3] or that He is a necessary truth of reason.[4] Yet his own view, by virtually turning the historical revelation into something timeless and static, approximates more closely than Vischer realizes to the views which he rejects. There is more than a little intermixture of Greek thought in Vischer's theology. One of its most serious defects is that so much of the richness and colour of the Old Testament is lost and its ability to mirror the abundant variety of human life. There is something singularly unconvincing about a theology which leaves the solid ground of history and turns its often grim reality into a shadow play. If the Old Testament is allowed to speak for itself, it will often point forward beyond itself, but the standpoint of the Christian who looks back from

[1] Op. cit., pp. 36 ff., E.Tr., pp. 30 f.
[2] Op. cit. ii, pp. 40 ff.
[3] Op. cit., pp. 12 ff., E.Tr., p. 11.
[4] Op. cit., p. 19, E.Tr., p. 17.

the vantage ground where Christ has placed him is not the same as that of those who strained their eyes to catch glimpses of what God had in store. It is interesting to note that Vriezen in his trenchant criticism[1] of Vischer and his Dutch follower Miskotte points out that this side of the Dialectic Theology is akin to medieval theory and so, not surprisingly, is handled with sympathy by the Roman Catholic press. It is possible to turn the Logos theology into a kind of Christian *gnosis* inconsistent with the general sense of scripture. To speak of Jesus Christ in the Old Testament, as Vischer does, is to do less than justice to the uniqueness of Jesus Christ the Incarnate Son. The impression left on one by much of Vischer's work is that here we have the writing of a consummate preacher who is not quite theologian enough to realize the consequences of some of the things he says.[2]

One of the ablest and most illuminating contributions to biblical theology in recent years has been made by C. H. Dodd in his little book *The Bible To-day*. A considerable part of it deals with the Old Testament. Dodd has no doubt at all that the historical element in the Bible is fundamental to it. 'The Church . . . offers the Bible, in both testaments, as the authoritative record of a divine revelation'.[3] 'The Bible comes to us . . . as a revelation of divine truth in the form of a history of events, the principle of succession in time is essential to it.'[4] Like Wheeler Robinson, Dodd recognizes that the historical movement in the Old Testament makes it easier to face the difficulties in it.

Dodd's method of handling the material of the Old Testament is suggestive. He deals first with that part of the Old Testament history which is directly illuminated by the insights of the prophets. He shows how this prophetic understanding of contemporary history was used to interpret the great creative period which preceded it, in particular the period of the Exodus. He

---

[1] *Hoofdlijnen*, pp. 70 ff.

[2] In his criticism of Vischer the writer desires to acknowledge his indebtedness to the brilliant little monograph by Volkmar Herntrich, *Theologische Auslegung des Alten Testaments? Zum Gespräch mit Wilhelm Vischer* (1936). Herntrich pleads for, not a christological, but a trinitarian, understanding of the Old Testament (p. 32).

[3] *The Bible To-day*, p. 15.　　　　　　　　　　　　[4] Op. cit., p. 27.

recognizes frankly the legendary element in these stories but emphasizes the importance of legend as a source of historical knowledge. Speaking of the account of the call of Moses Dodd writes: 'We can recognize, under the legendary form, the same kind of personal experience as that described in the classical passage in Isaiah. . . . As with the prophets, the call is an intensely personal experience, but has an immediate reference to the needs and the destiny of a people.'[1] In the same way, in the stories about an even earlier time, the historical note is not absent. In the story of Abraham God speaks and a man responds and so history is made. 'We have learned from the prophets how the Word of God makes history when it comes to a man as the meaning of the facts of his experience, and through his response gives a new direction to events. Here at the beginning of the Bible story we recognize the prophetic pattern at its simplest.'[2]

When Dodd comes to deal with the New Testament, the controlling thought is that the Christian Church is the Israel of God which looks back to the people of God into which Israel was shaped under the divine providence by the events of history, yet as something which was incomplete and pointed forward beyond itself. The Church is Isaiah's righteous Remnant, Jeremiah's people of the New Covenant, Ezekiel's new Israel risen from the dead, the 'ransomed' (liberated) people of the Second Isaiah, Daniel's 'people of the saints of the Most High'.[3]

Dodd maintains that a notable difference between the testaments is that the Old Testament tells the story of a community, whereas the New Testament tells the story of a Person and only secondarily of a community. It is in Christ that the Church has the attributes of the people of God. In Christ the kingdom of God has established in the world 'a living centre of creative energy, embodied in the action of Jesus Himself'.[4] The judgement foretold by the prophets has indeed come but it has fallen primarily on the Judge, on Christ Himself, who is the fulfilment of the Suffering Servant of the Second Isaiah.

In Dodd's discussion of the importance of history as the

---

[1] Op. cit., pp. 55-6.
[2] Op. cit., pp. 57-8.
[3] Op. cit., p. 70.
[4] Op. cit., p. 93.

medium of revelation, he shows how God's Word is the creative factor in history. It comes in any situation 'as the interpretation of the situation, requiring action in that situation'.[1] It comes as a word of judgement, but, when it meets with response, also as a word of renewal. We cannot get away from the fact that God's Word came in the first instance to a particular people and to the individuals within that people. It is in the nature of an historical revelation that things should happen this way. The Word finally evoked a perfect response, not from the whole people of Israel, not even from the Remnant, but from a Person who in His life demonstrated what God wished life to be and speaks to us the Word with final authority, because He is the Word. 'Here, then, we have the perfect meeting of God with men, towards which the whole course of events was tending. It is at last realized in the unity of a single Personality; and henceforward this becomes the centre about which the whole movement of history turns.'[2]

Having sketched the *Heilsgeschichte* from Abraham to Christ Dodd points out that 'it is set in a framework which is not, in the same sense, historical'.[3] The early chapters of Genesis which tell of the Creation and the Fall, the Deluge and the Tower of Babel serve to universalize the historical experience of Israel. The strange history of Israel which culminated in Christ and the rise of the Christian Church as the New Israel has significance for the whole world of men who fell in Adam and are all included in the covenant made with Noah. In a similar way the symbolic picture of the Last Things universalizes the end of the story. The *Heilsgeschichte* leads to a goal which concerns the whole creation.

The Bible, then, gives us the record of God's ways with a particular community, but the story is set in a universal framework. We can go farther. If the Bible is by implication the story of Everyman, then the individual believer may expect to find himself mirrored in it and to receive God's guidance in judgement upon his course through life. We are here reminded of the way in which Procksch believes that the Old Testament can be used.

---

[1] Op. cit., p. 105.
[2] Op. cit., p. 111.
[3] Op. cit., p. 112.

But Dodd makes here an important point. The biblical history became universal history through the emergence of the Church Catholic and it is still in the Church that history in the fullest sense is made, because it is primarily in the Church that man meets with God and makes the response which God demands. It is within the Church that the Bible is read and the Sacraments administered in the context of an act of worship through which believers are made contemporary with the great creative events of history constituting God's revelation of His will. God can reveal Himself in other ways, but here in the Church He does speak and here man can respond.

Perhaps we may break off here. From the foregoing discussion of different views certain things may have become clearer. There is legitimate ground for difference of opinion as to precisely where the line between Old Testament theology and dogmatic theology should be drawn. But we are not entitled to speak of a theology, if we mean no more than a history of beliefs about God which men at different times have held. At least, if we do so, we should recognize that we are not using the word in its full sense. We have come across a welcome emphasis on the fact that revelation is mediated in historical events when, through the divine–human encounter, a Word is spoken to which a response is made. This intimate response of man's whole being to God is what the Bible means by knowledge of God, and the classic record of such knowledge of God, culminating in the complete knowledge which Christ possessed, is contained in the Bible. Old Testament theology is essentially part of the critique of this knowledge and it can only be rightly undertaken from an inside point of view. As Wheeler Robinson said, the Old Testament theologian must at least be a resident alien in Israel's religion. If this means that there must be an existential element in Old Testament theology then we shall just have to accept the consequences of that. Would it be scientific to shirk facing up to the real religious object of knowledge? It will speak about God in His relationship to a people created by Him to exhibit a new way of life. It is within the fellowship of the Christian Church which succeeded the fellowship of Israel that we can serve ourselves heirs to the Old Testament and, surveying as its freemen its majestic structure, rightly understand what it is. A theology of the Old Testament, however, will not seek to obscure the fact that Christ did not merely decode the Old Testament but fulfilled it. The ultimate unity of such a theology is to be found, not in this or that idea or institution but in the purpose of God to create through His living Word a people for Himself. A theology of the Old Testament will be worthy of the attention of men today in the measure in which it keeps close to life and does not operate merely at the academic level where thought and action are apt to be divorced.

NORMAN W. PORTEOUS

BIBLIOGRAPHY

BAAB, O. G. *The Theology of the Old Testament* (1949).

BURROWS, MILLAR. *An Outline of Biblical Theology* (1946).

DAVIDSON, A. B. *The Theology of the Old Testament* (1904) (strictly speaking outside the period).

DENTAN, R. C. *Preface to Old Testament Theology* (Yale Studies in Religion, xiv, 1950).

DODD, C. H. *The Bible To-day* (1946).

EICHRODT, W. *Theologie des Alten Testaments* (i, 1933; ii, 1935; iii, 1939).

— *Das Menschenverständnis des Alten Testaments* (1944).

HEMPEL, J. *Gott und Mensch im Alten Testament* (B.W.A.N.T. iii, 2, 1926).

— *Das Ethos des Alten Testament* (B.Z.A.W. lxvii, 1938).

JOHNSON, A. R. *The One and the Many in the Israelite Conception of God* (1942).

KNIGHT, H. *The Hebrew Prophetic Consciousness*—Part II. Theology (1947).

KÖNIG, E. *Theologie des Alten Testaments* (1922).

NORTH, C. R. *The Thought of the Old Testament* (1948).

PHYTHIAN-ADAMS, W. J. *The Call of Israel* (1934).

— *The Fulness of Israel* (1938).

— *The People and the Presence* (1942).

PROCKSCH, O. *Theologie des Alten Testaments* (1949–50). (Completed while the present work was in the press.)

ROBINSON, H. W. *Record and Revelation*: Section V. The Theology of the Old Testament (1938).

— *Inspiration and Revelation in the Old Testament* (1946).

ROWLEY, H. H. *The Relevance of the Bible* (1941).

— *The Rediscovery of the Old Testament* (1945).

— *The Biblical Doctrine of Election* (1950).

SELLIN, E. *Alttestamentliche Theologie auf religionsgeschichtlicher Grundlage* (1933).

VISCHER, W. *Das Christuszeugnis des Alten Testaments* (i, 1934, E.Tr., 1949; ii, 1942).

VRIEZEN, TH. C. *Hoofdlijnen der Theologie van het Oude Testament* (1949).

WRIGHT, G. E. *The Old Testament against its Environment* (1950).

The following articles and pamphlets, not all referred to in the text, will be found relevant:

EICHRODT, W. 'Hat die alttestamentliche Theologie noch selbständige Bedeutung innerhalb der alttestamentlichen Wissenschaft?' (*Z.A.W.* xlvii, 1929, pp. 83–91).

— 'Zur Frage der theologischen Exegese des Alten Testamentes.' (*Theologische Blätter*, April 1938, Sp. 73–87).

EISSFELDT, O. 'Israelitisch-jüdische Religionsgeschichte und alttestament-liche Theologie' (*Z.A.W.* xliv, 1926, pp. 1–12).

HELLBARDT, H. 'Die Auslegung des Alten Testaments als theologische Disziplin' (*Theologische Blätter*, Juli/August 1937, Sp. 129–43).

HERNTRICH, V. *Theologische Auslegung des Alten Testaments? Zum Gespräch mit Wilhelm Vischer* (1936).

NORTH, C. R. 'Old Testament Theology and the History of Hebrew Religion' (*Scottish Journal of Theology*, vol. ii, No. 2, 1949, pp. 113–26).

PORTEOUS, N. W. 'Towards a Theology of the Old Testament'. (*Scottish Journal of Theology*, vol. i, No. 2, 1947, pp. 136–49).

— 'Semantics and Old Testament Theology' (*O.T.S.* viii, 1950, pp. 1–14).

STEUERNAGEL, C. 'Alttestamentliche Theologie und alttestamentliche Religionsgeschichte' (B.Z.A.W. xli, 1925, pp. 266–73).

WEISER, A. 'Die theologische Aufgabe der alttestamentlichen Wissenschaft' (B.Z.A.W. lxvi, 1936, pp. 207–24).

ZIMMERLI, W. *Das Menschenbild des Alten Testamentes* (Theologische Existenz heute: Neue Folge 14, 1949).

Other relevant literature is detailed on pages 325 and 326 of the text.

XII
EPILOGUE

THE OLD TESTAMENT AND THE MODERN WORLD

EARLIER chapters in this volume have dealt with a variety of subjects from the angle of the specialist. We have been shown in popular summary the kind of opinions reached by the students of archaeology, literary criticism, philology, and religion. Each and all of these may be profoundly interesting, and may open to us a world which is too often hidden from us. We have learnt much about the past, and something of a type of mind which is widely different from our own. It is never easy to think ourselves into the mental position of a bygone age, and even contemporaries in countries close at hand present us with psychological problems which to us seem insoluble. We may hope that the studies of the scholars who have contributed to this volume may have done something to enlighten us, and to let us feel what it was like to have been an ancient Israelite, living in Old Testament times.

But when we have done all this there still remains a pressing question: What is the use of all this for us today? All the characters mentioned in the Old Testament have been dead for thousands of years. The cultures and civilizations of which our records tell us have long since vanished from the face of the earth, and represent a stage in human development which has been superseded for centuries. Just as the archaeologist, excavating some oriental mound, finds the remains of one city superimposed on those of another, and may go deeper till he has a whole series on the same site, so one age after another has left its traces on history and has disappeared under the mass of material laid over it by later periods. It would seem as if we had little or nothing in common with these old documents and the story they tell us, interesting as these may be to us as relics of the past. And still we continue to study the Old Testament.

The fact is that the Old Testament is sacred literature for two of the world's great religions, though for one it is only a part of that literature, and cannot be separated from the rest. That is to say, that in it men recognize a unique revelation of God, an expression of His nature, His will, and His methods of dealing with men. Further, it may be expected to show us the truth about ourselves and our relation to Him. It may safely be said that most of the contributors to the present volume, perhaps all, would regard the Old Testament as the very word of God, ranking second only to the person of Christ Himself. It is, therefore, natural to assume that it is in some way or other valid for all generations of mankind and for all types of humanity. It has been said of Old Testament prophecy that it is a statement of eternal truth, presented in a form adapted to particular occasions. While this principle is less obvious in some other parts than it is in the prophetic writings, it still holds good. We may believe that the whole of the sacrificial system has been superseded, but some would find in it a foreshadowing of the Christian Atonement, and it certainly shows that the gulf between man and God, cleft by human sin, is not easily or lightly to be crossed.

For the Christian, the supreme importance of the Old Testament lies in the fact that it prepares for, and in large measure explains, the New Testament. As the late S. A. Cook so often insisted, the Bible as a whole presents us with a religious continuum in which there are clearly marked stages but no actual gap. We have often noticed how much in the Gospels is taken for granted. Nowhere do we find any attempt to prove the existence of God or the fact that He is one and there is no other. Jesus and His Jewish contemporaries were entirely agreed in their monotheism, however much they may have differed in other matters. Further, there was no dispute as to the moral character and demands of the one living and true God. In both these points the Jew stood alone in the world of his day. Everywhere else men recognized numerous objects of worship, and everywhere else the list included gods, goddesses, or spirits which could not be called moral by any stretch of language. It was to the religion of the Old Testament that the Jew owed this unique position, and it has so completely dominated the thought of the western world that few people are conscious of any distinction between sin and vice.

But there is another feature of the Old Testament attitude which is sometimes more open to challenge. It laid great stress on personality, human and divine. It could conceive of God only as a person, differing in many ways from human persons, but still a person. There is no room for any form of Pantheism in Jewish or Christian faith. It is a striking fact that this insistence on personality is not natural to the Indo-European mind. The Vedanta philosophy offers the most thorough type of Pantheism which we know, and in Greek thought we can see how easily men's minds drifted in the same direction, reaching in Neo-platonism a point not far removed from that taken by Indian thought. Certain modern developments in the west show signs of the same influence, and we constantly need to get back to the view which dominates the Old Testament. We can never allow Amos and Kant to be overshadowed by Plato and Hegel.

The Christian will freely admit, indeed he will claim, that the revelation of God in the Old Testament is incomplete, and that its precepts needed modification. What is more, the standards of life and conduct presented in the Old Testament vary a good deal. We have an instance of human sacrifice in the Book of Judges, which is passed over without explicit condemnation; in the eighth century the practice is regarded with such horror that it is indicated as one of the offences for which the punishment of exile was imposed (2 Kings xxi). At times we meet with discrepancies which are theological rather than ethical; in the story of David it is recorded that he took a census of the population. This was held to be a serious offence, probably because the actual size of the nation was a piece of knowledge which God had reserved for Himself, and it was punished with a severe pestilence which automatically invalidated the figures obtained by the census. In 2 Sam. xxiv. 1 it is God Himself who incites David to this sin, in order that He may bring trouble on Israel. But in 1 Chron. xxi. 1 the tempter is Satan, a change which strongly suggests that there had been an advance in the understanding of God. The second historian, it seems, could not endure the thought that God was in any way responsible for moral evil, nor could He induce men to sin simply that He might punish them. Even the prophet Ezekiel held the more primitive view, and actually ascribed to God's orders the institution of human sacrifice (Ezek. xx. 25 f.).

In these and other cases we surely have an illustration of the principle cited above; the revelation is always presented in a form adapted to a particular situation. We have to take into account a great deal of what has been said in earlier sections of this book. One of the important factors in the situation is the mind of the people to whom the revelation was first imparted. Too dazzling a light would have blinded them; it must come as the dawn and not as a lightning flash.

Other applications of this principle are less striking but none the less important. The language in which the Old Testament has come down to us is very different from our own or, indeed, from any Indo-European speech. It often has grammatical nuances which we feel as we read the Hebrew (or, in a few cases, the Aramaic), but which cannot be expressed in English grammatical forms. When, for example, a speaker or writer wished to emphasize some verb or in other ways to call special attention to it, he repeated the basic root in a form which admits of no inflection whatever, and is hard to define syntactically. Translators have always been in difficulties when trying to render this idiom. It sometimes appears in our versions as 'surely', but it does not necessarily imply certainty. It is commonly employed in legal phraseology, much as a headline might be used to indicate the special subject of a clause in some legal enactment. It means that the mind of the hearer or reader must for the moment be concentrated on that particular idea. Tense-forms, again, do not primarily indicate past, present, or future, but rather the mode of action; we may compare the difference between the Imperfect, the Aorist, and the Perfect in classical Greek.

We have also to take historical circumstances into account. In the narratives contained in the books from Joshua to 2 Chronicles we can see fairly well what was happening, and that discoveries of the last hundred years have given us much light from other lands and peoples which were contemporary with the events described in the Bible. In other cases we lack exact knowledge of the time or occasion to which particular parts of the Old Testament were directed. This is especially noticeable in the Psalter, and attempts to date individual Psalms are seldom widely accepted. But it is just those parts of the Old Testament in which we have the most general statements of truth that such uncertainty occurs, and it is usually a simple matter to see how the writer's point of view fits our own conditions.

More important, perhaps, than any of these points is the fact that we have to allow also for the individual character of the writer. Granted that the Old Testament is a God-given book, produced by divine inspiration, we must recognize the general principle that God works always through human agents, and that without eclipsing their personality. Some of the Old Testament writers are as well known to us as any persons in the ancient world, even though we may have fewer facts about their lives. We are impressed by the wide differences in temperament, even between men who were contemporaries of one another. There is a strong contrast between Hosea and Isaiah, or between Jeremiah and Ezekiel. There may well be differences of opinion as to the extent to which the human channel has shaped the divine message, but it can hardly be maintained that there was no influence at all, unless we are prepared for a purely mechanical inspiration or deny obvious facts. This is not a mere question of literary style; it goes much deeper, and a just appreciation of it demands insight into the character of the writers with an estimate of their peculiarities. Critical study of the prophets, for example, has shown us that their utterances were usually short, sometimes very short, and that each was the result of a separate act of divine inspiration in which the personality of the speaker was possessed by the divine Spirit to utter words which were in themselves effective and produced the events which they predicted. Such, at least, was the view held by the prophets themselves and their contemporaries, and we have no reason to doubt its correctness. But the prophet's own personality still contributed to the form of the utterance.

All this means that before we can see what bearing the Old Testament has on our own age, we shall have to allow for much that is temporary, racial, and personal, in the form which truth assumes in its pages. This is not an easy or a simple task, and requires of every serious interpreter a long course of study and the ability to think himself into the mind and circumstances of another age and of another people. Of course he may make mistakes; a sympathetic imagination, the *sine qua non* of a successful expositor, may easily go too far or take the wrong road, but this is a risk which has to be taken, and it is unlikely that every person who handles the Old Testament will make the same error.

Further, we have to consider the particular audience to which the divine message was in each case addressed. A primitive mind can recognize a truth only when it is expressed in a primitive form. This is not simply a matter of language, grammar, and vocabulary, but of the thought-shape. It is no use to offer a small child a student's text-book on Ethics; the training must be done through simpler means, often through stories which an adult mind would class only as parables. But the truth is there, and can be restated and adapted to each stage of the developing intelligence.

We may take one or two examples. It has long been recognized that it is difficult to reconcile in detail the two main parts of the creation story in Gen. i and ii. On the one hand we have a dignified, philosophical, scientific, almost evolutionary statement, in which the divine act of 'creation', i.e. the introduction of a totally new factor which cannot be explained by anything earlier, occurs only at three crucial points, the provision of sheer matter, the introduction of animal life, and the formation of that personality which man shares only with God Himself. What follows is a simple story in which God models the objects of creation as a potter fashions his vessels of clay. Many people, it is true, succeed in harmonizing the two, but to others the only valid explanation of the facts seems to be that the one is addressed to a highly 'sophisticated' audience, while the other is intended for hearers who are still in the intellectual nursery. But (and this is what matters) both insist that the physical universe and man himself are directly and expressly made by God; He is the author of all being other than His own, and He is eternal and self-existent. That truth is as valid today as it was when the Genesis stories were first told, though for its own sake the modern mind might need to have it expressed in terms which did not correspond to those either of Gen. i or of Gen. ii.

We may take another example from the chapter which immediately follows the story of creation. This describes the 'Fall', to use the common term. It gives us a picture of all the essential elements in temptation. First the forbidden thing is seen to be desirable; it will add to the fullness and richness of life as a human mind may regard it. In the second place it is within reach, the 'temptee' can simply put out her hand and take it. And in the third place there is the prospect of impunity; there has been fear of unpleasant consequences, but these are now felt to be avoidable if they exist at all, and, if not avoidable, then negligible. Again, we have in narrative form adapted to an early stage of development a statement of truth which is valid for all time, though we and others would naturally express it in different forms.

Of all the elements in religion that which today seems to need more emphasis than any other is the fact of sin. The modern world does not like any reference to it, though it seems to grow more and more tolerant of the thing itself. It offers and readily accepts many 'explanations' of what men used to regard with horror, and tries thereby to shelve responsibility. Yet sin is a universal fact of experience which all religions have to face, and the revolt against a theological conception of the thing is largely based on ignorance or muddled thinking. For every religion necessarily sets before its adherents an ideal relationship between the worshipper and that which he worships. No two religions present the same ideal, since no two religions agree as to the character of that which they worship, but there always is and must be an ideal. Now in human experience (and this applies to *all* religions) the ideal is never wholly reached or permanently maintained; there is always something in human life or character which interferes. That something, universal in man's experience, is *sin*. Of course the acts or states of mind which constitute sin will vary enormously; there is and can be no list of deeds which every religion would recognize as sin. But sin is always present as a real fact of experience, and until men recognize it there can be no recovery of the religious life, no diagnosis of the diseases which threaten humanity, and no hope of finding or applying a successful remedy.

Now it may fairly be claimed that the Old Testament has more to say about sin than about any other subject; it is equally true that few if any collections of religious literature have as much to say about it as does the Old Testament. Our dictionaries show us a long list of words describing it, each suggesting a special aspect. Sometimes it is a failure to reach an ideal, a missing of the mark. Sometimes it is something empty or vain, sometimes a twist in human nature or action, sometimes definite rebellion, pride, or self-will. And there are two kinds of result which accrue from it. It is important to bear in mind the distinction between the two, for there are few sides of Bible thought which are subject to more confusion than what we may call the 'punishment' of sin.

In the first place there is an inevitable and inexorable consequence of sin. This is the 'punishment' in the strict sense of the term. It cannot be too strongly stressed that there is no such thing as impunity. There are 'laws' in the moral and spiritual world which are just as rigid and certain in their application as those which 'control' the behaviour of physical nature. They may be more complicated and difficult to understand, but they are there. The Old Testament insists again and again that there is no escape from the consequences. The man who sins has let loose in the world a force which will, sooner or later, return, boomerang-fashion, and strike down the person who has sent it out. Our knowledge of the material world and its working is immeasurably greater than that of pre-exilic Israel, and we should state the matter for ourselves in rather different terms. Dominated by the conception of personality, the ancient Hebrew saw in the consequence of every deed a direct act of divine vengeance, and shaped his language accordingly. Of course it may be possible to modify in some way the effect of previous action, but only to a limited extent, and, apart from such action, there is no means of averting the consequences which follow disregard of God's laws.

But the inevitable suffering is not the only effect, or even the worst effect of sin. In the Hebrew view, especially as it is stated by great prophets like Jeremiah and Hosea, the most serious result is a breach in the relations which should exist between man and God. Again and again in Law, in Prophets, and in Psalms, we find the attitude of God to His people described as love. Sometimes it is the love of husband for wife, and sometimes it is the love of father for child. But always it is a love which not merely gives, but also asks for return, a love which cannot be satisfied, and which remains incomplete, until it is mutual. Now it is the rupture in this relationship of love which forms the real horror of sin, for it is here that the failure to reach the religious ideal most strongly manifests itself. At the same time, unlike the 'punishment', it is remediable and in a sense avoidable. For the relationship can always be restored. A sinner can always 'repent', i.e. turn back to his God, and seek for readmittance into the true fellowship. It is this which constitutes *forgiveness*, which has nothing to do with the remission of the necessary suffering. One of the misconceptions of the modern world is the idea that people can be 'let off' if they truly 'repent', and it cannot be too strongly insisted that this is not the essence of Old Testament teaching. Man must endure the effects of his own sin, as he must endure the effects of any act which ignores the principles of physical nature. But God is always more ready to *forgive* than man is to seek forgiveness. It may be remarked in passing that we have here the basis of New Testament thought, but with one striking and all-important difference. In Old Testament religion, as in every other except Christianity, the restoration can be made on the initiative of the sinner himself; he must first turn back to God to find forgiveness, while in Christian belief it is not man but God who takes the first step and makes the recovery of an ideal relationship possible. That is one of the truths which the Cross of Christ sets before us.

One further remark in this connexion must be made. The Old Testament frequently seems to represent God as a vindictive master who violently resents and arbitrarily punishes any offence against His will. Here we have an example of the language and still more of the thought-shape of Israel. We soon learn to recognize that the range of emotion covered by a Hebrew word may be very different from that which is indicated by the nearest English expression. The word rendered most naturally 'fear', for example, covers much more than what we mean by that term. 'Shame' often indicates a feeling which would not be rightly expressed by that term in modern speech. So, too, 'anger', even in its strongest forms, is used in general to express the divine reaction to human sin, though, as we have seen, deeper insight shows that it is often much nearer to extreme suffering than to what we call anger. At the same time we have to remember that the ancient Hebrew inevitably tended to interpret God's feelings by his own. To him, with his concentration on personality, it seemed as if the 'punishment', that is the inevitable suffering which follows sin, were an arbitrary penalty imposed by offended authority, and in their language the Old Testament speakers and writers often plead for remission of that penalty and for a return to the favour of their God. Nevertheless, if we look below the surface, and especially if we consider the greatest exponents of Hebrew thought, we realize that the essential message of the Old Testament, as valid today as when it was first delivered, embodies two essential elements, the Rule of Law and the Love of God.

We may pass on to consider another aspect of Old Testament belief and teaching. That is its moral element. Here, again, we have to recognize apparent inequalities in the course of the Bible. It is frequently pointed out that certain acts are recorded without reprobation which a more developed conscience would strongly condemn. In Deuteronomy, for example (cf., for example, vii. 24), the complete extermination of Israel's predecessors in Palestine is contemplated. Not only was this measure never carried into effect; it offends our modern sense of right and wrong. We sometimes have a kind of ethical correction in the pages of the Old Testament itself. The slaughter of Baal-worshippers by Jehu is highly commended by the contemporary historian (2 Kings x. 30), but is emphatically condemned a century or more later by the prophet Hosea (Hos. i. 4 f.), and is held to be a reason for the destruction of the northern kingdom. Here is a clear case of a growing moral sense which never reaches its full development in the Old Testament itself. The attitude towards sex relations, too, offers an instructive example of different standards. Adultery is always condemned, but we suspect that in the earlier stages it was regarded primarily as an intolerable violation of a husband's rights. Fornication, on the other hand, especially when it had some religious sanction (as it too often had in some Israelite circles), passes without special comment in such narratives as that of Gen. xxxviii, while prophets like Amos and Hosea contemplate it with horror. Again we can suggest only one explanation; there is a gradual revelation of the divine will as men were able to bear it.

At the same time, the Old Testament presents us with moral standards which have been universally accepted, even if they are not universally observed. The 'Ten Commandments' are still used as the minimum of what should be observed by every person, though the religious prescriptions with which the list begins are apt to take a second place. But murder, adultery, theft, and slander are still condemned by the modern world in theory, if not always in practice, while most people would admit that covetousness lies at the root of more than one of the other offences. But the Decalogue is far from being the only statement of an ethical standard which the Old Testament contains; it is, as has just been suggested, the minimum, and not the complete ideal. A far higher position is indicated in Job xxxi, where the sufferer, contemplating the possibility of stating his case before God, makes a great oath of purgation, listing the sins of which he has not been guilty. Here we note that the principle of the Tenth Commandment is carried to considerable lengths, and in some ways anticipates that 'fulfilment of the law' which we normally associate with the Sermon on the Mount. Certain points may be especially noted. In *vv.* 13–15 we have an attitude towards the slave which has few parallels in the ancient world. He has to receive exactly the same just treatment as the master would demand for himself, and the reason is that he can claim the same human nature, created by the same God. The needs of the destitute make a demand which Job has never refused to meet. Rich as he has been, he has never set a high value on money. Not only has he refrained from taking vengeance on those who have wronged him; he has never even felt any satisfaction when disaster has overtaken them from some other quarter. Here we have a description of the ethical life which goes far beyond the standard required by the Decalogue.

Yet even such a standard as that which is presented in Job xxxi does not exhaust the ethical principles involved in Old Testament teaching. It is notorious that a mere code, however complete it may be from the casuistic angle, can never by itself cover all possible contingencies, and is liable to be misused. When first promulgated it may be entirely suitable for existing circumstances, but other occasions are certain to arise when its use may violate the very principles which it was intended to maintain. Further, a measure which originally met a real grievance or deficiency may later become in itself an obstacle to moral progress. Of this we have more than one example in the Old Testament, and from time to time we find in the Gospels further expansion of the essential principles; the most obvious example is to be seen in that section of the Sermon on the Mount which deals with the contrast between the old law and the new (Mt. v. 17–48). We may select two examples. The law of divorce, imposing on the husband the duty of supplying the dismissed wife with a certificate, was in the first instance a protection, enabling the woman to marry again without incurring a charge of adultery. With the more perfect conception of the marriage relationship which our Lord stated, divorce in itself, especially if followed by remarriage of either party, comes under the condemnation of adultery. The old law had served its purpose for centuries, but was adapted to a stage in ethical development which had to be superseded by a nobler conception.

As a second example we may take the familiar *Lex Talionis*, 'an eye for an eye and a tooth for a tooth'. Originally this was clearly intended to be a limitation on vengeance and on the retribution which an injured party might claim. In future none might exact seven lives for one, as Cain might (Gen. iv. 15); still less the seventy for one demanded by Lamech (Gen. iv. 24). Again, the perfect law required that there should be no thought of vengeance whatever, but a willingness to endure any injury. After all, it is in the long run not the injured party, but the wrongdoer who is the real sufferer.

Within the Old Testament itself the problem is solved in another way. The prophets go past the actual words of the law to the spirit lying behind them. As we have seen, the law could be used, and too often was used, to defeat its proper ends. It forbade stealing, but there were ways of acquiring the property of others which were not legally stealing. We have reason to suppose that the laws of debt were employed for this purpose. An unfortunate farmer would find himself in difficulties, perhaps owing to a bad season, a raid by enemies, or his own extravagance. He would apply to a money-lender and give what he had as a pledge. If he failed to repay, the pledge would remain the property of the richer man. We have complaints of the way in which men of substance were able to get together large estates, depriving the original owners of the means of livelihood. There is a general statement in Isa. v. 8–10, and an account of a brutal eviction in Mic. ii. 9–10. A peasant or his family might even be reduced to slavery by such a process; we have in 2 Kings iv. 1–7 a story which may be taken as illustrating the kind of thing that might happen almost at any time. There is no expression of anger against the money-lender; he is simply a part of the countryman's normal background. Apparently judges might be bribed, and so small a gift as a pair of shoes would secure a verdict and even hand a man over to one who would enslave him (Amos ii. 6, viii. 6). It would seem that some kind of legal process was necessary before the debt could be claimed, and this suggests that all was done according to the forms of law. But to men like Amos, Isaiah, and Micah, the whole system involved breaking the spirit of the law which forbade theft, even though the letter of that and other laws were strictly observed. The Decalogue may have sufficed for a simple order of society, like that of Israel in the Mosaic age, but it needed to be reinterpreted and restated

as the economic order grew more complicated. That is characteristic of the true teaching of the Old Testament; it is the spirit
that matters, not the letter, and St. Paul summed up the principle
when he said 'the letter killeth, but the spirit maketh alive'
(2 Cor. iii. 6). This is one of those truths which the modern
world would do well to bear in mind.

So the ethic of the prophetic school was not based primarily
on any formal list of rules, though they would have been recognized as offering some expression of deeper principles. Their
teaching is summed up in a single verse in the Book of Micah:
'What doth the Lord require of thee, but to do justly and to love
mercy, and to walk humbly with thy God?' (vi. 8). Here we
note three stages. The first is that of action; the prophetic
demand is for fair, honest, and truthful dealing as between man
and man. But this does not stand alone, nor is it to be controlled by
legal precepts. It must be based on an attitude of soul, which is
indicated by one of the richest words in the whole vocabulary of
the Old Testament, a word here, as often, disguised by the
English 'mercy'. It is a form of love, that form of love which,
says Hosea, God prefers to sacrifice (Hos. vi. 6). But it is very
far from being a mere romantic sentiment. It is the kind of love
which is imposed by some relationship between two or more
people. It is the proper feeling of a father for a son, a son for a
father, a brother for a brother, a wife for a husband, a worshipper
for his God and God for His worshippers. It thus has a strongly
ethical content; it implies an obligation. One of our best-known
British scholars renders it as 'leal love', another finds the nearest
word to be 'devotion'. The truth is that it is all these and much
more. It involves consecration to a personality, a consecration
which will manifest itself in practical life. He who has this
quality and this attitude to those about him will be in no danger
of failing to meet the demand for justice.

But it is to be noted that the prophet does not stop here.
'Mercy' is something which is normally beyond the reach of the
common man, or, indeed, of any man. It is to be attained only
by unbroken contact with that God in whom alone it exists in its
perfection; man must 'walk humbly' with his God. Here we

have an adumbration of the feature which constitutes the unique feature of the moral teaching of our Lord. That uniqueness does not lie in the type of conduct which is produced in men; other great ethical systems set similar ideals before their pupils. The real distinctiveness of the Christian ethic lies in the means whereby the good life is to be attained. It is not, as it is in all other systems, the result of long training, stern repression of human desires and even instincts, but a change in the outlook and direction of life. In other words, it does not say 'Be good and you may get into contact with God', but 'get into contact with God and He will help you to be good'. It is an ethic, not of repression but of sublimation, and so avoids one of the supreme dangers which threaten men when they seek merely to attain a moral standard by their own efforts. And while this is not obvious in the greater part of the Old Testament, there are already (as in the passage cited) adumbrations of a truth which was fully stated only by Jesus and is still valid as the essential basis of any sound ethical teaching.

We have looked, then, at some of the religious truths of the Old Testament which need to be applied to our own age as much as to any other. But there is another aspect of the Old Testament which is apt to be overlooked except by people who are ready to study closely the principles underlying the social history of mankind. To appreciate this, it is necessary to take a cursory glance at the whole history of Israel down to the exile.

The Old Testament narrative is unintelligible until we remember that during the historical period we have mentioned there were two elements in the population. On the one hand we have the older inhabitants, designated by a number of different terms, Canaanites, Amorites, Hittites, and the rest; the full list includes seven names. For our present purpose, however, they may be regarded as constituting only a single factor in the situation. They were all more or less settled peoples, living the life of the farmer, city-dweller, and trader. They had a comparatively high standard of culture, and forms of religion which were characteristic of the nearer east. They had built cities, and though they had little or no political unity among themselves, each small place had developed some kind of organization. Nominally all had been under the domination of Egypt since the middle of the fifteenth century B.C., but, as in most early territorial empires, effective control was apt to be spasmodic, and even in times of stress the various little states were largely left to manage their own affairs. It is curious that we hardly hear of Egypt between the Exodus and the time of Solomon. But in every state there was some political and social organization, and in the main these were all of the one pattern, the pattern which was usual among agricultural communities in the ancient world. We may assume that this pattern included a system of civil law corresponding (with, perhaps, minor local variations) to that which we find in Mesopotamia, Anatolia, and, in a comparatively simple form, in that early Israelite code which is contained in Exod. xxi. 1–xxiii. 9. The common ideas of social life seem to have been much like those which we find elsewhere, with great stress on property of various kinds, and respect and obedience for authority, whether it were that of a 'king' or of 'elders', to use modern terms, whether it were autocratic or oligarchical.

Over against this we have the culture of the Aramaean invaders. The patriarchal narratives attest the fact that the genuine Israelite tradition was that of the pastoral nomad, and this was clearly the level of culture which is to be found all through the period between the Exodus and the entry into Palestine. The type of social order is today best exemplified by that of the Beduin, though we may allow for minor differences. Certainly there was no fixed home, and no solid building. Members of the tribe lived in tents, and were always liable to be on the move. Their property consisted of cattle (probably goats with a few sheep), and the conditions of life made it necessary to travel from one place to another in order to find sustenance for the flocks. The country of the 'wanderings' is far too dry to produce regular crops, though in favoured spots and in especially rainy seasons it may occasionally be possible to grow a little grain. But this cannot be regarded as a regular occupation or a normal means of life. Private property hardly exists; the flocks belong to the whole group. In contrast to the settled communities, the greatest stress is laid on the value of personality. This is essential in conditions where living is in any case hard, and there is a real danger that a group may be weakened or even disappear through lack of free members. In theory, all free members of the group are equal, though in times of emergency a strong individual will naturally come to the front and assume the duties of leadership. But it is his qualities which command respect, not his position or his ancestry. Except in such emergencies, no man has a right to command another or to insist on services rendered to him by his fellow-tribesmen. It will be remembered that the horror of Israel's residence in Egypt lay in the forced labour (an institution for which neither English nor Welsh has a term) which the Pharaohs exacted from the free nomadic shepherds. Here was a people who, in economic structure, in social outlook, and in culture, differed as widely as possible from the settled communities of western Palestine.

The centrifugal tendencies of the little Palestinian states made possible the conquest of the land by the Aramaean invaders from the eastern wilderness. But, as the opening chapters of Judges tell us, that conquest was neither sudden nor complete. It seems to have been most successful in the central mountain range, where the Ephraimite group established itself. In the better agricultural districts, however, especially on the coastal plain and in the Esdraelon area, the newcomers failed to expel or even conquer their predecessors, and had to settle down alongside of them where they were able to make good their footing at all. In the story of Deborah and Barak (Judges iv, v) we have a good illustration of actual conditions in and about the Kishon valley.

It was almost inevitable that, as time passed, the invaders should gradually accommodate themselves to the conditions which they found already in existence. There is plenty of evidence to show that they adopted to a large extent the culture and the religion of their predecessors and neighbours. But the process of assimilation was never quite complete. Palestine has always been exposed to raids and even invasion from the east, and in other cases the new element has been completely absorbed in the old. The case of Israel appears to be unique. Under Moses they had learnt to recognize a unity among themselves which was not due to a unified political organization, or even to a common ancestry. It rested on the fact that they had a common religion, a single national God who claimed the allegiance of every branch of the people, wherever they might be and on whatever scale they were living. Neglect of this God meant disunion, for the local fertility spirits of Palestine encouraged only a kind of village patriotism, and the high gods who were also worshipped in various places were too nearly universal to form a bond between different groups. But when men came at the call of the national God, with whom they had entered into a Covenant under the leadership of Moses, they could gather in strength, and had, too, the inspiration which enabled them to infuse the dreaded battle-panic into any foe who tried to withstand them. This is the key to the events described in the Book of Judges, with its repeated cycle of apostasy, oppression, repentance, and deliverance.

But the newcomers did more than defend themselves, they did much to protect other elements in the population. Only one Palestinian enemy is included in the list given in the Book of Judges; all but Sisera came from outside the land; they were Moabites, Ishmaelites, 'Easterners', Midianites, or Ammonites. Deliverance came always from Israel, united under her single God and fighting with wild *élan* under His inspiration. They thus attained a unique position in the land, and succeeded to a large extent in imposing on the mixed community their own ideas and their own traditions. It may almost be said that the Israelites conquered western Palestine, not by exterminating their predecessors but by defending them.

But, about the beginning of the twelfth century B.C. there came an enemy who was not to be overthrown by the old methods. This was the Philistine people, the last relics of the old Aegean civilization, who, driven from their ancient homes by the ancestors of those whom we know as Greeks, moved southwards along the coast towards Egypt. Turned back on the frontiers of that country, they made their new home in the coastal plain of Palestine, compelling at least one section of the Israelite group (the tribe of Dan) to take refuge in the far north, and establishing some kind of authority over the central range, though they never crossed the Jordan. The valour of Saul did something to check them, but it was the genius of David which secured a final victory over the invaders from the north and west. For the first time Palestine was united as a political entity, and maintained a more or less independent existence for some four centuries.

By the time of David's death the fusion of the two peoples seems to have been fairly complete. Such divisions as still existed were local, and perhaps to some extent tribal, but the separate layers could not easily be distinguished from one another. A common language had emerged, in which (as has happened in other cases of minority conquest) the speech of the older inhabitants had asserted itself, while that of the invaders had simply enriched the vocabulary. The sense of unity produced by a common religion and a common tradition was strong enough to outweigh the political division between north and south; the eighth-century prophets largely ignore it, except in so far as it may be necessary to mention individuals, or in special circumstances such as the attempt made by Pekah to force Ahaz into an anti-Assyrian coalition.

At the same time there was a real cleft in the nation. While a large part of the country, including all the good arable land, was occupied by people who had settled down to a life based on agriculture and trade, there were others who were still in the nomad stage or raised little above it. This was particularly true to the east of the Jordan (cf. the narrative of Num. xxxii), and to the south, where the agricultural land merged through a pastoral country into the comparative desert of northern Arabia. Here there was little temptation to adopt the theories and practices of the Canaanite cities, either in religion or in the social order. In the west it seems fairly clear that the local cults had exercised very considerable influence on that of Israel's God, which was in some ways hardly to be distinguished from the worship offered to the old Baals, except in the name of the Deity. The east and south, however, tended to maintain the Mosaic tradition in comparative purity, uncontaminated by intimate contact with the more highly developed civilization of the agricultural community. It was not an accident that Elijah and Amos, two of the first great champions of the old tradition in Church and State, came from the east and south respectively, not from the agricultural areas of western Palestine.

But even among the more highly developed community there were forces which made for the Mosaic tradition. We hear of Nazirites, who would not touch the grape or its products, since the vine, even more than corn, was a symbol of the cultivated land. They insisted on allowing their hair to grow, for razors are no part of the wilderness life, and we gather that the fierce warriors who followed Deborah also let their long locks stream in the wind of their charge. In the ninth and seventh centuries we meet with Rechabites, a group who, like the Nazirites, eschewed the vine, but also refused to live in solid houses, maintaining the tent-life of the pastoral age in the midst of a city-dwelling people. But above all there were the prophets, men (and sometimes women) who were subject to abnormal psychological experiences. These were always attributed to the access of the divine Spirit, which took possession of them and directed their acts and words. Prophets tended to gather into bands and seem to have had a recognized place in some of the sanctuaries. Their reputation was not high; it has happened elsewhere that 'holy' men may be revered on religious grounds but shunned and almost despised from the social point of view. But, whatever their faults may have been, these men did stand for the genuine Israelite tradition in religion and social life, insisting on the validity of that demand for the rights of humanity which so clearly marked the nomad Israelite in contrast with the Canaanite settled community.

Originally the Hebrew monarchy was an attempt also to maintain the old tradition in a centralized state. Israel loved to think of David as the shepherd lad who, through sheer personal ability, had raised himself first to high military rank and then to the throne itself. To a late period in his reign he maintained that respect for human rights which nomad Israel had so valued. The story of his great sin with Bathsheba is one of the most significant in the Old Testament. It shows the courage and stern devotion to principle which marked the God-inspired prophet, and, still more, the humility and contrition with which the king accepted Nathan's denunciation. Such an attitude would have been inconceivable anywhere else in the ancient east, and the facts are the more remarkable since the victim of royal oppression was not even an Israelite by race. But it is clear that circumstances compelled even David to assume a position which was in some ways nearer to that of normal autocracy; an example may be seen in the king's bodyguard, largely recruited from other peoples, which stood in contrast to the national levies. David's wealth, on the other hand, may well have been accumulated without wrong done to his own subjects, for he held control over practically all the great trade routes of the ancient east, and could levy tolls on every caravan passing between Asia or Europe and Egypt.

A change came with the accession of Solomon, a man who was in almost every way a contrast to his father. He was born in the purple, a couple of years after the last of David's serious wars, and knew by experience nothing of the struggles and principles which marked his father's early life. He had the support of the royal bodyguard, while his rival's adherents included the chief of the national levies and the priest who had followed David from the time when he had to escape Saul's jealous anger. Solomon's triumph was a victory for pure autocracy.

The results were soon manifest. Solomon erected great buildings, including the Temple in Jerusalem, and numerous military posts, but he was no warrior and was hardly faithful to the tradition of the national God. Worse still, from the average Israelite's point of view, he introduced the hateful system of forced labour, which was essential to his building projects. In the eyes of men like the prophets no splendour or 'wisdom' could justify the supreme wrong, and there were signs of discontent during the king's lifetime. After his death the smouldering dissatisfaction broke into open flame, and Rehoboam's refusal to abandon the practice of forced labour led to the disruption of the kingdom. The fidelity of Judah to the house of David seems to have been due to the fact that the south had enjoyed preferential treatment under Solomon; the list of administrative districts which had to supply the royal needs does not include Judah.

The principle of political freedom, thus established, was challenged only once again in the history of Israel. In the ninth century Ahab's marriage with Jezebel introduced a princess who had naturally been brought up in the normal conceptions of oriental despotism. The clash between her ideas and those of traditional Israel is exemplified for us in the story of Naboth. Four figures are worthy of attention. First we have the Israelite peasant farmer, insignificant in himself, but stubborn and independent, aware of his traditional rights, and determined to hold them even against the king. Secondly we have Ahab. Much as he dislikes the situation, he has to accept Naboth's refusal as final; there is no means by which he can overcome the opposition, for he has been reared in the old tradition. In the third place we have the foreign queen, unable to understand the position of a sovereign who could not do as he pleased with his subjects, but dimly aware that she must observe the forms of justice. Finally we have the prophet, who denounces the deed and proclaims a blood-feud against the new occupier of Naboth's ground, a feud which issued a few years later in an appalling massacre of all Ahab's kin. It was enough; the lesson was learnt, and we hear of no other attempt to enforce the claims of autocracy except, perhaps, during the short reign of Jehoiakim in Jerusalem.

But that was not the end of the struggle for human rights. Between Elijah and Amos it seems clear that the social and economic structure of Israel underwent a complete revolution. A new class sprang up, that of the wealthy merchant or property owner. The land of the peasants was absorbed in large estates; we have already glanced at the process. The eighth- and seventh-century prophets seldom denounce the domestic policy of the Crown. On the other hand, the rapacity of the wealthy is a frequent theme with them. The results of the process are obvious, and were stated in no uncertain terms by men such as Amos. The concentration of wealth and the normal means of livelihood in the hands of a few, and consequent depression of the great masses can have only one result, and that is the downfall of the society which allows this condition to exist. History has borne out the prophets' judgement. One of two things must happen. The repression of the 'lower classes' may be incomplete, and leave them with some spark of human feeling. Sooner or later this must end in an internal explosion such as that which wrecked French society in the eighteenth century and Russian in our own day. If, on the other hand, all sense of men's right to self-determination is lost, the country will fall an easy prey to the first invader who seriously attacks it. So came the end of the Graeco-Roman world, a slave society which ceased to produce its own fighting men. So, too, perished the Hebrew kingdoms. A coalition of the little western states, led by Israel and Damascus, had held at bay the advance of the Assyrian king in the ninth century; a hundred years later Tiglath-pileser overran the west with consummate ease. The vitality of the common people had been sapped, and there was no longer a force which could offer serious resistance to the conqueror. Surely the message here is plain enough. Success, even stability, is dependent on the maintenance of a spiritual coefficient in life. There is something in human nature which claims its right to live with a certain degree of freedom. The Israelite prophets succeeded in establishing this principle when they were facing autocracy, but they failed to make it good when it was threatened by a selfish plutocratic class; perhaps they realized the situation too late.

Today we are passing through a period of confusion. We cannot speak of a modern mind, because there is little or no unity of outlook or of purpose. All that seems certain is that a large proportion of the things we used to know has vanished for ever. Even the nineteenth century's confident belief in the better life to be won through fuller knowledge of the physical world has been shattered by the use of science for mass-destruction, and the boundless trust in the general goodness of human nature is giving way to a feeling that, after all, the heart of man is deceitful above all things and desperately wicked. Men are looking and longing for something on which they can build a new and stable society. The Old Testament offers us no blue-print of a new social order. But, once more, it does offer us eternal truths expressed in forms adapted to particular occasions. When the Israelites entered Palestine they embarked on a great experiment. It failed, because they neglected the central truth which was fundamental to their earlier thought, the supreme value of people as against things. Any social order which is to succeed must give full scope to the spiritual coefficient in life; the worst of disasters is the reduction of men and women to the rank of machines.

Further, some clear ethical standards must be maintained and, if necessary, restored. Wherever the Old Testament principles have been applied, they have been found successful, for they meet the essential needs of human nature. A social order without a moral sense would automatically become the most dangerous of machines. We may need to restate the Old Testament principles in modern terms, but they themselves are eternally valid, and can be disregarded only at peril of final calamity.

Most important of all, no social or political system can minister to the needs of man, no ethic can guide man's dealings with his fellows, unless they are based on knowledge of God and of His will, and enforced by direct personal communion with Him. An irreligious society is even more surely doomed than one in which human rights are ignored, for in the last resort it has no valid foundation whatever. The only hope for mankind lies in its acceptance of the principles laid down centuries ago by a prophet, and expanded by Christ: 'What doth the Lord require of thee but to do justly, and love mercy and walk humbly with thy God.'

Finally, we must not overlook the universalism which appears from time to time in Old Testament thought. It is true that most of the writers were concerned primarily, often solely, with their own people. But there is also a wider outlook, the hope and prospect of a time when Israel's God shall claim the allegiance of all the human race. We may, possibly, ascribe some of its forms to that ambition for universal dominion which actuated the great conquering nations and rulers of the ancient world; the spirit is not unknown in modern times. But in the prophets and elsewhere we sometimes meet with a nobler conception than that of an Israelite 'Herrenvolk'. Amos sees in the God of Israel not merely the patriotic deity of a small Palestinian kingdom, but also the controller of the great racial migrations. Others recognize the principle that there can be no good or safe life for any section of humanity till all accept the same divine authority. History has borne out the essential truth underlying this belief. Neglect of a geographical area left room for the outbreak of Islam. Failure to apply the prophetic lessons to the industrial revolution gave ground and opportunity for Marxism. It is not enough that the one living and true God should be recognized as supreme merely over a part of earth's surface, or over some aspects only of human life. He must be accepted by all men, and accepted fully, before the messianic vision of the prophet can be translated into achievement. The New Covenant will be fully valid only when 'one shall not say to another, Know the Lord, but all shall know' Him 'from the least of them unto the greatest of them'. The grand prediction of universal peace for nature and for man can never be fulfilled till the habitable world becomes God's 'holy mountain', and the earth is 'full of the knowledge of God as the waters cover the sea'. The Old Testament, as well as the New, attests the truth that some day, be it near or be it yet far distant in the future, the ideal of a redeemed humanity will become a fact of experience.   T. H. ROBINSON

INDEXES

(a) SUBJECTS

(b) AUTHORS

(Writers' references to themselves are not included here.)

(c) SCRIPTURE REFERENCES

(*d*) SEMITIC WORDS

PRINTED IN GREAT BRITAIN
AT THE UNIVERSITY PRESS, OXFORD
· BY VIVIAN RIDLER
PRINTER TO THE UNIVERSITY